Purnell's Concise Illustrated Dictionary

Purnell

ISBN 0 361 06256 7

This edition published 1984 by Purnell Books,
Paulton, Bristol BS18 5LQ, a member of
the BPCC Group.

Made and printed in Great Britain
by Purnell and Sons (Book Production)
Limited, Paulton, Bristol.

Contents

How to use the Dictionary

Purnell's Concise Illustrated Dictionary has been carefully planned to be as easy as possible to use. These hints may be useful:

1 Keywords — that is words which are important enough to be defined — are printed in bold, for example **danger**.

2 Some compound words are not regarded as keywords. But they can be found printed in semi-bold type under one part of the compound or the other. Under **sluice**, for instance, can be found **sluice-gate**.

3 Well-known expressions or phrases which include a keyword are also printed in semi-bold and explained. Thus under **beat** can be found **it beats me**.

4 Words which have the same spelling but a different meaning have a numeral following the keyword, for example **amount** 1) and **amount** 2).

5 The whole entry for a keyword should be read through. It may be the last part which best explains the usage you are looking for.

6 An abbreviation in brackets, e.g. (chem.), coming before a definition shows that the word is used in this sense only in connection with the subject for which the abbreviation stands.

7 You should carefully study the key to the pronunciation on page 247. The system is simple, easy to remember and shows clearly the generally accepted pronunciation of all the words included in this dictionary.

abandon 1) v.t. (*a băn'don*) To give up, *abandon a career, abandon hope*; to desert, *abandon his family*; to leave, *abandon his country*
abbey n. (*ăb'i*) Buildings occupied by monks or nuns
abbreviation n. (*a brē'vi ā'shun*) Act of shortening; an instance of this; writing part for the whole of a word, as *adj*. for 'adjective', *R.C* for 'Roman Catholic'
abdicate v.t. (*ăb'di kāt*) To resign from a position, to renounce power used esp. of monarchs, to give up throne
abdomen n. (*ăb'do men*) (anat.) The belly; part of the body between diaphragm and pelvis containing the urinogenital and digestive organs
abduction n. (*ăb duk'shun*) The forcible or fraudulent carrying off of a person
abhor v.t. (*ab haw(r)'*) To regard with loathing, disgust, horror
ability n. (*a bil'iti*) Capacity or means esp. to do a special thing; skill in performance; cleverness
able adj. (*ābl*) Have means or skill to do some (usually specified) thing, *I am able to read;* competent, talented, *an able performer;* good, showing ability, *an able performance*
aborigines n.pl. (*ăb'o rij'i nēz*) The original natives of a country, esp. Australian
about 1) adv. (*a bowt'*) Nearly, approximately, *about an hour;* on all sides, in various directions, *to look about, to stroll about;* here and there, *to order about, influenza is about;* in the opposite direction, as in (naut.) **about ship!** order to place ship on different tack; (milit.) **about turn!** order to face opposite direction
about 2) prep. (*a bowt'*) Around, *a garland about her neck;* here and there in, to and fro in, *to pace about the room;* somewhere in or at, *about the house, about town;* close to, with, *to keep one's wits about one;* on the subject of, *to talk about something;* concerning qualities of, *the best thing about her*
above 1) adv. (*a buv'*) In a higher place, overhead (of motion or rest), *the sky above, to fly above;* higher in power or rank, *those above, the class above*
above 2) prep. (*a buv'*) Higher than, *above our heads;* surpassing in quality, *he is above the rest in*

aborigine

intelligence; more than, *above fifty*
abroad adv. (*a brawd'*) Widely, over a large area, *to spread abroad;* current, *a rumour is abroad;* in foreign countries, *to take holidays abroad;* out of doors, away from home, *to be abroad early;*
abrupt adj. (*ab rupt'*) Broken off sudden, unexpected, *an abrupt departure;* (of behaviour) short, brusque
abscond v.i. (*ab scond'*) To go away secretly and suddenly esp to evade the law
absence n. (*ăb'sens*) Being away from a place, *absence makes the heart grow fonder;* the time of being away, *a short absence;* lack of something, *absence of the necessary funds;* mental distraction, esp. in *absence of mind*
absent 1) adj. (*ăb'sent*) Not present in a place, *absent friends*
absent 2) v. reflex. (*ăb sent'*) To keep deliberately away, *he absented himself from the meeting*
absolute adj. (*ăb'sol o͞ot*) Complete, perfect, *absolute freedom;* pure, *absolute alcohol;* unconditional, unqualified, *absolute pardon, absolute lie;* free from restraints, despotic, *absolute power;* positive, definite, *absolute fact;* complete in itself, self-existent, *absolute truth*
absorb v.t. (*ab zawb', ab sawb'*) To swallow up; (of heat, light, etc.) to take in; (of liquids) to suck up, *blotting-paper absorbs*

ink; (fig.) to take in, assimilate ideas etc., *to absorb the atmosphere of a place;* to engross, to occupy the mind, *his work completely absorbs him*
absorbent adj. and n. (*ab saw'bent, ab zaw'bent*) Tending to absorb readily, substance that absorbs
absurd adj. and n. (*ab surd', ab zurd'*) Incongruous; odd, eccentric; unreasonable; ridiculous. As n. in absolute sense *the absurd*
abuse v.t. (*a būz'*) To use wrongly or badly (esp. authority, power); to handle roughly or cruelly; to violate (a woman's virtue, etc.); to insult, revile; to presume upon (hospitality, etc.)
accelerate v.t. and i. (*ăk sel'er rāt*) To hasten, to quicken; to become or travel faster
accent n. (*ăk'sent*) National or local mode of pronunciation
accept v.t. (*ak sept'*) To agree to take something offered (gifts, honours, etc.)
acceptable adj. (*ak sep'tabl*) Worth accepting
access n. (*ak'ses*) The way of approach to a place, *access to this house is from the lake*
accident n. (*ăk'si dent*) Act with no apparent cause, hence unexpected, *I met him by accident;* a mishap, disaster
accidental adj. (*ăk'si dentl'*) Happening by chance
accompany v.t. (*a kum'pan i*) To go with, escort; (mus.) to play supporting part
accordion n. (*a kaw'di on*) (mus.) Portable wind-instrument worked on metallic reed principle by hand-operated bellows
account 1) n. (*a kownt'*) Record or calculation of money, esp. debit or credit with bank or tradesmen; bill; **account-book**, book for keeping such records; pl. *to keep accounts;* description, narrative, *he gave an account of his adventures*
account 2) v.t. and i. (*a kownt'*) To judge, estimate, *I account him guilty;* to give an adequate explanation for, *to account for one's behaviour*
accumulate v.t. and i. (*a kū'mū lāt*) To gather little by little, amass (wealth etc.); to increase, *dirt accumulates in corners*
accurate adj. (*ak'ur at*) Correct, precise (as of persons, descriptions; machines, methods)

accordion

accuse v.t. (*a kūz'*) To charge (a person) with an offence; to blame
accustom v.t. (*a kus'tum*) To make (person, oneself, or animal) used *to* something, *Caesar accustomed his men to long marches;* often p.p., *to be, to become accustomed to*
ace n. (*ās*) Unit; 'one', esp. one spot or mark on playing cards, dice; card so marked, *ace of diamonds;* (fig. from cards) highest, best, *an ace fighter-pilot*
ache n. and v.i. (*āk*) Dull, continuous pain; to suffer such pain or (of parts of body) to give it; (fig.) **to ache for** to long for
achieve v.t. (*a chēv'*) To finish, accomplish, gain (an effect, purpose, ambition)
acid 1) adj. (*ăs'id*) Sour, sharp to taste
acid 2) n. (*ăs'id*) Sour substance, as vinegar; (chem.) substance containing hydrogen and combining with salifiable bases to form salts
acknowledge v.t. (*ak nol'ij*) Admit the truth of; recognize (someone *to be* something, *as* something); confess (fault etc.); declare receipt of (letters etc.); reward (a service)
acorn n. (*ā'kawn*) Fruit of the oak
acquaint v.t. (*ak wānt'*) Inform (a person *with* a fact); reflex. to make *oneself* familiar *with*; (in pass.) have personal knowledge of
acquaintance n. (*ak wān'tans*) Direct but slight knowledge of person or fact; person known socially, not intimately
acquire v.t. (*ak wīr'*) Gain something by oneself, for oneself; come into possession of

acre n. (*ā'ker*) Measure of land 4,840 sq. yards
acrobat n. (*ăk'rō băt*) Skilled gymnast, tumbler, tight-rope walker
across adv. and prep. (*a kros'*) Crosswise, from side to side (of), running counter (to); forming a cross (with); on the other side (of)
act 1) n. (*ăkt*) Thing done, deed; process of doing, *caught in the act*; main division of a play; law, or document recording a law, *an Act of Parliament*
act 2) v.t. and i. (*ăkt*) To perform (a play); play (a part, on stage or in life); simulate (feelings etc.). As v.i. to perform actions, *now is the time to act*; with *as*, to fulfil the duties of, *to act as deputy*; to behave, *to act wisely*; with *on, upon*, to behave according to (orders etc.)
active adj. (*ăk'tiv*) Given to action, quick of movement; (of persons) energetic; working, effective, *an active volcano*
activity n. (*ăk tiv'i ti*) Agility, alertness; movement, liveliness; rate of working. In pl. **activities** specific doings in certain spheres of action, *sport is one of many activities*
actor n. (*ăk'ter*) Dramatic performer, professional stage player
actress n. woman actor
acute adj. (*a kūt'*) Sharp, pointed; (geom.) less than 90°; (of the mind) shrewd, perceptive; (of physical or emotional condition) severe, violent, as opposed to chronic; (of sound) high, shrill
add v.t. and i. (*ăd*) To join one thing to another, *add insult to injury*; combine two or more numbers (often with *up*); increase, augment, *rain added to our discomfort*; to say further
address 1) v.t. (*a dres'*) Communicate with (in speech or writing), *address a remark to, address an audience*; write postal directions on letters; apply (oneself to work etc.)
address 2) n. (*a dres'*) Person's residence described by street, number etc., esp. on letters; formal public speech
adenoids n.pl. (*ad'en oidz*) (med.) Enlarged growths of spongy tissue between back of nose and throat, often impeding breathing and speaking
adhesive adj. and n. (*ad hē'siv*) Sticky, made to stick, *he used an adhesive plaster*

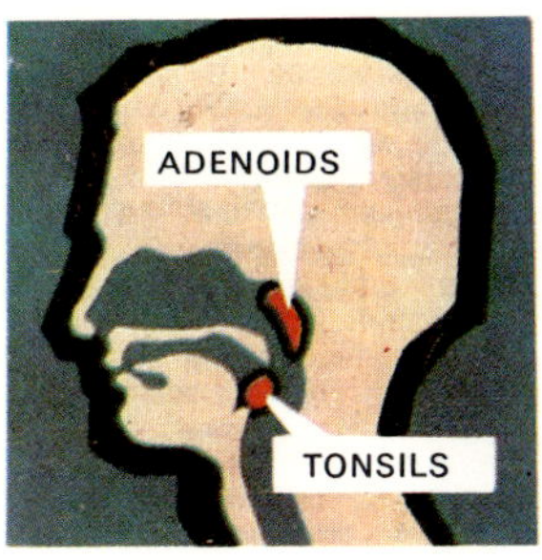

adjust v.t. (*a just'*) To arrange, put in order; settle differences; adapt (for a purpose etc.)
admiral n. (*ăd'mi ral*) Naval officer commanding a fleet; in the British navy there are four grades: *Admiral of the Fleet, Admiral, Vice-Admiral*, and *Rear-Admiral*
admiration n. (*ăd'mi rā'shun*) Act of admiring; delighted contemplation (of beauty, skill etc.)
admire v.t. (*ad mīr'*) To regard with admiration, pleasure etc.; have a high opinion of
admission n. (*ad mish'un*) Letting in, allowing to enter; acknowledgement that something is true, confession
admit v.t. (*ad mit'*) To allow to enter (place, institution, society etc.); confess, acknowledge as true
adore v.t. (*a daw(r)'*) To worship as divine; love to distraction, idolize. Hence: **adorable** adj. in above senses and also (colloq.) charming, pretty
adult adj. and n. (*a dult', ăd'ult*) Fully grown, mature; person who is so
advance 1) v.t. and i. (*ad vahns'*) To move, lead or put forward; (of plans, suggestions etc.) to propose; (of persons or their interests) promote, help forward; (of events) hasten; lend or pay money on security. As v.i. to move forward; make progress; (milit.) move to the attack; (of prices) to rise
advance 2) n. and adj. (*ad vahns'*) Act of moving forward; progress; loan of money, payment beforehand
advantage n. (*ad vahn'tij*) Favourable condition, circumstance likely to cause progress, benefit
adventure n. (*ad ven'cher*) Risk, danger; risky or exciting enterprise

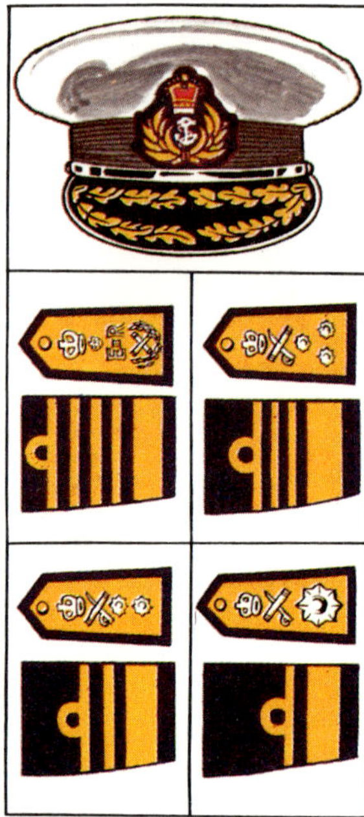

Admiral of the Fleet **Admiral**
Vice-Admiral **Rear-Admiral**

advertise v.t. and i. (*ad'ver tiz*) To announce publicly; display a public notice esp. in newspapers etc., putting forward supposed merits of a commercial product; as v.i. to insert notice in a newspaper etc. in order to obtain something (often with *for*), *to advertise for a house*. Hence: **advertisement** n. (*ad vur'tis ment*) public notice, esp. one aiming to promote sales
advice n. (*ad vis'*) Considered opinion given to someone about how he should think or act, *he acted on my advice*
advise v.t. and i. (*ad viz'*) To give advice to, *the doctor advised rest*; inform (a person *of* a thing), *we advised that the goods had been dispatched*
aeroplane n. (*ār'ō plān*) Heavier-than-air powered aircraft supported in the air by wings
affair n. (*a fār'*) Thing to be done; business, concern, *that is his affair*; used as vague reference to a happening or adventure, *what an extraordinary affair!*; romantic intrigue, esp. with intimate relationship; (colloq.) vague reference to material object, *her hat was a garish affair*; (pl.) public or private transactions or business, *affairs of State, his affairs are in disorder*
affect 1) v.t. (*a fekt'*) To act upon, produce a change in; move the emotions of; (of disease) attack
affection n. (*a fek'shun*) State of mind, disposition
whence **affectionate** adj. showing affection
afflict v.t. (*a flikt'*) To cause suffering of body or mind; often p.p. **afflicted** and pres.p. **afflicting**
afford v.t. (*a fawd'*) (with *can*) To be rich enough, *I can afford a new suit*; give, supply, *poetry affords me great pleasure*
afloat adv. and adj. (*a flōt'*) Floating; at sea, aboard ship
afraid adj. (*a frād'*) Frightened
after 1) adv., prep. and conj. (*ahf'ter*) (of place) Behind, *enter after me*; in pursuit of, *go after him*; (of time) later than, *a day after that*; concerning, *enquire after*; in imitation of, *an engraving after a picture by Reynolds*; in accordance with, *a man after my own heart*; **take after** resemble (generally parent or relation); **look after** take care of
afternoon n. (*ahf ter nōōn'*) Time between noon and evening
afterwards adv. (*ahf'ter werds*) Later, subsequently
again adv. (*a gen, a gān*) Once more, *do it again*; in addition, *half as much again*; back to the original condition or place, *home again*; moreover, besides; on the other hand, *he is bigger, but then again he is more stupid*; **again and again, time and again** repeatedly; **now and again** occasionally
against prep. (*a gānst', a genst'*) In opposition to, *struggle against*; in competition with, *play against*; in contrast to, *outlined against the sky*; contrary to, *against the grain*; in collision with, *bump against the post*; in contact with, *lean against the wall*; opposite to (usually with *over*), *over against the town hall*; in preparation for, *against his coming*; **run up against** meet unexpectedly (person, snag etc.)
age 1) n. (*āj*) Length of life or existence, esp. to the present or specified time, *the age of the earth, his age was then eighty years, what's his age?*; condition of being

THE AEROPLANE

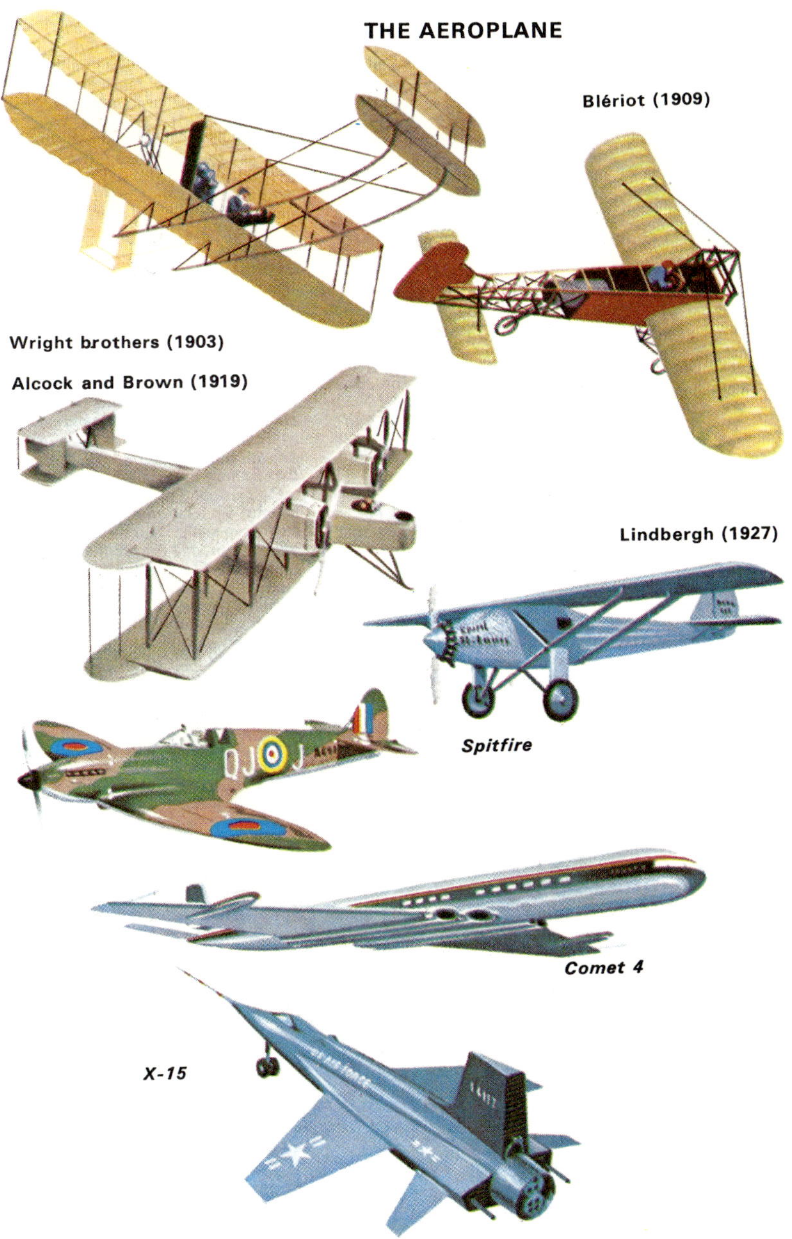

Wright brothers (1903)

Blériot (1909)

Alcock and Brown (1919)

Lindbergh (1927)

Spitfire

Comet 4

X-15

old, *age may bring wisdom*; major historical or geological period, *Ice Age*; generation, *the greatest man of his age*; (law) **of age** having reached the age (21) of legal rights and responsibilities; **under, over age** under, over twenty-one (colloq.) pl. **ages** a long time, *that was ages ago*. (OFr. *aage*
age 2) v.t. and i. (*āj*) To grow old or appear to have done so, *how he has aged!*; to cause to grow old, *wine aged in wood*
agency n. (*ā'jen si*) Motive power, *a free agency*; instrumentality, *he was repatriated through the agency of his consul*; (comm.) occupation of an agent; establishment for business purposes
agenda n. (*a jen'da*) Things to be done, list of items for business meeting
agent n. (*ā'jent*) One who performs an action or causes something to happen; business representative, acting for person or firm; force producing certain effects on matter, *chemical agent* etc
aggravate v.t. (*ăg'ra vāt*) To make worse, increase the gravity of (offence etc.); (colloq.) irritate, annoy; often pres. and p.p. **aggravating, aggravated**
aggressive adj. (*ag res'iv*) Pugnacious, disposed to attack
agitate v.t. and i. (*ăj'i tāt*) To shake, move; disturb, upset (persons, feelings); arouse public excitement, esp. for political reasons, *agitate for better working conditions*. Hence: **agitator** n
ago adv. (*a gō'*) Past, gone by, *a year ago*. (OE p.p. of *agan* pass
agony n. (*ăg'o ni*) Extreme physical or mental pain
agree v.i. (*a grē'*) To consent *to*, accept (proposition etc.), *he agreed to the motion*; concur with (a person), *I agree with you about that*; conform with, *his evidence did not agree with known facts*; get on together, *he and I do not agree*; come to terms; suit the constitution of, *fresh air agrees with me*; (gram.) correspond in number, gender, case, or person
agreeable adj. (*a grē'ab l*) Pleasant; willing, ready to agree, *I am agreeable to that idea*
agreement n. (*a grē'ment*) Harmony of feelings, opinions etc.; bargain, mutual understanding; (law) undertaking legally binding on the parties; (gram.) correspondence of number, gender, case, or person
agriculture n. (*ăg'ri kul cher*) Cultivation of the soil; theory and practice of farming. Hence: **agricultural** adj.; **agriculturalist** n
ahead adv. (*a hed'*) Further in advance, leading, *walk on ahead*; directly in front of, *there's a traffic-jam ahead*; in advance *of*, *ahead of his times*; (colloq.) **go ahead** start; continue; **get ahead** make progress, esp. in a career
aid 1) v.t. (*ād*) To help. (Fr. *aider*)
aid 2) n. (*ād*) Help; helper, or means of help; (law) legal help in defence of action, claimed by defendant; **first aid** on-the-spot medical attention in case of accident
ail v.t. and i. (*āl*) To trouble, afflict, *what ails you?*; to be ill, *ailing*. Hence: **ailment** n. slight illness
aim 1) v.t. and i. (*ām*) To point, direct (weapon, blow, etc.) *at*, also fig.; try to achieve a purpose or object; **aim high** be ambitious
aim 2) n. (*ām*) Pointing of weapon, missile etc., *take aim* (*at*); estimate of direction and range in order to hit an object; purpose, *an aim in life*
air 1) n. (*ār*) Gaseous substance composed largely of oxygen and nitrogen, forming atmosphere which envelops the earth; space above the earth, sky, *birds of the air*; outward appearance, manner, *air of distinction*; (pl.) affectation, *put on airs*; (mus.) tune, melody, esp. chief melodic part in harmonized piece of music; **open-air** adj. held out of doors; **in the air** (of rumours) current; (of projects) unsettled; **castles in the air** fanciful dreams; **on, over the air** broadcast by radio; **hot air** nonsense, boasting; **treading on air** in exhilarated state
air 2) v.t. and i. (*ār*) To put in fresh air to purify; to dry (beds etc.); let fresh air into (rooms etc.); (fig.) parade (grievances etc.), *he aired his feelings*
aisle n. (*īl*) (arch.) Side division of a church, running lengthwise and parallel to the nave; a passage between two blocks of pews in a church
ajar adv. (*a jah(r)'*) (of door or window) Slightly open
alarm 1) n. (*a lahm'*) A warning of danger, a call to arms; fear, apprehension, *cause for alarm*; also **alarum; alarm-clock,** clock with bell that rings at set time
alarm 2) v.t. (*a lahm'*) To arouse a feeling of danger, to frighten

albatross

albatross n. (*ăl'ba tros*) The largest sea-bird, related to petrels, found mostly in southern hemisphere. (Port. and Span. *alcatraz*

album n. (*ăl'bum*) Book with blank pages on which photographs, stamps etc. are fixed

alcohol n. (*ăl'ko hol*) Pure spirit, an intoxicating product of fermentation; any liquor containing this

alcoholic adj. and n. (*ăl ko hol'ik*) Of, pertaining to, alcohol; containing alcohol (of drinks). As n. a person addicted to alcoholic drinks.

alcoholism n. (*ăl'ko hol iz m*) The habit of taking alcoholic drinks; the harmful effect of this on the system

alcove n. (*ăl'kōv*) Vaulted recess in wall of room, in garden wall etc

alderman n. (*awl'der man*) Senior member of county or municipal council, elected for a term

ale n. (*āl*) Intoxicating fermented malt liquor, generally flavoured with hops etc.; beer

alert adj. and n. (*a lurt'*) Watchful, vigilant; lively, quick-witted. As n. a warning signal, esp. an air-raid warning; **on the alert**, ready to act

alga n. (*ăl'ga*) pl. **algae** (*ăl'jē*) (bot.) Order of plants including seaweeds

algebra n. (*ăl'ji bra*) Branch of mathematics dealing with relations and properties of numbers, and in which numbers are represented by symbols

alias adv. and n. (*ā'li as*) Otherwise called, *Jack Sprat alias 'the Shrimp'*. As n. an assumed name, *to use, go under, an alias*

alien adj. and n. (*a'li en*) Of another country, race etc., *an alien tongue, alien shores*; strange to, not natural to, repugnant to, *deceit is alien to his nature*. As n. a person living in a country who is not a citizen of that country

alike pred. adj. and adv. (*a lik'*) Similar, like. As adv. equally, similarly

algae

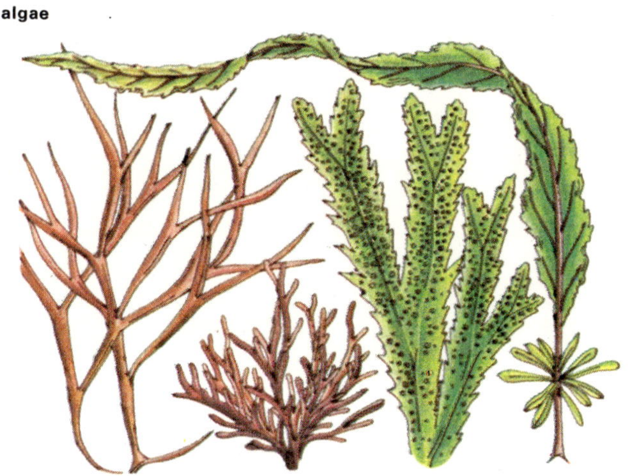

alive adv. and pred. adj. (*a liv'*) Living (as opposed to dead); in existence, action, operation etc. (of claims, hopes etc.); alert, brisk, *very much alive*; **alive to** fully aware of, *alive to the possibilities*; **alive with**, swarming with, *the place was alive with snakes*

all adj., n. and adv. (*awl*) The whole of (in extent, amount, or quantity), *all day, all your life*; (with pl.) every, every one of, *in all respects, all possibilities*; the greatest possible, *with all speed*; any whatever, *renounce all claim*; **for good and all** (colloq.) for ever; **once and for all** for the last time; **at all events** in any case. As n. the whole (quantity, amount, number), everything, everybody, *all is lost, all desire a happy life*; (fig.) the whole of one's property, *he lost his all*

allergy n. (*ăl'erji*) (path.) Extreme sensitivity to certain substances; (colloq.) a dislike for (someone, something). Hence: **allergic** adj. (*ăler'jik*) hypersensitive to

alliance n. (*a li'ans*) Union by marriage or between states, parties

alligator n. (*ăl'i gā'ter*) American and Chinese reptile of genus *Saurians* of the crocodile family

allow v.t. and i. (*a low'*) To permit, *you are allowed to smoke*; to admit, concede, *I allow that my work is not perfect, but . . .*; to make possible, provide, *mechanization allows us more leisure*; to make a regular payment (to a dependent), *his father allows him £400 a year*; to deduct (from payment due), *to allow so much in the pound*. As v.i. in **allow of**, admit, *these facts allow of various interpretations*; **allow for**, take into consideration, *buy more, so as to allow for waste*

allowance n. (*a low'ans*) A certain fixed ration of some substance periodically served out, esp. food and money

alloy n. (*ăl'oi*) Mixture of two or more metals

ally 1) v.t. (*a li'*) To unite or combine *with*, esp. (persons, families) in marriage or (states) by

ally 2) n. (*ăl'i*) A state allied by treaty with another; a friend, confederate

ALLOYS

almighty adj. (*awl mī'ti*) All-powerful, omnipotent; **The Almighty** God
almond n. (*ah'mund*) Tree related to the peach; the kernel of the stone-fruit of this tree, eaten as a nut
almost adv. (*awl'mōst*) Nearly, all but
along adv. and prep. (*a long'*) Lengthwise, from end to end of, through any part of the length of, *along the road;* onward, forward, *to go along, come along;* **along with** in company with; **to get along with** to be on friendly terms with
aloud adv. (*a lowd'*) Audibly, in a loud voice, not whispered, *to speak, laugh aloud*
alphabet n. (*ăl'fa bet*) The set of letters used in a written language
already adv. (*awl red'i*) Before a specified time, beforehand, *I have already finished*
Alsatian n. (*ăl sā'shun*) Large dog originally bred as a sheepdog in Alsace
also adv. and conj. (*awl'sō*) In addition, besides; as well; likewise
alter v.t. and i. (*awl'ter*) To change, vary, *to alter one's diet, one's opinion;* to modify, *to alter a dress etc.* As v.i. to become different (in appearance or character)
alternative adj. and n. (*awl tur'na tiv*) (with pl.) Offering a choice of two (possibilities); (with sing.) one (possibility) differing from that suggested. As n. a choice of one of two things; a second possibility; also used, though incorrectly, of more than two, *there are several alternatives.* Hence: **alternatively** adv. as an alternate way, on the other hand
although conj. (*awl thō'*) Though, notwithstanding, in spite of all the facts that
altitude n. (*ăl'ti tūd*) Height from bottom to top, esp. of high objects height above sea level
altogether adv. (*awl'to geth'er*) Wholly, entirely, *you are altogether wrong;* on the whole, *I don't altogether mind*
aluminium n. (*ăl ū min'i um*) A very light silvery metal
always adv. (*awl'wāz*) At all times, continually; on every occasion; in any circumstances
amateur n. and adj. (*ăm'a tur' ăm'a tūr', ăm'at yur'*) One who pursues an art or sport or study purely for the love of it; a non-professional (artist, sportsman etc.); one lacking professional skill. As adj. applied to non-professionals and their activities
amaze v.t. (*a māz'*) To fill with wonder, to surprise greatly
ambassador n. (*ăm băs'a der*) The permanent official representative of a state at a foreign court; minister sent on special mission abroad
ambiguous adj. (*ăm big'ū us*) Liable to be interpreted in more than one way
ambition n. (*ăm bi'shun*) The strong desire for success (in attaining wealth, position, ideals etc.)
ambitious adj. (*ăm bi'shus*) (of persons) Full of ambition
ambulance n. (*ăm'bū lans*) Mobile field hospital; vehicle for transport of sick or wounded
ambush v.t. and n. (*ăm'boosh*) To station troops in hiding ready for surprise attack; to lie in wait for, and attack from hiding. As n. the stationing of troops in hiding for surprise attack; the troops lying in wait; their hiding place; the attack itself
amethyst n. (*ăm'i thist*) A precious stone, purple or violet in colour; the colour of it
amicable adj. (*ăm'ik ab l*) Friendly; in a friendly way, *an amicable agreement*
amid, amidst prep. (*a mid', a midst'*) In the middle of; among
ammonia n. (*a mō'ni a*) A compound of nitrogen with three parts of hydrogen; the pungent volatile alkaline gas obtained from hartshorn
ammunition n. (*ăm'ū ni'shun*) Collective term for military projectiles and accessories, explosives, cartridges etc
amnesia n. (*ăm nē'zi a*) (med.) Loss of memory
amnesty n. (*ăm'nes ti*) Pardon, esp. for political offences
among, amongst prep. (*a mung', a mungst'*) Surrounded by, *the house among the trees;* in the number of, *blessed among women;* (expressing distribution), *we divided the food amongst us;* reciprocally, *they quarrelled among themselves*
amount 1) v.t. (*a mownt'*) To come to, add up to (of a number of things, sums of money etc.); to be equivalent to (in significance), *all this amounts to very little*
amount 2) n. (*a mownt'*) Sum total; *a quantity, a large or small*

amount
amp (*ămp*) Short form of **ampere**
ampère n. (*ăm'pār*) Unit of force in an electric current
amphibious adj. (*ăm fib'i us*) Capable of living both on land and in water
amphitheatre n. (*ăm'fi thē'a ter*) An oval or circular arena with tiers of seats
ample adj. (*ămp l*) Large, spacious, *ample rooms, ample proportions*; abundant, *ample supplies, stores*; sufficient, *ample for one's needs*
amputate v.t. (*ăm'pū tāt*) To cut off, esp. a limb of the body or larger branches of a tree. Hence: **amputation** n. (*am pū tā'shun*)
amuse v.t. (*a mūz'*) To occupy the attention agreeably; to entertain, divert; to provoke mirth. Hence: **amusement** n. the state of being amused, mirth; a pleasant diversion, pastime, entertainment
anaemia n. (*an ē'mi a*) Blood deficiency, lack of red corpuscles. Hence: **anaemic** adj
anagram n. (*ăn'a grăm'*) Word or phrase formed by transposing the letters of another word or phrase, e.g. *lump* to *plum*
analyse v.t. (*ăn'a līz*) To resolve a thing into its constituent elements; (chem.) to split a compound into its components; (fig.) to examine critically and minutely
anarchist n. (*ăn'ah kist*) One who believes that all organized government is evil
anarchy n. (*ăn'ah ki*) Absence of organized government; thus, social and political chaos; (fig.) lawlessness and confusion in general
anatomy n. (*ăn ăt'o mi*) Originally the dissection of bodies to study their structure; the art of dissection; the science of bodily structure; the bodily structure itself
ancestor n. (*ăn'ses ter*) One from whom a person is descended, a forebear; also used of animals, plants etc
ancestry n. (*ăn'ses tri*) Ancestral lineage, descent
anchor 1) n. (*ăng'ker*) A heavy iron bar with a ring for cable attachment at one end and two barbed arms or hooks at the other, for mooring ships to sea-bottom; **to cast anchor** to drop the anchor

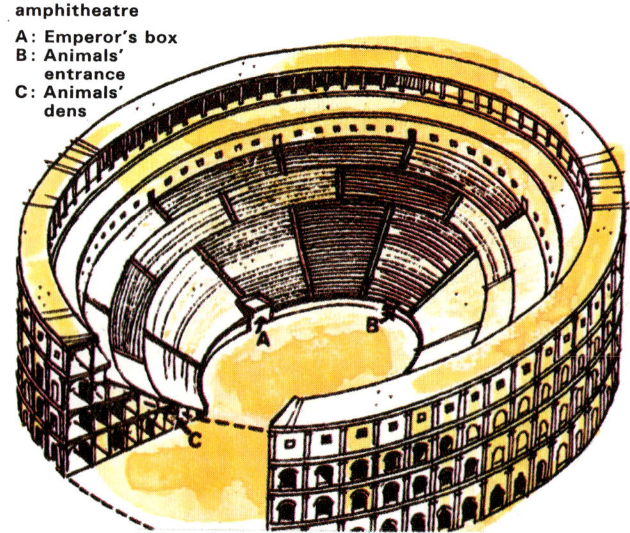

overboard; **to weigh anchor** to haul the anchor up; to begin a voyage
anchor 2) v.t. and i. (*ăng'ker*) To make fast by dropping the anchor. As v.i. to cast anchor, come to rest
ancient adj. and n. (*ān'shent*) Old; of former times
and conj. (*ănd*) Used to link words or sentences and express addition to what has gone before; (colloq. after certain verbs) in order to, *try and do it, come and see, go and tell him*
angel n. (*ān'jl*) In Jewish, Christian, and other theologies, an immortal spiritual being acting as messenger between God and man; (fig.) a good or beautiful person, esp. a child
anger 1) n. (*ăng'ger*) A passion of the mind prompted by a sense of wrong; wrath, indignation
anger 2) v.t. (*ăng'ger*) To provoke anger (n.) in a person.
angle n. (*ăng'gl*) (geom.) The inclination of one line to another which meets it; the space between two meeting lines or surfaces
angler n. (*ăng'gler*) One who fishes with rod and line
angry adj. (*ăng'gri*) Full of anger, enraged (*at, about* a thing, *at, with* a person); (fig.) enflamed. Hence: **angrily** adv
animal 1) n. (*ăn'im al*) Living creature having sensation and voluntary motion, as distinct from plants
animal 2) adj. (*ăn'im al*) Pertaining to living creatures, *animal life*
ankle n. (*ăng'kl*) The joint in human beings connecting the foot and the leg; the slender part of the leg below the calf
anniversary n. and adj. (*ăni vurs'a ri*) The yearly return of a date; the celebration of a particular date, such as that of a wedding
announce v.t. (*a nowns'*) To proclaim, *to announce an intention;* to make known the approach or presence of, *all eyes turned as the duchess was announced.* Hence: **announcement** n. a proclamation; the act of announcing; **announcer** n. one who announces, esp. over the radio
annoy v.t. (*a noi'*) To irritate, harass, worry. Hence; **annoyance** n.; **annoying** adj
annual adj. and n. (*ăn'ū al*) Returning every year, *an annual holiday;* reckoned by the year, *annual income.* As n. that which appears yearly (esp. books etc.); a plant living only one year. Hence: **annually** adv
anonymous adj. (*a non'i mus*) (of persons) Of unknown name; with the name not revealed; (of books etc.) of unknown or undeclared authorship
another pron. and adj. (*a nuth'er*) One in addition, *would you like another drink? Yes, I'd like another;* a different one, *if that racket is too heavy, try another*; (following *one*) reciprocally, *to cherish one another;* of the same kind, *he thinks he is another Napoleon, I'll never find another cook as good*
answer 1) n. (*ahn'ser*) Statement made in reply to a question
answer 2) v.t. and i. (*ahn'ser*) To speak, write, or act in consequence of another's words or actions; to reply to, *to answer a question;* to speak or write in return, *to answer a letter, to answer the phone* (not necessarily involving questions); to respond to, *to answer the call of duty;* to suit, be adequate for, *to answer one's requirements.* As v.i. to reply, *I asked but he did not answer*

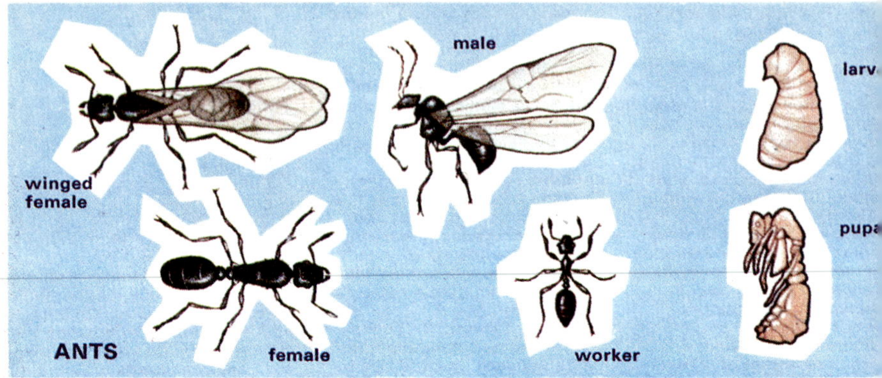

ant n. (*ănt*) A small social insect of the family Formicidae
antarctic adj. and n. (*ănt ahk'tik*) Of the south polar regions. As n. **the Antarctic** the south polar regions themselves, **Antarctica**; **Antarctic Circle** parallel of 66° 32' South
antelope n. (*ăn'ti lōp*) Horned ruminant animal akin to deer
antenna n. (*ăn ten'a*) pl. **antennae** (*ăn ten'ē*) A feeler (usually in pairs) on heads of insects
anthem n. (*ăn'them*) Passage set to music and sung in churches
anthology n. (*ăn thol'o ji*) A collection of specially chosen poems
anthropology n. (*ăn thro pol'o ji*) The study and science of mankind in all aspects
anticipate v.t. (*ăn tis'i pāt*) To use in advance, *to anticipate next week's wages;* to forestall, *he anticipated the enemy's attack*; to foresee (and take steps to meet or fulfil), *he anticipated the situation, anticipated your needs;* to look forward to, *I anticipate enjoying myself greatly;* expect (*that* something will happen)
antique adj. and n. (*ăn tēk'*) Belonging to, surviving from, old times, *an antique song;* old-fashioned, *in an antique style* an old object of furniture, etc. sought by collectors
antiseptic adj. and n. (*ăn ti sep'tik*) Counteracting putrefaction. As n. a substance which so acts
antler n. (*ănt'ler*) The whole, or any part, of a stag's horn
anxiety n. (*ăng zī'et i*) Distress, uneasiness of mind esp. about some future event
anxious adj. (*ăng'shus, ăngk'shus*) Troubled, uneasy esp. about some future event, *he is anxious about passing his exams;* intensely solicitous, concerned, *we are always anxious to please*
any adj., pron. and adv. (*en'i*) No matter what, *any help is better than none, ask any doctor;* (in interrog. and neg.) some, *have you any cigarettes? I haven't any;* **at any rate** at least; **in any case** in any circumstances; **anybody** any person, someone (chiefly interrog. and neg.); a person of importance; **anyhow** by any means, in any case; (fig.) carelessly; **anyone** anybody; **anything** whatsoever thing, no matter what; **anyway** in any case; **anywhere** in, to, any place
apart adv. (*a paht'*) (Of space) on

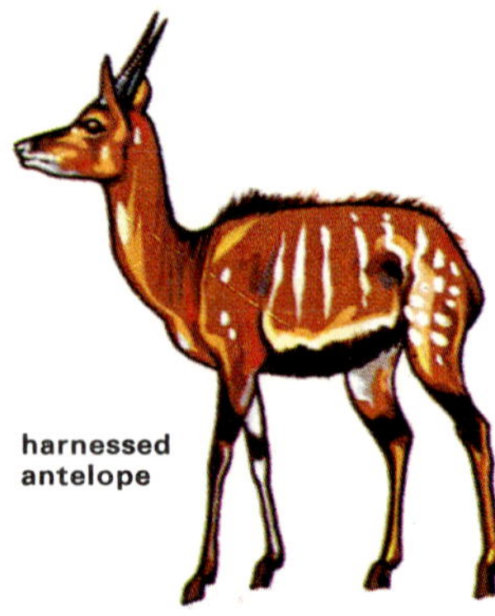
harnessed antelope

one side, *he stood apart from the rest;* (of purpose, thought etc.) separately, independently, *apart from the salary, the job is worth doing;* **to set apart** to reserve (for special purpose) ; **to take apart** to take to pieces, dismantle ; **joking apart** not meaning to joke, thus, seriously

apartheid n. (*a pah(r) tāt*) In South Africa, the political principle of total separation of European from African races

apartment n. (*a paht'ment*) A single, usually rather grand, room, *a spacious apartment;* (Scotland and U.S.) a flat ; (pl.) a set of rooms, suite, *the State Apartments*

ape 1) n. (*āp*) A monkey, esp. of the tailless species more closely related to man (gorilla, chimpanzee, orang-utan, gibbon)

ape 2) v.t. (*āp*) To imitate, mimic, *to ape one's betters*

apiary n. (*ā'pi a ri*) A place where bees are kept

apologize v.i. (*a pol'o jīz*) To express regret *for* an action, to say one is sorry

apology n. (*a pol'o ji*) The act, or an expression, of regret *for* injury inflicted etc. ; saying one is sorry ; a defence, explanation

apostle n. (*a pos l'*) One sent out to preach, esp. one of the twelve sent out by Christ

apparatus n. (*ăp a rā' tus*) The instruments or utensils for carrying out any given operation, experiment etc.

apparel n. (*a pă'rel*) Clothes, dress (archaic) ; ecclesiastical

apparent adj. (*a pă'rent, a pār'ent*) Visible, *apparent to the naked eye;* easily seen, obvious, *his failure was all too apparent;* seeming, *his apparent indifference is only an act*

apparition n. (*ăp a rish'n*) Appearance ; something which appears, esp. a ghost

appeal 1) v.i. and t. (*a pēl'*) To call upon (for aid), *to appeal for rescue funds;* (for a decision) *to appeal to the referee* ; (to a higher tribunal, to reverse the decision of a lower) *to appeal to the Lords* ; to attract, *the idea of a holiday appeals to me*

appeal 2) n. (*a pēl'*) An urgent demand for aid or for a decision ; (law) the bringing of a case for another judgement by a higher court ; thus, **Court of Appeal** ; attractiveness, *her voice has great appeal*

APPLES

appear v.i. (*a pēr'*) To become visible, *a small cloud appeared in the sky;* to present oneself publicly or formally, *Sarah Bernhardt appeared for the last time, Marshall Hall appeared for the defence;* to be published, *his new book will appear in the spring;* to be manifest, *it appears from your behaviour . . .;* to seem, *the conjurer appeared to cut the lady in half.*

appearance n. (*a pēr'ans*) The act of appearing (any sense of the verb); aspect, look, *his wretched appearance belied his true nature*

appendicitis n. (*a pen di sī'tis*) (med) Inflammation of the vermiform appendix. (As below)

appendix n. (*a pen'diks*) pl. **appendices** (*a pen'dis'ēz*) An addition, esp. to a book or document; **(vermiform) appendix** a very short, thin tube with closed end leading off the large intestine

appetite n. (*ăp'it it*) Natural desire for gratification, esp. of bodily needs such as hunger

appetizing adj. (*ăp'et īz ing*) Stimulating to the appetite

applaud v.t. and i. (*a plawd'*) To clap the hands to express approval; to praise, express approval in general

applause n. (*a plawz'*) The act of applauding; praise, approval

apple n. (*ăp l*) A round, firm, red and yellow fleshy fruit of the apple tree, genus *Malus*, cultivated in many varieties

appliance n. (*a plī'ans*) Mechanical device used for a particular purpose, *bulbs, sockets and other electrical appliances*

application n. (*ăp lik ā'shun*) The act of applying one thing to another; the thing applied (dressing to wound etc.); the act of making a request to obtain a job etc.; the letter etc. in which such a request is made; diligence, close attention (to study etc.); the testing of a theory by putting it into practice

apply v.t. and i. (*a plī'*) To lay or put on, to bring one thing into contact with another, *to apply a dressing to a wound, to apply a coat of paint, lipstick* etc.; to put into practice, bring to bear on, *to apply the rule;* to use (word etc.) as appropriate *to*, *the word 'reserved' is often applied to the English;* to devote *to* a specific end, *the government applies too little money to education;* to set (the mind, oneself) to, *he applied himself, all his energy, to learning Russian.* As v.i. to be relevant, *this regulation applies to everyone;* to make an application, ask in order to obtain something (*to* a person, *for* a thing), *he applied to my firm for a job*

appoint v.t. (*a point'*) To fix (time, place etc.) *for* a purpose, *the time appointed for the meeting;* to decree, settle, esp. in p.p., *one's appointed task;* to nominate a person to perform certain duties, *a new ambassador has been appointed;* (law) to determine the disposition of an estate; to arrange, set in order, *a well-appointed country mansion*

appointment n. (*a point'ment*) An arrangement to meet, to visit, *an appointment at 12 o'clock, a dentist's appointment;* appointing to an office, *his appointment was announced*

appreciate v.t. and i. (*a prē'shi āt*) To judge correctly, set a just value on, *I appreciate the difficulties of your position;* to set a high value on, be grateful for, *I appreciate your concern for my children;* to perceive the merits of, *I appreciate good music;* to perceive small differences. As v.i. to rise in value, as opposed to 'depreciate'

apprehend v.t. (*ăp ri hend'*) To take hold of, seize, arrest

apprentice n. (*a pren'tis*) One bound for a term of years to serve some craft or trade under a master who is in turn bound to instruct him. Hence: **apprenticeship** n. state of being an apprentice; term for which apprenticeship lasts

approach 1) v.t. and i. (*a prōch'*) To come near, nearer (place or time), *to approach the city, to approach middle age;* to approximate to, be similar to, *he answered with something approaching disdain;* to make advances or overtures to a person, *he approached his M.P. about it.* As v.i. to come nearer; (in time) to draw nearer, *death approaches*

approach 2) n. (*a prōch'*) The act of coming near or nearer (in senses of the verb above); the means of access (to a place), *the approach to the house is through an olive grove*

appropriate adj. (*a prō'pri āt*) Originally, set apart for a certain purpose; thus, suited *to* a certain purpose

approval n. (*a prōō'val*) Consent

to, sanction of, an act; critical examination (with favourable outcome implied); *to submit something for approval*; **on approval** (of goods) returnable if not satisfactory. (As below)
approve v.t. and i. (*a prōōv'*) To have, express, good opinion (*of*), *I approve of my son's fiancée;* to sanction formally, ratify, *Parliament approved the bill*
approximate adj. (*a prok'si māt*) Nearly exact, esp. coming near in amount, extent etc., *an approximate rendering of accounts, of the facts*. Hence: **approximately** adv
apricot n. (*ā'pri kot*) An orange-coloured, oval, soft stone-fruit allied to plum and peach
apron n. (*ā'pron*) Garment of cloth, leather etc. worn in front of the body to protect clothes
apt adj. (*ăpt*) Suitable, appropriate, *an apt remark;* skilled, promising, *an apt pupil;* liable, tending to, *he is apt to get his sums wrong*
aquarium n. (*a kwār'i um*) Tank or pond (usually with glass sides) for fish and water plants
aqueduct n. (*ăk'wi dukt*) Artificial channel or conduit for water, esp. one on raised structure of masonry

aqueduct

arable adj. and n. (*ă'rabl*) (Land) suitable for ploughing, ploughed
arbitration n. (*ah bi trā'shun*) Settlement of disputes by an arbiter chosen by the disputants jointly, *to go to arbitration*
arc n. (*ahk*) A segment of a circle or other curve; the apparent path of a heavenly body
arcade n. (*ah kād'*) A row of arches supported on columns; an arched walk; an arched gallery lined with shops
arch 1) n. (*ahch*) Curved overhead structure, esp. spanning doors, windows etc., or the span of a bridge; entrance or passage covered with an arch, an archway
arch 2) v.t. (*ahch*) To cover, span, with an arch; (fig.) to form into an arch, *the cat arched its back*

Roman arch

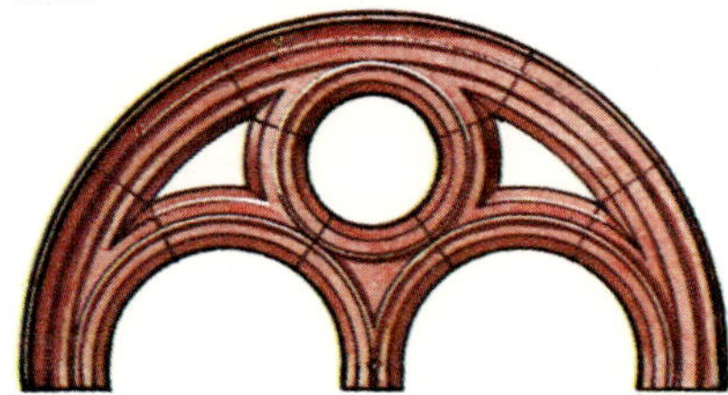

Venetian arch

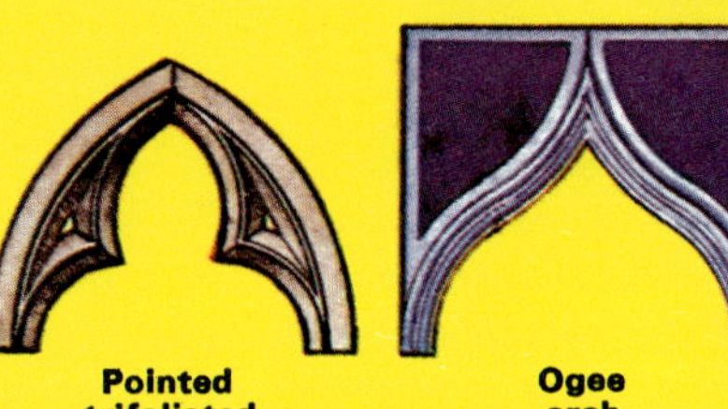

Pointed trifoliated arch

Ogee arch

archaeology n. (*ah ki ol'o ji*) The study of ancient history and culture by means of material remains
archbishop n. (*ahch bish'op*) Chief bishop
archer n. (*ah'cher*) One who shoots with bow and arrow Hence: **archery** n. the art of shooting with bow and arrow
architect n. (*ah'ki tekt*) One who designs buildings
architecture n. (*ah'ki tek cher*) The art and skill of building; the style, design of a building; construction, framework
arctic adj. and n. (*ahk'tik*) Belonging to the North Polar regions; (fig.) very cold. As n. **the Arctic** the North Polar regions; **Arctic Circle** parallel of $66\frac{1}{2}$°N
area n. (*ār'i a*) A measure of the extent of a plane surface, land etc., *London covers a large area;* a region, particular district, *a rural area*
arena n. (*a rē'na*) Space in the middle of an amphitheatre where combats and contests were held; (fig.) the scene of any active conflict, *the political arena.* (Lat.
argue v.t. and i. (*ah'gū*) To debate, bring reasons for or against, *the lawyer argued the case brilliantly;* to indicate strongly, *this argues him to be a fool.* As v.i. to maintain *that* a thing is so, *he argued that education was bunk;* to debate keenly (*with, against* a person, *about* a topic, *against* a position, opinion); to persuade someone by reasoning, *I argued him out of it*
argument n. (*ah'gū ment*) Line of reasoning put forward in support of a proposition etc., *he has a strong argument;* a debate, discussion, dispute, *we had a heated argument about who should pay*
arid adj. (*ă'rid*) Dry, parched with heat (lit. and fig.); (of land)

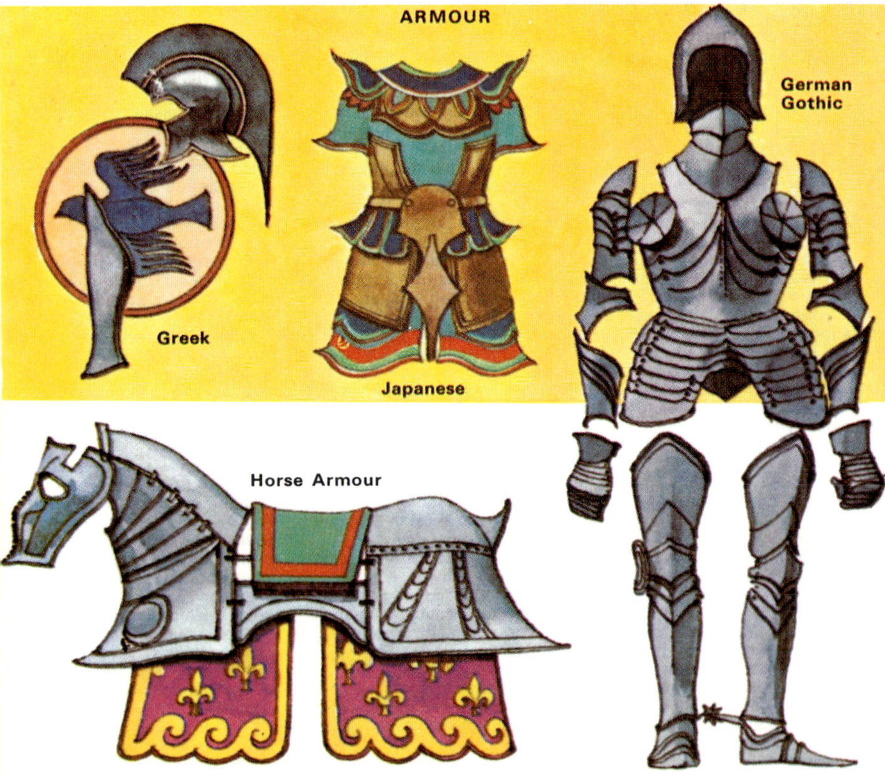

lacking precipitation, barren
arise v.i. (*a riz'*) **arose, arisen** To get up, rise (archaic); (fig.) to come into existence, into notice, *a murmur arose from the crowd, a doubt arose in his mind;* to result (*from, out of*), *one question arises from what he said*
arithmetic n. (*a rith'met ik*) The science of numbers; the art of computing, counting, calculating
ark n. (*ahk*) (bibl.) A chest, coffer; the vessel in which Noah escaped the Flood; **Ark of the Covenant** the holy chest containing the tablets of the Jewish Law
arm 1) n. (*ahm*) The upper limb of the human body from shoulder to hand; part of a garment covering this, a sleeve; part of a chair or seat supporting the arms
arm 2) n. (*ahm*) usually pl. A weapon, instrument for fighting
arm 3) v.t. and i. (*ahm*) To provide with arms, weapons; (fig.) to be equipped (with appropriate tools, mental preparation etc.) for a certain task, *he strode forth armed with the Bible and an umbrella.* As v.i. to take up, provide oneself with, arms
armistice n. (*ah'mis tis*) A truce, temporary suspension of hostilities by mutual agreement
armour n. (*ah'mer*) Protective covering for the body, worn in battle; steel plates protecting
army n. (*ah'mi*) Body of men organized for war on land
around adv. and prep. (*a rownd'*) Round about, in circles, *to walk around;* (colloq.) at random, *to fool around, play around.* As prep., on all sides of; on the other side of, *right around the corner;* about, *around two o'clock*
arrange v.t. and i. (*a rānj'*) To set in order, place systematically, to *arrange flowers, arrange one's ideas;* to settle (disputes etc.); to make preparations for, to *arrange a meeting;* (mus.) to adapt a work to some new purpose, as a quartet arranged for two pianos. As v.i. to come to an agreement, *he arranged with John to go to the sea;* to make plans, give instructions, *he arranged for flowers to be delivered*
arrangement n. (*a rānj'ment*) The act of arranging, putting things in order etc.; the order so produced
arrear(s) n. (usually pl.) (*a rēr(z)'*) That in which one has fallen behind, esp. in paying debts, rent, etc.; **in arrears** in debt
arrest v.t. (*a rest'*) To stop, check, hinder, *to arrest progress, decay;* (law) to seize (a person) on legal authority
arrival n. (*a rī'val*) The act of arriving, coming to one's destination; advent, appearance; person or thing that has arrived, *new arrivals;* (in pl.) trains, ships, etc., due to arrive shortly
arrive v.i. (*a riv'*) To come to a destination, *we arrived in Paris at 6 o'clock;* to appear on the scene, *he arrived just in time to prevent a massacre;* to reach (conclusion, etc., a certain time of life)
arrogant adj. (*ă'ro gant*) Insolently superior, overbearing
arrow n. (*ă'rō*) Slender shaft, sharp at the tip and feathered at the tail, to be shot from a bow; an object resembling this, esp. a sign indicating direction etc
arson n. (*ah'son*) The act and offence of wilfully setting fire to property, one's own or another's
art n. (*aht*) Craft or skill, esp. human skill as opposed to the works of nature; collective term for a number of human activities requiring sensibility and imagination in addition to skill, esp. the so-called *Fine Arts* of poetry, painting, sculpture, music, architecture
artery n. (*ah'ter i*) A large blood-vessel carrying blood from the heart to all parts of the body
article n. (*ah'tikl*) An item, a particular thing, *an article of clothing;* a separate portion or clause of a document
artificial adj. (*ah ti fish'l*) Made by art or skill, not by nature; contrived to imitate the real, *artificial teeth, flowers;* real, but produced by skill, *artificial insemination;* (of persons, manners) unnatural, forced, false, *an artificial smile;* **artificial respiration** forced inducement of breathing in suffocated persons
artillery n. (*ah til'er i*) Big guns discharging shells, missiles, as opposed to *small arms;* the branch of the army that manages these
artist n. (*ah'tist*) One who practises one of the fine arts (esp. painting) as a profession; one skilled in such arts; one who
as adv., conj., and rel. pron. (*ăz, az*) Expressing equality in comparisons, *as good as gold,* or equality, identity of manner, degree, etc., *do as you please, as a stag turns at bay, so he stood against his enemies, as far as*

ash

mountain ash

possible in the capacity of, *he joined the firm as a director;* having the appearance of, *he dressed up as a soldier;* since, seeing that, because, *as he disliked the host, he declined the invitation;* for instance, *some birds, such as the ostrich and the kiwi, cannot fly;* when, while, *as he was crossing the road he was hit by a car*

asbestos n. (*ăs bes'tos*) An incombustible greyish-white fibrous mineral, capable of being woven into fireproof fabric

ascend v.t. and i. (*a send'*) To climb, go up, *to ascend the stairs*. As v.i. to move upwards, *ascend into heaven*

ascent n. (*a sent'*) The act of ascending

ash 1) n. (*ăsh*) Tree of the genus *Fraxinius*; the wood of this tree; **mountain ash** the rowan tree

ash 2) n. usually pl. **ashes** (*ăsh, ăsh'iz*) The greyish powdery material left after combustion

ashamed pred. adj. (*a shāmd'*) Stricken with shame, feeling consciousness of guilt

ashore adv. (*a shaw*(r)') On, to, the shore

aside adv. (*a sīd'*) On or to one side, (lit. or fig.) *he stepped aside to let her pass,*

ask v.t. and i. (*ahsk*) To beg to be told, request information, *to ask a question, to ask the time;* (with person as direct obj.) to put a question to, *I asked him how he felt;* to beg, urge upon (a person), beg for (a thing), *I asked him to do his best, he asked a favour in return;* to demand a price for, *he is asking £10,000 for his house;* to invite, *she asked me to dinner;* to publish banns of marriage. As v.i. (followed by *for*), *to ask for help,* (or, *after, about*), *to ask after a person*

asleep adv. and pred. adj. (*a slēp'*) Sleeping; (of limbs) numb

asphalt n. and v.t. (*ăs'fălt*) Mineral pitch, a hard, brittle, bituminous substance; as mixed with sand, gravel, etc., for surfacing roads

aspirin n. (*ăs'pi rin*) Trade name for a compound of salicylic acid used to relieve pain and reduce fever

ass n. (*ăs*) The donkey, a quadruped related to the horse, with long ears and a tufted tail; (fig.) a stupid, ignorant person

assassin n. (*a săs'in*) A murderer, esp. with political motives

assassinate v.t. (*a săs'in āt*) To murder for political reasons, to kill a public figure

assault n. and v.t. (*a sawlt'*) A violent or sudden attack (lit. and fig.); (law) performance or threat of injury to another person. As v.t. to make such an attack

ass

assemble v.t. and i. (*a sem'bl*) To bring together, collect (persons or things), *to assemble the troops;* to put together the parts of a machine, *to assemble a motor*. As v.i. to come together, meet, *a crowd assembled in the square*
assembly n. (*a sem'bli*) Gathering, or being gathered, together; a concourse, meeting, for a specific purpose, *a legislative assembly*
assent v.i. and n. (*a sent'*) To agree, consent (*to*) proposals, etc. As n. the act of agreeing, agreement, *to give one's assent*
assess v.t. and i. (*a ses'*) To estimate the value of
assign v.t. and n. (*a sīn'*) To allot as a share *to*; (law) to make over (property) to another; to appoint (a person to a special duty, etc.); to ascribe (event, work of art, etc
assignment n. (*a sīn'ment*) Allotment (of work, duties, etc.)
assist v.t. and i. (*a sist'*) To help. As v.i. to take part *in*; to be present *at*. Hence: **assistance** n. help; **assistant** n. helper, junior co-worker
associate 1) v.t. and i. (*a sō'shi āt*) To join (person or thing) *with* another; to connect by thought, *we associate Italy with wine and sunshine*
associate 2) adj. and n. (*a sō'shi at*) Closely connected, *associate companies;* co-operating, connected, but without full power etc., *associate professor, associate membership*. As n. a partner, a companion in common activities, a colleague
assort v.t. and i. (*a sawt'*) To arrange into groups, to classify according to character, appearance etc. Hence: **assortment** n. the act of assorting; a group or collection of assorted objects
assure v.t. (*a shōōr'*) To make a thing certain, ensure, *Ariadne's thread assured his safe return;* to assert confidently to, *I assured him that it was a bargain;* to promise, *I assure you I will do my best;* to insure
asthma n. (*ăs'ma*) (med.) Chronic or recurrent spasm of the bronchial tubes, causing difficulty in breathing, etc
astonish v.t. (*as ton'ish*) To surprise, amaze greatly. Hence **astonishment** n
astray adv. (*a strā'*) Off the right track, in the wrong direction (lit. and fig.), *to go, be led, astray*
astrology n. (*as trol'o ji*) Primitive astronomy; the art or practice of predicting events, etc., by study of the stars. Hence: **astrologer** n
astronaut n. (*ăst'rō naut*) Person trained in astronautics
astronautics n. (*ăstro naw' tiks*) Science that deals with travel in outer space
astronomy n. (*as tron'o mi*) The scientific study of the heavenly bodies. Hence: **astronomer** n.
astute adj. (*a stūt'*) Shrewd; crafty
asylum n. (*a sī'lum*) A place of sanctuary, refuge, *to seek asylum, political asylum;* obsolete term for institution for the care of the infirm, esp. the insane, *lunatic asylum*
at prep. (*ăt*) Expressing place in which a thing is, *at Windsor*, or position, *at the top, at the end;* expressing motion or direction towards, *to jump at, to point at;* expressing time when, *at 4 o'clock, at Easter;* expressing and governing number, price, etc., *at two shillings a pound;* in many adverbial phrases denoting relations in space, *at a distance*, time, *at once*, manner, *at least*, or position, *at home*
athlete n. (*ăth'lēt*) One skilled in physical exercises, esp. running, jumping, and throwing
athletic adj. (*ăth let'ik*) Pertaining to athletes; vigorous and strong. Hence: **athletically** adv.; **athleticism** n. devotion to, practice of **athletics** n.pl. physical sports, esp. track and field events (running, jumping, throwing)
atlas n. (*ăt'las*) Bound collection of maps
atmosphere n. (*ăt'mos fēr*) The gaseous envelope surrounding some planets, esp. the Earth
atom n. (*ăt'om*) (chem.) The smallest particle in which an element combines with itself or another
atomic adj. (*a tom'ik*) Pertaining to, consisting of, atoms; **atomic bomb** earliest type deriving energy from nuclear fission
attach v.t. and i. (*a tăch'*) To fasten (a thing to another) Hence: **attachable** adj.; **attachment** n
attack v.t. and n. (*a tăk'*) To assault, assail (in any sense, lit. and fig.). As n. the act of attacking, assault; an instance of this; mode of beginning (esp. mus. and dram.). Hence: **attacker** n. assailant
attempt 1) v.t. (*a tempt'*) To try, seek to obtain a thing or perform an action, *to attempt a hard task*

to attempt to swim the Channel
attempt 2) n. (*a tempt'*) An endeavour to do something
attend v.i. and t. (*a tend'*) To pay good heed (to), *attend to what you are doing;* to apply oneself to, perform, *I must attend to this matter;* to wait *upon* in order to serve, *four royal dukes attended upon the king.* As v.t. to be present at, *to attend church, a lecture;* to accompany, wait upon, *a footman attended the royal party;* to visit in order to render service, *a doctor attended him night and day;* to accompany in fig. sense, *attended by misfortune*
attendance n. (*a ten'dens*) Act of attending, serving, being present, *to be in attendance, attendance is compulsory;* those present at a meeting, cinema, etc., *there was a good attendance at the performance*
attention n. (*a ten'shun*) State or act of mental application, watchful notice, *to pay attention;* awareness, *to call, attract attention;* care, solicitude, *your wound needs attention*
attic n. (*ăt'ik*) Top storey of a house, or room in this, immediately under the roof, a garret
attitude n. (*ăt'i tūd*) Posture of body, disposition of limbs, etc.; way of thinking, feeling, behaving, *what is your attitude to this problem?*
attract v.t. and i. (*a trăkt'*) To draw towards (of physical forces), *a magnet attracts iron;* (fig.) to arouse interest and admiration in a person, to charm, allure; to draw attention, etc
attractive adj. (*a trăk'tiv*) Having the power to attract; (fig.) charming, pleasant, pretty
auction n. and v.t. (*awk'shun*) Public sale at which asking price is raised until a buyer is found; As v.t. to sell by auction. Hence: **auctioneer** n. one whose business is to auction goods
audible adj. (*aw'dib l*) Loud enough to be heard
audience n. (*aw'di ens*) A hearing; a formal interview (with king, pope, etc.); a judicial session to hear cases; an assembly of listeners (to play, concert, etc., but also applied loosely as in *a writer's audience*)
audio adj. (*aw'dyō*) Relating to the reproduction of sound
audio-visual adj. (*aw'dyō vizh'u al*) Involving both hearing and sight; descriptive of teaching aids involving film strips, recordings, etc.
audition n. (*aw dish'n*) The act or capacity of hearing; a trial given to a singer, dancer, etc., by a prospective employer
auditorium n. (*aw di taw'ri um*) Building or part of building in which an audience sits
aunt n. (*ahnt*) Sister of one's father or mother; wife of an uncle
author n. (*aw'ther*) Creator, originator, of anything; esp. of a literary work
authority n. (*aw thor'i ti*) The power or legal right to command and be obeyed, *the authority of the law;* (often pl.) person or group having power, *the Port of London Authority, the local authorities* (i.e. County Council); influence, etc. derived from knowledge, experience, etc., *an opinion of great authority;* an expert, *an authority on French wines;* books, etc., in which reliable opinions are expressed
authorize v.t. (*aw'thor iz*) To give authority to (a person); sanction, allow (an action)
autobiography n. (*aw tō bī og'ra fi*) Writing the history of one's own life; an instance of this
autograph n. and v.t. (*aw'to grahf*) A person's own writing, esp. his signature As v.t. to write one's name as a favour in a book, album, etc
automatic adj. and n. (*aw to măt'ik*) Working of itself, *automatic gear-change;* (of movements, actions) involuntary. As n. a self-loading, quick-firing pistol
automobile n. (*aw tō mō bēl'*) Motor-car
autopsy n. (*aw'top si*) Personal inspection, esp. post-mortem examination
autumn n. (*aw'tum*) The third season of the year, between summer and winter
auxiliary adj. and n. (*awg zil'i a ri*) Helping; subsidiary; **auxiliary verb** (such as 'be', 'have', etc.) that helps to form tenses of other verbs. As n. a helper; an auxiliary verb; (pl.) foreign troops
avalanche n. (*ăv'a lahnch*) A mass of loosened snow and ice hurtling down a mountainside; (fig.) as in *an avalanche of letters*
avenge v.t. (*a venj'*) To exact satisfaction, inflict retribution, for an injury
avenue n. (*ăv'en ū*) Tree-lined

driveway to country house; tree-lined street; wide roadway
average 1) n. (*ăv'er ij*) Medial estimate, as *average of 4 and 2 is 3;* generally prevailing standard, *up to, about, average*
average 2) adj. (*ăv'er ij*) Obtained by average, *average expenditure;* ordinary, standard, *average height*
average 3) v.t. and i. (*ăv'er ij*) To estimate the average of
aviary n. (*ā'vi a ri*). Place for keeping birds
avoid v.t. (*a void'*) To keep away from (place); to shun (persons); refrain from (doing); escape from (consequences, trouble, etc.)
await v.t. (*a wāt'*) Wait for, *I will await you;* (of things) to be in store for, *death awaits us at the end*
awake 1) (**awoke, awaked**) v.t. and i. (*a wāk'*) To rouse from sleep or lethargy; to make a person aware, *awake him to the dangers;* to revive (feelings, etc.) As v.i. to wake up, come out of sleep; (with *to*) to become aware of
awake 2) pred. adj. (*a wāk'*) Not sleeping; (fig.) mentally alert
awaken v.t. and i. (*a wā'ken*) To awake, but esp. in sense of to make, become aware, *awaken to the possibilities*
award 1) v.t. (*a wawd'*) To grant, assign, *to award damages;* to give as a prize
award 2) n. (*a wawd'*) Decision, grant, by judges; payment by arbiters; prize, medal, etc
aware adj. (*a wār'*) Conscious, knowing, *aware of the dangers.* Hence: **awareness** n
away adv. pat. (*a wā'*) At or to some distance from a given person or place, *far away, to go away;* not at home, absent, *he is away, an away match;* denoting continuity of action, *to work away;* without delay as in *right away* get going as in *away with you;* much the best as in *far and away;* **to explain away** to excuse; **to get away with** escape the consequences of; **to pass away** to die
awe n. and v.t. (*aw*) Fear mixed with reverence, *to stand in awe of*
awful adj. (*aw'fo͞ol*) Inspiring awe, dreadful, *awful majesty;* (colloq.) used as an intensive (bad sense implied) *an awful noise, I had an awful time.* Hence: **awfully** adv. in an awful way; (colloq.) very
awhile adv. (*a wīl'*) For a short time
awkward adj. (*awk'werd*) (of things) Ill-fitted for use, *an awkward suitcase to carry;* (of non-material things) embarrassing, inconvenient, *an awkward situation;* (of persons, actions) clumsy, ungainly, *an awkward movement;* (colloq.) difficult to deal with, *an awkward customer*
axe n. and v.t. (*ăks*) Tool with heavy sharp-edged head at right-angles to long handle, for cutting trees, etc
As v.t. to cut down (public expenditure)
axis n. (*ăk'sis*) pl. **axes** (*ăk'sēz*) Imaginary central line of a body, esp. (astron.) hypothetical line about which a body appears to rotate; the line which divides a body into two symmetrical halves
axle n. (*ăks l*) **axle-tree** Pin or rod on which a wheel or pair of wheels revolves

B

babble v.t. and i. and n. (*băb l*) To speak incoherently or indistinctly, as an infant; (often with *away*) to chatter foolishly; to reveal secrets indiscreetly; (of streams, etc.) to make the gentle murmuring sound

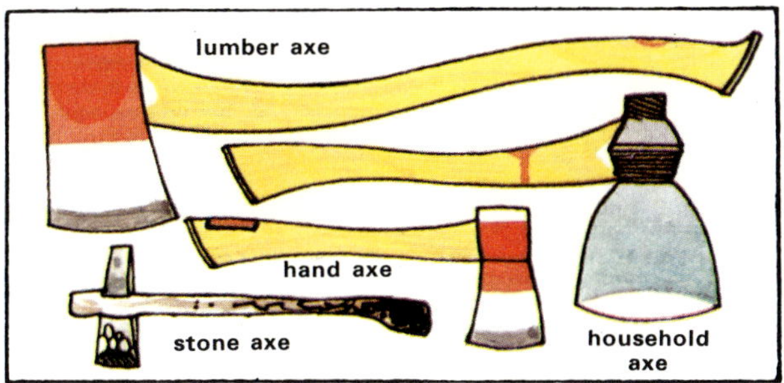

of flowing water. As n. incoherent speech; childish prattle; idle talk; murmur of running water

baby n. (*bā'bi*) Very young child

bachelor n. (*băch'el er*) Unmarried man; holder of lowest university degree

back 1) n. (*băk*) Hinder part of human body from base of neck to base of spine; corresponding part in animals; part of object most distant from observer, *the back of the stage;* part of a chair, etc., supporting the back of sitter; part of a thing opposite the operative part, *back of a knife, of the hand;* (in football, hockey, etc.) position in the rear, defensive, lines of players

back 2) v.t. and i. (*băk*) To provide or form a back or lining for; to give moral, legal, or material support to; to bet money on (horses or other contestants); to cause to go backwards, reverse (cars, etc.); to endorse (documents). As v.i. to move backwards (in a car, on horseback, etc.)

back 3) adj. (*băk*) Situated in the rear, *back yard;* overdue, *back payment;* no longer current, out of date, *back number*

back 4) adv. (*băk*) To the rear, *to look back, move back;* returning to the original place, state, etc., *to go back home, to give back;* into the past, *to think back;* away from, at a distance, *back from the road*

backbencher n. (*băk bĕn'cher*) Member of Parliament sitting on the back (i.e. less important) benches of the House of Commons

backbone n. (*băk'bōn*) The spinal column; (fig.) firmness of character, determination; (fig.) the main support, foundation, constituent of a thing

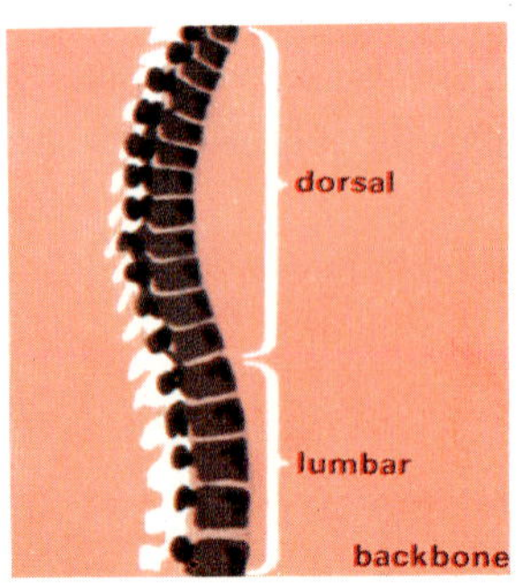

background n. (*băk'grownd*) More distant part of scene, painting etc., against which the main figures or objects stand out; obscure position, *to keep in the background;* (fig.) general knowledge, cultural environment, of a subject, *the historical background of Shakespeare's plays*

backward(s) adv. **backward** adj. (*băk'werd*(z)) Towards the back, *to lean backwards;* with the back foremost, *to walk backwards;* in the reverse direction to the normal, *he counted backwards from ten to one*. As adj. turned towards the back, *a backward glance;* behindhand in mental, educational, or social development, *a backward child, a backward nation;*

bacon n. (*bā'kun*) Cured back and sides of a pig

bacterium n. (*băk tēr'i um*) pl. **bacteria** Microscopic living vegetable organisms found almost everywhere

bad adj. (**worse, worst**) and n. (*băd*) Wicked, immoral, *bad habits, language;* worthless, corrupt, *bad faith, bad coin;* offensive, disagreeable, *bad feeling, bad temper;* decayed, *bad meat, a bad tooth;* unsound, *bad health, a bad leg;* (of things in themselves not good) severe, *a bad headache;* inadequate, below standard, *a bad dinner, with bad grace;* unfortunate, *bad luck;* unfavourable, *in a bad light;* (with *for*) harmful, *bad for the health*

badge n. (*bădj*) Distinguishing mark or token of rank, membership of society, etc

badger n. (*băd'jer*) Small grey nocturnal animal with long coarse hair, living in earth-burrow or set

badminton n. (*băd'min ton*) Game in which a shuttlecock is hit to and fro across a net

baffle v.t. (*băf l*) To puzzle, bewilder (persons); to hinder, bar progress of (efforts, etc.); often pres.p. **baffling** adj. *a baffling question*

bag n. (*băg*) Receptacle, with opening at the top, made of paper, cloth, leather, or other flexible material, *travelling-bag, shopping-bag*

baggage n. (*băg'ij*) Collection of travelling-bags, luggage (now chiefly U.S.)

bagpipe n. (*băg'pīp*) Musical wind instrument, the player blowing into a leather bag which is pressed to provide an even flow

bagpipe

balalaika

of air into pipes fitted with reeds and finger-holes

bail 1) n. (*bāl*) Sum of money paid as security for a prisoner's appearance at his trial

bail 2) v.t. (*bāl*) Usually **bail out.** To secure (or grant) release of a prisoner awaiting trial by paying bail 1)

bail 3) n. (*bāl*) (cricket) cross-piece laid on top of stumps;

bail 4), **bale** v.t. and i. (*bāl*) To ladle water out of a boat, using bucket, cupped hands, etc

bait 1) v.t. and i. (*bāt*) To worry, harass (bulls, bears, etc.) with dogs; (fig.) to tease, provoke; to put bait (n.) in trap or on hook to catch animals or fish

bait 2) n. (*bāt*) Real or imitation food used to lure animals to traps, fish to hooks

bake v.t. and i. (*bāk*) To cook by dry heat in closed space or oven; to dry and harden by heat. As v.i. to become baked (cakes, earth, etc.); (fig.) to get very hot

baker n. (*bā'ker*) Professional maker of bread, cakes, etc.; **baker's dozen** thirteen

bakery n. place where bread is baked or shop where it is sold

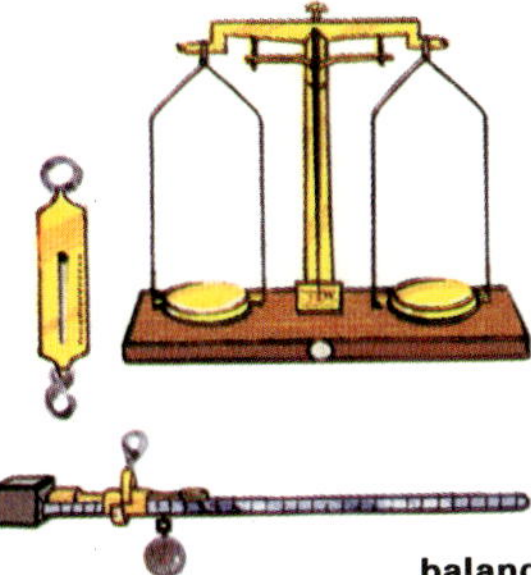

balance

balance 1) n. (*băl'ans*) The condition of equilibrium between two opposing forces, weights, etc.; equality of weight or quantity; a weighing apparatus, pair of scales; the amount required to make two weights or quantities equal to each other, esp. the sum of money required to equalize two sides of a credit and debit account; (pop.) the remainder, or the sum remaining on the credit side (in a bank account, etc.); (fig.) mental equipoise, reasonable and normal state of mind; (fig.) poise, steadiness, *to keep one's balance;* (fig.) harmony of proportion (i.e. in a picture, orchestration, etc.)

balance 2) v.t. and i. (*băl'ans*) To bring to, keep in, a state of equilibrium

balcony n. (*băl'ko ni*) Balustraded platform outside upper-storey windows; in theatres, seats between dress-circle and gallery

bald adj. (*bawld*) Lacking hair on the head; bare, without vegetation (mountains, etc.); simple, unadorned, undisguised, *bald statement*

bale n. (*bāl*) Large bundle of goods, wrapped in canvas and corded or metal hooped.
to escape by parachute from an aircraft

ball 1) n. (*bawl*) Spherical or roundish object, solid or hollow, of any size or substance; sphere (large or small, hard or soft, solid, hollow, or inflated) used in many games A social assembly for dancing, dancing party

ballad n. (*băl'ad*) Poem in short stanzas and simple metre relating popular or traditional story (originally sung); a simple song with repetitive melody and narrative words

ballet n. (*băl'ā*) Elaborate and stylized dance performance to music, often representing some dramatic action; the art of this type of dancing
balloon n. (*ba lōōn'*) Inflated bag filled with lighter-than-air gas which causes it to rise
ballot n. and v.i. (*băl'ot*) Paper (orig. a ball) used in secret voting; secret voting in general; the total of votes cast; **ballot-box** in which voting papers are put. As v.i. to vote by ballot
balm n. (*bahm*) Sap, juice, or gum resin obtained from various aromatic or healing shrubs and trees; fragrant healing ointment; **balmy** adj. soothing, *balmy breezes*
balustrade n. (*băl us trād'*) Row of balusters supporting a rail or canopy
bamboo n. (*băm bōō'*) Genus of tropical giant grass of the family Gramineae with hard, jointed stalks; the stalk of this plant

balustrade

bamboo

ban v.t. (*băn*) To forbid, prohibit
banana n. (*ba nah'na*) A tropical fruit-tree; the long finger-shaped fruit of this, with soft flesh and rubbery greenish-yellow rind
band 1) n. (*bănd*) Thin strip of material used for binding objects together, esp. flat strip, hoop (of metal, elastic, etc.); any flat strip (as on hats, clothes, etc.); a stripe a company of persons, *band of brothers, robber band;* a company of musicians, *brass band*
band 2) v.t. and i. (*bănd*) To collect together (of persons); usually **to band together** unite for a purpose
bandage n. and v.t. (*băn'dij*) Strip of fabric to dress and bind up wounds and injuries. As v.t. to apply a bandage to a wound, etc
bandit n. (*băn'dit*) pl. **banditti, bandits** An outlaw, brigand, armed robber usually member of a gang under a recognized leader
bang 1) v.t. and i. (*băng*) To strike forcibly and noisily
As v.i. to explode, to make a loud noise
bang 2) n. (*băng*) Sudden loud noise, report, explosion; a violent blow
bangle n. (*băng'gl*) Slender bracelet or anklet
banish v.t. (*băn'ish*) To expel, drive out, esp. to exile a person from his country
banister n. (*băn'is ter*) Handrail of a staircase and its supporting uprights (usually pl. **banisters**)
banjo n. (*băn'jō*) pl. **banjos, banjoes** Stringed instrument with body like a tambourine and neck like a guitar
bank 1) n. (*băngk*) Mound of earth, snow, sand, etc.; raised shelf on sea- or river-bed; sloping edge of river, lake, etc

banjo

bank 2) v.t. and i. (*băngk*) To heap up into a bank (often with *up*)
bank 3) n. (*băngk*) An establishment that trades in, receives, lends, or exchanges money; the building occupied by such an institution
bank 4) v.t. and i. (*băngk*) To keep (money) in a bank; to carry on the business of banking
banker n. (*băng'ker*) One who keeps, carries on the business of, a bank
bankrupt n., adj. and v.t. (*băng'krupt*) An insolvent person one not able to pay his debts
banner n. (*băn'er*) Flag, ensign, usually symbolic of country, cause, etc.; representative flag (carried on two poles) or placard with slogan borne in religious, political, etc., processions
banquet n. and v.t. and i. (*băng'kwet*) A sumptuous feast, often official or as celebration
banter n. and v.t. and i. (*băn'ter*) Good-humoured teasing and raillery. As v.t. to tease. As v.i. to joke
baptism n. (*băp'tizm*) Sacrament of initiation into the Christian Church (by sprinkling of water or immersion)
baptize v.t. and i. (*băp tīz'*) To administer the sacrament of baptism; to christen, name (person)
bar 1) n. (*bah(r)*) Long narrow piece of wood, metal, or other rigid material; such a thing in many special uses, e.g. for obstruction (on doors, windows, etc.); for closing a road, *toll-bar;* gatehouse in fortified town, *Temple Bar;* bank of sand in river or harbour mouth; railing in court of justice dividing off the places where the judges sit and where the accused stands; a counter (or room containing it) at which drinks are served in hotels and public-houses, *saloon bar;* (law) the whole body of qualified barristers; a plea that completely destroys a plaintiff's claim or action; a railing in the House of Commons, etc., beyond which non-members may not go; (fig.) a moral or intellectual restriction, a barrier or obstacle to progress; (mus.) vertical line drawn across stave dividing it into sections of equal time-value, such a section, *the opening bars of the National Anthem*
bar 2) v.t. and prep. (*bah(r)*) To fasten (door, window, etc.) with a bar; to obstruct in general, *to bar the way;* to exclude, rule out, forbid, *politics and religion are barred from this discussion*
barbarian n. and adj. (*bah bār'i an*) Originally used by Greeks and Romans of foreign, thus rude and uncivilized, people and nations; a rough, uncouth, uncultured person. As adj. rude, uncivilized; cruel
barbarous adj. (*bah'ba rus*) Wild, savage; coarse, unrefined; cruel
barbecue n. and v.t. (*bah'bi kū*) Wooden frame for smoking and roasting meat, vegetables, etc., open-air function at which such fare is prepared and served
As v.t. to roast an animal whole
bare adj. (*bār*) Naked, without normal covering, *bare feet;* without ornament, *a bare wall;* devoid (of), empty, *the cupboard was bare;* just enough, mere, *a bare handful;* slight (often super.), *the barest chance;* exposed, *to lay bare;* **bareback** without a saddle; **barefaced** insolent, unashamed, *a barefaced lie;* **barefoot** adj. and adv. and **barefooted** adj. without shoes or stockings; **bareheaded** without hat; **barelegged** without stockings. Hence: **barely** adv. nakedly; scarcely, only just, *he barely succeeded;* **bareness** n
bargain 1) n. (*bah'gen*) An agreement, pact, usually concerning buying and selling; a thing thus acquired; *good, bad, bargain;* a thing acquired or offered cheap, *this is a bargain – it's worth double*
bargain 2) v.i. (*bah'gen*) To argue over price or terms (*with* a person, *about* price, etc.)
barge n. (*bahj*) Large flat-bottomed freight-boat used on canals, rivers, etc.
richly decorated vessel for use on ceremonial occasions
bark 1) n. (*bahk*) Outer protective rind of trees
bark 2) v.i. and t. (*bahk*) Of dogs, foxes, etc., to utter the sharp, explosive cry natural to them
barley n. (*bah'li*) Cereal plant of the genus *Hordeum* whose grain is used as food and for malt in brewing and distilling; its grain
barn n. (*bahn*) Building for storing grain, hay, etc.; (fig.) large, bare, draughty room or building
barometer n. (*ba rom'it er*) Instrument for measuring

atmospheric pressure
barrack(s) n. (usually pl.) (*bă'raks*) Large building housing troops
barrel n. (*bă'rel*) Cylindrical vessel or cask of hooped wooden staves, with flat ends and bulging sides; the contents of a barrel, *a barrel of beer;* hollow metal tube in firearm through which projectile passes after firing
barren adj. and n. (*bă'ren*) Not, or incapable of, producing young, fruit, vegetation; unproductive land; (fig.) unfruitful, unprofitable
barricade n. and v.i. (*bă ri kād'*) Improvised barrier, obstruction, across street, etc. As v.t. to block (street, etc.) or defend (place, etc.) with a barricade
barrier n. (*bă'ri er*) Obstacle, obstruction, to prevent approach or access; (fig.) hindrance, obstacle to progress; any obstacle, boundary
barrow n. (*bă'rō*) Small hand-cart with one or two wheels and two legs to support it when at rest
barter v.t. and i. (*bah'ter*) To exchange goods *for* other goods
base 1) n. (*bās*) Bottom, lowest part of a thing; foundation, what an object rests on
base 2) v.t. (*bās*) To found (anything) on another, to use as a starting point (largely fig.), *to base one's hopes on;* (usually p.p.) (milit.) to station at
basement n. (*bās'ment*) Storey of house below ground level
bash v.t. and n. (*băsh*) (colloq.) To strike violently; to beat, thrash (person). As n. a violent blow; **to have a bash** try, have a go
bashful adj. (*băsh'fool*) Shy shame-faced
basic adj. (*bā'sik*) Fundamental, *basic principles;* forming the base, *basic structure*

basin n. (*bā'sin*) Hollow round vessel less deep than wide, with sides curving in towards small circular base; hollow or depression of this shape, such as a pool; land-locked harbour or dock closed with flood-gates; area drained by a river
basket n. (*bahs'kit*) Hollow receptacle of cane, rushes, etc., usually with handle; the contents of this, *a basket of eggs;* receptacle of other materials resembling this, *fire-basket*
bass adj. and n. (*bās*) (mus.) Low in pitch, deep-sounding, *a bass voice, aria*. As n. the lower part of the musical register; the deepest male voice or a singer with such a voice
bat 1) n. (*băt*) Nocturnal flying mammal of order Chiroptera with mouse-like body and large membranes attached to fore and hind legs to form wings
bat 2) n. and v.t. and i. (*băt*) Wooden club for striking in various ball-games, esp. cricket and baseball
batch n. (*băch*) Loaves made at one baking; any group of things made, put, arriving, etc., together
bath n. and v.t. (*bahth*) Large metal, porcelain, or wooden tub containing enough water to immerse whole body; the act or fact of washing in this, *to have, take, a bath;* immersion in mud, etc., for medical purposes; a swimming-pool; (pl.) (*bah*thz) building in which various kinds of bath may be taken; (phot.) solution in which prints or plates are steeped. As v.t. to give a bath to (child, invalid, etc.)
bathe 1) v.i. and t. (*bā*th) To immerse oneself in water, the sea, etc., to wash or for recreation; to expose the body to the sun, usually *sun-bathe*. As v.t. to pour liquid over, soak; (of rivers, etc.) to flow by, wash, *Hawaii is bathed by the blue Pacific*. Hence: **bather** n
bathe 2) n. (*bā*th) The act of bathing; a swim. (From the above)
baton n. and v.t. (*bătn*) Short staff as symbol of office, *Field-Marshal's baton;* short staff passed from hand to hand in relay race; police truncheon (as v.t. to strike with this); slender wand used by orchestral conductors
battalion n. (*ba tăl'yon*) (milit.) Body of infantry consisting of several companies
batter 1) v.t. and i. (*băt'er*) To strike violently and repeatedly, *batter someone about, storm-battered*. As v.i. to make a loud noise by violent blows, *batter at the door*
batter 2) n. (*băt'er*) Mixture of flour, milk, and eggs whipped together
battery n. (*băt'er i*) (law) Unlawful attack, or threat of it, on another person, esp. *assault and battery;* (milit.) artillery unit (also fig. of arguments, etc.); (elect.) group of connected cells for generating current
battle 1) n. (*bătl*) A particular conflict between large opposing armed forces
battle 2) v.i. (*bătl*) To struggle *with*, fight *against*
bawl v.i. and t. and n. (*bawl*) To shout or cry loudly and harshly; to speak, sing, noisily. As n. a loud, harsh shout
bay 1) n. (*bā*) Large indentation in coastline or (of lake) shoreline
bay 2) v.i. and n. (*bā*) To bark continuously (as hounds in pursuit of their quarry). As n. bark of large dog, esp. continuous chorus of barking as hounds come upon hunted animal
bayonet n. and v.t. (*bā'o net*) Long dagger attachable to rifle muzzle
bazaar n. (*ba zah(r)'*) Eastern market; large store fitted up with fancy-goods stalls; a sale-of-work, jumble sale
be substantive, copulative, and auxiliary verb (*bē*) (pres. **am, is, are**; pret. **was, were**; pres.p. **being**; p.p. **been**) As v.subst. to exist, live, *I think therefore I am*, *there is a tavern in the town;* to remain, continue, *long may it be so;* to happen, *it can never be;* (in perfect tense) to have gone and returned, *have you been to Paris?* As v.cop. (linking subject and predicate) indicates a quality, *I am tall;* expresses identity, *this is the man I spoke of*, or cost, amount, *this book is two shillings, twice two is four*. As v.auxil. used with p.p. of verbs to form passive voice, *he was beaten;* with pres.p. of verbs to form continuous tenses, *he was working* (also in passive, *the road was being cleared*)
beach n. and v.t. (*bēch*) The edge of sea, lake, etc., esp. strip of land there covered with water-worn pebbles or sand As v.t. to drag (boats, etc.) up onto the

beach; run aground
beacon n. and v.i. and t. (*bē'kon*) Signal, warning fire on hill-top; lighthouse or prominent landmark, warning light at pedestrian crossings
bead n. and v.t. and i. (*bēd*) Small pierced ball of glass, etc., for threading with others to make a necklace
beagle n. and v.i. (*bēgl*) Small smooth-haired hound for hunting hares, accompanied on foot
beak n. (*bēk*) The sharp, often hooked, horny projections from the mouths of birds
beaker n. (*bē'ker*) Drinking cup; cylindrical glass vessel, with lip, for laboratory experiments
beam 1) n. (*bēm*) Long piece of heavy squared timber, ray of light; (fig.) warm, happy smile
beam 2) v.i. (*bēm*) To shine; (fig.) to smile cheerfully, radiantly
bean n. (*bēn*) One of several kinds of leguminous seeds grown in pods
bear 1) n. (*bār*) One of many kinds of mammals of the genus *Ursus*
bear 2) v.t. and i. (*bār*) (**bore**, **borne** or **born**, see below) To carry, support, sustain (lit. and fig.), *to bear a heavy load, to bear responsibility, it doesn't bear* (i.e. stand up to) *close scrutiny*
beard n. (*bērd*) Hair on lower part of the face
bearer n. (*bār'er*) Person who carries anything
bearing n. (*bār'ing*) Connection, relation, *this has no bearing on the problem;* deportment, behaviour, *a military bearing, a dignified bearing;* direction, relative position, *I took a bearing on the North Star, I had lost my bearings;* action of giving birth to (children) or producing (fruit)
beast n. (*bēst*) Animal, esp. mammals as distinct from birds, fish, insects, etc.; cattle; (fig.) a person of filthy habits or brutal character; the animal part of man's nature. Hence: **beastly** adj. and adv. like a beast, but also used colloq. of anything unpleasant, *a beastly job, beastly weather*
beat 1) v.t. and i. (*bēt*) (pret. **beat**, p.p. **beaten**) To strike repeatedly, thrash, *he beat her black and blue;* to defeat, surpass, *Ireland beat England by 22 points to nil;* to baffle, *it beats me how he does t!;* to stir rapidly, whip up (eggs, etc.); to shape (metal, etc.) by hammering; to rouse game from coverts. As v.i. to throb, pulsate
beat 2) n. (*bēt*) Regularly recurring stroke, pulsation, or throb (of the heart, etc.); recurring rhythmical stress in music; path or course habitually traversed (by policemen, etc.)
beautiful adj. and n. (*bū'ti fōōl*) Endowed with beauty, delightful to the senses (esp. the eye and ear)
beauty n. (*bū'ti*) A combination of qualities or attributes arousing a sense of aesthetic satisfaction or affording keen pleasure and delight to the senses, as in a work of art, or a woman's face; a beautiful feature, outstanding attraction, *her hair is her chief beauty;* a beautiful woman; an excellent example of its kind, *I love all roses, but this is a beauty*
beaver n. (*bē'ver*) Large rodent living by lakes and rivers; its fur; a hat made of this fur
because adv. and conj. (*be koz'*) For the reason that, since, inasmuch as
beckon v.t. and i. (*bek n*) To summon a person by a gesture, esp. of hand or crooked fingers.
become v.i. and t. (*bi kum'*) (pret. **became**, p.p. **become**) To come to be, *he became a lawyer;* to develop into, *he became a new man.* As v.t. to suit, look well on, be fitting, *her new dress becomes her, charity becomes the rich*
bed n. (*bed*) Thing on which a person or animal may rest or sleep, esp. a framework with mattress, etc.; plot of ground for cultivation, *flower-bed;* bottom of river, lake, sea
bee n. (*bē*) Small flying insect making wax and honey, equipped with sting, esp. the honey-bee
beehive wooden house for bees

beaver

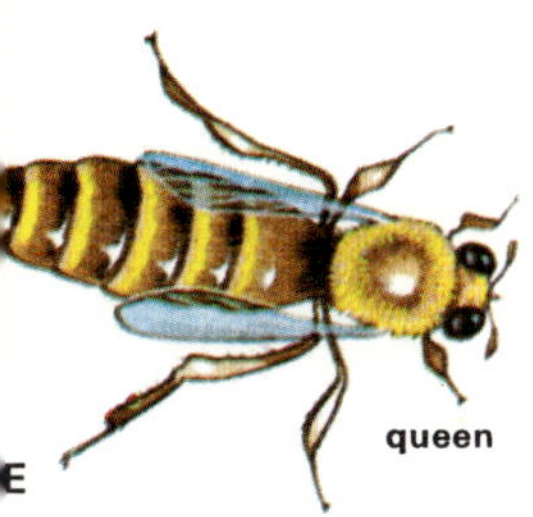
queen

drone

worker

E

beech n. (*bēch*) Smooth-barked tree of the genus *Fagus*, with oval-shaped leaves; its wood
beef n. (*bēf*) pl. **beeves** (*bēvz*) Formerly, an ox; now, the flesh of an ox, bull or cow
beer n. (*bēr*) Alcoholic beverage of fermented malted barley flavoured with hops
beet n. (*bēt*) Two plants, one with red roots eaten as a vegetable (also *beetroot*), the other with white roots used for making sugar
beetle n. (*bētl*) Insect of the order *Coleoptera*, with hard, scaly wing coverings; (pop.) only of large black varieties and (wrongly) of the cockroach
before adv., prep., and conj. (*be faw(r)'*) Ahead, *those who have gone before;* earlier, already, *I have heard that before;* on the front, *he wore armour before and behind*. As prep. ahead of, *a drummer marched before the victims to the scaffold;* in front of, *a tree stands before the house;* in the presence of, *before the king;* under the impulse of, *to sail before the wind;* earlier in order or precedence than, *your turn before mine;* earlier in time than, *before Christmas, before Christ* (B.C.), *I must finish this before going to bed* (also as conj. *. . . before I go to bed*); rather than, *he would resign before betraying his principles*
beg v.t. and i. (*beg*) To ask for, esp. charity, alms; to implore, entreat earnestly, *I beg you to spare my life;* to ask politely, *I beg your pardon*. As v.i. to live by asking for alms
beggar n. (*beg'er*) One who lives by soliciting alms
begin v.t. and i. (*bi gin'*) (pret. **began**, p.p. **begun**) To commence an action, start (doing a thing), *to begin speaking, to begin to speak, to begin a book* (i.e. to read it); to initiate, be the first to do, a thing, *the Athenians began the idea of democracy*. As v.i. to start, to come into being, *it's beginning to rain, since the world began;* **to begin with** in the first place. Hence: **beginner** n. one who begins, thus (fig.) a learner, novice; **beginning** n. the start, origin
behave v.i. and reflex. (*bi hāv'*) To act, conduct oneself, *he behaved with great dignity* (absolute, of children only, *did little Tommy behave?*); (reflex.) to act with good manners; **well-(ill-, badly-) behaved** with good (or bad) manners
behaviour n. (*bi hāv'yer*) Manner; manners; way of acting
behind adv., prep. and n. (*bi hīnd'*) In, to, the rear (of), on the further side (of), at the back (of), *behind the house, to fall behind;* on the other side (of), *he hid behind a bush;* remaining after a departure, *to leave a thing behind;* past in time, *our joys are before us, our cares are behind;* in arrears, *behind with the rent;* in support (of), *the City is behind the Tory party*
behold v.t. (*bi hōld'*) (pret.

TLE

bark beetle

ladybird

Colorado beetle

beheld) To see; (imper. used absolutely) look!; consider!
being n. (*bē'ing*) Existence, life in the abstract; a living creature, esp. *human-being*
belfry n. (*bel'fri*) Bell tower; part of tower where bells hang
belief n. (*bi lēf'*) Something held by a person to be true, esp. of religious doctrines; a firm conviction, esp. when arrived at by intuition rather than knowledge, *to the best of my belief*
believe v.t. and i. (*bi lēv'*) To hold a thing to be true, esp. a religious doctrine; to trust (a person's word etc.); to think, be under the impression that, *I believe it is going to rain*. As v.i. to have faith in (person, principle, God, etc.); to set store by (with *in*), *I believe in moderation*
bell n. (*bel*) Hollow bowl-shaped metal vessel emitting a clear note when struck with a clapper; anything resembling a bell in shape, *diving-bell*, etc
bellow v.i. and n. (*bel'ō*) To roar (as a bull); to shout, sing, loudly. As n. noise a bull makes
belly 1) n. (*bel'i*) Lower part of the trunk in mammals, below the diaphragm; the stomach
belly 2) v.i. (*bel'i*) To swell out, esp. of sails in the wind
belong v.i. (*bi long'*) To be appropriate, pertain, *to* (of rights, duties, etc.); to be the property of, *this book belongs to me;* to be in place, *this book belongs on the shelf, we all belong in society;* to be a member of (club, etc., with *to*). Hence: **belongings** n. pl. possession
beloved p.p. used as adj. and n. (as p.p. in pass. *bi luvd'*, as adj. and n. *bi luv'id*) Loved. As n. a much loved person
below adv. and prep. (*bi lō'*) At, to, a lower level (in relation to a given position); later in a book, *see below;* (naut.) underneath main deck; **here below** on earth, in this life. As prep. lower than (in position); down stream, *below the bridge;* inferior to (in merit, morals, rank, etc.)
belt n. (*belt*) Waist-band of leather, etc., to confine garments or support garments or weapons; girdle indicating rank of earl or knight; in machines, band connecting and driving wheels, shafts, etc.; any broad strip of approximately uniform width, *belt of trees, Green Belt*
bench n. (*bench*) Long wooden seat, often backless table of carpenter, etc
bend 1) n. (*bend*) A curve; (part of) something not straight
bend 2) v.t. and i. (*bend*) (pret. and p.p. **bent**) To curve, make crooked (of rather rigid material); to stoop (often with *down*)
beneath adv. and prep. (*bi nēth'*) Below, lower (than); (of merit or social position) inferior (to), *beneath one's notice, he married beneath him*
benefactor n. (*ben'i făk ter*) Person who gives one help or money, or does one a service
benefit 1) n. (*ben'i fit*) A generous action, favour, *to confer benefits upon;* advantage, *this is greatly to my benefit;* theatrical performance, sporting event, etc., from which money is given to charity or particular player
benefit 2) v.t. and i. (*ben'i fit*) To do good to. As v.i. to derive advantage (*by* a thing)
bereave v.t. (*bi rēv'*) (p.p. **bereaved, bereft**) To deprive of, usually in p.p., **bereaved** being used more of deprivation (of relatives, friends) by death, **bereft** in more general senses, *bereft of hope*. Hence: **bereavement** n
beret n. (*be'rā*) Soft, round peakless cap, as worn by Basque peasants
berry n. and v.i. (*be'ri*) Small, spherical pulpy fruit of some trees and shrubs; (bot.) soft fleshy fruit containing seeds
berth n. and v.t. and i. (*burth*) Room for ship to swing at anchor or manœuvre, *give a wide berth to;* ship's place at wharf; sleeping-place, esp. on ship; situation, employment. As v.t. and i. to moor (a ship) alongside a wharf
beside prep. (*bi sīd'*) Close to, by, *beside the fire;* alongside, *I'll walk beside you;* on a level with, *there is nothing to put beside his achievements;* wide of, *beside the point;* **beside oneself** uncontrollably enraged, out of one's mind
besides prep. and adv. (*bi sīdz'*) In addition (to); other than. As adv., moreover
best adj. (sometimes used as n.) and adv. (*best*) Superlative of 'good' and 'well'; of the highest excellence; most advantageous, suitable or appropriate. As adv. in the most excellent, suitable, way
bet n. and v.i. and t. (*bet*) A wager, mutual agreement that

winner of some argument, etc., should receive a certain reward, usually money, from loser; the amount wagered. As v.i. and t. to make a wager (with a person); to make a practice of wagering; to lay (money, etc.) as a wager
betray v.t. (*bi trā'*) Treacherously to deliver (person, thing, secret) into enemy hands; to be unfaithful, disloyal, to
better 1) adj. (sometimes as n.) and adv. (*bet'er*) Comparative of 'good' and 'well'; of greater excellence *than*, superior to; more advantageous, suitable or appropriate. As adv. more excellently, in a superior way; in the more advantageous or suitable way
better 2) v.t. and i. (*bet'er*) Improve; (reflex.) **to better oneself** get better pay, social position, etc
between prep. and adv. (*bi twēn'*) Flanked by, having one person, object, etc., on each side (rest or movement), *he was marched off between two policemen;* in an intermediary position, *between 6 and 7 o'clock, he stood between the door and the window;* restricted to, shared by, *divide the cake between the children;* separating, *there was bad blood between them;* connecting, *a hammock slung between two trees;* implying a choice (strictly) of one of two possibilities, *to choose between;* by the combined efforts of, *we managed to do it between us*
bevel n., adj. and v.t. and i. (*bev'el*) In carpentry, masonry, a sloping edge As v.t. and i. to cut, provide with, have, a sloping edge (usually in p.p. **bevelled**)
beverage n. (*bev'erij*) Liquid for drinking; a drink
beware v.i. and t. (*bi wār'*) To guard against, be wary of (used only where 'be' is the appropriate verbal particle), *beware of the dog, you should beware of half-truths*
bewilder v.t. (*bi wil'der*) To puzzle, baffle, confuse
beyond adv., prep. and n. (*bi yond'*) On, to, the farther side (of), farther on (than), *the river lies beyond the church;* (of time) later than; out of reach, exceeding the range or limit of, *beyond my understanding;* surpassing, *beyond doubt;* besides, in addition to, *I know nothing beyond what I have said*
bi- pref. (*bī*) Two, twice, twofold, having two

biceps

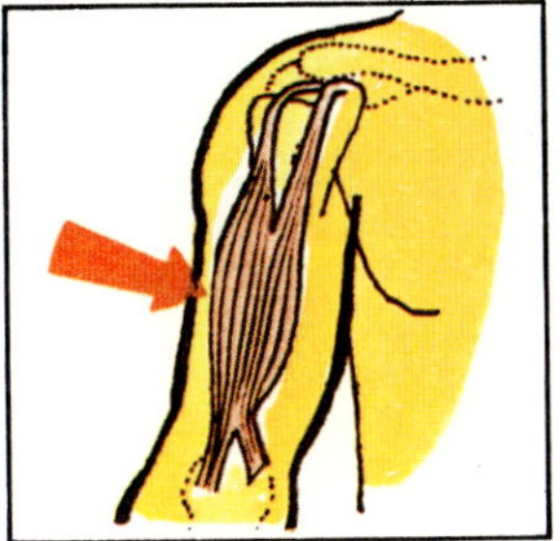

bib n. (*bib*) Cloth worn by infants to protect dress-front while eating
Bible n. (*bibl*) The collection of the sacred Scriptures of the Christian religion; a copy of this
biceps n. (*bī'seps*) A muscle with two heads or attachments, esp. the flexor muscle of the upper arm
bicycle n. and v.i. (*bī'sikl*) Vehicle with two wheels in line, propelled by rotating foot-pedals. Hence: **bicyclist** n
bid 1) v.t. and i. (*bid*) pret. **bade, bad, bid,** p.p. **bidden** To command, order; to invite; to proclaim, *bid defiance;* to offer (price) *for*
bid 2) n. (*bid*) Offer of a price, as at an auction
big adj. and adv. (*big*) Large in size, power or quality, great in bulk; tall, broad, capacious; (fig.) generous, *big-hearted;* grown up
bigamy n. (*big'a mi*) Having two wives or husbands at the same time
bilingual adj. (*bi ling'gwal*) (Of persons) speaking two languages naturally, esp. from childhood; (of texts, etc.) written, spoken, in two languages. (Lat. *bi-* two + *lingua* language)
bill 1) n. and v.i. (*bil*) Bird's beak
bill 2) n. (*bil*) Written list or statement of particulars, *bill of fare, bill of lading;* draft of proposed Act of Parliament; account of money due for services or goods; proclamation or advertisement, *theatre bill*
billiards n. pl. (*bil'yerdz*) Game played by striking ivory balls with cues upon a rectangular flat table with four corner and two side pockets; **billiard ball, cue, table, room** items used for playing billiards
billow n. and v.i. (*bil'ō*) Large rolling wave; (poet. often pl.) the

sea; (fig.) surge, roll, of smoke, flame, etc. As v.i. to form into billows; to surge, roll like waves

billy-goat n. (*bil'igōt'*) Male goat

bin n. and v.t. (*bin*) Receptacle with lid for storing bread, grain, etc.; receptacle for dust, ashes, etc., esp. *dustbin;* division of wine cellar

binary adj. (*bī'nari*) Dual, composed of two

bind v.t. and i. (*bīnd*) pret. and p.p. **bound** (*bownd*) To fasten together, (with *up*) to bandage, wrap round; to strengthen the edge of something with a strip of material, *brass-bound, iron-bound;* (reflex.) to pledge (oneself); to fasten the leaves of a book in a cover

billy-goat

binding n. (*bin'ding*) material used to bind a book, manner and style in which it is bound

biography n. (*bī og'rafi*) An account of a person's life and character; branch of literature consisting of such accounts

biology n. (*bī ol'oji*) The study of living animals and plants, their relationship, distribution, origin, structure, functions and way of life

biplane n. (*bī'plān*) Aeroplane with two wing-planes, one above the other

birch n., adj. and v.t. (*burch*) Genus of trees of the order Betulaceae, with smooth whitish bark; the wood of this tree; a bundle of twigs for thrashing schoolboys, etc. As adj. made, consisting of, birch trees or wood.

birch

As v.t. to thrash with a birch
bird n. (*burd*) Two-legged feathered vertebrate animal that lays eggs
biro n. (*bīro*) Ball-point pen. (Trade name, from that of inventor)
birth n. (*bŭrth*) Act of bringing forth offspring or process of being born **birthday** anniversary of one's birth
biscuit n. (*bis'kit*) Thin, hard, crisp cake made of flour, water, eggs, etc
bishop n. (*bish'op*) Priest with charge over spiritual matters and responsibility for supervising a diocese
bison n. (*bī'sun*) (orig.). A European wild ox; North American species popularly known as 'buffalo'
bit 1) n. (*bit*) Cutting edge of tool; boring tool used with drill, brace, etc.; part of key that grips lock-lever; metal mouthpiece of bridle
bit 2) n. (*bit*) Small portion, piece or amount
bitch n. (*bich*) Female dog, wolf, or fox
bite 1) v.t. and i. (*bīt*) pret. **bit** (*bit*) p.p. **bitten** (*bitn*) To pierce, cut into, with the teeth; (with *off* etc.) sever with the teeth; (of dogs, etc.) to snap at (or be in the habit of snapping); (of snakes, insects, etc.) to sting, bloodsuck; (of anchor, motor tyres, etc.) grip; to take a bait (lit. and fig.); to corrode (of an acid, etc.); to cause pain, smarting, etc. (of cold wind, taste, etc.)
bite 2) n. (*bīt*) A mouthful (of food); wound made, pain caused, by teeth or sting
bitter adj., adv., and n. (*bit'er*) Having an acrid taste, sour, opposite of sweet; (fig.) harsh, distressing, *bitter news*
bivouac v.i. and n. (*biv'o͞o ăk*) To camp out for the night, usually without tents. As n. a temporary encampment
bizarre adj. (*bi zah(r)'*) Eccentric, odd (of persons); grotesque, fantastic (of things).
blab v.i. and n. (*blăb*) To reveal secrets, etc. As n. one who does so
black 1) adj. (*blăk*) Completely absorbing light, and thus colourless; soot-coloured, the opposite of white; of the darkest colour; very dark complexioned; (fig.) unpropitious, gloomy, *a black outlook;* wicked, *black deeds;* sullen, angry, *black looks*
blackmail (hist.) tribute demanded by bandits in return for immunity; now, money demanded under threat of exposure, etc. (as v.t. to demand this from a person); hence: **blackmailer**
black 2) n. (*blăk*) The colour black, soot-colour
bladder n. (*blăd'er*) (anat.) Thin membranous bag in human and animal bodies (esp. that containing the urine); such a bag used for various purposes, e.g. bagpipes; inflatable bag of rubber, etc. (for football, etc.)
blade n. (*blād*) Narrow leaf of grass or corn; anything similar to this in shape, as the cutting part of sword or tool, the flat part of oar, bat, propeller, paddle-wheel, etc
blame 1) v.t. (*blām*) To censure, find fault with; to pin responsibility on (someone) (*for* offence, bad situation, etc.), to accuse
blame 2) n. (*blām*) responsibility for offence, bad situation, etc., *to take the blame, lay the blame on*
blancmange n. (*bla monj'*) Opaque jelly pudding of cornflour milk, etc
blank 1) adj. (*blănk*) Vacant, void; (of paper) not written on; (of facial expression) nonplussed, expressionless; (of cartridge) with powder but no bullet; (of cheque) with amount to be filled in by possessor
blank 2) n. (*blănk*) An unmarked surface; emptiness, void, *my mind is a blank;* empty space in document (for signature, etc.) blank cartridge; space where something is left out, *to leave a blank*
blanket n. (*blănk'it*) Large woollen cloth used esp. as bed-covering
blast 1) n. (*blahst*) Sudden strong gust of wind; strong air-current forced into furnace, etc.; loud sound of wind (esp. brass) instruments, a long blast on the ship's siren; wave of compressed air radiating outwards from an explosion; the explosion in a rock-splitting operation, etc., or charge used for one such operation
blast 2) v.t. (*blahst*) To break, blow up by explosives curse, damn
blaze 1) n. (*blāz*) A burst of flame, stream of light from a fire; a fire, esp. an intense one; a bright glare as of this, *a blaze of light, colour*

blaze 2) v.i. and t. (*blāz*) To burst into flame, burn intensely: shine brightly
blazer n. (*blā'zer*) Light sports jacket often distinctive of club, school, etc
bleach 1) v.t. and i. (*blēch*) To whiten, in the sun or by chemical action. As v.i. to become whiter in this way
bleach 2) n. (*blēch*) Chemical agent for whitening esp. linen, etc
bleak adj. (*blēk*) Cheerless; bare, exposed
bleat v.i. and t. and n. (*blēt*) To utter the cry of a sheep
As n. the cry of a sheep; a feeble wail
bleed v.i. and t. (*blēd*) pret. and p.p. **bled** (*bled*) To emit, lose, blood; (bot.) to lose sap. As v.i. to take blood from a patient
bleep n. (*blēp*) Sound of radio signals from artificial satellite, etc
blend v.t. and i. and n. (*blend*) To mix things together, esp. so that the components are indistinguish-able. As v.i. to mingle easily together, unite perfectly. As n. a mixture of things or types of things, as different teas, whiskies, etc. Hence: **blender** n. person who blends; machine for blending
bless v.t. (*bles*) p.p. **blest, blessed** (*blest*) To consecrate, pronounce holy; to invoke divine favour upon, *bless you!* (*God* understood); to praise, worship, *we bless Thee, O Lord;* to thank, remember with gratitude, *I often bless the day I met you;* to make happy or prosperous, *he is blest with good health, he is blest in his good health*
blessing n. (*bles'ing*) Prayer, an advantage, cause of happiness; a thing to be glad of, *it's a blessing that you came;* **a blessing in disguise** unpleasant thing that turns out for the best
blind 1) adj. (*blind*) Deprived of sight **blind-alley** passage that does not go through to anywhere **blindfold** with the eyes covered with bandage, etc. (as v.t. to cover a person's eyes) **turn a blind eye to** overlook. Hence: **blindly** adv. **blindness** n. (OE *blind*)
blind 2) v.t. and i. (*blind*) To deprive of sight
blind 3) n. (*blind*) A screen for windows, esp. of cloth or shutters lowered from a spring-roller
blink v.i. and t. and n. (*blink*) To close and open the eyelids rapidly (usually involuntarily); to shine fitfully (of lights, etc.)
bliss n. (*blis*) Perfect happiness; the state of souls in paradise. Hence: **blissful** adj
blister n. and v.t. and i. (*blis'ter*) Bladder-like protuberance on skin, containing fluid and caused by burn, friction, etc.; similar swelling on painted surface, wall-paper, etc. As v.t. and i. to raise, come out in, blisters
blitz n. and v.t. (*blits*) Sudden attack, esp. from the air
blizzard n. (*bliz'erd*) A violent, driving snowstorm
bloc n. (*blok*) Group of allied political parties; group of countries acting in concert, as in *sterling bloc*
block 1) n. (*blok*) Log, stump, or squared lump of wood; squared mass of stone; large piece of wood for chopping on, for beheading people on; group of buildings uninterrupted by streets
block 2) v.t. (*blok*) To obstruct (passage, pipe, vision, etc.); to prevent, delay (progress, parlia-mentary bill, etc.); (cricket) to stop ball dead with bat
blockade n. and v.t. (*blo kād'*) Closing off of a port by hostile warships; sealing off supplies from an area to force surrender
blood n. (*blud*) The red fluid circulating through the arteries, veins, etc., of bodies **blood donor** person who gives blood for trans-fusing to another **blood-group** (med.) class of persons having the same type of blood **blood- hound** large floppy-eared dog used for tracking criminals, etc.; (fig.) detective, sleuth **blood-sports** hunting, killing, animals for pleasure
blood-transfusion (med.) infusion of one person's blood into another person
bloom 1) n. (*bloōm*) Blossom or flower of plant
bloom 2) v.i. (*bloōm*) To blossom, put forth flowers

bloodhound

blossom n. (*blos'um*) The flower of shrub or tree preceding the fruit; the mass of flowers on certain trees, esp. almond, apple, cherry

blot 1) n. (*blot*) Spot, stain, esp. of ink on paper; a disfiguring mark, *a blot on the landscape*

blot 2) v.t. (*blot*) To make blots on, esp. with ink **blotting paper** absorbent paper for drying ink. Hence: **blotter** n. pad, etc., covered with blotting paper

blouse n. (*blowz*) Woman's loose bodice or shirt of light material

blow 1) v.i. and t. (*blō*) pret. **blew** (*bloo͞*) p.p. **blown** (*blōn*) To cause a gust or current of air (of wind, etc.); to expel air forcibly through mouth or nose, to puff, pant; As v.t. to drive air from the lungs, upon or through (an object) **to blow over** to pass by, *the storm blew over*; **to blow up** destroy by explosion

blow 2) n. (*blō*) A hard knock, esp. with fist, weapon, etc.; (fig.) an unpleasant shock, sudden calamity

bluff v.t. and n. (*bluf*) To disguise one's real intentions, give a misleading impression of one's strength As n. the act of doing this or an instance of it

blunder v.i. and t., and n. (*blun'der*) To flounder, stumble, *about;* to make a careless, tactless, mistake; (with *upon*) to find by chance

blunt adj., v.t., and n. (*blunt*) Not sharp, dull (of objects with point or cutting edge); (fig.) stupid, dull; (fig.) abrupt in manner, plain-speaking. As v.t. to dull the edge or point of (also fig. of mind, sensibilities, etc.)

blush v.i. and n. (*blush*) To grow red in the cheeks, esp. through

modesty, embarrassment, shame; (fig.) to feel ashamed. As n. the redness suffusing a person's cheeks when moved by emotion, esp. modesty, embarrassment, shame
bluster v.i. and t., and n. (*blus'ter*) To rage boisterously (of winds, waves, etc.); (fig. of persons) threaten, scold, boast in a boisterous manner. As v.t. (with *out, forth*) utter threateningly, noisily. As n. roaring of waves or wind; (fig.) noisy talk, boasting, etc
boar n. (*baw(r)*) Male uncastrated pig
board 1) n. (*bawd*) Plank; long, narrow strip of timber
a table, and thus the food received at table, as in **bed and board** bed and meals (in lodging house); rectangle of wood, etc., for posting notices, also **notice board**; thin piece of wood or cardboard on which certain games are played, *chessboard;* an official body of persons, often a government department or management committee of firm, *Board of Trade, board-meeting* (of company directors, etc.)
board 2) v.t. and i. (*bawd*) To cover with boards (of gaps, etc., often with *up*); to provide (lodger, etc.) with regular meals in return for payment (*full board* all meals); to go on board ship, enter train, bus, etc. As v.i. to receive regular meals in return for payment
boast n. and v.i. and t. (*bōst*) Arrogant expression of self-conceit; proud assertion or cause for this. As v.i. to brag, praise oneself; assert arrogantly
boat n. (*bōt*) Water-craft of any description with the essential properties of buoyancy and the ability to transport at least one person
bob 1) v.i. and t. (*bob*) To move up and down with quick, jerky motion (as a cork on water)
bob 2) n. (*bob*) A short, jerky ducking motion woman's hairstyle in which the hair is cut off straight at neck-level
bobbin n. (*bob'in*) Cylinder on which thread, wire, etc., is wound
bob-sled, -sleigh n. (*bob'sled, -slā*) Sleigh holding two or more persons
bodice n. (*bod'is*) Close-fitting woman's garment covering upper part of body; upper part of a woman's dress
body n. (*bod'i*) The material, physical structure of living creatures; the trunk, as distinct from head and limbs; a corpse; the main portion of a work, object, or structure as distinct from appendages, *the body of a book, car, hall;* a number of persons, or mass of something, *a body of troops, of men, of water, a legislative body*
bog n. (*bog*) Marshy place, quagmire
boil 1) n. (*boil*) An inflamed swelling on the skin, filled with pus
boil 2) v.i. and t., and n. (*boil*) (Of a liquid) to be heated to a temperature at which bubbles form (i.e. change to gas) (of water 100°C., 212°F.); to reach this temperature; to be cooked by boiling As v.t.
to heat (liquid) to boiling point; to cook (food) in boiling water; to immerse anything (laundry, etc.) in boiling liquid As n. boiling point, *on the boil.* Hence: **boiler** n. vessel in which water is boiled
bolt 1) n. (*bōlt*) metal bar sliding in groove to fasten door headed metal pin used to fasten metal plates, etc., together and locked by means of screwed shank and nut; lightning, a thunder-bolt; a sudden dash; a long roll of fabric
bolt 2) v.t. and i. (*bōlt*). To fasten with a bolt (door, things together, etc.); to swallow hastily, *he bolted his breakfast.* As v.i. to run away, dart off, *he bolted down the garden;* (of horse) run out of control
bomb n. and v.t. (*bom*) Metal case fitted with explosive, etc., which detonates or catches fire
bombshell bomb; (fig.) surprise, a shock. Hence: **bomber** n. aircraft designed for dropping bombs
bond n. (*bond*) Thing which binds, chain, cord (only in pl.), *to break one's bonds*
connecting link, thing that unites, *the bond of friendship;* (law) a written agreement to pay money, esp. by government or public company to repay loan **bondage** n. slavery, captivity (also fig.)
bone 1) n. (*bōn*) The hard substance forming the skeleton of mammals and other vertebrates; one of the parts of this skeleton
bone 2) v.t. (*bōn*) To remove the bones from (fish, fowl, etc.)

bonfire n. (*bon'fīr*) Large fire for open-air celebration, or to destroy leaves, rubbish, etc

bonnet n. and v.t. (*bon'it*) Kind of head-dress, esp. fitting cap fastened under the chin as worn by women and babies; a Scotsman's flat cap; various other coverings such as cover or hood over a motor-car engine

bonus n. (*bō'nus*) Additional payment over and above salary

bony adj. (*bō'ni*) Like bone; full of bones (of fish, etc.); having prominent bones (of people, their features, etc.)

boo inter., and v.t. and i. (*boo*) Exclamation of disapproval. As v.t. and i. to exclaim thus; to show disapproval of (speaker, play, etc.) by shouting *boo;* to scare (animal) away thus; **he wouldn't say boo to a goose** he is very timid

book 1) n. (*book*) Collection of blank, printed, or written sheets bound together into a volume **bookmaker** one whose occupation is to take bets on sporting events (thus **bookmaking**) **booklet** n. small book, pamphlet. (OE *boc*)

book 2) v.t. (*book*) To enter or write down in a book; to order in advance, reserve (seat, room, dinner, tour, etc.)

boom v.i. and t., and n. (*boom*) To give out a deep, resonant humming sound; (fig.) to prosper, increase rapidly in value, popularity, etc. As n. deep humming sound, as of bass drum, thunder, etc.; (fig.) sudden rapid activity in trade, etc., resulting in prosperity

boomerang n. and v.i. (*boo'merăng*) Curved flat hardwood missile that returns to the thrower if it misses its mark, used by Aust. aborigines

boost v.t. and n. (*boost*) To lift, hoist, by pushing; to increase popularity, value, power of (a commercial product, political personality, etc.) As n. a lift, help-up; an advance in value, popularity, etc

boomerangs

boot n. and v.t. (*boot*) Article of footwear, esp. of leather, extending at least over the ankle (often to knee or above); luggage compartment in motor-car

booth n. (*booth*) Covered market-stall, temporary stall, etc., at fairground; cubicle (for telephone); **polling-booth** for voting at elections

booze v.i. and n. (*booz*) (colloq.) To drink (alcohol) too much. As n. alcoholic liquor

border 1) n. (*baw'der*) Edge, margin, of a thing; frontier, boundary (of country, territory); ornamental edging, as on a dress, etc.; a flower-bed forming an edge to a lawn or path in garden

border 2) v.t. and i. (*baw'der*) To provide with a border, edging; (with *on*) to be adjacent to (of land, etc.)

bore 1) v.t. and i. (*baw(r)*) To drill a hole into, usually with revolving tool, (fig.) to weary (person) by tedious talk or repetition. As v.i. make a hole, burrow

Hence: **boredom** n. state of being wearied by talk, inactivity, etc.; **boring** n. process of drilling holes; adj. dull, tedious

bore 2) n. (*baw(r)*) Instrument used for drilling holes; a hole made by this; the hollow inside of tube or gun-barrel; (fig.) dull, tedious person, job, etc

borough n. (*bu'ra*) A town or city; having certain privileges granted by royal charter

borrow v.t. and i. (*bo'rō*) To take, accept, a thing or the use of a thing, on condition that it is returned later

bosom n. and adj. (*booz'um*) The human breast (now, esp. of women)

boss n. and v.t. (*bos*) (colloq.) Master, employer. As v.t. to supervise; (colloq.) to bully, domineer, *to boss someone about.* Hence: **bossy** adj. domineering

botany n. (*bot'a ni*) The science of the structure, growth, and function of plants

both adj., pron., and adv. (*bōth*) The two together, the one and the other, *I have read both volumes.* As pron. the one and the other (with or without *of*), *both are bad, both of them are bad.* As adv

equally of two things, *he is both a soldier and a scholar*
bother v.t. and i. and n. (*both'er*) To worry, pester. As v.i. to worry oneself, take trouble; as mild expletive, *bother it!* As n. worry, fuss, trouble
bottle 1) n. (*botl*) Hollow narrow-necked vessel, usually of glass, for holding liquid, fruit, etc. **bottleneck** narrows in roadway, becoming easily congested with traffic; what holds up flow (of production, etc.)
bottle 2) v.t. (*botl*) To fill bottles with liquid, fruit, vegetables, etc
bottom n. and adj. (*bot m*) Lowest part of anything; bed of sea, etc.; farthest from front, *bottom of the garden;* seat of a person or chair; keel of ship; (fig.) foundation, *get to the bottom of this problem;* (as adj.) last, *his bottom dollar;* lowest, *his bottom price*
bough n. (*bow*) A large branch of a tree
boulder n. (*bōl'der*) Large rock worn smooth by water
bounce v.i. and t. and n. (*bowns*) To rebound on striking anything (of a ball, etc.); to move about boisterously, violently, *he bounced into the room* As v.t. to cause (ball, etc.) to bounce
bound 1) n. and v.t. (*bownd*) Limit, boundary (esp. pl. as in **out of bounds**). As v.t. to mark the boundary of, limit; (fig.) confine, restrain
bound 2) v.i. and n. (*bownd*) To leap, spring, move with springy motion; to bounce. As n. a leap, an upward springing motion
bound 3) adj. (*bownd*) Prepared to start on a journey; having started, *homeward bound*
boundary n. (*bown'da ri*) Line, etc., marking the limits (of estate, country, etc.); (cricket) limit-line of field of play; stroke causing ball to cross this, scoring 4 or 6 runs
bouquet n. (*bōō kā'*) Bunch of flowers
boutique n. (*bōō tēk'*) Small shop or department selling fashionable clothes
bow 1) n., and v.t. and i. (*bō*) Weapon for shooting arrows, consisting of a curved (usually wooden) flexible rod with tips joined by a taut string which, pulled back and released, propels the arrow; anything shaped like this, esp. a rainbow; (mus.) slender rod strung with horsehair for playing certain stringed instruments; the curved front of a

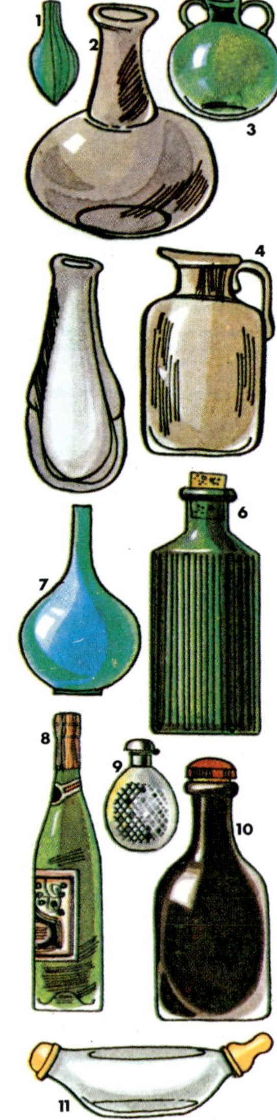

Bottles. 1. Egyptian. 2. Early English. 3. Greek. 4. and 5. Roman. 6. Medicine. 7. Chinese. 8. Wine. 9 Perfume. 10. Liqueur. 11. Baby's.

saddle; a double-looped slip-knot, or necktie, etc., tied with such a knot

bow 2) v.i. and t., and n. (*bow*) To incline the head or bend the body in sign of respect, as greeting, acknowledgement, etc., or in submission As n. inclination of head or body in sign of respect, greeting, etc

bow 3) n. (*bow*) Fore-end of ship or boat, which cuts through the water

bowel n. (*bow'el*) A division of the intestines; usually pl., **the bowels** the intestines generally; (fig.) the depths, interior, *the bowels of the earth*

bowl 1) n. (*bōl*) Basin (of various sizes and materials); drinking vessel; basin-shaped part of various objects, as of pipes, spoons, etc

bowl 2) n. (*bōl*) Heavy wooden ball with bias, used in game of **bowls**

bowl 3) v.t. and i. (*bōl*) To roll hoop or ball along the ground; to play bowls; (cricket) to deliver the ball; to hit the batsman's wicket in so doing (often with *out*); as v.i. **to bowl along** move quickly and smoothly in wheeled vehicle; **to bowl over** knock down; to upset, disconcert. Hence: **bowler 1)** n. (cricket) player who delivers the ball to the batsman.

bowler 2) n. (*bō'ler*) Hard round felt hat

bowling n. (*bō'ling*) Game of bowls; playing at this; (cricket) act or style of delivering ball; skittles; **bowling-alley** long narrow enclosure for skittles or ten-pin bowling; **bowling-crease** (cricket) line from behind which ball is bowled; **bowling-green** smooth lawn for playing bowls

box 1) n. (*boks*) Case, receptacle, usually lidded and rectangular, made of wood, cardboard, etc.; the contents of this, *a box of chocolates*
separate compartment in theatre, in horse's stable (also **loose box**)

box 2) n., and v.t. and i. (*boks*) A slap with the open hand, esp. **box on the ear.** As v.t. to deliver such a slap. As v.i. to fight with the closed fists, esp. for sport and wearing padded gloves. Hence: **boxer** n. pugilist, one who boxes for sport or as a profession; kind of smooth-haired dog of German origin; **boxing** n. the art of fighting with the fists

boy n. (*boi*) Male child Hence: **boyhood** n. The period of a male child's life up to puberty; **boyish** adj. like, characteristic of, a boy

boycott v.t. and n. (*boi'kot*) To refuse to speak to a person, have dealings with him, etc

brace 1) n. (*brās*) Anything used as a support, stay, etc.; rope to adjust ship's sails; cord to keep drum tight; carpenter's drilling tool, esp. **brace and bit;** (print.) bracket shaped thus { }; a pair of (birds, pistols, etc.); (pl.) **braces** shoulder straps for holding trousers up

brace 2) v.t. (*brās*) To fasten together, support, steady

bracelet n. (*brās'let*) Ornamental band for wrist or arm

bracket n. (*brăk'et*) Angular piece of metal or wood projecting as support from a wall; (arch.) flat-topped projecting support for arch, shelf, etc.; hinged wall-fixture for gas lamp, jet, etc.; hinged shelf on wall with under-prop; (print.) the marks ( ), used to enclose parentheses, etc., or (math.) group of symbols in relationship to preceding or succeeding symbol

brag v.i. and n. (*brăg*) To boast

braid v.t. and n. (*brād*) To weave by intertwining strands, to plait (hair); to trim or bind with braid. As n. a plait (of hair); a narrow band of woven silk, thread, etc., for trimming or binding

Braille n. (*brāl*) A system of

Braille alphabet, with detail of three-line system.

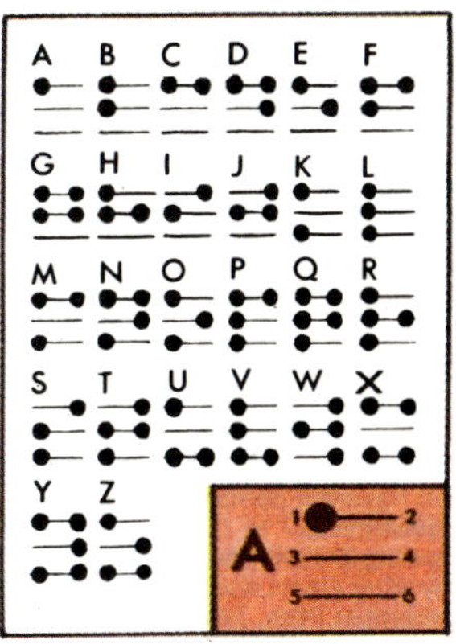

printing for the blind using an alphabet of raised dots read by touch
brain n. and v.t. (*brān*) Convoluted mass of soft substance enclosed in the skull, the centre of the nervous system and of mental processes **brainwave** a bright idea
brake and v.t. (*brāk*) Device for slowing down or stopping the motion of a wheel or a moving body (often pl.); (fig.) to slow down course of action, *to apply the brakes*. As v.t. to apply the brake, stop or slow by so doing
bramble n. (*brămb l*) The common name for some plants of the genus *Rubus*, particularly the wild-blackberry bush
bran n. (*brăn*) The husks of oats, wheat, etc., separated from the flour after grinding, used as meal
branch 1) n. (*brahnch*) Limb or arm of tree, springing from the trunk or from a bough; an offshoot, outgrowth (of a river, road, etc.); subdivision, extension, *the Hampstead branch of Barclays Bank;* division, group, of some subject of study, knowledge, etc., *ethics is a branch of philosophy*
branch 2) v.i. (*brahnch*) To put forth, separate into, branches; (with *out*) to extend, turn in new directions, launch out
brand 1) n. (*brănd*) A burning piece of wood; mark made by burning, esp. with hot iron, as on cattle for identification or on criminals; from last meaning (fig.) stigma, mark of infamy; trade-mark; type of goods produced by a particular firm, *this is a good brand of marmalade*
brand 2) v.t. (*brănd*) Mark with a brand; attach a stigma to, *he was branded a coward*
brandy n. (*brăn'di*) A strong spirit distilled from wine
brass n. and adj. (*brahs*) An alloy of copper and zinc
brave 1) adj. and n. (*brāv*) Courageous, gallant (of persons); requiring courage (of actions) brave men collectively, *Toll for the brave;* a Red Indian warrior. Hence: **bravely** adv.; **bravery** n. courage
brave 2) v.t. (*brāv*) To face boldly, defy; **to brave it out** to face suspicion or blame with defiance
brawl v.i. and n. (*brawl*) To quarrel loudly; to take part in a rowdy fight. As n. a loud quarrel; a general rowdy fight, esp. in a

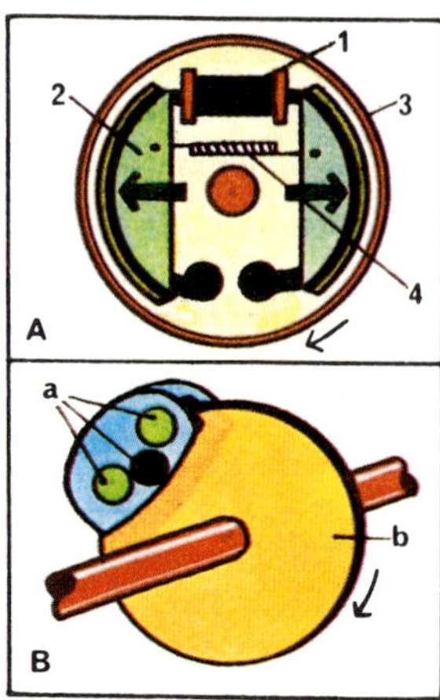

A. Hydraulic brake. 1. ***Hydraulic chamber.* 2. *Shoe.* 3. *Drum.* 4. *Return spring.*** **B. Disc brake. a.** ***Friction pads.*** **b.** ***Disc.***

public place
bray n. and v.i. and t. (*brā*) The cry of the ass; the blare of a trumpet. As v.i. to utter these sounds (of persons, always derogatory); (with *out*) to utter stridently
brazier n. (*brā'zi er, brā'zher*) Open pan containing burning coals or charcoal
breach n. and v.t. (*brēch*) A breaking, infringement, of law, obligation, etc. **breach of the peace** (law) riot, disorderly conduct
bread n. (*bred*) Foodstuff of flour and water kneaded (usually with yeast) and baked
bread-winner person supporting a family by working
breadth n. (*bredth, bretth*) Width, broadness, measure from side to side of an object, as distinct from *length*
break 1) v.t. and i. (*brāk*) pret. **broke**, p.p. **broken** (*brōk, brōkn*) To divide forcibly into pieces (esp. by sudden blow, impact, etc.); to smash, shatter; to injure, put out of action (machine, watch, etc.) to interrupt (journey, etc.); to violate (law, etc.). As v.i. to come to bits (as result of impact, etc.)
break 2) n. (*brāk*) Forcible division, fracture; place at, manner in, which a thing is broken, *a clean break;* interruption in time or continuity, speil of rest or

recreation between office, factory, or school periods of work, *tea-break;* (of ball) change in direction on pitching
breakfast n. and v.i. (*brek'fast*) First meal of the day. As v.i. to eat this
breast n. and v.t. (*brest*) The front of the body between throat and waist, chest, bosom
breath n. (*breth*) The air drawn into and exhaled from the lungs; this when perceptible to sight or smell; one act of respiration, in and out; (fig.) a light breeze, puff of wind; slight suggestion (of rumour, etc.); **to take one's breath away** utterly astound one; **out of breath** panting; **below one's breath** in a whisper. Hence: **breathless** adj. panting
breathe v.i. and t. (*brēth*) To take in and expel air from the lungs; (fig.) to live; to blow gently (on). As v.t. to utter softly, *don't breathe a word!*
breech n. (*brēch*) pl. **breeches** (*brich'iz*) trousers ending below knee and fastened there
breed 1) v.t. and i. (*brēd*) pret. and p.p. **bred** (*bred*) To produce, bear, rear offspring; to educate, bring up; (fig.) to give rise to (results), *idleness breeds discontent;* to propagate (animals) by selective mating. As v.i. to beget, propagate the species, *rabbits breed like wildfire;* also fig., *desperate thoughts breed in loneliness*
breed 2) n. (*brēd*) Race or stock; racial variety, *a breed of cattle;* (fig.) a group possessing common qualities, *Caesar, Napoleon, and men of their breed.*
breeze n. and v.i. (*brēz*) Gentle wind
brew v.t. and i. and n. (*broo*) To make beer and similar liquor by boiling and fermenting from malt or hops; loosely, to prepare by boiling and infusing (tea, etc.); (fig.) to plot, contrive, mischief. As v.i. to undergo the process of brewing; also fig. *mischief, a storm, is brewing*
briar, **brier** (*bri'er*) The wild rose; any prickly bush or shrub; a thorn or prickle
bribe n. and v.t. (*brīb*) Money, reward, offered or given to a person to induce him to act illegally or dishonestly. As v.t. to offer or give a person money, etc., to this end
brick n. and adj. (*brik*) Rectangular block of hard-baked clay used for building; the material of which bricks are composed; a block of any substance shaped like a brick
bride n. (*brīd*) A woman on her wedding-day; a newly married woman
bridegroom a man on his wedding day or shortly after; **bridesmaid** unmarried woman or girl attending bride
bridge 1) n. and v.t. (*brij*) Structure carrying road, railway, across gap, river, ravine, etc.; thing resembling this in shape or purpose; raised deck from which a ship is navigated; bony upper structure of nose; wooden support for taut strings of violin, etc. As v.t. to build a bridge over; (fig.) to surmount, overcome
bridge 2) n. (*brij*) Card game
bridle n. and v.t. and i. (*brīdl*) Headgear of horse's harness, to which reins are attached
brief 1) adj. (*brēf*) Short, concise.
brief 2) n. (*brēf*) (law) Statement of client's case given to barrister
brief 3) v.t. (*brēf*) To instruct barrister in the facts of a case; to employ a barrister; (R.A.F.) to instruct aircrews before a flying mission (also used generally of instructions before any task)
brigade n. and v.t. (*bri gād'*) Military unit smaller than a division and commanded by a brigadier; an organized, usually uniformed, semi-military body, as *fire-brigade*
brigand n. (*brig'and*) Bandit, robber, esp. member of outlaw band in southern Europe
bright adj. (*brīt*) Reflecting, giving out, much light; vivid, vividly coloured; (of manner) cheerful (of persons, their intelligence) quick, lively Hence: **brighten** v.t. and i. make or become bright (v.i. often with *up*)
brilliant adj. (*bril'yant*) Shining, sparkling; (of persons) exceptionally talented; splendid, showy. Hence: **brilliance** n
brim n. and v.t. and i. (*brim*) Edge of rim round cup, bowl, etc.; flattish rim round crown of hat; edge of sea, river, etc., or chasm, pit. As v.t. and i. to fill, be filled, to the brim
brine n. (*brīn*) Water saturated with salt, as used for pickling; sea-water

rope
plank
stone single-span
stone arched
arched beam
beam
lattice
suspension
cantilever
swing
bascule
deck

bring v.t. (*bring*) pret. and p.p. **brought** (*brawt*) To convey (by any means) towards the speaker; to produce, cause to arise, *good work brings satisfaction*

brisk adj. and v.t. and i. (*brisk*) Lively, spirited, quick in movement, a brisk pace; enlivening, stimulating (of air, etc.)

bristle 1) n. (*brisl*) A short stiff animal hair, as on pigs; any such hair (on the chin, etc.); stiff hair in a brush

bristle 2) v.i. (*brisl*) To stand on end, as the hair of angry or frightened animals; (fig.) to show anger

brittle adj. (*britl*) Fragile, apt to break

broad adj. (*brawd*) Wide, extensive from side to side, opposite of *narrow*

broadcast adj., adv., v.t. and i., and n. (*brawd'kahst*) (Of seed) scattered by hand (as adv. thus sown); (fig.) widely disseminated; transmitted by radio. As v.t. and i. to sow by scattering; (fig.) to transmit (speeches, music, etc.) by radio

broccoli n. (*brok'oli*) Hardy species of cauliflower bearing numerous small sprouts

brochure n. (*brō'shōōr*) Pamphlet, esp. of description, advertisement, etc

broke pret. of 'break', and archaic p.p. used as adj. (colloq.) penniless bankrupt

broken adj. (*brō'ken*) In verbal senses of 'break'; also, crushed, dispirited, *a broken man;* uneven, *broken ground;* interrupted, *broken* time

bronco n. (*brong'kō*) (U.S.) An untamed horse

bronze n. and adj. (*bronz*) Alloy primarily of copper and tin

brooch n. (*brōch*) Ornamental clasp or pin worn on the clothes at the breast or throat

brood 1) n. (*brōōd*) Young birds hatched at one sitting; all the offspring of one parent

brood 2) v.i. (*brōōd*) Sit on eggs to hatch them; to meditate almost obsessively (esp. *on* or *over* injuries, etc.), *he brooded on his fate*

brook n. (*brŏŏk*) Small stream

broom n. (*brōōm*) Shrub of genus *Cytisus* or *Genista*, having short spiky leaves and bearing yellow flowers; long-handled sweeping implement

broth n. (*broth*) Water in which meat has been cooked, stock; this with chopped vegetables, etc., in it

brother n. (*bruth'er*) Male person having the same parents as another

brotherhood n. (*bruth'erhŏŏd*) State of being a brother (any sense); a society, association

brow n. (*brow*) The forehead, esp. that part of it just above the eyes; the arch of hair on the bone ridge above the eye (usually **eyebrow**); top edge of steep hill

bruise v.t. and i. and n. (*brōōz*) To injure, discolour, but not break, the skin by blow (human skin, but also of fruit, etc.). As v.i. to become thus discoloured. As n. a contusion, discolouring of the skin due to blow

brunch n. (*brunch*) (slang) Combined breakfast and lunch

brunette n. and adj. (*brōōnet'*) (Woman) with dark hair and complexion

brush 1) n. (*brush*) Hand utensil made of bunch of bristles, hair, etc., set in wood, etc., with handle, used for sweeping, cleaning, applying paint

brush 2) v.t. and i. (*brush*) To clean, etc., with a brush

brutal adj. (*brōō'tal*) Characteristic of a brute; cruel, rough, savage

brute n. and adj. (*brōōt*) Beast, as distinct from a man; a rough, cruel person

bubble 1) n. (*bubl*) Thin spherical skin of liquid inflated with air or gas; small air- or gas-filled pocket in liquid or solid

bubble 2) v.i. (*bubl*) To make, produce, bubbles

buck 1) n. (*buk*) Male of the deer family (esp. fallow-deer), of rabbits and hares

broom

buck 2) v.i. and t. (*buk*) (Of horse) to jump up and down, back arched and all four feet leaving ground

bucket n. (*buk'it*) Vessel with hoop-handle for carrying water, etc

buckle 1) n. (*bukl*) Metal frame with hinged spike for fastening belt, strap, etc

buckle 2) v.t. and i. (*bukl*) To fasten with a buckle; to bend, crumple, under pressure (also **buckle under**); **to buckle to** get to work

bud n. and v.i. and t. (*bud*) (bot.) Embryonic growth of compact leaves or flower breaking out of stem; half-opened flower. As v.i. to put forth buds

budgerigar n. (*buj'eri gah(r)*) Small green parakeet, the Australian love-bird

budget n. and v.i. (*buj'it*) Originally small bag or its contents; now an estimate of expenditure, esp. that presented to Parliament by the Chancellor of the Exchequer; in general, any person's financial reckonings. As v.i. to estimate finances

buffalo n. (*buf'a lō*) Wild ox of various kinds; incorrectly used of American bison

buffet 1) n. and v.t. and i. (*buf'it*) A blow with the hand; (fig.) misfortune, calamity. As v.t. to strike, knock. As v.i. to contend *with* (esp. waves)

buffet 2) n. (*bo͞o'fā*) Sideboard; refreshment bar (at railway station, etc.)

buffoon n. (*bu fo͞on'*) Clown, jester; clownish person

bug 1) n. (*bug*) Verminous, flat, blood-sucking wingless insect infesting dirty houses, esp. beds; loosely, any small insect

bug 2) v.t. and n. To install secretly or conceal listening or recording device in a room. As n. such a device

buffalo

bugle n. and v.i. (*būgl*) Small brass (esp. military) trumpet. As v.i. to sound, play, the bugle

build v.t. and i. (*bild*) pret. and p.p. **built** (*bilt*) To construct by putting together component parts (esp. of houses, etc., but also of machines, bridges, etc.); to develop gradually, improve (often with *up*, of reputation, position, etc.)

builder n. esp. contractor for building houses, etc.; **building** n. esp. edifice (house, church, etc.)

bulb n. and v.i. (*bulb*) Enlarged spherical base of stem of plants such as onion, daffodil; a similar shaped

bulge n. and v.i. (*bulj*) A swelling. As v.i. to swell out, expand in irregular way, *his cheeks bulged with Christmas pudding*

bull n. and adj. (*bo͝ol*) Uncastrated male ox or male of any of the bovine group; also of whale, elephant, walrus, etc

bullet n. (*bo͝ol'it*) Round or conical lead pellet fired from rifle or revolver; **bullet-proof** able to resist impact of a bullet

bulletin n. (*bo͝ol'it in*) Official report of news, often of condition of an invalid

bullion n. (*bo͝ol'yon*) Uncoined gold or silver; gold and silver money assessed in its raw material value

bully n. and v.t. and i. and adj. (*bo͝ol'i*) Blustering, overbearing person, cowardly tyrant, esp. boy who persecutes smaller boys
As v.t. and i. to oppress

bump v.i. and t. and n. (*bump*) To strike dully *against, into* a solid thing; to jolt along
As v.t. to hurt by striking against a thing, *he bumped his head on the low doorway* As n. a dull blow, or thudding sound made by this; a swelling caused by a blow

bumper n. and adj. (*bum'per*) Metal fender at front and back of motor-car

bun n. (*bun*) Small, soft, round cake often with currants; small round bunch, as of hair

bunch n. and v.t. and i. (*bunch*) Cluster of things growing (grapes etc.) or gathered (flowers, etc.) together; knot of material, etc. closely gathered together; (slang) a group of people, *best of the bunch*

bundle n. and v.t. and i. (*bundl*) A number of things bound together (sticks, old rags, etc.); clothes etc. tied loosely together for carrying. As v.t. to make up into a bundle; (with *out, off*) to dismiss (person) unceremoniously

bungalow n. (*bung'ga lō*) One-storeyed house, in English sense usually small

bungle v.i. and t. and n. (*bung'gl*) To perform badly, blunder. As v.t. to spoil by clumsy performance. As n. a blunder, bad performance. Hence: **bungler** n

bunk n. and v.i. (*bungk*) Sleeping-berth, esp. on a ship or train

bunting n. (*bun'ting*) Coarse brightly coloured cloth used for flags and streamers; decorative flags made of this

buoy n. and v.t. (*boi*) Floating sphere or drum indicating rocks, shoal, etc., or marking navigable channel; (usually **life-buoy**)

burden, burthen n. and v.t. (*burdn, burthn*) Thing carried, load, weight; also fig., *burden of responsibility;* (naut.) ship's freightage capacity

bureau n. (*būr'ō*) Writing desk with drawers; a public office, government department

bureaucracy n. (*būr ok'ra si*) Administration of government by central offices; officials as a body; control by officials

burglar n. (*burg'ler*) One who breaks into a house by night, esp. to steal

burglary n. the act of breaking into a house by night with intent to steal

burgle v.i. and t. (*burgl*) To commit burglary

burial n. (*be'ri al*) Act of burying underground, esp. of dead body; funeral

burn 1) v.t. and i. (*burn*) pret. and p.p. **burnt, burned** (*burnt, burnd*) To consume, destroy, by fire; to injure by exposure to fire or heat (person, part of body, food, etc.); to make (hole, etc.) by heat; to put to death by burning (heretics, etc.); to use as fuel for heat or lighting, *this stove burns wood* (also fig. of energy, etc.); (of the sun) to tan the skin, *she burns easily;* to harden, produce, (bricks, etc.) by heat; to parch, crack, dry up, wither, by heat (earth, plants, etc.); to give the sensation of heat (of acids, flavours, etc.). As v.i. to be on fire; to be capable of combustion, *dry wood burns quickly;* (fig.) to feel excessive heat; to be inflamed with passion, etc., *burning with shame*

burn 2) n. (*burn*) Injury, mark, caused by burning

burr, bur n. (*bur*) Prickly, sticky seed-vessel of certain plants, which clings to clothes, etc

burrow n. and v.i. and t. (*bu'rō*) Hole made in ground by rabbits, foxes, etc. As v.i. and t. to make a burrow; to dig one's way *into* (lit. and fig.)

burst v.t. and i. (*burst*) pret. and p.p. **burst** To break, cause to break, violently open or apart, *Samson burst his bonds, the floods burst the dam gates.* As v.i. to break open violently, explode, fly to pieces (bomb, bubble, etc.); to open out (buds, leaves, etc.); to overflow with, *bursting with energy, joy;* to appear suddenly, *he burst into the room;* to become suddenly and violently active, *to burst into flame, burst out laughing*

bury v.t. (*be'ri*) To deposit (esp. corpse, but also anything) under-ground, in sea, etc.; to hide away, immerse (face in hands, oneself in studies, etc.); to cover up, submerge (under pile of stuff, etc.)

bus n. (*bus*) pl. **buses** (*bus'iz*) Short for omnibus

bush n. (*bo͝osh*) Shrub with dense foliage; wild uncultivated

region with thick undergrowth (esp. in Africa and Australia); anything thick or bushy (hair, etc.)
business n. (*biz'nis*) Trade or profession followed for a livelihood; trading, commercial transactions as a whole; a commercial enterprise, a firm; task, duty, concern, *to make it one's business;* a subject, affair, *a mysterious business*
busy adj. and n. (*biz'i*) Working hard, actively employed, *go away, I am busy;* habitually occupied (of person or occupation), *his is a busy life*
butcher n. and v.t. (*bŏŏ'cher*) One who slaughters animals for meat; a dealer in meat
butter 1) n. (*but'er*) Firm, fatty substance obtained by churning cream; similar foodstuff obtained from other materials, *peanut butter*
butter 2) v.t. (*but'er*) To spread with butter
button n. (*butn*) Disk or knob of metal, bone, etc., on dress, etc., and used to fasten it by passing through a hole; similar disk, etc., worn as ornament; object resembling this (as on bell, end of fencing foil, etc.)
buy v.t. and n. (*bī*) pret. and p.p. **bought** (*bawt*) To obtain in exchange for money
buzz v.i. and t. and n. (*buz*) To make a humming sound, as that of a bee As n. the humming sound made by bee, etc.; similar sound made by people talking together, etc., or by a machine
by prep. and adv. (*bī*) Near, close to, *he stood by the window;* handy, *I always keep one by me;* of direction, along, through, across, via, past, *we came by the main road, we walked by his house;* of time, during, *by night,* for a certain period, *to pay by the week,* not later than, *I'll finish by tea-time;* expressing agency, means, method, manner, *Hamlet was written by Shakespeare, I did it by myself, the engine is worked by steam, to hang by a thread;* expressing multiplication, division, etc., *six feet by two;* according to, *by my watch, by rights, they called him by his name;* through the authority of, *by God;* in the measure of, *sold by the pound, one by one;* in accordance with, *by request;* to the extent of, *he won by a yard.* As adv. near, *to stand by;* aside, to one side, *to lay by;* past, *to walk by, times gone by;* **by and by** presently
by-election n. (*bī'i lek'shun*) An election held due to special vacancy in Parliament or Council, not at a General Election
by-pass n. and v.t. (*bī'pahs*) Pipe, outlet, etc., used when main supply or current is cut off; an arterial road to divert through-traffic from a town. As v.t. to divert by means of a by-pass; to make a detour round a town, etc

C

cab n. (*kăb*) Small vehicle plying for public hire, taxi; driver's shelter on locomotive
cabaret n. (*kăb'a rā*) Restaurant providing entertainment, singing, dancing, etc.; the entertainment provided
cabin n. (*kăb'in*) A hut; small wretched dwelling; room (esp. bedroom) on ship; other uses in sense of 'small shelter'
cabinet n. (*kăb'in et*) Small private room; piece of furniture designed for keeping or displaying objects, curiosities, etc.; (pol.) the committee of ministers holding the principal government offices, presided over by the Prime Minister, and responsible to Parliament for the government of the country
shadow cabinet (pol.) made up of prospective ministers when in opposition
cable 1) n. (*kăbl*) Rope of twisted hemp or wire over 10″ in circumference; insulated wires for transmitting electricity; a message transmitted by such a cable
cable 2) v.t. and i. (*kābl*) To secure or provide with a cable; to transmit (message), communicate (with person), by telegraphic cable
cactus n. (*kăk'tus*) pl. **cactuses, cacti** (*kăk'tī*) Family of succulent plants with thick fleshy leaves and stems covered with prickles

cacti

caddy 1), **caddie** n. (*kăd'i*) Golfer's attendant who carries clubs, etc

caddy 2) n. (*kăd'i*) A container for tea, also **tea-caddy**

cadet n. (*ka det'*) Younger son; pupil at naval or military college

Cadet Corps body of schoolboys formed for military training

café n. (*kăf'ā*) Coffee-house; restaurant for light meals

cafeteria n. (*kăf i tēr'i a*) Restaurant where customers serve themselves from counters

cage n. and v.t. (*kāj*) Construction wholly or partly of bars or wire, for confining animals or birds; thing resembling this, esp. lift cage. As v.t. to confine in a cage (lit. and fig.)

cake n. and v.t. and i. (*kāk*) Kind of confectionery made of flour, butter, eggs, and sugar baked in a mould, often with flavouring, raisins etc.; the substance this is made of, a *slice of cake;* compact mass of other food (*fishcake*) or other substance (*cake of soap*)

calamity n. (*ka lăm'i ti*) Sudden, overwhelming misfortune or disaster

calculate v.t. and i. (*kăl'kū lāt*) To reckon by mathematics; to foresee, work out beforehand; to plan for a particular purpose, *calculated to give satisfaction* (often in p.p. **calculated** deliberate, cold-blooded, *a calculated murder*). Hence: **calculating** adj. that calculates, *calculating machine;* (of person, etc.) cautious, shrewd, cunning

calculation n. process or result of calculating; a forecast; forethought, *planned with great calculation*

calculator n. person or machine that calculates

calendar n. and v.t. (*kăl'en der*) System of fixing the beginning and end of the year together with its subdivision into months, etc.; list of days and months in a given year, often giving prominence to days of special interest

calf 1) n. (*kahf*) pl. **calves** (*kahvz*) A young bull or cow, though also used of elephants, seals, etc

calf 2) n. (*kahf*) pl. **calves** (*kahvz*) The fleshy back of the leg between ankle and knee

call 1) v.i. and t. (*kawl*) To cry out, esp. for affection or help, *he called but no one heard him;* to pay a brief visit (*on* a person, *at* a house), *the vicar called at tea-time;* to come and fetch (with *for*) As v.t. to summon, esp. by the voice, *come when I call you, call the police!*; to give a name to, *call me Ishmael;* to waken from sleep, *call me at seven o'clock;* to telephone (also with *up*); to reckon, regard as, *I call him an utter scoundrel;* to summon to a position, profession, etc., *to call to the Bar;* to summon, *he called a committee meeting*

call 2) n. (*kawl*) Shout, cry, esp. to attract attention; signal, summons, message (on bugle, telephone, etc., or in general, *give me a call in the morning*); bird or animal cry; short visit, *to pay a call on;* vocation, *a call to the ministry;* strong attraction, *the call of the sea;* claim, demand, *many calls on one's time*

callous adj. (*kăl'us*) Hardened (of skin); (fig.) unfeeling, hard-hearted

calm 1) n. (*kahm*) Stillness, tranquillity (lit. of weather, wind, etc.; fig. of the mind, passions, state of affairs)

calm 2) adj. and v.t. and i. (*kahm*) Quiet, peaceful, unruffled (lit. and fig.) As v.t. and i. to pacify or be pacified (often with *down*)

calorie n. (*kăl'o ri*) A unit of heat, the quantity of heat required to raise the temperature of 1 gram of water by 1°C

camel n. (*kăm'el*) Large, ruminant quadruped with long neck, thick coarse coat, large flat feet, and one hump (**Arabian camel** or dromedary) or two humps (**Bactrian camel**), much used in desert regions

camel

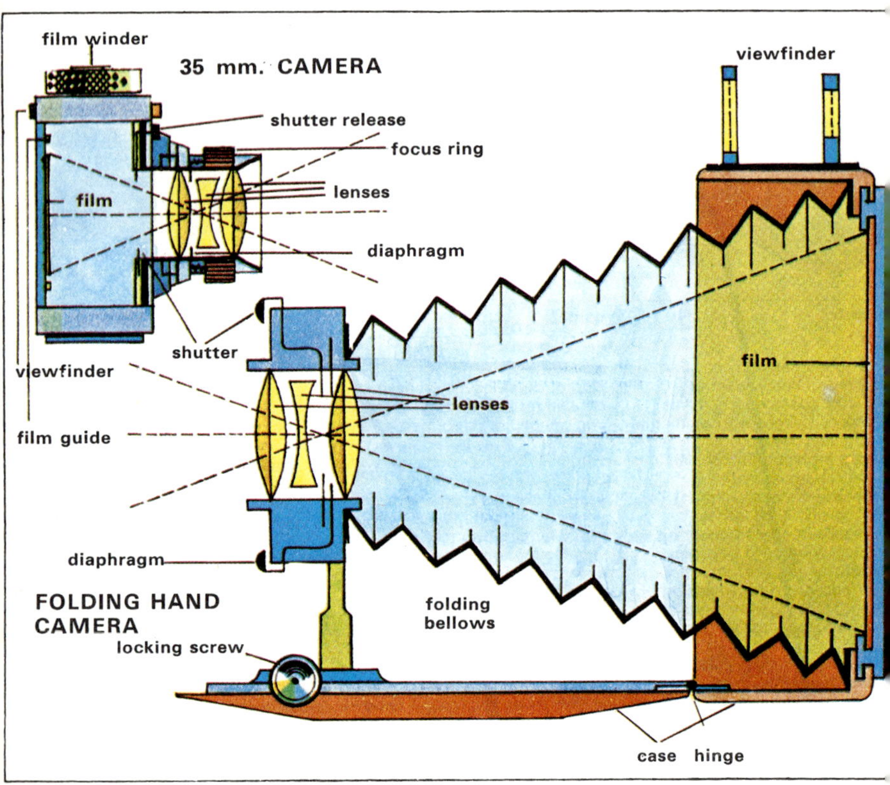

camera n. (*kăm'er a*) (phot.) Light-tight apparatus with lens at one end to throw inverted image of what is before it onto sensitized plate or film at other end

camouflage n. and v.t. (*kăm'o͞o flahzh*) Disguise, concealment, of guns, tanks, ships, etc., by painting, covering with boughs, etc.; also fig. of ideas, intentions, etc. As v.t. to hide by camouflage

camp 1) n. (*kămp*) Place where troops are lodged in tents, huts, etc.; similar place used as prison (**prison-, concentration-, internment-camp**); any temporary shelter in open country, for gypsies, hunters, etc

camp 2) v.i. (*kămp*) To pitch a camp; to take up temporary quarters; (with *out*) to live, sleep, in tent or open air.

campaign n. and v.i. (*kăm pān'*) Series of military operations towards a single object; (fig.) any series of actions planned in the same way, esp. in politics and advertising. As v.i. to direct or work in a campaign (in either sense)

can 1) v. auxil. (*kăn*) (3rd person sing. **can,** pret., pres. conditional and past subj. **could,** neg. forms **cannot, can't** (*kahnt*)) Defective verb used in the above tenses for be able to, be allowed to, know how to

can 2) n. and v.t. (*kăn*) Metal container for liquids, etc.; air-tight box for preserving foods. As v.t. to put (food, etc.) into air-tight tin boxes to preserve it

canal n. (*ka năl'*) Artificial water-

course for navigation or irrigation
canary adj. and n. (*ka nār'i*) From the Canary Islands, esp. (as noun) a bright yellow songbird (also **canary-bird**)
cancel v.t. and i. (*kăn'sel*) To cross out, delete (word, etc.) ; to annul, countermand (order, reservation, etc.) ; to neutralize, balance (often with *out*, of two things, *they cancel each other out*)
cancer n. (*kăn'ser*) malignant tumour that gradually consumes the tissues of the body
candidate n. (*kăn'di dat, kăn'di dāt*) Person offering himself or put forward for an appointment, election, examination, etc
candle n. (*kăndl*) A lighting device consisting of a wick embedded in a cylinder of wax, tallow, etc
cane n. (*kān*) Hollow jointed hard stem of bamboo, etc., or the sugar-cane ; length of this or similar material as walking-stick or for beating small boys
cannabis n. (*kăn'a bis*) Hemp plant ; preparation of hemp smoked for its hallucinatory properties
cannibal n. and adj. (*kăn'i bal*) Human being who eats human flesh ; animal that eats its own kind
cannon n. (*kăn'on*) Large mounted gun for heavy ammunition
canoe n. and v.i. (*ka nōō'*) Light boat propelled with paddle(s)
canopy n. and v.t. (*kăn'o pi*) Covering forming roof over bed, throne, etc
canteen n. (*kăn tēn'*) Refreshment bar, lunch-counter, etc., esp. in barracks, factory, etc. ; soldier's drinking bottle ; chest of knives, forks, spoons
canvas n. and adj. (*kăn'vas*) Strong coarse cloth of hemp or flax or cotton used for tents, sails, etc., for painting on, and for tapestry
canvass v.t. and i. (*kăn'vas*) Discuss thoroughly ; to solicit votes, orders, opinions, etc., *canvassing is forbidden, he canvassed the constituency.* Hence: **canvasser** n.
canyon n. (*kăn'yon*) A steep-walled gorge
cap 1) n. (*kăp*) Head-dress, usually of cloth, without brim ; formerly ladies' indoor headgear of muslin, lace, etc. ; now usually for men's wear, with peak ; special cap awarded to member of cricket, etc., team ; a round covering over numerous objects

sugar-cane

cap 2) v.t. (*kăp*) To put a cap upon, in any sense ; to cover
capable adj. (*kā'pabl*) Competent, qualified, clever (of person)
capacity n. (*ka păs'i ti*) Power of holding or containing, (of material things) *this jug has a capacity of two pints,* (or of mental ability) *children have great capacity for learning;* cubic content ; position, relation to circumstances, *in his capacity as a lawyer;* (elect.) output of a generator, etc. ; storage power of capacitor, number of ampère-hours of fully charged battery ; **capacity crowd** completely filling stadium, etc. ; **filled to capacity** full up
cape 1) n. (*kāp*) Short sleeveless cloak, as separate garment or attached to longer garment
cape 2) n. and adj. (*kāp*) Head-land, promontory
capital 1) adj. (*kăp'itl*) Relating to life, esp. to the loss of it, *capital offence, punishment;* of first importance, chief, *capital*

14th-century messenger's cape

city; standing at thé head, *capital letter*
capital 2) n. (*kăp'itl*) Chief city of a country, seat of government; a capital letter; stock of money, property, etc., used to carry on a business; accumulated wealth
capitalism n. (*kăp'it al izm*) The economic system based on private ownership of wealth. Hence: capitalist n. one who owns accumulated wealth; a believer in capitalism as a system
capitulate v.i. (*ka pit'ū lāt*) To surrender, give in, esp. (milit.) to surrender on terms
capsize v.t. and i. (*kăp sīz'*) Upset, overturn (esp. of boats)
capsule n. (*kăp'sūl*) Small case or vessel (in special senses) (bot.) seed-vessel; (med.) gelatinous case in which medicines are swallowed; space-craft designed for orbiting Earth, etc., detached from rocket motors
captain n. and v.t. (*kăp'tin*) An officer (in navy) between commander and commodore, (in army) between lieutenant and major; commanding officer of merchant ship; leader of team in sports; a great leader, soldier, etc., *captains of industry, 'The captains and the kings depart'*. As v.t. to lead, be captain of
captive adj. and n. (*kăp'tiv*) Taken prisoner, captured; **captive audience** unable easily to stop listening or watching As n. a prisoner. Hence: **captivity** n. (*kăp tiv'i ti*)
capture n. and v.t. (*kăp'cher*) Act of seizing, taking prisoner; person or thing seized or taken. As v.t. to seize, catch, take as prisoner or prize
car n. (*kah(r)*) A wheeled vehicle esp. an automobile; special railway-carriage, as *dining-car, sleeping-car;* (in U.S.) any railway carriage or wagon
carafe n. (*ka rahf'*) Glass bottle for wine, etc., at table
caramel n. (*kă'ra mel*) Burnt sugar used for colouring or flavouring; kind of toffee
carat n. (*kă'rat*) Measure of weight for precious stones, about 3⅛ grains; measure of purity in gold, pure gold being 24 carat
caravan n. (*kă'ra văn*) Party of travellers, esp. across desert, covered wagon used as home by gypsies, etc.; automobile trailer equipped for sleeping, etc
carcass, carcase n. (*kah'kas*) Dead body of animal, esp. when prepared by butcher
card n. (*kahd*) Piece of thin pasteboard, esp. a playing card; also, one bearing name and address (*visiting card*), celebrating a special occasion (*birthday, Christmas, card*), bearing programme of events or scores (*race-card, score-card*), etc.; short for postcard
cardboard stiff paper or paste-board
cardigan n. (*kah'di gan*) Short knitted waistcoat
care 1) n. (*kār*) Attention, caution, *take care, with care* anxiety, worry, or occasion for these, *free from care* (often pl.); responsibility, charge, *they were left in my care*
caretaker person looking after unoccupied house, museum, etc
care 2) v.i. (*kār*) To feel interest or concern, *he cares a lot about his appearance, who cares?;* (often neg.) *he doesn't care at all;* (with *for*) to be fond of, to like, *you never cared for me!;* to look after, *he cared for his old mother till she died;* to be willing, *would you care to go for a walk?*
career n. (*ka rēr'*) A rapid motion onwards, impetuous course, *in full career;* way of life, profession etc., esp. as means of personal advancement in life; a person's course or progress through life
careful adj. (*kār'fo͞ol*) Originally, full of care; now (of persons) cautious, painstaking, (of acts) done with care, thorough
careless adj. (*kār'les*) Care-free, lighthearted; negligent, thoughtless, unconcerned, heedless, *careless of the consequences*
cargo n. (*kah'gō*) pl. **cargoes** Freight, the goods carried by a ship
carnival n. (*kah'ni val*) revelry, riotousness, in general
carol n. and v.t. and i. (*kă'rol*) Joyful song, esp. Christmas hymn
carpenter n. and v.i. and t. (*kah'pen ter*) Worker in wood, making esp. fittings for buildings, floors, doors etc
carpet n. and v.t. (*kah'pit*) Floor covering of heavy woven fabric; smooth covering for the ground, *a carpet of leaves*. As v.t. to cover with a carpet
carriage n. (*kă'rij*) Act of carrying, transporting; charge made for this; way of holding head or body, bearing; wheeled passenger vehicle, esp. four-wheeled and

horse-drawn; passenger compartment on train
carry v.t. and i. (*kă'ri*) To bear, transport, convey a thing, to lift and move a thing, *he carried his bride over the threshold*; also of immaterial things, *to carry a message*; to support, *this beam carries a lot of weight*; to bear about with one, possess, *to carry a stick, to carry heavy insurance*; to hold head or body in a certain way, *he carries himself well*; to extend, *he carried the line across the page, to carry a fence round a field, to carry things too far*; (milit.) to take by storm (town etc.); to retain (in the memory), *to carry a thing in one's head*; to gain approval for, *to carry a resolution, carry one's point*; to involve, imply, *this job carries responsibility*; (math.) to transfer to column of higher value. As v.i. to perform act of carrying, esp. *to fetch and carry*; to reach to, be audible at, a certain distance, *the shot carried for miles, his voice was loud enough to carry across the river*
cart n. and v.t. and i. (*kaht*) Horse-drawn wheeled vehicle for transport; light two-wheeled passenger vehicle, also **dog-cart**; **cart-horse** heavy type capable of drawing heavy loads; **cart-wheel** wheel of cart; sideways somersault; **cartwright** maker of carts As v.t. and i. to carry in a cart, work with a cart
carton n. (*kah'ton*) Small cardboard box or container
cartoon n. and v.t. and i. (*kah to͞on'*) Design or sketch expressing views, comments, on political affairs etc. a film made from a succession of drawings, also **animated cartoon**
cartridge n. (*kah'trij*) Container of metal, paper, plastic, holding esp. explosive charge for a firearm
carve v.t. and i. (*kahv*) To cut, chisel, engrave design, figure, inscription etc. in wood, stone etc.; to cut up meat, fowl, at or for the table; (fig. esp. with *out*) to shape, acquire, *to carve out a career for oneself*
case 1) n. (*kās*) That which happens; actual state of affairs, fact, *that is the case*; special circumstances, *in this case*; position, predicament, *in a bad case*; instance, example, *a case in point*; (med.) instance of disease in person; thus, the person having the disease
case 2) n. and v.t. (*kās*) Box, chest, receptacle for almost anything
cash n. and v.t. (*kăsh*) Ready money in coin or notes; (colloq.) money generally As v.t. give or get ready money for cheque etc
cashier n. (*kă shēr'*) Person in charge of cash in bank etc., or receiving cash in shop etc
casino n. (*ka sē'nō*) Place of public entertainment esp. with facilities for gambling
casket n. (*kahs'kit*) Small case for jewels and other precious objects
casserole n. (*kăs'er ōl*) Fire-proof cooking vessel of earthenware etc.; dish cooked in this
cassock n. (*kăs'ok*) Long (black) tunic worn by clergy
cast v.t. and i. (*kahst*) pret. and p.p. **cast** To throw to mould (molten metal) into shape
castaway n. (*kahs'ta wā*) Shipwrecked person
castle n. and v.i. (*kahsl*) Large, strongly fortified building, a fortress; large house once a castle or like one; chess-piece shaped like a castle tower, the rook
casual adj. and n. (*kăzh'ū al*) Accidental, happening by chance, *a casual meeting*; irregular, occasional, *casual labour*; without method or intent, *casual conversation*; careless, slack, offhand, *casual manner*
casualty n. (*kăzh'ū al ti*) Accident, mishap; person injured in accident, war etc. (often pl.)
cat n. (*kăt*) Small domesticated carnivorous quadruped of genus *Felis* (**tom-cat** male); **Wild Cat** larger species found wild in British Isles; (zoo.) any member of genus *Felis*, as lion, tiger etc. **cat's eye** small glass reflector marking centre of roadway
catalogue n. and v.t. (*kăt'a log*) Systematic list or register (of books, objects for sale etc.)
catamaran n. (*kăt a ma răn'*) Raft of logs lashed together; boat consisting of two hulls side by side
catapult n. and v.t. and i. (*kăt'a pult*) Forked stick with elastic strung between the fork tips, for propelling stones etc
cataract n. (*kăt'a răkt*) Large waterfall; downpour of water, rain etc.; (med.) disease of eye
catastrophe n. (*ka tăs'tro fi*) A

disaster, terrible calamity
catch 1) v.t. and i. (*kăch*) pret. and p.p. **caught** (*kawt*) To seize, to pursue and capture, *the cat caught a mouse*; to ensnare, trap (fish, rabbit etc. but also fig. of persons, *his question really caught me, and I couldn't answer*); to snatch (often with *at, up*); to draw level with (often with *up*); to receive in communication, in various senses: (of illness) to be infected with, (of sound) to succeed in hearing, (of meaning) to succeed in understanding, (of inflammable substances) to kindle, *the wood caught fire*; to intercept motion of, grasp, entangle, *he caught the ball, the thorns caught my sleeve*; to hit, *he caught me a blow*; to gasp, *catch one's breath*; to be in time for, *catch a train*; (of senses) to seize, *catch a glimpse*; to attract (eye, fancy etc.); to detect, discover, *to catch someone in the act*. As v.i. to become entangled, fastened etc., *my sleeve caught on the thorns*
catch 2) n. (*kăch*) Act of seizing, grasping; sudden halt or break (in breath etc.); thing that catches, esp. mechanical contrivance for door, necklace etc.; (fig.) trick to deceive or trap, *there's a catch in this somewhere*; thing caught, esp. amount of fish, but also thing, person, worth having, *her fiancée is a good catch: he's a millionaire*
category n. (*kăt'i go ri*) A class, group, division based on common qualities
cater v.i. (*kā'ter*) To provide food *for*; provide amusement, satisfaction *for*, *to cater for all tastes*. Hence: **caterer** n.
caterpillar n. (*kăt'a pil er*) Larva of butterfly or moth; endless jointed band running over wheels of vehicle (tank, tractor etc.)
cathedral n. and adj. (*ka thē'dral*) The principal church of a diocese, containing bishop's throne
catholic adj. and n. (*kăth'o lik*) Universal, applicable to all; liberal, broad-minded (of views, tastes etc.) As n.
Catholic a member of the Catholic Church; a Roman Catholic
cattle n. pl. (*kătl*) Bovine animals (cows, bulls, oxen) esp. domesticated
cauldron, caldron n. (*kawl'dron*) Large deep bowl-shaped kettle or pan of copper or iron, for cooking
cause 1) n. (*kawz*) What produces an effect; person, thing, producing, contributing to, an effect, *dangerous driving is the cause of accidents, she was the cause of my downfall*; reason, motive, *cause for alarm*; adequate reason, *to show cause*; a principle, ideal etc. to which a person or group of persons is devoted, *freedom is a noble cause*; lawsuit, reason for going to law, *to plead one's cause*
cause 2) v.t. (*kawz*) To bring about an effect, induce, motivate
causeway n. and v.t. (*kawz'wā*) Raised roadway across stretch of water, marsh, or low ground
caution n. and v.t. (*kaw'shun*) Prudence, carefulness; a warning
cavalry n. (*kăv'al ri*) Troops mounted on horseback
cave 1) (*kāv*) Underground hollow in rock, cliff etc., whether natural or artificial, usually with horizontal entrance
cave-dweller one living in a cave, esp. primitive man; **cave-man** primitive man (lit. and fig.)
cave 2) v.i. and t. (*kāv*) **cave in** to subside, fall in (earth, roof etc.); (fig.) give in, cease resistance. As v.t. to cause to fall in, to smash in
cavity n. (*kăv'i ti*) Internal hollow,

external depression, in solid body
cease v.i. and t. (*sēs*) To desist *from*; to come to an end. As v.t. to stop, leave off
ceiling n. (*sē'ling*) Inside surface of house roof; lining of wood, plaster etc. on upper side of a room; upper limit
celebrate v.t. and i. (*sel'i brāt*) (slang) to have a spree to mark some occasion. Hence: **celebrated** adj. famous; **celebration** n.; **celebrity** n. (*se leb'ri ti*) state of being famous; *a* well-known person
cell n. (*sel*) Small room in prison or monastery; hermit's one-roomed dwelling; small unit of a whole composed of similar units, as in honeycomb etc.; subsidiary unit of (esp. revolutionary) political organization; (biol.) smallest unit of living tissue; (elect.) one complete unit in a battery, single source of electric potential; storage unit in computer
cellar n. (*sel'er*) Underground room in house, esp. for storage
cement n. and v.t. (*si ment'*) Substance of ground limestone and water which, applied wet and soft between bricks etc., dries hard and binds them together; any bonding substance that binds as it dries As v.t. to unite by, cover with, cement; (fig.) to unite, consolidate (friendship etc.)
cemetery n. (*sem'it er i*) Burial ground other than churchyard
censor n. and v.t. (*sen'ser*) An official authorized to suppress books, films, plays etc. (or parts of these) on grounds of morality
census n. (*sen'sus*) Official count of population
centigrade adj. (*sen'tigrād*) Temperature scale divided into 100 degrees between freezing point of water, 0°, and boiling point, 100°.
central adj. (*sen'tral*) At, in, near, of, the centre
centre 1) n. and adj. (*sen'ter*) The middle point
centre-forward player in middle of forward line in football and hockey
centre 2) v.t. and i. (*sen'ter*) To place in, on, the centre
century n. (*sen'cher i*) Period of a hundred years, esp. any one of such periods reckoned from the birth of Christ, *20th century*; a hundred of one thing, esp. runs at cricket
cereal adj. and n. (*sēr'i al*) Of, to do with, edible grain. As n. (often pl.) kind of plant producing edible grain, as wheat, barley, rice etc.; the grain itself; (esp. breakfast-) food made from this
ceremony n. (*se'ri mun i*) Public or religious rite or rites, formal observances; public function at which these are used
certain adj. (*sur'tn, sur'tin*) Sure, positive (of state of mind); undisputed, beyond doubt (facts etc.); sure to happen, inevitable (future events); fixed, agreed upon, *a certain date*; some unspecified, *a certain person* Hence: **certainly** adv. undoubtedly, *he will certainly fail*
certificate n. (*ser tif'i kat*) and v.t. (*ser tif'i kāt*) Document formally declaring a fact, esp. the bearer's status, qualifications etc., *birth certificate, health certificate*
chain 1) n. (*chān*) Connected series of (esp. metal) links a connected series of objects, mountains, human beings, events, ideas etc
chain 2) v.t. (*chān*) To fasten, secure, confine, with a chain (lit. and fig.)
chair n. and v.t. (*chār*) Movable seat for one, with back rest; (fig.) a seat of authority, post of university professor, position of person presiding at meeting etc
chalet n. (*shă'lā*) Swiss mountain cottage; house in this style; summer bungalow
chalk 1) n. (*chawk*) A soft white limestone; this or synthetic substance prepared for writing or drawing
chalk 2) v.t. (*chawk*) To mark, rub, with chalk; (with *up*) to record score, bill for drinks etc
challenge n. and v.t. (*chăl'inj*) A call to account (by sentry or fig.); provocation, summons, to duel, game, trial of skill or worth etc; to make a challenge (any of above senses)
chamber n. (*chām'ber*) Room in house or public building; (pl.) judge's private room at law court, *to hear a case in chambers*; hall used for legislative assemblies etc.; the assembly itself, *the Lower Chamber, Chamber of Commerce*; (pl.) rented apartments, esp. in Inns of Court; a hollow space; compartment in gun's breech to hold projectile or charge
chamois n. (*sham'wah*) A mountain goat-like antelope, found in southern Europe; (pron. *shăm'i*) soft leather made from skin of this animal or other, used for polishing etc

chamois

champagne n. (*shăm pān'*) Wine from Champagne district in E. France, usually white and sparkling

champion n. and adj. (*chăm'pi un*) Defender of cause, other person etc.; person, animal etc. of proven superiority over others. winner of first prize (esp. in sport). As adj. excellent. Hence: **championship** n.

chance 1) n. and adj. (*chahns*) The course of events, way things happen; unforeseen, undesigned occurrence, accident, luck, *by chance, leave things to chance*; opportunity, *a chance to make good*; possibility, probability, *there's a good chance*

chance 2) v.i. (*chahns*) To happen; to do, experience, by accident, *I chanced to see him*; (with *upon*) find, meet, unexpectedly

chandelier n. (*shăn del ēr'*) Branched hanging support for lights

change 1) n. (*chānj*) An alteration; substitution of one thing for another, variety, novelty, *for a change, a change is as good as a rest* coins of small value; money in excess of purchase price returned to buyer

change 2) v.t. and i. (*chānj*) To make a change, modify; substitute or adopt one thing *for* another

changeable adj. liable to change, inconstant; able to be changed

channel n. and v.t. (*chăn'el*) Watercourse, bed of running water, natural or artificial; navigable waterway in river, estuary, harbour etc. providing best passage for ships; narrow body of water joining two larger seas, *English Channel* (elect.) a band of frequencies for transmission of radio, television signals; (fig.) means of communication

chapel n. (*chăp'el*) Place of Christian worship, various senses: part of larger church or cathedral, private place of worship in college, institution, large house etc

chapter n. (*chăp'ter*) Main section of book

character n. (*kă'rik ter*) Inscribed mark, letter, alphabetical symbol; mode of writing; distinguishing mark, essential quality, kind, nature; (biol.) characteristics of a species; moral strength; reputation; testimonial; eccentric individual, well-known person; fictitious person in play or novel

charge 1) n. (*chahj*) Full loading, esp. of something later emptied, as fire-arm, glass, electric battery etc.; price asked for thing, service etc.; liability, tax, on property etc.; task, duty, responsibility, care for something, *to be in charge of*; thing to be cared for (esp. child etc.)

charge 2) v.t. and i. (*chahj*) To load fully (*with*); to ask a certain price for thing or service; to command, *I charge you to do your duty*; to entrust *with* thing, undertaking etc.; to accuse, *he was charged with murder*; to attack with sudden rush (v.t. and i.) As v.i. to demand a price, *he charges for his services*

charity n. (*chă'ri ti*) Love of fellow men; generosity of feeling, benevolence, tendency to judge favourably (motives etc.); liberality to the poor and needy; alms, money given to help poor and needy; institution for distributing this or other work of benevolence

charm 1) n. *chahm*) Incantation, formula, object etc. with supposed magical power

charm 2) v.t. and i. (*chahm*) To bewitch, influence by magic; (fig.) to enchant, fascinate, delight

chart n. and v.t. (*chaht*) Navigator's map of sea, coast etc. showing rocks, depths etc.; any detailed map or plan; graph showing fluctuation in temperature, price, population etc.; table of information, statistics etc.
As v.t. to make a chart of, map out

chase 1) v.t. and i. (*chās*) To

pursue, try to catch, *to chase a rabbit*; to drive away, drive out, *the dog chased the wolf away*; (fig.) dispel, drive out (gloom, fear etc.) As v.i. to rush *about, up and down* etc

chase 2) n. (*chās*) Act of chasing

chassis n. (*shăs'i*) Supporting framework of motor-car etc

chatter v.i. and n. (*chăt'er*) To talk rapidly

chauffeur n. (*shō'fer*) Man employed to drive private car

cheap adj. and adv. (*chēp*) Low in price; worth more than cost; of little value

cheat n. and v.t. and i. (*chēt*) A fraud, deception; a swindler, person who cheats. As v.t. to swindle, deceive, trick (person *out* of a thing)

check 1) n. (*chek*) pattern of squares, chess-board pattern; cloth woven in such a pattern

check 2) v.t. and i. (*chek*) To obstruct, restrain; to verify, test

cheek n. and v.t. (*chēk*) One of the two fleshy sides of human face, below the eye; (colloq.) insolence, impertinent speech

cheer 1) n. (*chēr*) State of mind *of good cheer*

cheer 2) v.t. and i. (*chēr*) To encourage, gladden; to shout applause (v.t. and i.)

cheetah n. (*chē'ta*) Very swift kind of leopard found in India and Africa

chef n. (*shef*) Head (male) cook

chemist n. (*kem'ist*) Person skilled in chemistry; dealer in drugs

chemistry n. (*kem'is tri*) The science of the properties of elements and their combinations, and of the behaviour and reactions of substances to each other

cheetah

cheque n. (*chek*) Order to banker to pay a certain sum to a named person out of the drawer's bank account; printed form so used; **cheque-book** booklet of these forms issued by banks to clients

cherish v.t. (*che'rish*) To hold dear, show great solicitude for; to cling to (hopes etc.)

chess n. (*ches*) Game played by two players, each using 16 pieces **(chessmen)**, on a board of 64 squares coloured alternately black and white

chest n. (*chest*) Large heavy box with lid, for storage
part of body enclosed in rib-cage

chestnut n. and adj. (*chest'nut*) The edible nut of the Spanish sweet chestnut *Castanea vulgaris*; the inedible or horse-chestnut *Aesculus hippocastanum*; the trees bearing either of these

chew v.t. and i. and n. (*choo͞*) To bite and grind up with the teeth

chicken n. (*chik'en*) Young bird, esp. of domestic fowl; flesh of this as dish

chief n. and adj. (*chēf*) Headman of tribe, clan etc.; leader, ruler; (colloq.) boss, head of firm or department

child n. (*chīld*) pl. **children** (*chil'dren*) Young human being

chessmen: **King, Queen, Bishop, Knight, Castle, Pawn**

offspring, son or daughter (any age)
chill 1) n. and adj. (*chil*) Sensation of cold; internal inflammation, feverish shivering, caused by cold, damp etc., *to catch a chill*; (fig.) depressing atmosphere, *cast a chill over*
chill 2) v.t. and i. (*chil*) To make (v.i. become) cold
chime n. and v.i. and t. (*chīm*) Set of tuned bells; series of notes played on this; a bell-like sound, harmony, agreement. As v.i. and t. to make bell-sound, to ring or strike chimes (bells or clock)
chimney n. (*chim'ni*) Hollow shaft above fire to carry away smoke, fumes etc: **chimney-pot** earthenware tube at top of house chimney, projecting above roof
chin n. (*chin*) Front part of lower jaw
china n. and adj. (*chī'na*) Glazed porcelain ware; household crockery in general
chink n. (*chingk*) Long narrow opening, crack
chip 1) n. (*chip*) Thin shaving cut from wood or broken from brittle substance (as china); the dented place left by such a fragment; thin slice of potato, fried
chip 2) v.t. and i. (*chip*) To cut or knock chips off (wood, china etc.); to slice and fry potatoes. As v.i. to be liable to be chipped at edge, *these cups chip easily*
chiropody n. (*kī rop'o di*) Treatment of the feet, toe-nails, corns etc. Thus: **chiropodist** n.
chirp v.i. and t. and n. (*churp*) Utter sharp shrill cry of small bird
chisel n. and v.t. (*chizl*) Tool with square bevelled cutting edge at tip of blade, for wood, stone etc. As v.t. to cut, shape with a chisel
chocolate n. and adj. (*chok'o lat*) Sweetmeat of hard paste made from cacao beans; this dissolved in hot milk as drink; the dark brown colour of this
choice n. and adj. (*chois*) Act or process of selecting, deciding, between alternatives; the thing selected; a chance to choose, *I offer you first choice, I have no choice* As adj. carefully selected, excellent, *choice fruit*
choir n. and v.t. and i. (*kwīr*) Band of singers esp. in church
choke v.t. and i. (*chōk*) To stop passage of breath, by squeezing or blocking windpipe or introducing fumes into lungs; to impede any passage partly or completely, *choked with dirt*; to stifle, smother through lack of air or light (fire, plants etc.); (fig.) to suppress (one's feelings). As v.i. to suffer a stoppage of breath, *he choked on a fishbone*; (fig.) to be rendered speechless etc., *he choked with anger*
choose v.t. and i. (*chōōz*) pret. **chose** (*chōz*) p.p. **chosen** (*chō'zen*) To pick out, select from greater number, *to choose a book*; to elect, *they chose a new leader*; to decide *to* do thing, *he chose to disobey*, or *between* alternatives
chop 1) v.t. and i. (*chop*) To cut by striking with axe or knife
chop 2) n. (*chop*) Cutting blow with axe etc.; thing chopped off, esp. slice of meat on rib-bone
chopsticks n. pl. (*chop'stiks*) Two thin wood or ivory sticks used by Chinese instead of fork
chord n. (*kawd*) String of musical instrument; thing resembling this, *spinal, vocal, chord*; (mus.) group of notes sounded simultaneously
chore n. (*chaw(r)*) Task, job of work (esp. in house)
chorus n. and v.t. and i. (*kaw'rus*) band of singers, choir; words, music, performed by a chorus in above senses; recurring refrain of song
christen v.t. (*krisn*) To make (person) Christian by baptism; to name (person) at baptism; (loosely) give name or nickname to. Hence: **christening** n. baptism
Christian adj. and n. (*kris'chun*) Concerned with, characteristic of, Jesus Christ, his teaching, or a believer in this
As n. a believer in Christ, a member of a Christian church or community; a person living in accordance with Christ's teachings

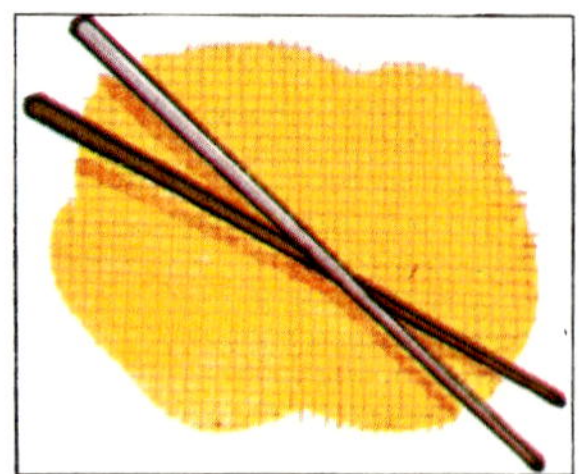

chopsticks

Christianity n. (*kris ti ăn'i ti*) The doctrine of Christ, the Christian faith
Christmas n. (*kris'mas*) Festival of the birth of Christ, observed on December 25th
chromium n. (*krō'mi um*) (chem.) The chemical element denoted by Cr; greyish-white metal used to give hardness to alloys
chubby adj. (*chub'i*) Plump, round-faced
chuckle v.i. and n. (*chukl*) Laugh to oneself, As n. the sound thus made. (Imitative)
chum n. and v.i. (*chum*) An intimate friend, pal
chunk n. (*chungk*) Thick lump or block (bread, wood etc.)
church n. (*church*) Building for public Christian worship; the whole body of Christians; any one organized body, sect, of Christians
churchyard ground surrounding church, often used for burial
churn n. and v.t. and i. (*churn*) Rotating drum etc. for agitating cream to make butter; a large milk-can. As v.t. and i. to agitate cream in buttermaking; to stir (liquid) violently (often with *up*)
cider n. (*sī'der*) Drink made of fermented apple juice
cigar n. (*si gah(r)'*) Roll of tobacco-leaf for smoking
cigarette n. (*si ga ret'*) Small cylinder of finely-cut tobacco-leaf in roll of fine paper
cinder n. (*sin'der*) Residue of coal or wood after burning but before being reduced to ashes
cinema n. (*sin'i mah*) Theatre for showing of motion pictures; the art or industry of motion picture making
cipher, cypher n. (*sī'fer*) The arithmetical symbol 0, zero code, secret method of writing, or key to this secret
circle 1) n. (*surkl*) (geom.) A perfectly round plane figure or line enclosing this; anything similar to this, as a ring group of persons associated in some way, *a circle of friends*
circle 2) v.t. and i. (*surkl*) To go right round, *the wall circles the city*. As v.i. to move in a circle, *the aeroplane circled for an hour*
circular adj. and n. (*sur'kū ler*) Round, having the shape of a circle; moving in a circle, *circular tour*; sent to a number of persons, *circular letter*
circulate v.i. and t. (*sur'kū lāt*) To move around, *the blood circulates in the body*; to pass freely (traffic etc.); to be handed round (wine, news); (math.) to recur. As v.t. to spread, give currency to (rumour etc.); to hand round (book etc.)
circumference n. (*sur kum'fer ens*) The line enclosing a circle; the length of this line
circumstance n. (*sur'kum stans*) (usually pl.) The accidental accompaniments of an event, as time, place etc.; external conditions affecting an act, *in the circumstances*; a detail, a factor, *a peculiar circumstance*; (pl.) material prosperity, *in easy, troubled circumstances*
circus n. (*sur'kus*) spectacular show consisting of trick-riding and other tricks, gymnastic feats, wild animals, clowning etc
cistern n. (*sis'tern*) Water-tank, esp. at top of house
citizen n. (*sit'i zen*) Inhabitant of a city, esp. one having full rights and duties in a certain city; a national or native or member of a State
city n. (*sit'i*) A great town
civilization n. (*siv il i zā'shun*) Act of making or becoming civilized; high level of social development; any stage in such a cultural development
civilize v.t. (*siv'i līz*) To raise from barbarism, educate in social and moral values; (fig.) to educate, refine
claim 1) v.t. and i. (*klām*) To demand as a right, *to claim a reward, damages*; demand recognition of (a fact), *to claim that something is so*; to assert one's ownership of (lost property etc.); (of things) to call for, deserve, *to claim attention*
claim 2) n. (*klām*) Act of demanding a right; the right demanded, *to have a claim on a person, to a thing*
clamber v.i. and n. (*klăm'ber*) To climb with difficulty, scramble *up*
clamp 1) n. and v.t. (*klămp*) Device, usually of wood or metal, for holding things together, esp. while being assembled
clamp 2) n. and v.t. (*klămp*) A pile of bricks; heap of potatoes etc. stored under straw and earth; dung heap. As v.t. to store (potatoes etc.) in a clamp
clan n. and v.t. (*klăn*) Tribal group, esp. in Scotland, united by

common ancestry; (loosely) a family
clank n. and v.i. and t. (*klănk*) Dull, heavy metallic sound, such as made by iron chains. As v.i. and t. to make, cause to make, this sound
clap 1) n. (*klăp*) Explosive sound of thunder, striking palms of hands together etc.; a friendly slap (on shoulder etc.)
clap 2) v.i. and t. (*klăp*) To make the sound of a clap esp. by striking the palms of the hands together; to applaud in this way (v.t. and i.); to slap in a friendly, encouraging way (esp. *on the back*)
clarinet n. (*klă ri net'*) Woodwind instrument with single-reed
clash v.i. and t. and n. (*klăsh*) To make a loud, harsh metallic sound, as of swords struck together; to collide, disagree, come into conflict, *the two armies clashed*; (of events) to coincide As v.t. to cause to clash. As n. harsh, violent metallic sound; a sudden conflict of opinions, armed forces etc
clasp n. and v.t. (*klahsp*) A secure grasp, strong handshake; device of interlocking metal pieces for closing, fastening (brooch, book-covers etc.)
As v.t. to grasp firmly, hug; to grasp hands; to fasten with a clasp
class n. and v.t. and adj. (*klahs*) Category, type, sort group of students studying together, *top of the class*
classroom where a class of pupils is taught
clatter v.i. and t. and n. (*klăt'er*) To make a repeated, hard, rattling noise. As v.t. to cause to make this noise. As n. such a noise, *a clatter of dishes, of footsteps*
claustrophobia n. (*klaws'tro fō'bi a*) Neurotic fear of small or confined spaces. (Lat. *claustrum* enclosed space
claw n. and v.t. and i. (*klaw*) Sharp nail on foot of bird or other animal
clay n. (*klā*) material used to make pottery, bricks etc
clean 1) adj. (*klēn*) Free from dirt, impurities etc
clean 2) v.t. and n. (*klēn*) To make clean, free from dirt, to polish; **to clean up** tidy; **to clean out** empty. As n. process of cleaning, *she gave the house a good clean*. Hence: **cleaner** n.

clarinet

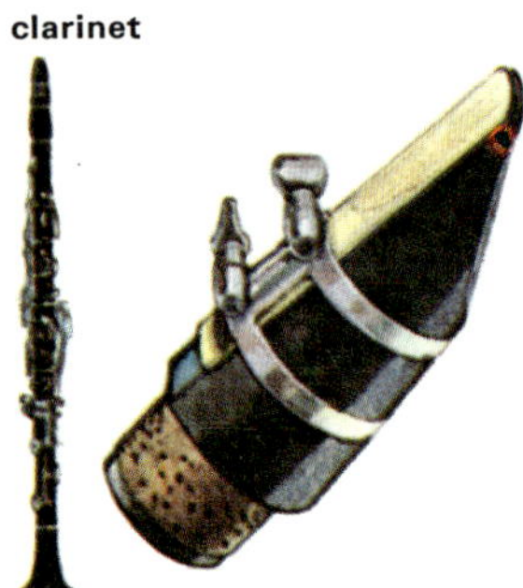

clear 1) adj. and adv. (*klēr*) Transparent, translucent, *clear water*; bright, unclouded, *clear sky*; lucid, intelligible, *a clear explanation*; distinct, *a clear outline, a clear voice*; free (from), *clear of debt* (also as n. *in the clear*); unobstructed, *the coast is clear*; complete, *a clear month's notice*; (of things) certain, obvious, *a clear case of murder*
clear 2) v.t. and i. (*klēr*) To make clear, *to clear the air* (also fig.); to remove, get rid of (obstacle, anything unwanted), *they cleared the trees before building*
clergy n. (*klur'ji*) Body of ordained ministers in Christian churches Hence:
clergyman n. ordained minister
clerk n. (*klahk*) Religious, legal or political official whose duties formerly involved writing, recording etc. employee of bank, business etc. performing routine tasks, copying, accounting etc
clever adj. (*klev'er*) Intelligent, quick-witted (of persons); adroit, skilful with the hands etc.; (of actions, products) displaying intelligence, skill etc
click n. and v.i. and t. (*klik*) Short sharp sound to make this sound
cliff n. (*klif*) Steep rock-face, esp. bordering the sea
climate n. (*klī'mat*) General or habitual weather conditions, *a good climate*; region having a certain climate, *to live in a warm climate*
climb v.t. and i. and n. (*klīm*) To go up, mount, esp. using hands, *climb a tree, a mountain*; to ascend in general, *the plane climbed steadily* As n. a place to be climbed, the act of climbing, *a stiff climb*
cling v.i. (*kling*) pret. and p.p.

sand glass
lamp
clock
graduated
candle clock
ship's clock
lantern
clock
pendulum
clock
with brass
weights
water clock
Egyptian shadow clock

clung (*klung*) To stick, adhere *to*; to grasp
clinic n. (*klin'ik*) Medical etc. institution, often a specialist one; centre for medical care (esp. of children etc.)
clip 1) v.t. and n. (*klip*) To grip tightly; to fasten *together* or *to*, esp. with a clip (n.) As n. a device for holding things together (esp. papers); a brooch
clip 2) v.t. and n. (*klip*) To cut or trim with scissors or shears (hair, sheep, hedge, edge of lawn etc.)
clique n. (*klēk*) Small exclusive set of people
cloak n. and v.t. (*klōk*) Long loose garment without arm-holes **cloak-room** repository at stations etc. for coats, baggage etc.; a toilet
clock n. and v.t. and i. (*klok*) Device for measuring time and showing it on a dial As v.t. to record a time in racing, *he clocked* 9.5 *seconds for the* 100 *yards*. As v.i. **to clock in, out** (of employees) record time of arrival at, departure from, factory etc
close 1) adj. and adv. (*klōs*) Near, in various senses: near *to*, *close to the road*; intimate, *close friends*; almost identical, *a close copy*; solid, compact, *close texture* (also fig. of reasoning etc.); thorough, careful, *close attention*; shut, in various senses: restricted, *close quarters*, *close scholarship*; confined, *close prisoner*; secluded, *keep oneself close*; sultry, stuffy (of atmosphere)
close 2) v.t. and i. and n. (*klōz*) To shut (door, lid etc.); to shut up, enclose completely, exclude customers etc. from (house, shop etc.); to make access impossible to (road, area etc.); to finish, bring to an end (discussion, bargaining etc.); to bring into contact, *close ranks*. As v.i. to come to an end, finish; become closed, be capable of closing, *this door doesn't close*
As n. conclusion, end, *close of play*
cloth n. and adj. (*kloth*) Pliable fabric of various materials, chiefly used for garments; a piece of this, esp. used for dusting etc. or as a covering, *table-cloth*
clothe v.t. (*klōth*) To supply with clothes, to put clothes upon
Hence: **clothing** n. articles of dress in general
clothes n. pl. (*klōthz, klōz*) Garments, articles of dress; linen etc. esp. for bed (also **bed-clothes**)
cloud n. and v.t. and i. (*klowd*) Mass of condensed water-vapour, esp. suspended in atmosphere; mass of similar appearance, *a cloud of dust, of flies*; (fig.) a vast multitude; (fig.) something that shadows, disgraces, threatens, *a cloud has come over his life*
clown n. and v.i. (*klown*) Buffoon, jester, esp. in circus or pantomime
club 1) n. (*klub*) Wooden stick with one large, heavy end; stick with heavy head used in various games, such as golf; (pl.) lowest suit at playing cards
group of persons associated for social, sporting, or other purposes, and usually bound by self-devised rules; the premises where such a group meets etc
club 2) v.t. and i. (*klub*) To beat with a club
clue n. (*kloo*) Fact throwing light on some puzzle or mystery.
clumsy adj. (*klum'zi*) Awkward in movement or appearance
cluster n. and v.i. and t. (*klus'ter*) Group of persons or objects; bunch of fruit etc. growing on one stem; mass of bees etc. As v.i. to grow, gather, in clusters. As v.t. to bring together
clutch 1) v.t. and i. (*kluch*) To seize, grab eagerly or desperately *at*; **to clutch at a straw** seize on any help when desperate
clutch 2) n. (*kluch*) Act of seizing, grasping, snatching; a tight grasp; device for connecting and disconnecting moving parts of a machine, esp. driving gear and wheels of car etc
coach n. and v.i. and t. (*kōch*) Large closed horse-drawn carriage; long-distance motorbus; passenger railway-carriage; a private tutor, esp. engaged to prepare pupil for a particular examination; trainer of athletics team etc. As v.i. to travel by coach. As v.t. to prepare pupil for examination; to train athletics team etc
coal n. (*kōl*) Solid black combustible mineral, chiefly carbon, burnt as fuel; piece of this, esp. while burning **coalfield** district where there are seams of coal
coalition n. (*kō a lishn'*) Act of

fusing, uniting; a temporary union of political parties for particular ends, esp. to form government
coarse adj. (*kaws*) Rough, harsh vulgar, rude (persons, behaviour etc.)
coast n. (*kōst*) That part of the land bordering on the sea
coat n. and v.t. (*kōt*) Sleeved outer garment buttoning up front, furry or hairy skin of an animal a layer of some substance spread over any body, *a coat of paint*
As v.t. to put a coat on something, esp. layer of paint etc.; often p.p. coated (with mud etc.)
coax v.t. and i. (*kōks*) To persuade
cobbler n. (*kob'ler*) Mender of shoes
cobweb n. (*kob'web*) Network of fine threads spun by spider to catch insects
cock 1) n. (*kok*) Male bird, esp. of domestic fowl
cock 2) v.t. and i. (*kok*) To set erect; set (hat etc.) at an angle
cocksure adj. (*kok shoo͞r'*) Confidently certain (of something); conceitedly sure (of oneself)
cocktail n. (*kok'tāl*) Short iced mixed drink of gin or other spirit etc
cocoa n. (*kō'kō*) Powder made from beans of cacao tree; chocolate-flavoured drink made from this
coconut n. (*kō'ker nut*) Fruit of coconut palm, with hard brown shell and white hollow kernel containing milky juice
cocoon n. (*ko koo͞n'*) Small silken case spun by caterpillars etc. to protect them in chrysalis stage
cod (*kod*) Large sea fish
codliver oil employed medicinally
code n. and v.t. (*kōd*) System of laws, *Penal Code*; accepted social customs, *code of behaviour, of honour*; set of special symbols for conveying messages etc. rapidly or secretly. As v.t. to put (message) into code
co-education n. (*kō ed ū kā'shun*) Education of girls and boys together
coffee n. (*kof'i*) Evergreen shrub with highly flavoured beans; these beans, raw, roasted, or ground; drink made from the ground and roasted beans
coffin n. and v.t. (*kof'in*) Case (now usually of wood) in which corpse is buried
cohabit v.i. (*kō hăb'it*) To live together, esp. unmarried but as husband and wife
coil 1) v.t. and i. (*koil*) Gather, arrange, rope etc. in spiral loops. As v.i. to wind (oneself), become wound (of ropes, snakes etc.)
coil 2) n. (*koil*) Series of spiral rings or loops, placed next to or on top of each other
coin 1) n. (*koin*) Piece of metal, usually circular, stamped and issued officially as money
coin 2) v.t. (*koin*) To stamp (money) out of metal, to mint; (fig.) to invent, *to coin a phrase*
coincide v.i. (*kō in sīd'*) To occupy same position, correspond, come together (in time or place); to agree, harmonize *with* (of tastes, opinions etc.)
cold 1) adj. (*kōld*) Of low temperature, esp. compared with body heat, tested by feel etc
cold 2) n. (*kōld*) Low temperature; sensation of this
collapse n. and v.t. (*ko lăps'*) Act or fact of falling down v.t. to fall to pieces etc
collar n. (*kol'er*) Neckband of various kinds, esp. on man's shirt, coat etc
colleague n. (*kol'ēg*) Professional associate; holder of joint office
collect v.t. and i. (*ko lekt'*) Assemble, accumulate, bring (v.i. come) together; to accumulate specimens as a hobby (stamps, paintings etc.)
collection n. (*ko lek'shun*) Act or process of collecting group of things collected (stamps, paintings etc.)
college n. (*kol ij*) institution for higher education
collide v.i. (*ko līd'*) To be in violent collision (*with*); (fig.) to clash, conflict (of wills, aims etc.)
collision n. (*ko lizhn'*) Violent impact between objects, esp. moving vehicles
colonel n. (*kur'nel*) Officer commanding regiment in British Army
colony n. (*kol'o ni*) Settlement established esp. in distant and sparsely inhabited country; the settlers of this; overseas territory governed by the home government; group of people of one nation living in foreign city etc.; (biol.) body of organisms closely grouped together
colour 1) n. (*kul'er*) Sensation produced on retina of eye by light waves of various frequencies; the

hue, tint, thus seen a military standard, *regimental colours*
colour 2) v.t. and i. (*kul'er*) To paint, stain, tint, with colour
colour-blind unable to distinguish certain colours (thus, **colour-blindness**)
colourless adj. (*kul'er les*) Without colour; dull, drab; (fig.) lifeless, characterless
colt 1) n. (*kōlt*) Young horse
column n. (*kol'um*) Pillar, upright shaft of stone etc., esp. bearing arch or roof; thing resembling this, *column of mercury*; vertical division of page of print, as in newspapers; set of figures arranged vertically
coma n. (*kō'ma*) Trance-like stupor caused by disease or injury
comb 1) n. (*kōm*) Instrument with row of long fine teeth for arranging or securing hair, or separating and cleaning wool, flax etc.; crest of cock-bird; cellular store-place built by bees for their honey
comb 2) v.t. and i. (*kōm*) Arrange, separate, cleanse, with a comb; (fig.) to search a place minutely
combat 1) v.t. and i. (*kom'băt, kom băt'*) To fight against, oppose
combat 2) n. (*kom'băt*) A fight, battle
combination n. (*kom bi nā'shun*) Act, process, of combining; result of combining, union
combine v.t. and i. (*kom bin'*) To bring (v.i. come) together, unite, mix, (cause to) coalesce
come v.i. (*kum*) pret. **came** (*kām*) p.p. **come** (*kum*) To approach, be in motion towards (esp. towards speaker or person addressed), *come and see me, I will come and see you*; to arrive, reach, *the post comes at nine o'clock*; to occur, happen, *to take what comes;* to originate in, result from, *he comes from Ireland, no good comes of idleness*; to amount *to* (of price, bill)
comedian n. (*ko mē'di an*) Comic actor or entertainer
comet n (*kom'it*) Heavenly body with star-like nucleus and long gaseous tail
comfort n. and v.t. (*kum'fert*) Consolation, solace, ease from affliction; person who brings this, *he is a great comfort to me*; well-being, physical satisfaction and ease; a thing that helps to make life easy. As v.t. to bring

comet

comfort to
comfortable adj. (*kum'fer tabl*) Providing, enjoying, comfort
comic adj. and n. (*kom'ik*) Relating to comedy; funny, laughable. As n. a music-hall comedian; a comic paper, esp. for children
comma n. (*kom'a*) Punctuation-mark (,) separating phrases and clauses of a sentence
command v.t. and i. (*komahnd'*) To order (person to do something)
commander n. (*ko mahn'der*) One who commands
commence v.t. and i. (*ko mens'*) To begin
commentator n. (*kom'en tā ter*) eyewitness giving running commentary on ceremony, sporting event etc., esp. on radio
commerce n. (*kom'urs*) Trade, exchange of merchandise, esp. on large scale
commercial adj. and n. (*ko mur'shal*) Relating to, engaged in, commerce
commit v.t. (*kom it'*) To perform an act, *he committed a crime*; to entrust to the care of, *he was committed to prison*
committee n. (*kom it'i*) Group of persons appointed by larger group to report on or manage branch of administration or with special terms of reference
common adj. (*kom'un*) Shared by several or many persons, *his death brought common sorrow to the nation*; open to all, not private; plentiful, widespread, familiar, *the buttercup is a common flower*
Commons pl. n. (*kom'unz*) esp. in **House of Commons** British parliamentary assembly sharing legislature with House of Lords

Commonwealth n. (*kom'un welth*) Nations recognizing King or Queen of United Kingdom as head of (British) association of nations

communicate v.t. and i. (*kom yōō'ni kāt*) To pass or exchange messages, ideas, information

communication n. (*kom yōō ni kā shun*) The act of communicating; the message communicated; the means of communication (esp. in pl.)

communism n. (*kom'yōōn izm*) Political theory that all property should be held in common; esp. theory and way of life developed in U.S.S.R. since Russian revolution in 1917. Hence: **communist** n. and adj

community n. (*kom yōōn'i ti*) A group considered as a whole that lives in same location

companion n. and v.t. (*kum păn'yan*) One who accompanies another

company n. (*kum'pa ni*) A group of people in one place with common bond; being together with another, *to keep company, to part company, good company*; the crew of a ship; the actors in a production; an association of shareholders in a business

compare v.t. and i. (*kom pār'*) To examine one thing in relation to another, to note the resemblance between (persons, things)

comparison n. (*kom pă'ri san*) Act of comparing; state of being compared; relative resemblance of one thing with another

compass n. (*kum'pas*) Instrument with magnetic needle that always points to North Magnetic Pole; (pl.) instrument for drawing circle or measuring distances on plan

compass

compete v.i. (*kom pēt'*) To strive against others in some common end; to take part in a sporting contest.

competition n. (*kom pe tish'an*) Act of competing; activity in which persons compete; contest for a prize

complain v.i. (*kom plān'*) To express discontent about something; to grumble, find fault

complaint n. (*kom plānt'*) The act of complaining; what is complained about, the grounds of discontent; an illness, *a heart complaint*

complete 1) v.t. (*kom plēt'*) To make an end of, to finish

complete 2) adj. (*kom plēt'*) Whole, entire, lacking nothing; finished, ended; utter, *a complete stranger*

complexion n. (*kom plek'shun*) The colour and appearance of the skin, esp. of the face

complicate v.t. (*kom'plik āt*) To make complex, difficult. Hence: **complicated** adj.; **complication** n. (*kom pli kā'shun*) (also med.) a new illness developing in the course of another

compliment n. and v.t. (*kom'pli ment*) Praise with intention to please; (pl. n.) polite greetings, *compliments of the season*

complimentary adj. (*kom pli men'ta ri*) Expressing praise; given free with the compliments of the donor, *complimentary ticket*

component n. and adj. (*kom pō'nant*) One of the parts of which something is composed.

compose v.i., n., and adj. (*kom pōz'*) To make up, put together, *it is composed of pure water*; to create a work of music, art, poem, etc
to get feelings under control, *compose yourself!* Hence: **composer** n. one who composes, esp. music

composition n. (*kom po zish'an*) The act of composing; the thing composed, esp. music or an exercise in writing

compost n. and v.t. (*kom'post, kom'pōst*) Mixture of rotted organic matter for working into soil in gardens

comprehend v.t. (*kom pre hend'*) To understand; to include within. **comprehension** n. act or power of understanding

compute v.t. and i. (*kom pūt'*) To count, calculate, estimate **computer** n. machine for computing, esp. electronic machine that digitally stores, sorts, analyses, and correlates data, producing selective information as required

conceal v.t. (*kon sēl'*) To hide; to keep secret

conceit n. (*kon sēt'*) Vanity, self-admiration

conceive v.i. and t. (*kon sēv'*) To form an idea in the mind, *he conceived a plan*; (of a woman) to become pregnant

concern 1) n. (*kon sern'*) What one is concerned or interested in, *it's no concern of mine*; anxiety, *he was full of concern*; a business, *his grocery concern was prospering*

concern 2) v.t. (*kon sern'*) To relate to, have to do with, affect, *this hardly concerns me*; to cause feeling of responsibility and anxiety, *don't let my illness concern you*

concerning prep. (*kon sern'ing*) About, with regard to, *I have no information concerning your plans*

concert n. (*kon'sert*) Musical performance, esp. one given in public place

conclude v.t. and i. (*kon kloōd'*) To bring to an end, *the chairman concluded the meeting*; to come to an opinion, *he concluded he was right*

concrete n. and v.t. (*kon'krēt*) Building material made of cement, sand, gravel, and water, hardening to a stone-like mass

condemn v.t. (*kon dem'*) To declare guilty

condition n. (*kon dishn'*) State of being, manner of existence; state of health, rank, social and financial standing etc.; (pl.) environment, circumstances, *bad living conditions in the slums*

conduct 1) n. (*kon'dukt*) Direction, guidance, management, *the conduct of the war*; behaviour

conduct 2) v.t. and i. (*kon dukt'*) To lead, escort (often p.p., *conducted tour*); to direct, manage (campaign etc.); (mus.) to direct a performance, orchestra etc. (also **conductor** n. (*kon duk'ter*) Guide; (mus.) director of orchestra etc.; collector of fares on bus etc.; substance etc. capable of conducting heat, electricity etc

cone n. (*kōn*) Solid (or hollow) body tapering to point from circular base; thing of this shape, *ice-cream cone, storm cone*; fruit of pine or fir

confer v.t. and i. (*kon fur'*) To bestow *on*, award (title etc.). As v.i. to discuss, take counsel, talk over *with*

conference n. (*kon'fer ans*) Consultation; formal gathering for discussion, exchange of opinions; a meeting, *the director is in conference*

confess v.t. and i. (*kon fes'*) To admit, acknowledge (error, that something is true etc.), esp. to make a formal admission of sin to a priest

confession n. (*kon feshn'*) Acknowledgement of guilt etc

confetti n. pl. (*kon fet'i*) Tiny pieces of coloured paper (originally plaster) thrown over people at revels etc., and esp. at newly married couples

confidant n. (*kon fid ănt'*) fem. **confidante** Familiar trusted friend

confide v.i. and t. (*kon fīd'*) To put confidence *in*, trust with secrets etc. As v.t. to tell (secrets,

CONES

troubles) *to, he confided his story to me*
confident adj. (*kon'fi dent*) Assured, convinced (of success etc.); assured of one's powers
confidential adj. (*kon fi den'shal*) Told, written etc., in confidence
confuse v.t. (*kon fūz'*) To mix up, throw into disorder (esp. of ideas, the mind etc.); to mistake one thing for another
confusion n. (*kon fū'zhun*) Muddle, disorder (lit. and fig.)
congratulate v.t. (*kon grăt' ū lāt*) To express pleasure at another's success; to wish joy to (engaged couple etc.); to compliment
congregate v.t. and i. (*kong'gri gāt*) Collect, bring (v.i. come) together, esp. of a group of people
congregation n. (*kong gri gā'shun*) Assembly of persons, esp. in church for religious service
congress n. (*kong'gres*) A gathering, conference, esp. a formal meeting of delegates
conjure v.t. and i. (*kon jōōr'*) To
connect v.t. and i. (*ko nekt'*) To join (things) together; to associate mentally, *I connect sunshine with holidays abroad* As v.i. to join on, make a connection
conquer v.t. and i. (*kong'ker*) To overcome by force, defeat (enemy)
conquest n. (*kong'kwest*) Act, process, of conquering
conscience n. (*kon'shens*) Moral sense of right and wrong
conscious adj. (*kon'shus*) Having the power of thought, *a conscious being*; aware, possessing knowledge *of, conscious of my duty towards you*; with mental faculties awake, alert, *fully conscious*
conscript v.t. (*kon skript'*) To enlist (soldiers) by compulsion. Hence: **conscription** n. (*kon skrip'shun*)
consent v.i. (*kon sent'*) Acquiesce, agree (*to, to do,* something)
conserve v.t. and n. (*kon surv'*) To keep unchanged, preserve from loss or destruction. Hence: **conservation** n. (*kon sur vā'shun*) act of conserving; preservation; prevention of loss, damage etc., *the conservation of woodland*
conservative adj. and n. title of British political party; member of this party
consider v.t. and i. (*kon sid'er*) To think about, meditate on; to take into account, make allowances for, *the judge considered his youth*: to hold, be of the opinion
consist v.i. (*kon sist'*) To be made up
consonant n. (phon.) any letter of alphabet other than a vowel
constable n. (*kun'stabl, kon'stabl*) A policeman
constellation n. (*kon stel ā'shun*) (astron.) A group of stars
constitution n. (*kon stit ū'shun*) Law or rules according to which a state, society etc. is governed; a person's physical condition
construct v.t. (*kon strukt'*) To build, form; to fit together
consul n. (*kon'sul*) An agent of a State in a foreign country
consult v.t. and i. (*kon sult'*) To refer to for information; to go to for advice etc., *I wish to consult my solicitor about that question*
consultant n. (*kon sul'tant*) Expert, esp. in medicine or surgery, advertising, etc. who is consulted for professional advice
consume v.t. and i. (*kon sūm'*) To take into one's system, to eat; to destroy, *fire consumed the building*; to waste, use up
contact n. and v.t. (*kon'takt*) A state of touching (elect.) that part of two conductors which is made to touch the other when current is to be passed between them As v.t., to get in touch with someone, *where can I contact you tomorrow?*
contagion n. (*kon tā'jun*) (med.) Communication of disease by direct contact between two persons
contain v.t. (*kon tān'*) To hold; to include, comprise; to have capacity for, *this jug will contain a pint*; restrain, keep under control, *you must contain your enthusiasm*
container n., vessel, box etc. designed to hold something
contaminate v.t. (*kon tam'in āt*) To make impure by addition of unclean matter
contemplate v.t. and i. (*kon'tem plāt*) To observe, look at intently; to meditate, reflect deeply upon
contemporary adj. and n. (*kon tem'per er i*) Living, existing or occurring at the time or period referred to
contempt n. (*kon tempt'*) Scorn, disdain
content 1) n. (*kon'tent*) (usually

pl., of material things) That which is contained in something, *the contents of this room*
content 2) adj., n., and v.t. (*kon-tent'*) Satisfied, not wanting more
contest 1) v.t. and i. (*kon test'*) To fight or struggle for; to dispute
contest 2) n. (*kon'test*) Struggle, competition.
continent n. (*kon'ti nent*) Continuous large stretch of land, esp. major divisions of land-surface of world (Africa, Antarctica, Asia, Australasia, Europe, North America, South America); **the Continent** European mainland
continual adj. (*kon tin'ū al*) Persistently repeated, very frequent, *continual troubles*
continue v.t. and i. (*kon tin'ū*) To go on with, keep up (action); to resume (interrupted action) to go on, be prolonged, remain
continuous adj. (*kon tin'ū us*) Connected in unbroken series, uninterrupted
contraception n. (*kon tra sep'shun*) Practice or method of avoiding conception, birth control
contract 1) n. (*kon'trăkt*) Solemn agreement between parties, states etc. to do or refrain from doing; business agreement
contract 2) v.t. and i. (*kon trăkt'*) To arrange (marriage, alliance etc.) by formal agreement (v.i.) to engage, make a contract, to do something to shorten, make smaller
contractor n. (*kon trăk'ter*) Person who contracts to do work or supply goods; a builder and house repairer
contrary adj., n. and adv. (*kon'tra ri*) Opposed to by tendency or character, *contrary to custom, our hopes, and our best interests*; unfavourable (of wind); (pop. *kon trār'i*) perverse
contribute v.t. and i. (*kon trib'ūt*) To give money, help etc. to common fund, esp. for charity etc.; to supply (ideas, knowledge etc.); to supply (esp. regular) literary articles to magazines etc. As v.i. in above senses but with *to, he contributed to our paper for ten years*; to help to bring about, *the rain contributed to our discomfort*
contribution n. (*kon tri bū'shun*) Act of contributing; thing, help, amount etc., contributed
control 1) n. (*kon trōl'*) Power of authority and guidance
controls instruments for handling machines
control 2) v.t. (*kon trōl'*) To curb, restrain (oneself, others, one's passions etc.); to dominate, command, *the enemy controlled the high passes*; to check by an accepted standard (quality of goods etc.); to regulate (prices etc.)
controversy n. (*kon'tro ver si, kon tro'ver si*) Dispute
convalesce v.i. (*kon va les'*) To regain health gradually after illness, operation etc
convenient adj. (*kon vē'ni ent*) Suitable, conducive to ease and comfort; near at hand, easy of access, use etc
convention n. (*kon ven'shun*) formal assembly to conduct business etc.
conversation adj. (*kon ver sā'shun*) Talk, talking together
convict 1) n. (*kon'vikt*) Person found guilty of crime and undergoing penal servitude
convict 2) v.t. (*kon vikt'*) To find person guilty of crime after trial in court
cook 1) n. (*kŏŏk*) Person who cooks food, esp. one employed to do so
cook 2) v.t. and i. (*kŏŏk*) To prepare food for eating by boiling, roasting, frying etc
cooker n. (*kŏŏk'er*) Stove for cooking on
cool 1) adj. and n. (*kōōl*) Pleasantly cold (contrasted with hot, warm), *a cool summer evening, cool white wine*; clear-headed, calm; not ardent or passionate; unfriendly, *he was quite cool towards me*
cool 2) v.i. and t. (*kōōl*) Become (as v.t. make) cool,
co-operate v.i. (*kō op'er āt*) To work together *with* person, *in* a task, *to* a common end
co-operation n. (*kō op er ā'shun*) Working together to a common end
co-operative adj. (*kō op'er a tiv*) Working, tending to work, together; (of a person) willing to help; **co-operative society** commercial enterprise in which customers are members and share in the profits (pop. as n.)
copper n. and adj. (*kop'er*) Reddish-brown malleable ductile metal; the chemical element denoted by Cu
As adj. made of copper

copy 1) n. (*kop'i*) Reproduction, imitation
copy 2) v.t. and i. (*kop'i*) Make a copy, imitation, transcript of (document etc.) ; to imitate (person, manner, style etc.) As v.i. to be an imitator
coral n. and adj. (*ko'ral*) Sea-water polyp, akin to sea-anemones, found in tropical seas ; the pink, red, white calcareous substance formed by these polyps
cord n. and v.t. (*kawd*) Thin rope, very thick string ; parts of body resembling string, *spinal cord* ; ribbed cloth, esp. corduroy ; (pl.) **cords** trousers or breeches of this
core n. and v.t. (*kaw(r)*) Innermost part of a thing, its heart ; horny inner part of apples, pears etc., containing the pips
cork n., adj. and v.t. (*kawk*) The light, resilient bark of the cork-oak, *Quercus suber* ; piece of this put to various uses, esp. as stopper for bottle As adj. made of cork. As v.t. to stop (bottle) with a cork
corn n. (*kawn*) Grain, the seed of cereal plants
corner 1) n. (*kaw'ner*) The place where two converging lines or surfaces meet, an angle (football, hockey) free kick, hit, from one of opponent's corners of the field
corner 2) v.t. (*kaw'ner*) To drive into a corner, trap (often fig.) ; (comm.) to control the market in some commodity
coronation n. (*ko ro nā'shun*) Act, ceremony, of crowning a sovereign
corporal n. (*kaw'po ral*) Non-commissioned officer ranking below sergeant
corpse n. (*kawps*) Dead body, esp. human
correct 1) adj. (*ko rekt'*) Free from error, right, true, *a correct statement, correct aim* ; conforming to a recognized standard or convention, proper, in good taste, *correct behaviour*
correct 2) v.t. (*ko rekt'*) To put right, remove errors
correction n. (*ko rek'shun*) Act of correcting ; corrected version
correspond v.i. (*ko res pond'*) To agree, be in accordance (*with, to*), *his version corresponded with mine;* to be similar equivalent *to* ; to communicate *with* person by exchange of letters

coral

correspondence n. (*ko res pon'dens*) letters exchanged between persons,
correspondent n. and adj. (*ko res pon'dent*) One who writes letters to another or to newspaper , person writing articles for newspaper, esp. from particular place etc., *our Middle East correspondent*
corridor n. (*ko'ri daw(r)*) Long passage (in building) with rooms opening off it (in train) running from end to end of coach
cosmetic adj. and n. (*koz met'ik*) Designed to heighten beauty of skin, hair etc. As n. substance (powder, ointment etc.) applied for this purpose (often pl. cosmetics)
cosmopolitan adj. and n. (*koz mo pol'itan*) Common to (of persons, at home in) all parts of the world
cosmos n. (*koz'mos*) The universe as a well-ordered whole
cost 1) v.t. (*kost*) To involve the expenditure of, be obtainable at (a certain price), *this costs five shillings, food costs money* ; (also fig. of effort etc.), *writing this book cost me a lot of trouble* ; to result in the loss of, *his folly cost him his life*
cost 2) n. (*kost*) Price charged for an article, expense expenditure or sacrifice in order to obtain some end, *at great cost*
costume n. and v.t. (*kos'tūm*) Fashion or mode of dress, esp. characteristic of people, period etc
cottage n. (*kot'ij*) Small, rather humble house in village or country
cotton n. and adj. (*kot'on*) Plant of the genus *Gossypium* ; soft downy hairs on the seeds

cotton

of this plant; thread made from these fibres; cloth woven from this thread. As adj. made of cotton

couch n. (*kowch*) Piece of furniture, like sofa, but with half-back and head-end only

cough v.i. (*kof*) To expel air from lungs by sudden spasm, clear throat this way, make the accompanying harsh barking sound

count 1) v.t. and i. (*kownt*) To name the numerals in correct sequence up to a certain number, *to count twenty*; to reckon an amount, enumerate, *he counted his winnings*; to take into account, include, *there were six of us, counting myself*; to esteem, set value on, *I count good health a blessing*

count 2) n. (*kownt*) Counting; result of this, a reckoning, *to take a count, lose count*; the total counted

counter n. (*kown'ter*) long flat-topped slab etc. in shop, bank etc. over which business is transacted

counter- pref. expressing opposition, rivalry, opposite direction, correspondence, substitution etc.; used freely in compounds **counterfeit** adj., n. and v.t. (thing) made in imitation, not genuine, forged (thing), impostor; as v.t. to forge (coins, writing etc.)

country n. (*kun'tri*) Territory of a particular nation, *Britain is a small country*; the people occupying this territory, *the whole country is behind the government*; land of birth or citizenship, *my country right or wrong*; rural districts as opposed to towns, *to live in the country* (also, anywhere but the capital); the physical nature of such districts, *open country, wooded country, hilly country*

county n. (*kown'ti*) (In British Isles) administrative division of country

couple 1) n. (*kupl*) A pair, brace; husband and wife, *married couple*

couple 2) v.t. and i. (*kupl*) To join, link, connect together

courage n. (*ku'rij*) Bravery, pluck

courageous adj. (*ku rā'jus*) (Of persons) brave; (of deeds) requiring courage

courier n. (*kōō'ri er*) Express messenger; person, firm, employed to make travelling arrangements for conducted tours abroad, acting as or providing guide

course n. (*kaws*) Onward movement, progress, trend; route traversed, direction taken, *to change course*; specially prepared ground for racing and other games, *race-course, golf-course*; channel for flowing water, watercourse; duration, period of time, *in the course of his career*; method of procedure, line of action, *his best course is to keep silent*; a series, *a course of lectures*; one of the dishes comprising a meal

court 1) n. (*kawt*) Small open space surrounded by buildings special walled-in area for squash racquets, fives etc.; marked-out lawn for tennis
sovereign's residence or household, including officials etc.; assembly, reception, held by sovereign, *to hold court*; place, hall, where justice is administered, cases heard etc

court 2) v.t. and i. (*kawt*) Pay court (to), try to gain favour (of); (fig.) to invite, run risk of, *to court disaster*

courteous adj. (*kur'ti us, kaw'ti us*) Polite, well-mannered

courtesy n. (*kur'ti si, kaw'ti si*) Courteous behaviour

courtier n. (*kawt'yer*) Person attached to royal court

cousin n. (*kuzn*) Child of one's uncle or aunt

cover 1) v.t. (*kuv'er*) To place one thing over another so as to hide it wholly or in part (face *with* hands, table *with* cloth etc.); to lie over, extend over, *snow covered the ground*; to shield, protect (person with one's body etc.) to stain, splash etc., all over, *covered in mud*; to travel a certain distance, *he covered six miles in an hour*

cover 2) (*kuv'er*) n. Thing made to cover an object, a lid, wrapper, case etc.; binding of book (or each board, *from cover to cover*) or outer pages of magazine; hiding place, shelter, *take cover, under cover*; envelope, *under separate cover*; place laid for each person at table (thus, **cover-charge**)

cow n. (*kow*) Female of the ox tribe, esp. when domesticated; also of elephant, seal, whale etc

coward n. and adj. (*kow'erd*) (One) lacking courage, fainthearted

cowardice n. (*kow'er dis*) Lack of courage, faintheartedness

cox n. and v.t. (*koks*) Steersman of racing row-boat. As v.t. to act as cox to (boat, crew)

coy adj. (*koi*) Shy, modest

crack 1) v.t. and i. (*krăk*) To cause a split, fissure, in (esp. glass and other brittle substances); to break by pressure or sudden blow, *crack a nut, a skull*

crack 2) n. and adj. (*krăk*) Sudden, sharp report (of whip, rifle); sharp blow, *a crack on the head*; a chink, narrow opening, slit, *open the door a crack*; fissure, break, in brittle substance (glass etc.), leaving the parts still together; (slang) an attempt, shot, *have a crack at it*; (slang) expert performer (as adj. expert, first-rate, *a crack shot*)

crackle v.i. and n. (*krăkl*) To give forth a series of sharp, faint reports (as does a fire). As n. such a sound

crackling n. (*krăk'ling*) Making of crackling sound (see above); the crisp skin of roast pork

cradle n. and v.t. (*krādl*) Baby's cot or crib, often on rockers As v.t. to rock (infant) in cradle, lull him in one's arms

craft n. (*krahft*) Skill, workmanship; cunning, guile; a skilled trade, or members of this organized into guild; a boat (pl. the same); **craftsman** skilled worker

cram v.t. and i. and n. (*krăm*) To squeeze, stuff, into a small space, *he crammed the sweets into his pocket* to coach (pupil) intensively for exam. As v.i. to eat greedily; to study quickly and intensively for exam etc

cramp 1) n. (*krămp*) Sudden, painful, muscular contraction, often due to cold

crane n. and v.t. and i. (*krān*) Large wading bird with long legs, neck and bill, machine for moving, raising, heavy weights As v.t. and i. to stretch (the neck) out full length

crash v.i. and t. and n. (*krăsh*) To fall with a loud noise, esp. to break, *the vase crashed to the ground*; to collide with something (of vehicles); (of aircraft) to fall violently to earth; (fig.) to collapse, be ruined (of financial schemes etc.); (slang) to gate-crash, go to party uninvited (v.t. and i.) As v.t. to cause to crash, *he crashed his new car.* As n. loud explosive sound as of breakage etc.; violent noisy impact; accident involving fall of aircraft, collision etc. of car, train etc.; ruin, collapse (esp. financial); **crash helmet** strong padded helmet worn by motor-cyclists etc., to protect head in case of crash

crate n. (*krāt*) Framework, packing-case, or basket for transporting fragile goods

crater n. (*krā'ter*) Mouth of volcano; similar cavity in ground formed by explosion

crawl v.i. and n. (*krawl*) To move slowly on hands and knees or with body on ground; to walk, drive etc. very slowly, *the traffic simply crawled along* to be infested with, swarming with, *crawling with lice* As n. act of crawling swimming stroke

crayon n. and v.t. and i. (*krā'on, -o(ng)*) Coloured pencil or chalk etc. used for drawing to draw with crayons

crazy adj. (*krā'zi*) Mad; scatter-brained; wildly enthusiastic *about*; (of building etc.) decrepit, broken down; (of pavement, quilt etc.) made of irregularly shaped pieces

creak n. and v.i. (*krēk*) (To make) a harsh sound as of unoiled hinges, new boots, bending floorboards

cream n. (*krēm*) Rich, fatty part of milk, from which butter is made; a sauce, dressing, cosmetic ointment etc. resembling this in consistency the best part of anything

crease n. and v.t. and i. (*krēs*) Line made by folding (esp. material) and pressing (cricket) parallel lines drawn across pitch at either end, marking positions of batsmen and bowlers. As v.t. to

press (trousers etc.) into creases
create v.t. and i. (*krē āt'*) To bring into being, cause to exist
creation n. (*krē ā'shun*) Act or process of creating, esp. of the world; the thing created
creature n. (*krē'cher*) Created thing, living being
credit n. (*kred'it*) good reputation, honour, *a person of credit*; what adds to honour of person etc., *he is a credit to his family and his country, it does you credit*; just reward, recognition of merit, *to get the credit for* lending of money on trust in person's or firm's promise and ability to pay later, *to get goods on credit*; reputation for solvency; the sum standing in one's favour in bank account etc
creek n. (*krēk*) Narrow inlet in coast; small narrow harbour; small tributary river
creep v.i. (*krēp*) pret. and p.p. crept (*krept*) To move with belly on ground, on hands and knees etc.; to move silently, stealthily (of plants) to grow along ground or wall
cremate v.t. (*kri māt'*) To consume to ashes with fire, esp. a corpse. Hence: **cremation** n. act, practice, of so doing
crematorium n. (*kre ma taw'ri um*) an authorized place for cremating bodies
crest n. (*krest*) Tuft of hair or feathers on head of certain birds etc.; cock's comb; plume of feathers, device, on top of helmet; thus, the helmet itself (chiefly poet.); (her.) device above shield and helmet on coat of arms (also used separately, as on notepaper etc.); top or highest point of a thing, *mountain crest, crest of a wave*
crew n. (*kroo̅*) Body of men manning ship or boat; (also) this excluding officers; gang of workmen; body, group, of persons
crib 1) n. (*krib*) Manger, rack for fodder; child's cot, with barred sides literal translation of foreign (esp. classical) author (as used by schoolboys) (OE *cribb*)
crib 2) v.t. and i. (*krib*) to copy (author's works, examination paper etc.) and pass off as one's own work
cricket 1) n. (*krik'it*) Small brown insect of Gryllidae family, which produces chirruping noise by rubbing fore-wings together
cricket 2) n. (*krik'it*) Open-air game played between two teams of eleven players each, using a ball, bats, and wickets
crime n. (*krim*) Offence against community's well-being punishable by law
criminal adj. and n. (*krim'in al*) Of the nature of a crime As n. person guilty of crime
crinkle v.t. and i. and n. (*kringkl*) Wrinkle, twist. Hence: **crinkly** adj. wrinkled
cripple n. and v.t. (*kripl*) Maimed, disabled, person esp. lame. As v.t. to disable, maim, *the accident crippled him for life*; also, fig., *crippled with debt*
crisp adj. and n. (*krisp*) Brittle, hard and dry (of crust, biscuits etc.) (of atmosphere) bracing; (of manner, talk, style) sharp, clipped, clear-cut. As n. a shaving of potato fried until crisp
critic n. (*krit' ik*) Person who criticizes; person judging works of art, literature etc. or reviewing books, films etc. for newspapers, etc
criticism n. (*krit'is izm*) Guiding principles of a critic; the art of judging works or art, literature etc.; an expression of adverse opinion
criticize v.t. (*krit'is iz*) To express judgement on, give critical estimate of
croak n. and v.i. and t. (*krōk*) Harsh sound made by frog or raven. As v.i. to make this sound. As v.t. to utter (words) in tone of voice resembling this
crochet n. and v.t. and i. (*krō'shā*) Needlework made with a small hook. As v.t. to make thing (v.i. work) in this way
crockery n. (*krok'eri*) Household earthenware or china vessels, used loosely for all plates and cups etc
crocodile n. (*krok'o dil*) Large lizard-like amphibious reptile
crook n. and v.t. and i. (*kro͝ok*) Stick with top bent into hook, esp. as used by shepherds; any bent thing, a hook; (colloq.) a swindler, cheat etc
crooked adj. (*kro͝ok'id*) Not straight, bent, not in line; (of persons, limbs etc.) deformed; (fig. of persons or acts) dishonest
crop 1) n. (*krop*) Pouch-like swelling in gullet of birds, the craw produce of cultivation, *a crop of potatoes*; (pl.) the season's total yield of produce a very short haircut
crop 2) v.t. and i. (*krop*) To cut off

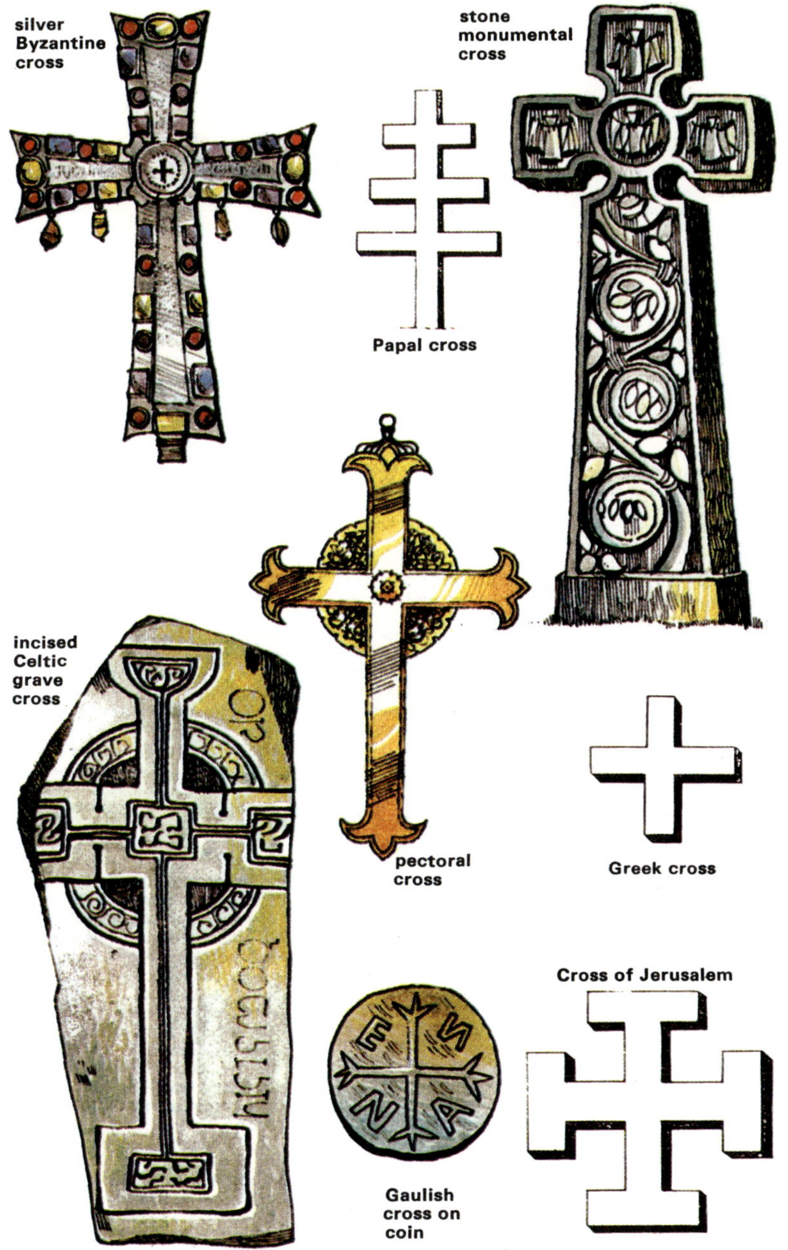
silver
Byzantine
cross
stone
monumental
cross
Papal cross
incised
Celtic
grave
cross
pectoral
cross
Greek cross
Cross of Jerusalem
Gaulish
cross on
coin

cross 1) n. (*kros*) Wooden stake (usually with transverse bar) used for executions in ancient times, esp. that on which Christ was crucified; model, representation of this, the symbol of Christianity; (fig.) suffering, affliction, *to bear one's cross patiently*; anything (mark, monument etc.) formed of two intersecting lines or having this basic shape; mixing of breeds in plants or animals, or a product of this, *a cross between a horse and an ass*
cross 2) v.t. and i. (*kros*) To place crosswise, to make sign of cross (*cross oneself*) to meet and pass (of persons, letters), *my letter crossed yours*; to obstruct, thwart (person, plans etc., *don't cross me*); to interbreed (plants, animals etc.)
cross 3) adj. (*kros*) (of persons) irritable, annoyed.
crouch v.i. and n. (*krowch*) To stoop down, esp. to bend body and legs in huddled position; (of animals) to lower body towards ground before springing etc
crow 1) n. (*krō*) Large black bird of genus *Corvus*
crow 2) v.i. and n. (*krō*) To utter the cry of the cock; to utter cry of joy (esp. of child); to express satisfaction, gloat (also, **crow over**). As n. the cry of the cock
crowd 1) n. (*krowd*) Large dense mass of people
crowd 2) v.i. and t. (*krowd*) To collect in a crowd, throng, swarm (often with *round, together*); to press forward (with *into, through*), *they crowded into the train*
crown 1) n. (*krown*) Wreath etc. worn on head as mark of honour; richly ornamented head-dress worn as emblem of sovereignty; (fig.) sovereignty, the king or queen, regal power, *an officer of the Crown, loyal to the Crown* top of thing (esp. of skull, hat, roadway etc.)
crown 2) v.t. (*krown*) To place crown on person's head, thus making him (or her) king (or queen); to reward, honour
crucify v.t. (*kroo'si fi*) To put to death by fastening to a cross
crude adj. (*kroōd*) Raw, in natural state (of food, minerals etc.)
cruel adj. (*kroō'el*) Willing, liking, to cause pain etc. to others; (of actions etc.) producing, meant to cause, pain or sorrow; painful, distressing, *a cruel blow, a cruel fate*

cruiser

cruise v.i. and n. (*kroōz*) To sail about, calling at various ports, for the pleasure of the voyage rather than to reach a destination
cruiser n. (*kr'oōzer*) Ship that cruises, esp. warship
crumb n. and v.t. (*krum*) Small fragment of bread
crumble v.t. and i. (*krumbl*) To break (as v.i. to disintegrate) into crumbs or small fragments
crumple v.t. and i. (*krumpl*) To press carelessly into creases, to rumple (of cloth etc.); to squeeze (esp. paper) into a crushed ball; (fig.) to cause (person's resistance etc.) to collapse
crunch v.t. and i. and n. (*krunch*) To crush noisily with the teeth (biscuit, apple etc.); to grind underfoot etc. with similar noise (gravel etc.)
crusade n. and v.i. (*kroō sād'*) Military expedition by Christians to conquer Holy Land from the Moslems; any holy war; (fig.) enthusiastic campaign against some public evil. As v.i. to take part in a crusade. Hence: **crusader**
crush v.t. and i. and n. (*krush*) To press, squeeze, so as to break, reduce to powder etc., destroy, kill; to crease, rumple (cloth etc.) As n. act of crushing; dense crowd of people
crust n. and v.t. and i. (*krust*) Hard outer part of bread: similar covering, shell etc
crutch n. (*kruch*) Staff with padded top which rests under armpit, used by the crippled as support in walking (often pl. **pair of crutches**)
cry v.i. and t. (*kri*) To utter, call loudly; to weep, sob, express grief by shedding tears. As v.t. to proclaim, announce
crystal n. and adj. (*kris'tal*) Clear transparent variety of quartz; a piece of this
cub n. and v.i. (*kub*) Young of fox, bear, lion etc

cubs

cube n. and v.t. (*kūb*) Regular six-sided solid with all sides square and identical; anything resembling this; (math.) the third power, the product of the square of a number multiplied by the number itself (the cube of 2 is 8, 2 being the **cube-root** of 8)
cuckoo n. (*ko͝ok'o͞o*) Migratory bird laying eggs in other birds' nests
cuddle v.t. and i. and n. (*kudl*) Hug, embrace
cue n. (*kū*) Last words of a speech in a play etc., upon which another actor enters
cuff 1) n. (*kuf*) Open end of sleeve, esp. when starched or ornamented
cuff 2) v.t. and i. (*kuf*) (To deliver) a blow, esp. with open hand to head
cul-de-sac n. (*ko͞ol'de săk*) Street etc. that has no through way
culprit n. (*kul'prit*) Offender, (the) guilty person
cultivate v.t. (*kul'ti vāt*) To prepare land for crops; to grow crops; (fig.) to improve, develop (the mind, studies etc.); (fig.) to pursue, cherish, aim to obtain (manner, person's friendship etc.)
cunning adj. (*kun'ing*) Crafty, sly; skilful, ingenious
cup n. (*kup*) Small drinking vessel, usually with handle; contents of this, *a cup of tea*; large (esp. gold or silver) vessel given as prize in sport
cupboard n. (*kub'erd*) Cabinet or wall-recess with shelves and doors, for storage
cure 1) n. (*kūr*) Remedy, esp. for disease; course of medical treatment
cure 2) v.t. and i. (*kūr*) To heal, restore (patient) to health; to remedy (disease, bad habit etc.); (also v.i.) to preserve by salting, drying, pickling (esp. fish and meat)
curfew n. (*kur'fū*) (hist.) Bell rung at fixed time in evening as signal that all fires must be put out (the signal, the bell itself, or the time when rung); (under martial law) time after which everyone must stay indoors
curiosity n. (*kūr i os'i ti*) Desire to find out
curious adj. (*kūr'i us*) (Of things, events etc.) rare and strange, odd, unusual, *a curious sight, a curious thing happened, a curious fellow;* (of persons) eager to find out; (in bad sense) inquisitive
currant n. (*ku'rant*) Dried grape of small and seedless variety
currency n. (*ku'ren si*) the particular form of money used in a country, *foreign currency*
current 1) adj. (*ku'rent*) In general use or circulation (money, words, idioms, opinions etc.); (of time) present, now in progress, *the current month*; of the present time, *current issue (of magazine etc.)*
current 2) n. (*ku'rent*) Continuous flow, esp. of water, air, or electricity; massive and continuous flow of body of water in sea or ocean
curriculum n. (*ku rik'ū lum*) Course of study, training etc.; *curriculum vitae* (*ku rik'ū lum vē'ti*) concise written account of personal history used in application for position
curry n. and v.t. (*ku'ri*) Dish of stewed meat, chicken etc. highly

seasoned with various hot spices
curse 1) n. (*kurs*) Utterance calling down evil, wrath, misfortune upon a person etc
curse 2) v.t. and i. (*kurs*) To utter curse against person or thing
curtain n. and v.t. (*kur'tn*) Piece of cloth hung across windows, round bed etc. or as partition etc.; this between stage and auditorium in theatre
curve n. and v.t. and i. (*kurv*) Line of which no part is straight As v.t. and i. to bend into a curve
cushion n. (*kŏŏshn*) Bag, case, of material stuffed with soft padding and sewn up, for sitting, reclining etc., on
custard n. (*kus'terd*) Mixture of sweetened milk and eggs boiled or baked until thick
custodian n. (*kus tō'di an*) Guardian, keeper, esp. of public building etc
custody n. (*kus'to di*) Care, guardianship, responsibility for, *a parent has custody of his child*; detention by police, *taken into custody*
custom n. (*kus'tom*) Habit, usual practice (pl.) duty levied on foreign goods
customer n. (*kus'tu mer*) Buyer (esp. habitual) or intending buyer from tradesman etc
cut v.t. and i. (*kut*) pret. and p.p. **cut** To gash, wound, make incision in with sharp-edged instrument; to divide, carve into pieces, with knife, scissors etc to abridge (book, article, film) or omit (passage, item); to reduce in amount (money, time etc.) to ignore, refuse to recognize, an acquaintance
cyclone n. (*sik'lōn*) Violent tropical storm with winds rotating round centre of low pressure

cygnet

cygnet n. (*sig'net*) Young swan

D

dab v.t. and i. and n. (*dăb*) To touch, apply lightly, *dab paint on a picture*. As n. a light tap, gentle
dagger n. (*dăg'er*) Short, double-edged stabbing weapon
daily adj., adv. and n. (*da'li*) Happening, done, appearing every day, *a daily event* As n. newspaper published every day
dainty 1) adj. (*dān'ti*) Delicate, neat, elegant
dainty 2) n. A delicacy, something agreeable to the taste
dairy n. (*dār'i*) Building or room for making and storing butter and cheese; shop for the sale of dairy produce
dale n. (*dāl*) A valley
dam n. and v.t. (*dăm*) An embankment or other construction built to control the flow of water. As v.t. to make a dam across; to obstruct by a dam
damage n. and v.t. (*dăm'ij*) Harm or injury to a person or object; (pl.) (law) money claimed or awarded as compensation for injury As v.t. to injure, cause damage to
damp 1) adj. and n. (*dămp*) Moist, *the rain has made my hat damp*
damp 2) v.t. and i. (*dămp*) To make damp
dance 1) v.i. and t. (*dahns*) To move or leap in an ordered series of rhythmical steps and body movements, esp. with musical accompaniment
dance 2) n. (*dahns*) Series of rhythmical movements and steps made in dancing; social gathering for dancing
danger n. (*dān'jer*) Risk of injury, suffering, or death; menace, cause of peril, *a danger to peace*
dangerous adj. (*dān'jer us*) Likely to cause danger, unsafe
dare v.i. and t. (*dār*) To have the courage or audacity to do something; to challenge a person to do something by implication of cowardice, *I dare you to jump that stream*
dare-devil bold, reckless person
daring n. and adj. (*dār'ing*) Courage; audacity. As adj., brave
dark 1) adj. (*dahk*) With little or no light; not reflecting light, nearly black, *dark hair*; (of the skin) not fair, *a dark complexion*; hidden,

mysterious, *a dark secret*; obscure; unenlightened, *the Dark Ages*; gloomy, sad Hence
darkness n. the state of being dark
dark 2) n. (*dahk*) Absence of light, darkness
darn 1) v.t. and i. (*dahn*) To mend a hole or tear in material by imitating its weave with new threads
darn 2) Place mended by darning
dart 1) n. (*daht*) Pointed weapon thrown by hand, now used with a target in the game of darts; a sudden rapid forward movement
dart 2) v.i. and t. (*daht*) To move like a dart, shoot forward suddenly
data n. (pl.) (*dā'ta*) Facts, from which inferences may be drawn and conclusions formed
date 1) n. (*dāt*) Indication of the day, month, or year, or all three; the day, month, and year when something occurred; period of history, *the pottery is of Roman date*; (colloq.) appointment, *I have made a date for next week*
date 2) v.t. and i. To assign a date to, *can you date this object?* (colloq. esp. U.S.) to make an appointment for young man to meet girl
date 3) n. Sweet, elongated stone fruit of the date palm
daughter n. (*daw'ter*) Somebody's female child
dawn n. (*dawn*) Daybreak, first light of day; (fig.) beginning
day n. (*dā*) The period of the earth's rotation on its axis; the time from midnight to succeeding midnight, *there are seven days in a week*; the sunlit part of a day, from sunrise to sunset, *he walked all day*
daylight n. (*dā'līt*) The light of the sun; natural light; dawn, *we must leave before daylight*
daze 1) v.t. (*dāz*) To stupefy, stun, bewilder
daze 2) n. (*dāz*) State of confusion; bewilderment
dazzle v.t. and i. (*dăzl*) To render unable quickly to see clearly, by exposing the eyes to brilliant light, esp. headlights of motor vehicle
dead adj. (*ded*) No longer living no longer used or practised, *a dead language*
deaden v.t. (*ded'n*) To lessen the force of, *drugs will deaden the pain*
deadlock n. (*ded'lok*) Complete failure to reach agreement
deadly adj. and adv. (*ded'li*) Causing, likely to cause, death, *deadly weapons*
deaf adj. and n. (*def*) Unable to hear well or at all; (fig.) disregarding, wilfully ignoring, *deaf to all entreaties*; **deaf-aid** device to help a deaf person to hear; **deaf-mute** one who is deaf and dumb. As n., those who are deaf. Hence: **deafness** n.
deafen v.t. (*defn*) To make deaf; to make so much noise that specific hearing is impossible
deal 1) v.t. and i. (*dēl*) To give, share out, esp. cards; **to deal with** to do business with; to manage, take in hand; to treat, behave towards, *how will you deal with him?*; to discuss, *deal with a subject*; **to deal in** to trade in. Hence: **dealer** n. trader; one who deals out playing cards
deal 2) n. (*dēl*) A business transaction; (colloq.) a bargain settled, *it's a deal*
dear adj. (*dēr*) Loved, lovable; charming, attractive, *a dear little house*; costly, expensive; in excess of the normal or reasonable price; polite form of address in letters, *Dear Sirs*
death n. (*deth*) Permanent and complete cessation of the functions of living matter; (fig.) end, destruction, *the death of his hopes*
debate 1) v.t. and i. (*di bāt'*) To discuss thoroughly, argue; to consider; to engage in a formal discussion
debate 2) n. (*di bāt*) A formal discussion, esp. at a public meeting or in Parliament
debt n. (*det*) Something owed or due to be paid to another
decade n. (*dĕ kād'*) Period of ten years
decathlon n. (*dec ăth'lon*) Ancient and modern Olympic contest in which each competitor takes part in ten different events
decay 1) v.i. (*di kā'*) To rot; deteriorate; lose power
decay 2) n. (*di kā'*) State or process of decaying; decline, loss of power etc., *the empire fell into decay*
deceit n. (*di sēt'*) Act of deceiving
deceitful adj. (*di sēt'fo͞ol*) Given to deceiving
deceive v.t. (*di sēv'*) To cause to believe what is false
decent adj. (*dē'sent*) Respectable,

modest, chaste; seemly; (colloq.) satisfactory, likeable, *he's a decent fellow*. Hence: **decently** adv. in a decent manner
deception n. (*di sep'shun*) The act of deceiving
deceptive adj. (*di sep'tiv*) Tending to deceive, misleading
decide v.t. and i. (*di sīd'*) To settle; to judge between possible alternatives; to determine, resolve; to cause to decide, *what decided you to take the job?*
decimal adj. and n. (*des'i mal*) Based on a system of numbers in which each unit is 10 times the next smaller one; **decimal fraction** in which denominator is taken as 10 or a power of 10; **decimal system** one in which weights and measures and/or coinage are reckoned in powers of 10
decimalize v.t. to turn measures into a decimal system; **decimalization** n.
decision n. (*di si'zhun*) Judgement, settlement of a question
declaration n. (*de kler ā'shun*) The act of declaring; what is declared
declare v.t. and i. (*di klār'*) To make known publicly to make a statement of dutiable goods brought into a country, or of one's income to a Tax Inspector; (cricket) to announce that one's innings is closed
decline 1) v.i. and t. (*di klīn'*) To slope; to deteriorate, become weaker, lower, *his powers declined with age*; to diminish, *the fever has declined*; to refuse, reject, *I declined the invitation*
decline 2) n. (*di'klīn*) Gradual and continued falling off in strength
decorate v.t. (*dek'or āt*) To adorn, place ornaments on or in; to paint and paper the interior of a house; to award a medal or other mark of distinction, *he was decorated for bravery*. Hence: **decoration** n. (*dek or ā'shun*) decorating, being decorated; something used for decorating; medal etc. given as an honour
decorator (*dek a rā'ter*) n. person employed in decorating a house
decrease v.t. and i. (*di krēs'*) To cause to become less, smaller
dedicate v.t. (*ded'i kāt*) To devote exclusively to a noble cause or purpose, *he dedicated his life to painting*; (of an author) to inscribe a person's name in a book in honour of them. Hence:
dedication n. (*ded i kā'shun*) the act of dedicating
deduct v.t. (*di dukt'*) To take away, subtract, *money deducted from wages for insurance*
deep adj. (*dēp*) Extending far down, *a deep well*
colours) rich in pigment, *deep brown*; (of sounds) low in tone, *a deep voice* Hence: **deepen** v.t. and i. make or become deep
deep-freeze n. (*dep frez'*) Refrigerator for quick-freezing and storing food at very low temperatures
defeat 1) v.t. (*di fēt'*) To conquer
defeat 2) n. (*di fēt'*) The act of defeating or being defeated
defect n. (*dē'fekt*) Imperfection, flaw, *a defect in his character*
defective adj. and n. (*di fek'tiv*) Having defects; imperfect
defence n. (*di fens'*) The act of defending; that which defends; (law) case stated in favour of a defendant in a court of law
defend v.t. (*di fend'*) To guard, protect, shield against attack; to speak in support of, repel charges against; (law) to endeavour to establish the innocence of a defendant in a court of law Hence: **defendant** n. one who defends; (law) person against whom a legal action is brought
define n. (*di fīn'*) To mark clearly the limits or outlines of, *a well-defined footprint*; to describe exactly, *can you define his duties?*; to state the exact meaning and uses of a word, term etc
definite adj. (*def'in it*) Clearly defined, having exact limits; exact
definition n. (*def in ish'n*) Act of defining; process of being defined; clearness of outline; power of a lens (telescopic, photographic etc.) to show clear outlines
defy v.t. (*di fī'*) To challenge, resist; to be in open disobedience to, *he defied his father*; to baffle, *the problem defies solution*
degree n. (*dig rē'*) Amount, extent of, stage reached in a line of development, *a high degree of skill*; status, rank, *a man of low degree*; grade or rank given by a university to one who has passed an examination, *studying for a degree*; a unit of measurement of angles, arcs, temperature etc., *water freezes at 0° Centigrade, there are 360 degrees in a circle*
delay 1) v.t. and i. (*di lā'*) To

retard, postpone, *I must delay my departure*; to linger, be slow
delay 2) n. Delaying or being delayed; an instance of this, *there was a delay of three hours*
delegate n. (*del'i gat*) Person appointed as a representative, deputy
delete v.t. (*di lēt'*) To expunge, take out, *delete the second sentence of that letter I have dictated*
deliberate 1) v.i. and t. (*di lib'er āt*) To reflect upon carefully, talk about, *they were deliberating whether to go on strike or not*
deliberate 2) adj. (*di lib'er at*) Intentional
delicate adj. (*del'i kat*) Fine in texture, soft, *delicate material* sensitive, finely adjusted, *a surgeon's delicate instruments*
delicatessen n. (*del ik at es'en*) A shop selling cooked foodstuffs; goods sold by such a shop
delicious adj. (*di lish'us*) Giving delight to the palate, taste, or senses, *it has a delicious smell*
delight 1) v.t. and i. (*di lit'*) To please greatly, *to delight the ear*; to find great pleasure in, *I delight in music*. Hence: **delighted** adj. glad, very pleased, *I am delighted at the news*
delight 2) n. (*di lit'*) Great pleasure, *to his delight he won the game*; source of great pleasure, *the delights of city life* Hence: **delightful** adj. giving delight
delinquent n. and adj. (*di ling'kwent*) One who neglects a duty or commits a fault; one who commits a social or criminal offence
deliver v.t. (*di liv'er*) To set free, rescue from something harmful, *he was delivered from captivity*; to take, hand over, distribute, *to deliver letters, milk*; (esp. with up) to hand over, surrender, *he delivered up his seal of office*; to pronounce, utter, *deliver a speech*; to aim, send against, *deliver a blow*; to help in childbirth, *deliver a baby*
demand 1) v.t. (*di mahnd'*) To ask to ask for as a right, *I demand an apology from you*; to need, require, *a task demanding great care*
demand 2) n. Act of demanding; something demanded, *a demand for higher pay*; requirements of consumers, *a demand for sugar.*
democracy n. (*di mok'ra si*) Form of government in which all citizens participate, either directly or through elected representatives; a state having this form of government
democrat n. (*dem'ō krăt*) One who favours or supports democracy
democratic adj. (*dem ō krăt'ik*) Of, based on, democracy
demolish v.t. (*di mol'ish*) To pull down, destroy **demolition** n. (*dem o lish'n*) demolishing or being demolished, esp. of buildings; instance of this
demonstrate v.t. and i. (*dem'on strāt*) To show, prove by argument and evidence, *demonstrate that the earth is round*; to make known one's feelings etc., *he demonstrated his sympathy*; to make a public exhibition of sympathy and support for something, *the students demonstrated against government policy*. Hence: **demonstration** n. (*de mon strā'shun*) demonstrating
den n. (*den*) Lair, hiding-place of a wild animal
denial n. (*di ni'al*) The act of denying
dense adj. (*dens*) Packed together, *a dense crowd*; impenetrable, *a dense fog*
density n. (*den'sit i*) The quality of being dense
dentist n. (*den'tist*) Person who treats diseases and irregularities of the teeth professionally
denture n. (*den'cher*) A set of false teeth
deny v.t. (*di ni'*) To say that something is false, contradict; refuse a request, *he could deny his children nothing*
deodorize v.t. (*dē ō'de riz*) To take away odours, esp. bad smells. Hence: **deodorant** n. substance that removes or conceals bad smells
depart v.i. and t. (*di paht'*) To go away from, leave,
department n. (*di paht'ment*) A separate part, division of a government, business etc
department store where various kinds of goods are sold in different departments
departure n. (*di pah'cher*) The act of departing, going away
depend v.i. (*di pend'*) (archaic) to rely on for support, *I depend on your help*; to trust, *you can depend on him*
dependent 1) adj. (*di pen'dent*) relying on for support

dependent, dependant 2) n. (*di pen'dent*) One who depends on another for support, a home etc
deport 1) v.t. (*di pawt'*) To expel, esp. an unwanted person from a country. Hence: **deportation** n. (*dē paw tā'shun*) act of deporting
deport 2) v.t. (reflex.) (*di pawt'*) To behave, *he deported himself with dignity*. Hence: **deportment n.** behaviour; way of holding oneself in standing and walking, *she is taking lessons in deportment*
deposit 1) v.t. (*di poz'it*) To place, put down
entrust for safe keeping
deposit 2) n. (*dipoz'it*) What is deposited; the sediment from a liquid; money paid into a bank, **deposit account** in bank on which interest is paid; money paid in advance, to secure a contract
depress v.t. (*di pres'*) To press down, lower to make
sad, lower the spirits of
depression n. (*di presh' un*) The act of depressing; being depressed, low spirits; a dip, hollow in a surface, esp. (geog.) in which surface is below sea-level; period of low activity in business; (meteor.) an area in which atmospheric pressure decreases to a low at the centre
deprive v.t. (*dipriv'*) To take away from, prevent the use or enjoyment of, *he was deprived of his pocket-money as a punishment*
depth n. (*depth*) The condition of being deep; at a great distance from the surface
deputy n. (*dep'ū ti*) One to whom functions, authority etc. are deputed, *I need a deputy during my absence*
descend v.t. and i. (*di send'*) To go down, *he descended the stairs*. As v.i. to come down, move downwards, *he descended from the hill*; to slope downwards; to have as ancestors, *descended from a noble family* Hence: **descendant** n. Person or thing descended from another
descent n. (*di sent'*) The act of descending, a going or coming down
describe v.t. (*dis krib'*) To say what someone or something is like
description n. (*dis krip'shun*) The act or process of describing; a word-picture
desert 1) v.t. and i. (*di zurt'*) To go away from, abandon, *he deserted his family*; to fail, *his courage deserted him*; to run away from, esp. from milit. service
desert 2) n. and adj. (*de'zert*) Barren, waste, lifeless, uninhabited, *a desert island*; esp. as noun an extremely arid area, *the Sahara desert*
deserve v.t. and i. (*di zurv'*) To earn, be entitled to, *he deserves his reward*; to merit, *he deserves well of his firm*
design 1) v.t. and i. (*di zīn'*) To plan out, draft a scheme for, *to design a stage-setting*; to make a plan or pattern for, *design a dress*
design 2) n. (*de zin'*) A mental plan, scheme; intention, *by design and not accident*; a pattern, plan, or outline of something, to aid in its construction; a pattern, arrangement of line, shape etc., *the design on a carpet*
desirable adj. (*di zīr'abl*) Causing desire, worth having, *a desirable house*
desire 1) v.t. (*di zīr'*) To wish, long for
desire 2) n. (*di zīr'*) Strong longing, powerful wish to obtain, *his only desire was for peace and quiet*
despair 1) v.i. (*dis pār'*) To have no hope, to lose hope
despair 2) n. (*dis pār*) Hopelessness
desperate adj. (*des'per at*) Beyond hope, extremely serious, *it was a desperate state of affairs*; reckless of danger, sticking at nothing
despise v.t. (*dis pīz'*) To look down on, feel contempt for, *they despised him for his meanness*
destination n. (*des tin ā'shun*) The place to which a person or thing is going or being sent
destine v.t. (*des'tin*) To decide or ordain in advance (of fate etc.)
destiny n. (*des'tin i*) Pre-ordained fate
destroy v.t. (*di stroi'*) To ruin, demolish, pull to pieces
destruction n. (*di struk'shun*) Destroying or being destroyed
destructive adj. (*dis truk'tiv*) Tending to destroy, harmful; in the habit of destroying, *a destructive child*
detail 1) v.t. (*dē tāl'*) To make a full report on, to describe minutely; to appoint for special duty, *he was detailed to collect the rations*
detail 2) n. (*dē'tāl*) Particular fact or item, section of a whole; something of slight importance, *that is only a detail*

detain v.t. (*di tān'*) To hold or keep back, *he was detained by an unexpected visitor*
detect v.t. (*di tekt'*) To discover, to expose, discover, *detect someone in a dishonest act.* Hence: **detection** n. the act or process of detecting, esp. criminal investigation
detective adj. and n. (*di tek'tiy*) Of or pertaining to detection; dealing with detection; **detective story** one in which the interest centres in the investigation of a puzzling crime. As n., police officer or private person engaged in the investigation of criminal cases
detention n. (*di ten'shun*) The act of detaining esp. the keeping in of school-children after hours as a punishment
deter v.t. (*di tur'*) To hold back, cause to hesitate
detergent n. (*di tur'jent*) A cleansing agent
deteriorate v.t. and i. (*di tē'ri a rāt*) To lower the value of; to become lower in quality, *the boy's work deteriorated rapidly*
determination n. (*di tur min ā'shun*) firmness of purpose, resolution
determine v.t. and i. (*di tur'min*) To delimit, fix the extent of; be the deciding factor, *the size of your head determines the size of your hat*; to make up one's mind, *he determined to succeed*
deterrent adj. and n. (*di te'rent*) Tending to deter, what deters
detonate v.t. and i. (*de'ton āt*) To cause to explode; to explode with a sudden loud noise. Hence: **detonation** n. explosion; noise of this; **detonator** n. that which initiates an explosion
detour n. (*dē'toor*) A diversion, departure from the direct approach
develop v.t. and i. (*di vel'op*) To cause to grow, unfold, expand, *they developed the business*; to bring out, cause to appear or become clearly defined, esp. to treat a photographic film so that the picture can be seen
device n. (*di vīs'*) Something thought out, a plan, scheme, trick
devil n. (*de'vil*) The spirit of evil, Satan
devote v.t. (*di vōt'*) To give up, dedicate, *devote one's spare time to study*; (reflex.) give oneself to. Hence: **devoted** adj. given up to; very loyal or loving, *a devoted friend*
devotion n. (*di vō'shun*) State of being devoted to someone or something; strong affection, unselfish attachment, *devotion of a mother for her child*
devour v.t. (*di vow(r)'*) To eat hungrily and greedily; consume, destroy, *trees devoured by fire* (fig.) to absorb mentally, read, look at, *she devoured the novel in one evening*
devout adj. (*di vowt'*) Reverently attentive to religious duties, pious
diabetes n. (*dī a bē'tēs*) Disease characterized by excess of sugar in urine, which is passed too often. Hence: **diabetic** adj. and n. (*dī a bet'ik*) of diabetes; as n. one suffering from diabetes
diagnose v.t. (*dī ag nōz'*) To identify (disease) by studying symptoms. (As below)
diagram n. (*dī'a grăm*) (geom.) Figure drawn to help in demonstration of proof; explanatory sketch, picture to represent statistics etc
dial n. and v.t. and i. (*dī'al*) Face of sundial, clock etc. marked for telling time of day; round flat scale with pointer showing weight, pressure etc.; movable disk on telephone for operating automatic number-calling system
dialect n. (*dī'a lekt*) Variation in pronunciation, grammar, or vocabulary within a language, distinct mode of speech characteristic of a certain region, class etc
dialogue n. (*dī'a log*) Conversation in speech or writing
diameter n. (*dī ăm'it er*) Straight line passing through centre and from side to side of a geometrical figure, esp. one bounded by curves, circle, sphere etc
diamond n., adj., and v.t. (*dī'a mund*) A precious stone, playing card with red lozenges (pl. suit so marked)
diarist n. (*dī'a rist*) One who keeps a diary
diary n. (*dī'er i*) Daily record of events, journal; book made for keeping such a record, with dated pages
dictate v.t. and i. (*dik tāt'*) To read, say, aloud (for another to put down in writing); to command, prescribe, *to dictate terms*. As v.i. to read dictation; to lay down the law. Hence: **dictation** n. matter read aloud and to be written down; act of dictating.

dictator n. (*dik tā'ter*) Despot, tyrant, absolute ruler; also fig., *my boss is a regular dictator*
diction n. (*dik'shun*) Choice of words or phrases, style of writing or speaking
dictionary n. (*dik'shun a ri*) Book containing a (usually alphabetical) list of the words of a language or deliberate selection of them, with explanations of their meanings in the same language or equivalent words in another language
die 1) n. (*dī*) (rare) Singular of pl. dice (*dīs*); with pl. **dies** (*dīz*) engraved metal stamp for making coins, embossing paper etc
die 2) v.i. (*dī*) To cease to live (of humans, animals)
diet n. and v.t. and i. (*dī'et*) Habitual way of feeding; special course of food for medical etc. reasons, *a slimming diet*. As v.t. and i. to prescribe (v.i. give oneself) special food, esp. in sense of eating less
differ v.i. (*dif'er*) To be unlike, distinct from, *tastes differ*; to disagree, take issue with, *I beg to differ*
difference n. (*dif'er ens*) Unlikeness, state of not being the same
different adj. (*dif'er ent*) Not the same, unlike (*from, to*); changed, altered, *you look different*
difficult adj. (*dif'i kult*) Hard to do, troublesome, needing skill (of task etc.) (of persons) hard to please, irritable, easily offended
difficulty n. (*dif'i kul ti*) difficult thing, obstacle, hindrance, *the main difficulty is*
dig 1) v.t. and i. (*dig*) pret. and p.p. **dug** (*dug*) To break up the ground with spade or other tool, or with claws etc
dig 2) n. (*dig*) A piece of digging, place dug, archaeological site
digest v.t. and i. (*di-, dī jest'*) To convert food in stomach and intestines into a form that can be assimilated into the system; (fig.) to absorb knowledge etc
digestion n. (*di jes'chun*) Process of digesting; ability to digest, *a good digestion*; also fig. of mental processes
diligence n. (*dil'i jens*) Steady application to work
diligent adj. (*dil'i jent*) Hard-working, displaying diligence
dilute v.t. and adj. (*di lūt'*) To weaken, thin, water down
dim adj. and v.t. and i. (*dim*) Faint, ill-defined, not bright or clear (of sights or sounds); (of eyes) not seeing clearly; (fig. of ideas, understanding etc.) obscure, ill-defined; (colloq. of persons) stupid. As v.t. and i. to make or become dim
dimension n. (*di men'shun*) Measurement of extent in length, breadth, depth, height, area etc
diminish v.t. and i. (*di min'ish*) To make, become, smaller
din n. and v.t. and i. (*din*) Loud, persistent noise, continued clamour
dine v.i. and t. (*dīn*) To eat dinner
dinghy n. (*ding'gi*) Small ship's boat; **rubber dinghy** collapsible rubber boat used by airmen crash-landing on water
dingy adj. (*din'ji*) Dull coloured, drab; (of places) dirty, gloomy
dinner n. (*din'er*) Main meal of day; formal banquet (in evening)
dinosaur n. (*dī'nō saw(r)*) Huge extinct reptile
diocese n. (*dī'o sis*) District over which a bishop has ecclesiastical authority
dip 1) v.t. and i. (*dip*) To plunge (thing) into liquid, immerse briefly to lower and raise quickly; to lower beam of headlights of car. As v.i. to slope downwards, *beyond the farm the road dips* (also geol. of strata); to sink below a certain level (sun below horizon, bird below level of flight etc.)
dip 2) n. (*dip*) Act of dipping or being dipped, brief immersion; a short bathe
diphtheria n. (*dif thēr'i a*) Serious infectious disease attacking throat and air-passages
diplomacy n. (*di plō'ma si*) Management of international affairs
diplomat n. (*dip'lō măt*) Person officially employed in diplomacy
direct 1) v.t. and i. (*di rekt'*) To manage, control, supervise (a business, a concerted action or operation); to give orders, command; to turn (attention, eyes etc.) to something; to address (letters etc., remarks *to* person); to point out the way to; (cinema) to co-ordinate actors, cameras and other activities involved in making a film. As v.i. to perform the act of directing
direct 2) adj. and adv. (*di rekt'*) Straight, *the direct route*
direction n. (*di rek'shun*) Management, control, guidance etc.; managing body; (often pl.)

instructions, orders; line along which a body moves, point to or from which a body is moving (also fig.); address on letter etc

directly adv. and conj. (*di rekt'li*) In a direct manner; at once, *I will come directly.* As conj. (colloq.) as soon as, *directly I have finished*

director n. (*di rek'ter*) Manager controller

dirty adj. and v.t. (*dur'ti*) Covered with, containing, dirt, not clean

disability n. (*dis a bil'i ti*) Being disabled, incapacity; what disables, legal disqualification, physical defect

disable v.t. (*dis ābl'*) To render physically unfit, maim; to render or pronounce legally incapable

disagree v.i. (*dis a grē'*) To differ, conflict (of two or more things or persons); to hold different opinions (*with* another); to quarrel (*with*); to be unsuitable, to upset (of food, climate etc.)

disagreeable adj. (*dis a grē'abl*) Distasteful, unpleasant

disappear v.i. (*dis a pēr'*) To vanish from sight

disappearance n.

disappoint v.t. (*dis a point'*) Not to fulfil expectations or desires of Hence: **disappointed** adj.

disappointment n. being disappointed; what disappoints

disarm v.t. and i. (*dis ahm'*) To deprive of weapons reduce military strength (v.t. and i.) Hence: **disarmament** n

disaster n. (*di zah'ster*) Calamity, sudden great misfortune, ruinous event. Hence: **disastrous** adj

disciple n. (*di sipl'*) Follower, student, adherent of any leader in thought, art, religion etc., esp. one of the first followers of Christ

discipline 1) n. (*dis'i plin*) Systematic mental and moral training, esp. teaching restraint, respect for authority etc.; result of this, restraint, obedience, steadiness under fire (lit. and fig.) etc.; control over group of persons (troops, class etc.), *to keep discipline*

discipline 2) v.t. (*dis'i plin*) To subject to discipline, bring under control; punish

discontent n., adj. and v.t. (*dis kon tent'*) Lack of contentment, dissatisfaction, grievance. As adj. dissatisfied

discontinue v.t. and i. (*dis kon tin'ū*) To stop, interrupt, break off (action, habit etc.) As v.i. to cease

discothèque n. Club or bar where dancing to popular recorded music takes place

discount n. (*dis'kownt*) Deduction from price of goods on account of prompt payment etc

discourage v.t. (*dis ku'rij*) To dishearten, deprive of courage, confidence etc.; to try to prevent (action) or deter (person) *from* doing thing. Hence: **discouragement** n

discover v.t. (*dis kuv'er*) To find out

discovery n. (*dis kuv'er i*) Act of discovering; thing discovered

discus n. (*dis'kus*) Originally stone or metal quoit thrown in ancient Greek athletic contests; in modern athletics a circular wooden disk with metal rim of standard size and weight

discuss v.t. (*dis kus'*) To debate, examine, a subject (in speech or writing). Hence: **discussible** adj.;

discussion n. (*dis kushn'*) debate, examination of problem etc., argument

disease n. (*di zēz'*) Deviation from normal healthy state (of body, mind, plant, or (fig.) society etc.); specific form of this, illness, particular disorder of an organ, etc. Hence: **diseased** adj. afflicted with disease

disfigure v.t. (*dis fig'er*) To spoil the beauty of, deface, make ugly

disgrace 1) n. (*dis grās'*) Discredit, loss of honour or favour; shame

disgrace 2) v.t. (*dis grās'*) To bring disgrace upon

disguise 1) v.t. (*dis gīz'*) To alter appearance of (oneself, *as* someone else etc.) for concealment or deception

disguise 2) n. (*dis gīz'*) Dress, manner, appearance, adopted for concealment or deception

disgust n. and v.t. (*dis gust'*) Strong feeling of repugnance, loathing, nausea (physical or moral). As v.t. to arouse these feelings in

dish n. (*dish*) Flat-bottomed shallow vessel of china, glass etc. for serving food at meals; the food contained in this; a particular kind of food or food prepared in a certain way

dishonest adj. (*dis on'ist*) Not honest, inclined to cheat, lie etc.

disinfect v.t. (*dis in fekt'*) To free from infection, cleanse, sterilize (wound, room etc.) Hence: **disinfectant** adj. and n. (substance) preventing or destroying infection

food dish
with
cover
pewter
dish
stainless steel divided veg. dish
glass ovenproof
dish
stainless steel spliced meat dish
soap dish
glass sweetmeats
dish
cheese dish

DISHES

dismal adj. (*diz'mal*) Gloomy, depressing, drear (of places, weather, persons, states of mind)
dismiss v.t. (*dis mis'*) To send away; to release, allow to go (from one's presence); to discharge from employment, service etc.
(cricket) to end the innings of batsman or team
disobedience n. (*dis o bē'di ens*) Not obeying orders or rules, refusal to do what one is told. Hence: **disobedient** adj.
disobey v.i. and t. (*dis o bā'*) To be guilty of disobedience. As v.t. not to obey a person, disregard orders, laws etc
disorder n. and v.t. (*dis aw'der*) Lack of order, untidiness; political or social unrest, riot; a breach of public order; disease, illness. As v.t. to throw into disorder, upset, disarrange
dispensary n. (*dis pen'sa ri*) Place where medicines are made up and sold or distributed
display 1) v.t. (*dis plā'*) To show, exhibit; to spread out so as to show prominently
display 2) n. (*dis plā'*) A show, exhibition
disposable adj. (*dis pō'zabl*) What can be got rid of, sold etc
disposal n. (*dis pō'zal*) Getting rid of
dispose v.t. and i. (*dis pōz'*) To arrange, set out in order
to dispose of get rid of
dispute v.i. and t. and n. (*dis pūt'*) To argue, debate; to quarrel
disqualify v.t. (*dis kwol'i fī*) To render or declare unfit or ineligible *for*; debar (esp. for breaking rules etc.) Hence: **disqualification** n
dissect v.t. (*di sekt'*) To cut in pieces, esp. (anat.) cut up body, plant etc. for examination; (fig.) to analyse, study, or criticize in detail. Hence: **dissection** n. dissecting or part dissected
dissolve v.t., i. and n. (*di zolv'*) To cause to melt, become liquid or be absorbed in liquid
distance n. and v.t. (*dis'tans*) Remoteness, degree of separation in space or time
distant adj. (*dis'tant*) Far off, remote
distinct adj. (*dis tingkt'*) Separate, different, distinguishable, *two distinct ideas*; clear, well defined, *the footprints in the sand were quite distinct*; marked, positive, *a distinct improvement*
distinction n. (*dis tingk'shun*) Act of distinguishing; distinguishing mark, point of difference, *to draw a distinction*
distinguish v.t. and i. (*dis ting'gwish*) To recognize a difference *between* (or one thing *from* another) to bring credit, eminence, or notoriety tc (often reflex., *he distinguished himself in battle*)
distort v.t. (*dis tawt'*) To twist out of shape; to misrepresent, warp (facts, motives etc.)
distract v.t. (*dis trăkt'*) To draw, divert (attention, mind) *from* object of thought
distress 1) n. (*dis tres'*) Grief, affliction of mind; thing causing this; physical exhaustion; severe poverty and need; difficulty, peril, *ship in distress*
distress 2) v.t. (*dis tres'*) To grieve, afflict with sorrow etc.; to cause suffering, anxiety
distribute v.t. (*dis trib'ūt*) To share out, divide amongst a number, to place, deliver (leaflets etc.), at various points; to spread out over a surface
distribution n. (*dis tri bū'shun*) Distributing, being distributed; way in which, extent to which, something is distributed, *wide distribution*
district n. and v.t. (*dis'trikt*) An area of territory defined esp. for administrative purposes, administrative division, *urban, rural, district*; region, locality
distrust n. and v.t. (*dis trust'*) Lack of trust, suspicion. As v.t. to doubt, suspect, not trust
disturb v.t. (*dis turb'*) To trouble, disquiet, agitate; to interrupt (person working etc.); to cause (thing) to alter position or condition
disturbance n. (*dis turb'ans*) Act of disturbing; thing that disturbs; disorder, uproar; breach of the peace
ditch n. (*dich*) Long narrow trench, esp. for drainage, as watercourse or as boundary
dive 1) v.i. (*dīv*) To plunge head first into water, to submerge thus while swimming; to swoop down with similar motion through air (of birds, aircraft etc.); to go down into deep water, esp. in special water-tight suit **diver** n. esp. one working under water in special suit
diversion n. (*di-, dī vur'shun*) alternative route to by-pass road obstruction etc
divide 1) v.t. and i. (*di vīd'*) To

separate or mark out into parts
divine 1) adj. and n. (*di vin'*) Of, proceeding from, like, God or a god, *divine attributes*
divine 2) v.t. and i. (*di vin'*) To foretell, predict, esp. by intuition or magic
division n. (*di vizhn'*) Dividing, being divided
divorce 1) n. (*di vaws'*) Legal dissolution of marriage
divorce 2) v.t. (*di vaws'*) To obtain a divorce from (husband or wife)
dizzy adj. and v.t. (*diz'i*) Giddy, suffering from vertigo
do v.t. and i. and auxil. (*do͞o*) pres. 3rd sing. **does** (*duz*), pret. **did** (*did*), p.p. **done** (*dun*) To perform an act, be occupied with, engaged on, *did you do this?*; *what are you doing?* to make, produce, *he did her portrait*; to cook, esp. to a certain degree, *pork should be well done, beef under-done* As auxil. verb in the negative and interrogative of simple present and past, *do you like music?*; *he didn't eat his dinner*; to indicate emphasis, urgent request etc., *I did at least think . . . do come to tea*
dock 1) n. and v.t. and i. (*dok*) Place, berth, in which ships are loaded, repaired etc
As v.t. and i. to bring (ship) into dock; (of ship) to come into dock
dock 2) n. (*dok*) Enclosure for prisoners in criminal court
doctor 1) n. (*dok'ter*) holder of highest university degree in any faculty, *Doctor of Philosophy*; medical practitioner, whether Doctor of Medicine (M.D.) or not
doctor 2) v.t. and i. (*dok'ter*) To treat medically

dock

document n. and v.t. (*dok'ū ment*) Writing, inscription etc., esp. giving evidence of or establishing a fact. As v.t. (also *dok'ū ment'*) to furnish evidence from documents. Hence: **documentary** adj. and n. (*dok ū men'ta ri*) of, supported by, documents, *documentary evidence*; as n. factual report in film, radio, or television
dog n. (*dog*) Carnivorous quadruped of genus *Canis*, existing in many breeds wild and domesticated
doll n. and v.t. (*dol*) Small model of person for child to play with
dollar n. (*dol'er*) Unit of coinage in U.S.A., Canada, Australia etc
domestic adj. and n. (*do mes'tik*) Of the home, household or family, *domestic joys, domestic appliances*
As n. servant in a household
domesticate v.t. (*do mes'ti kāt*) To make fond of home (esp. p.p.); to tame (animals) for man's advantage
dominate v.t. and i. (*dom'i nāt*) To rule over, exercise influence over As v.i. to wield most influence, be the highest
domination n. (*dom i nā'shun*) Ascendancy, act of dominating, rule
donkey n. (*dong'ki*) Common word for the ass
doom n. (*do͞om*) Fate, ruin, evil destiny
doomsday n. (*do͞omz'dā*) The Day of Judgement
door n. (*daw(r)*) Hinged or sliding structure of wood, metal, glass etc. closing the opening to a house, room, cupboard, vehicle etc
dope n. and v.t. (*dōp*) A thick oily liquid; varnish used to coat and tighten fabric shell of aircraft; (colloq.) narcotic drug, artificial stimulant etc. (also fig.); (slang) information. As v.t. to apply or administer dope to; (colloq.) to hoodwink, deceive
dormitory n. (*daw'mi ter i*) Sleeping-room with several beds (in school etc.)
dose n. and v.t. (*dōs*) Amount of medicine to be taken at any one time
dot n. (*dot*) Point, small round mark, made with pen etc., esp. as over letter i To mark with dot or dots
double 1) adj. and adv. (*dubl*) Twice as much (of quantity, quality, size, strength, appearance etc.)

double 2) n. (*dubl*) Twice the amount,
double 3) v.t. and i. (*dubl*) To make double, multiply by two
doubt 1) n. (*dowt*) Tendency to disbelieve; uncertain state, lack of conviction, hesitation, *to be in doubt*
doubt 2) v.i. and t. (*dowt*) To be uncertain, waver in opinion, be disinclined to believe (esp. in religion); to be undecided *whether, if*, have misgivings about, *I doubt if we should go*
doubtful adj. (*dowt'ful*) Uncertain, not proven, not clear in meaning (of statements etc.); uncertain, hesitating (of persons); undecided, full of uncertainty
doubtless adv. (*dowt'les*) Certainly; probably
dough n. (*dō*) Mass of flour etc. and water kneaded for baking
dove n. (*duv*) One of many kinds of bird of order Columbae
down 1) n. (*down*) First plumage or soft under-feathers of birds; soft substance resembling this, as first hair on youth's face, covering of certain plants, seeds etc
down 2) n. (*down*) Open treeless high land; the rolling chalk hills of southern England, *North, South Downs*
down 3) adv. (*down*) (With verbs of motion) to a lower position, *come down*; from vertical to horizontal, *knock down*; to place of less importance, *down to the country, go down from Oxford*
down 4) prep. (*down*) (Of motion) from higher to lower position on, towards the bottom etc. of, *walk down the hill, paddle down the river*; along, esp. away from speaker or given point, *walk down the road*; (of position) lower on, further along, *the house down the road*; from earlier to later time in, *down the ages*
downcast adj. (*down'kahst*) Looking down (of eyes); dispirited
downfall n. (*down'fawl*) Act of falling; thing which falls, esp. heavy snow etc.; (fig.) ruin, overthrow
downward adj. and adv.
downwards adj. (*down'werd(z)*) Moving, tending to something lower (*downward path*) As adv. to lower place etc
doze v.i. and n. (*dōz*) To sleep lightly, be half asleep. As n. a light sleep

dove

dozen n. (*duzn*) Group of twelve, *a dozen eggs*
draft 1) n. (*drahft*) Body of men detached from larger body for special service outline or first version of letter, memorandum, article etc., *a rough draft*
draft 2) v.t. (*drahft*) To detach body of men for special service to prepare, make first tentative version of letter, memorandum, etc
dragon n. (*drăg'un*) Fabulous monster like fire-breathing, winged crocodile
drain n. (*drān*) Channel, conduit, pipe etc. for carrying away liquid, sewage etc. (fig.) constant demand, expenditure etc., *a drain on my resources*
drama n. (*drah'ma*) Play for stage performance; the art of the theatre as a whole
dramatic adj. (*dra măt'ik*) Of, like, in the form of, a drama
dramatist n. (*drăm'a tist*) Playwright
dramatize v.t. and i. (*drăm'a tiz*) To cast (novel etc.) into play form
drape v.t. (*drāp*) To cover with cloth that hangs in loose folds
draper n. (*drā'per*) Dealer in cloth and fabrics
draught n. (*drahft*) Act of drawing, pulling; thing drawn, esp. amount of liquid swallowed at one time; dose of medicine; amount of water displaced by ship, amount required to float her; current of air through crack, hole etc. or in furnace
dread v.t. and i. and n. (*dred*) To fear, esp. some future event or possibility, be apprehensive of, *she dreads growing old*. As n. a settled fear of some future event
dreadful adj. (*dred'fōōl*) Inspiring dread, terrible
dream n. (*drēm*) Series of

images, events, sensations, arising from unconscious of a sleeping person

dreary, drear adj. (*drēr'*(*i*)) Gloomy, tedious

dredge n. and v.t. and r. (*drej*) Device for scraping objects from sea-bottom etc. As v.t. to fetch something *up* with a dredge Hence: **dredger** n. ship equipped for dredging work

drench v.t. (*drench*) To soak, saturate

drift 1) n. (*drift*) Being driven by wind or current in sea etc

drift 2) v.i. and t. (*drift*) To be carried along by current of water, wind etc

drill 1) n. and v.t. and i. (*dril*) Tool with revolving point for boring holes. As v.t. and i. to bore holes (in) with this

drill 2) v.t. and i. and n. (*dril*) To train (soldiers etc.) by repetitive exercises in marching, handling weapons etc

drink n. (*dringk*) Liquid for drinking; a portion of this, *a drink before dinner*; alcoholic liquor, *he's taken to drink*. (See above)

drip v.i. and t. and n. (*drip*) (Of liquid) to fall drop by drop; (of tap etc.) to let (liquid) fall so (also v.t.) As n. action of falling drop by drop, liquid so falling, or sound made by this

drive 1) v.t. and i. (*drīv*) pret. **drove** (*drōv*) p.p. **driven** (*driv'en*) To force into motion, by blows, cries etc. (cattle etc.), with a hammer (nail), with a hard stroke of bat, racket etc. (ball); to control the motion of (vehicle, animal drawing this etc.); to cause (machine etc.) to move, to power (esp. p.p. *driven by steam*); to

drill

dredge

compel, force, *drive a man to drink, the enemy back*; to cut through by steady effort, *drive a road through the jungle*; to effect, conclude, *drive a hard bargain*

drive 2) n. (*drīv*) A trip in a vehicle, *go for a drive*; private road up to house hard striking of ball in various games

driver n. (*drī'ver*) Person or thing that drives, esp. person driving a vehicle

droop v.i. and t. and n. (*dro͞op*) To hang down, sag (of head, eyelids, leaves etc.)

drop 1) n. (*drop*) Small globule of liquid falling, about to fall, or adhering to window etc. (*of* water, sweat, rain etc.)

drop 2) v.t. and i. (*drop*) To let fall; (of liquid) let fall in drops

drought n. (*drowt*) Lack of rain

drown v.t. and i. (*drown*) To (cause to) suffocate to death in water; to flood, drench (esp. fig., *drowned in tears*); to blot out (sorrows *with* or *in* drink, sound with louder one)

drug n. and v.t. and i. (*drug*) A medicine; substance producing unnatural excitement or other effect in the body, esp. **narcotic drugs**; abundant but unsaleable goods, *drug in the market*. As v.t. to administer (v.i. to be in the habit of taking narcotic) drugs

drunk pred. adj. and n. (*drungk*) Overcome by alcohol, under the influence of drink, *he is drunk* Hence: **drunkard** n. person habitually drunk

dry adj. (*drī*) comp. **drier** (*drī'er*) super. **driest** (*drī'ist*) Without moisture, as opposed to *wet*

duck n. (*duk*) One of many kinds of broad-beaked water-birds

due adj. and adv. (*dū*) (Of debt, money) owing, to be paid now
duel n. and v.i. (*dū'el*) Private fight between two armed persons according to set rules
duet n. (*dū et'*) Musical composition for two performers
dull adj. and v.t. and i. (*dul*) Obtuse, stupid (of persons or their minds); boring, commonplace (of books, lectures, persons etc.); (of senses) not vivid; (of light, colour etc.) dim, not intense; (of knife) not sharp; (of trade) slow; (of weather) overcast
dumb adj. and v.t. (*dum*) Unable to or not having learned to speak
dunce n. (*duns*) Stupid, ignorant person
dungeon n. (*dun'jn*) Underground prison-cell in castle
duplicate 1) adj. and n. (*dū'pli kat*) Double, with two corresponding parts
duplicate 2) v.t. (*dū'pli kāt*) To make double; to make an exact copy of. Hence: **duplication** n.; **duplicator** n machine for making copies of documents
durable adj. (*dūr'abl*) Hard-wearing (of substances); lasting (of friendships etc.)
dusk n. (*dusk*) Late twilight; near-darkness esp. before nightfall
duty n. (*dū'ti*) Task, obligation, conduct etc.
dwarf n., adj. and v.t. (*dwawf*) (myth.) Small supernatural being person, animal, or plant of much less than normal size
dye 1) n. (*dī*) Substance for colouring fabrics etc
dye 2) v.t. and i. (*dī*) pres.p. **dyeing** To colour, stain esp. by dipping

E

eager adj. (*ē'ger*) Keen, impatient, strongly desirous
ear n. (*ēr*) The organ of hearing
early adj. and adv. (*ur'li*) (Occurring) towards the beginning of a given or understood period of time, *early dinner, an early riser, to get up early*; before the usual or expected time, *the train arrived early, an early death*
earn v.t. and i. (*urn*) To get (money) by working
earnest adj. and n. (*ur'nist* Serious, zealous
earth n. (*urth*) The planet we live on as opposed to other planets; the world as opposed to heaven etc., *life on earth*; the dry, hard surface of the globe as opposed to sea, air etc., *he fell to (the) earth*; ground, soil, *a shovelful of earth*
easel n. (*ēzl*) Adjustable wooden frame holding artist's canvas or blackboard
east n., adj. and adv. (*ēst*) One of the cardinal points of the compass, at which sun rises at equinoxes
easy adj. and adv. (*ē'zi*) Not difficult, simple
eat v.t. and i. (*ēt*) pret. **ate** (*et*) p.p. **eaten** (*ē'ten*) To consume as food by chewing and swallowing
echo 1) n. (*ek'ō*) pl. **echoes** Sound or signal repeated by reflection
echo 2) v.i. and t. (*ek'ō*) To resound, produce an echo, *the valleys echoed*; (of sound) be repeated, *his voice echoed*
eclipse n. (*ik lips'*) Total or partial interception of the light of sun (by moon passing between it and earth) or of moon (by earth coming between it and sun)
ecology n. (*ē kol'o ji*) Study of organisms in relation to environment
economy n. (*ē kon'o mi*) Management of finances of household, community etc
edible adj. (*ed'ibl*) Fit to eat
edit v.t. (*ed'it*) To prepare (work of others) for publication, *he has edited Pope and several anthologies*; to cut, select from, arrange a book, document, film etc., *published in a much edited version*; to direct and be responsible for a newspaper etc.
educate v.t. (*ed'ū kāt*) To train, instruct, bring up (young people)
education n. (*ed ū kā'shun*) Bringing up, instruction, of the young; system of instruction

eclipse

effect 1) n. (*i fekt'*) Result, consequence of something
effect 2) v.t. (*i fekt'*) To bring about, *effect a change*. (As above)
effective adj. and n. (*i fek'tiv*) Having a result
efficient adj. (*i fish'ent*) Producing an effect, effective, good at the job (of means, machines etc.) ; (of persons) capable, competent
effort n. (*ef'ert*) Exertion of strength (mental or physical)
elaborate 1) adj. (*i lăb'er at*) Complicated
elaborate 2) v.t. and i. (*i lăb'er āt*) To work out in detail
elbow n. (*el'bō*) Joint between forearm and upper arm, esp. point of this
elder adj. and n. (*el'der*) Older of two persons
official of Presbyterian Church
elect v.t. and i. (*i lekt'*) To choose (person) by vote ; to make
election n. (*i lek'shun*) Act of choosing, being chosen, esp. by vote
elector n. (*i lek'ter*) Person who has right or duty of electing (esp. Members to Parliament)
electric adj. and n. (*i lek'trik*) Of, producing, worked by, electricity
electrician n. (*el ek trishn'*) A student of electricity ; one who makes, mends, electrical appliances
electricity n. (*el ek tris'i ti*) A form of energy, due to the presence or flow of electrons and convertible into physical phenomena in heat, light and sound
electrocute v.t. (*i lek'trō kūt*) To kill by electric shock, esp. as capital punishment
elegant adj. (*el'i gant*) Graceful, refined in manner, speech, appearance etc. (of persons)

elephant

elevator

element n. (*el'i ment*) Basic constituent part of anything, essential ingredient
elephant n. (*el'i fant*) Huge tusked quadruped with long trunk
elevate v.t. (*el'i vāt*) To lift up
elevator n. (*el'i vā ter*) Person or thing that lifts ; (U.S.) a lift
elf n. (*elf*) pl. **elves** (*elvz*) (myth.) Small supernatural woodland creature
eliminate v.t. (*i lim'in āt*) To remove, get rid of
ellipse n. (*i lips'*) Plane curved symmetrical figure longer than broad, an oval
elocution n. (*el o kū'shun*) Manner of speaking, oral delivery study or art of this
elope v.t. (*i lōp'*) To run away (from home etc.) with one's lover (esp. to marry)
eloquence n. (*el'o kwens*) Power of easy, forceful, persuasive speech
embark v.i. and t. (*em bahk'*) To go, or receive, on board a ship ; start on a journey ; engage in, *embark on a venture*
embarrass v.t. (*embă'ras*) To cause confusion of mind
emblem n. (*em'blem*) Symbol ; visual representation of something abstract
embroider v.t. and i. (*em broi'der*) To decorate a fabric with designs made with needle and thread
emerge v.i. (*im urj'*) To come into view from concealment
emigrate v.i. (*em'i grāt*) To leave one country in order to settle in another
eminent adj. (*em'i nent*) Renowned, distinguished
emotion n. (*i mō'shun*) Mental state characterized by excitement and strong feelings
emperor n. (*em'per or*) Ruler of an empire
emphasis n. (*em'fa sis*) Special importance, weight, stress laid on

embroidery

an idea or feeling
employ v.t. (*em ploi'*) To make use of a person's services, give work to
empty adj. (*em'ti*) Containing nothing, without contents
enchant v.t. (*en chahnt'*) To cast a spell over; (fig.) delight, charm, captivate, *the scenery enchanted him*
enclose, inclose v.t. (*in klōz'*) To surround completely
encounter n. (*en kown'ter*) A meeting, confrontation; conflict
encourage v.t. (*en kur'ij*) To inspire with courage, hope, confidence
end n. (end) Conclusion, finish
enemy n. (*en'e mi*) One who hates or attempts to injure another; foe, opponent; nation at war with another
energy n. (*en'er ji*) Power, force, causing action or motion
engine n. (*en'jin*) Machine in which power is applied to do work
engineer n. (*en jin'ēr'*) Person trained in the design, construction, and control of machines
enjoy v.t. (*en joi'*) To derive pleasure from, take delight in
enlighten v.t. (*en līt'en*) To impart knowledge, information
enlist v.t. and i. (*en list'*) To take into, join, the armed forces
enormous adj. (*i nawm'us*) Huge, immense, *an enormous animal*
enough adj. (*i nuf'*) As much as is necessary or desirable, sufficient, *we have enough bread*
enquire, inquire v.t. and i. (*in kwīr'*) To ask, *he insisted on enquiring the reason*; to ask questions *about*
entangle v.t. (*en tăng'gl*) To catch in a mesh or by winding round
enter v.t. (*en'ter*) To go or come in, pass inside, *enter a room*; to penetrate, *the bullet entered his brain*; to become a member of, *enter a society*; to write, record, names etc. in a list or book, *enter an event in a diary*
enterprise n. (*en'ter prīz*) Undertaking, esp. something daring or difficult
entertain v.t. and i. (*en ter tān'*) To provide hospitality for amuse, divert
enthusiasm n. (*en thū'zi ăzm*) Keen zeal or admiration
entire adj. and n. (*en tīr'*) Whole, complete
envelope n. (*en'vel ōp*) Wrapper or covering, esp. paper cover for sending a letter in
environment n. (*en vī'ron ment*) That which surrounds, esp. (biol.) conditions in which an organism lives; external conditions of life
envy n. (*en'vi*) Feeling of grudging ill-will caused by the contemplation of another's better fortune, *he was consumed by envy*
epidemic n. and adj. (*ep i dem'ik*) Outbreak of infectious disease widespread among many people at the same time in a region
episode n. (*ep'i sōd*) One of a series of events
equal 1) adj. (*ē'kwal*) Of like amount in number, size, degree, quality, force, etc
equal 2) v.t. (*ē kawl*) To be equal to in quality etc., *equal someone in intelligence*; be the same in size, number etc., *if x equals y, if x = y.* (As above)
equator n. (*i kwā'tor*) Imaginary circle on the surface of the earth, equidistant from the north and south poles
equip v.t. (*i kwip'*) To supply with what is necessary. Hence: **equipment** n.
erase v.t. (*i rāz'*) To scratch out, rub out, *erase an inscription*
erect 1) adj. (*i rekt'*) Upright,
erect 2) adv. (*i rekt*) In an upright, vertical, position, *to stand erect*
erect 3) v.t. (*i rekt'*) To put up, raise into an upright position, *erect a flagstaff*; to construct, build, *erect a house*
errand n. (*e'rand*) A mission, charge, *errand of mercy*, short journey entrusted to a messenger, *to run errands*
error n. (*e'rer*) Mistake,
erupt v.i. (*i rupt'*) To break out, burst forth, esp. of a volcano

escape 1) v.i. and t. (*es kāp'*) To get free, get out of confinement
escape 2) n. (*es kāp'*) Act of escaping
escort n. (*es'kawt*) Person or number of persons or troops, warships, etc., accompanying other persons or vessels etc. to afford protection or company
essay n. (*e'sā*) An attempt; piece of writing upon a particular subject
essence n. (*e'sens*) Fundamental nature or character of a thing
establish v.t. (*es tăb'lish*) To settle, place, on a firm basis
estate n. (*es tāt'*) Landed property, esp. in the country
esteem v.t. and n. (*es tēm'*) To have a high opinion of, respect; to consider, value, *I esteem this*
estimate v.t. and i. (*es'tim āt*) To form a judgement of the value of something; to calculate roughly, *estimate the cost of a job*
estuary n. (*es'tu a ri*) Broadening mouth of river where outflow joins sea
eternal adj. (*i ter'nal*) Everlasting, *eternal life*
ethnic, ethnical adj. (*eth'nik, eth'nik al*) Of a race, or its distinctive features
evacuate v.t. (*i văk'ū āt*) To empty out, rid of its contents, esp. the stomach or other bodily organ; to withdraw troops from untenable positions; to remove inhabitants from a dangerous area. Hence: **evacuation** n. (*i văk ū ā'shun*); **evacuee** n. (*i văk ū ē'*) one who is evacuated
evaporate v.t. and i. (*i văp'er āt*) (of liquid) To change into vapour, at a temperature below boiling point; (fig.) disperse, disappear, *his hopes evaporated*
even adj. (*ē'ven*) Level, smooth, flat, *an even surface*
evening n. (*ēv'ning*) Time of the day from sundown to the early night
event n. (*i vent'*) A happening, incident, occurrence
evergreen adj. and n. (*e'ver grēn*) Bearing leaves all year round. As n., a plant of this type
evidence n. (*ev'i dens*) Fact etc., that proves or tends to prove something
evil adj. (*ē'vil*) Bad, wicked, sinful
exaggerate v.t. and i. (*eg zăj'er āt*) To think of, represent as, greater than the reality

an evergreen

rhododendron

example n. (*eg zampl'*) Instance that illustrates or confirms a statement or rule
excavate v.t. (*eks'ka vāt*) To dig out; dig a pit
exceed v.t. (*ek sēd'*) To go beyond a limit or what is permitted
excel v.i. and t. (*ek sel'*) To surpass, rise above, do better than
except v.t. and i. (*ek sept'*) To leave out, exclude
exchange v.t. and i. (*eks chānj'*) To give one thing in return for another
excite v.t. (*ek sit'*) To rouse something into activity, increase its activity, *excite the mob to a riot*; stimulate, *the patient needs quiet, and must not be excited*; to provoke
exclaim v.t. and i. (*eks klām'*) To cry out suddenly, esp. from pain, fear, surprise
excursion n. (*eks kur'shun*) A journey, esp. a pleasure trip
excuse n. (*eks kūs'*) Reason, explanation, given in defence of one's conduct
execute v.t. (*eks'i kūt*) To carry out, perform, *execute a task* to carry out punishment by death upon, *to execute a criminal*
exercise 1), n. (*eks'er siz*) Bodily activity for health, strength, etc
exert v.t. (*eg zert'*) To put forth, bring into active operation
exhibit v.t. and i. (*eg zib'it*) To show publicly, display
exhibition n. (*eks i bish'un*) Act of

exhibiting; collection of things displayed publicly
exist v.t. (*eg zist'*) To be, occur, *slum areas still exist in many cities*; to have material or spiritual being, *ghosts do not exist*; to live, *he exists on very little*
exit n. and v.i. (*ek'sit*) Way out
expel v.t. (*ek spel'*) To compel to leave, drive out by force, *expel the enemy from a position*; to eject, esp. of pupil from school, as a punishment
experience n. (*ek spēr'i ens*) Process of acquiring knowledge, skill, etc. by doing or observing things
experiment n. (*ek sper'i ment*) Trial, test, carried out under scientifically controlled conditions, to ascertain the result of certain actions or conditions upon substances or organisms
explain v.t. (*ek splān'*) To make clear, plain, intelligible
explode v.t. and i. (*ek splōd'*) To burst, cause to burst, with a loud report
explore v.t. and i. (*ek splaw(r)'*) To search into, investigate thoroughly travel through a country and investigate its geography, geology, etc
export v.t. (*ek spawt'*) To send (goods) out of a country in the course of trade
expose v.t. (*ek spōz'*) To uncover
express v.t. (*ek spres'*) To make known, set forth, reveal, in words or visual images or actions
extend v.t. and i. (*eks tend'*) To reach or stretch out, *extend one's hand to someone*; to lengthen, prolong, continue, *extend the time of one's visit*
extinguish v.t. (*ek sting'gwish*) To quench, put out, *extinguish a fire*
extra adj. (*eks'tra*) Additional to; more than
extract v.t. (*eks trăkt'*) To draw out, esp. by force or persuasion, *to extract a tooth*; to distil, press out, *extract oil from olives*; to take out or select a part from, *extract passages from a book*
extraordinary adj. (*ek straw'din a ri*) Out of the ordinary, unusual
extravagance n. (*eks trăv'a gans*) Quality of being extravagant; lavish wastefulness of money or means
extravagant adj. (*eks trăv'a gant*) Exceeding normal limits
extreme adj. (*ek strēm'*) Furthest off, outermost
eye n. (*ī*) The organ of sight

F

fable n. (*fābl*) Story, esp. one with animals, intended to convey a moral
fabric n. (*făb'rik*) Structure, framework, *the fabric of society*; construction, *the fabric of a building*; woven material, *silk and woollen fabrics*
fact n. (*făkt*) Something that has happened or been done, *accessory before the fact*; something known
factory n. (*făk'ter i*) Building(s) where commodities are manufactured
fade v.i. and t. (*fād*) To lose or cause to lose strength, vigour, freshness
faint 1) adj. (*fānt*) Weak, not clear, *a faint sound*; feeble
faint 2) v.i. (*fānt*) To grow weak, *faint with hunger*; fall unconscious, swoon
fair 1) n. (*fār*) Periodical gathering for the sale of various kinds of articles, often accompanied by entertainments and sideshows; gathering of
fair 2) adj. (*fār*) Just, equitable, unprejudiced, *it was a fair decision*
moderately good, *he has a fair chance of success*; light-coloured; having light hair and complexion
fairy n. (*fār'i*) Small supernatural being in human form.
faith n. (*fāth*) Confidence, trust, *have faith in*
system of belief, religious doctrine, *the Christian faith*
fall 1) v.i. (*fawl*), pret. **fell**, p.p. **fallen**. To pass through space freely from a higher to a lower level, drop
fall 2) n. (*fawl*) Act of falling; a drop
falter v.i. and t. (*fawl'ter*) To move or act uncertainly and hesitatingly, *his stride faltered*
fame n. (*fām*) Good repute, renown, *his fame is widespread*
familiar adj. (*fa mil'ya*) acquainted with, having a good knowledge of, *I am not familiar with that subject*
family n. (*făm'i li*) Parents and children, *the family next door is a very noisy one*; children of the same parents, *she has a big family*; all the descendants of a common ancestor

famine n. (*făm'in*) Extreme scarcity, esp. of food, in a district; starvation
far adv. (*fah*) At a distance, remote, in space or time or fact
farce n. (*fahs*) Dramatic work, characterized by boisterous humour and ludicrous situations; an absurd proceeding
fare 1) n. (*fār*) Money charged for carrying a passenger; one who pays a fare for being carried in a hired vehicle
fare 2) n. and v.i. (*fār*) Food, provisions
farm n. (*fahm*) Land and buildings forming a single property and worked for agricultural purposes **farm-yard** space enclosed by farm buildings. **farmer** n. one who owns or manages a farm
fascinate v.t. (*făs'i nāt*) Exercise a powerful influence over attract, charm. Hence: **fascinating** adj. exercising fascination; strongly attractive; **fascinatingly** adv.; **fascination** n. (*făs i nā'shun*) fascinating or being fascinated; power to fascinate
fashion 1) n. (*făsh'on*) Manner of making or doing something, *she behaved in a strange fashion*; the style, mode of behaviour, habit etc., that prevails or is considered to be the most admirable at a given time, *the latest fashions*
fashion 2) v.t. (*făsh'an*) To form, shape, make
fast 1) adv. and adj. (*fahst*) Firm, secure, *make the boat fast*
fast 2) adj. and adv. (*fahst*) Rapid, swift, *a fast car*
fast 3) v.i. and n. (*fahst*) To abstain from eating
fasten v.t. and i. (*fah'san*) To make fast
fat 1) adj. (*făt*) Covered with fat having much fat, *fat meat*
fat 2) n. (*făt*) Oily or greasy substance found in parts of the animal body
fatal adj. (*fātl*) Causing death or disaster, *a fatal accident*
fate n. (*fāt*) Supposed power that orders events beforehand
father 1) n. (*fah'*ther) Male parent priest, *father confessor*
fatigue n. (*fa tēg'*) Exhaustion, weariness
fatten v.t. and i. (*făt'en*) To make or become fat
fault n. (*fawlt*) Imperfection, flaw, *his only fault is shyness*; liability for blame, *it's all my fault*

favour 1) n. (*fā'ver*) Goodwill, approval, *look on something with favour*
token or decoration usually worn as sign of membership, *the party favours are yellow*
favour 2) v.t. (*fā ver*) To show favour, support, *I favour the idea*
favourite adj. and n. (*fā'verit*) Preferred, *my favourite uncle*. As n., person preferred above all others, *he is a favourite of mine*
fear 1) n. (*fēr*) Mental distress caused by impending danger, pain etc
fear 2) v.t. and i. (*fēr*) To feel fear of, be afraid of, *fear danger*
feat n. (*fēt*) Act or deed, esp. one showing strength, skill, or courage
feather n. (*fe'*th*er*) One of the external growths forming the body covering of birds
feature n. (*fē'cher*) A part of the face, *her eyes are her best feature*; part of something, esp. that which attracts attention, *the main feature in a programme*; prominent article in a newspaper etc., *this feature on architecture is well-written*; full-length film in a cinema programme
fee n. (*fē*) Feudal benefice; sum payable to a professional man, public body, etc., for services or privileges
feeble adj. (*fēbl*) Weak; infirm
feed 1) v.t. and i. (*fēd*) pret. and p.p. **fed** (*fed*) To give food to, *feed a baby*; supply as food, *feed oats to a horse*; supply with material, *feed flames with wood*
feed 2) (*fēd*) Act of feeding; food for animals; channel or other means by which material is carried to a machine; material supplied to a machine
feel v.t. and i. (*fēl*) pret. and p.p. **felt** (*felt*) To have a physical sensation of, *feel the cold*; have an intellectual, emotional sense of, *she felt delighted*; to perceive, experience, by touch, *he felt the edge of the knife*
be in a certain moral, emotional, or physical state, *I feel very cold*
feeler n. (*fē'ler*) Organ of touch in certain insects
feeling n (*fē'ling*) Physical or emotional sensation
feline adj. and n. (*fē'lin*). Of cats or the cat family
fellow n. (*fel'ō*) Partner, sharer in anything, *fellows in misery*
general term for a male person
fellowship n. (*fel'ōship*) State of

being fellows; companionship; group of people bound by a common ideal, belief; society
felt n. (*felt*) Fabric made by pressing wool, hair etc. and mixing with glue into a compact mess
female 1) adj. (*fē'māl*) Of the sex that bears offspring
female 2) n. (*fē'māl*) Female person or animal. (As above)
feminine adj.
Pertaining to women, characteristic of, or suitable for, women
feminism n. (*fem'i nizm*) Movement for equality of rights between the sexes. Hence:
feminist n. supporter of feminism
fence 1) n. (*fens*) Barrier, wall enclosing a piece of land, esp. one made of wood (colloq.) receiver of stolen goods; his place of business
fence 2) v.i. and t. (*fens*) To enclose with a fence; practise the art of swordsmanship
fender n. (*fen'der*) Protective frame round an open fireplace; device such as mass of rope to protect side of ship from damage alongside wharf or another ship
fern n. (*fern*) Large flowerless plant
ferocious adj. (*fe rō'shus*) Fierce, brutal, savage
ferry n. and v.t. and i. (*fe'ri*) System of transport, esp. by boat, for conveyance of passengers, goods, vehicles across a river, short sea passage; boat used for such transport; place where such boats are used. As v.t. and i., to convey in a ferry, go across in a ferry; **ferry-boat** n.; **ferry-man** n
fertile adj. (*fer'tīl*) Productive, fruitful, *fertile land*; inventive, full of ideas, *a fertile mind*. Hence:
fertility n. (*fer til'i ti*) state of being fertile
fertilize v.t. (*fer'til īz*) To render fruitful, fertile
fertilizer n. that which fertilizes; artificial manure, or substance of this kind
festival adj. and n. (*fes'ti val*) Of a feast, festal. As n., joyful celebration; day, season for celebration, *Easter is a Church festival*
fetch v.t. and i. (*fech*) To go for and bring back someone or something
fête n. (*fāt*) Festival or entertainment, esp. for charitable cause
feud n. (*fūd*) Bitter quarrel between two persons, families, or groups, esp. one kept alive for a long period by desire for revenge
fever n. (*fē'ver*) Reaction of the body to infection, associated with a rise in temperature; one of the various diseases characterized by a rise in temperature, *rheumatic fever*; state of great nervous

excitement, *a fever of impatience*
few adj. (*fū*) Not many, *he has few friends*; a small number of, *it only cost a few shillings.* Hence
fiancé n. fem. **fiancée** (*fē ahn'sā*) Person to whom one is engaged to be married
fickle adj. (*fik'l*) Changeable in affections and purpose
fiction n. (*fik'shun*) Something imagined, invented, *fact is stranger than fiction*; a fictitious account; type of literature, e.g. novel, which consists of fictitious narrative
fictitious adj. (*fik ti'shus*) Unreal, imaginary, *fictitious characters*
fiddle 1) n. (*fid'l*) instrument of the violin family; a small swindle
fiddle 2) v.t. and i. (*fid'l*) To play upon the fiddle, *fiddle a tune* (colloq.) falsify records etc., *fiddle an Income Tax return*
fidget v.i. and t. (*fi'jet*) To move about restlessly and
field 1) n. (*fēld*) Piece of land enclosed by boundary fence, hedge, etc. and used for agricultural purposes, *a field of wheat* open space or wide area, *snow-field* area of operation, *cricket field*
field 2) v.t. and i. (*fēld*) (cricket, baseball) To stop the ball and return it
fiend n. (*fēnd*) Evil spirit, demon
fig n. (*fig*) Juicy, sweet, pear-shaped fruit of *Ficus* the fig-tree
fight 1) v.t. and i. (*fit*) To struggle against
fight 2) n. (*fit*) Act of fighting; struggle, contest, *a dog-fight*
figure 1) n. (*fig'er*) Human form, bodily shape, *she has a good figure* person in the light of his influence, *a great figure of his age* design, drawing, diagram, *refer to the figure on the next page*; written symbol, esp. one representing a number; price
figure 2) v.t. and i. (*fig'er*) To imagine, think out, *figure it out!*; play a part, appear, *the son figures largely in the story*
fill 1) v.t. and i. (*fil*) To cram, stuff to utmost capacity, occupy a space completely, *fill a bottle with milk*; to make full, pervade, *smoke filled the room*; to occupy a place, position, *he fills the office satisfactorily*
fill 2) n. (*fil*) That which fills; a full supply or amount, *eat one's fill*
filly n. (*fil'i*) Female foal
filth n. (*filth*) Foul, disgusting matter; (fig.) obscenity. Hence: filthy adj.
final 1) adj. (*fi'nal*) Last
final 2) n. (also pl.) (*fi'nal*) That which is final; the concluding stage of a series, esp. examinations or contests Hence: **finalist** n. competitor who is in the finals of a series of contests
finance 1) n. (*fi năns'*) revenue, money,
finance 2) v.t. and i. (*finans'*) To provide money for,
financial adj. (*fi năn'shal*) Of finance, money matters,
financier n. (*fi năn's ier*) One skilled in finance
find 1) v.t. (*find*) To discover as a result of deliberate search something lost or forgotten, *I cannot find the pen I lost this morning* provide, furnish with, *find the money for a business venture* succeed in obtaining, *he found the courage to go on fighting*
find 2) n. (*find*) Something found
fine 1) n. (*fin*) Sum of money paid as punishment
fine 2) v.t. (*fin*) To punish by a fine.
fine 3) adj. (*fin*) Slender, delicate, thin, *a fine thread* minute, in small particles or drops, *fine rain* clear, not raining, *a fine day* well developed, in good condition, *a fine animal*; enjoyable, *have a fine time*
finger n. (*fing'ger*) One of the five separate members in which the hand terminates
finger-print mark made by the finger-tip when pressed on a surface, used as a means of identifying criminals
finish v.t. and i. (*fin'ish*) To bring to an end, complete, *finish one's work*; come to the end of, *finish a book* make as perfect as possible, *he finished the cabinet beautifully*
fire 1) n. (*fīr*) The active principle of combustion, producing heat and light shooting, *exposed to enemy fire*
fire-arm weapon from which a missile is discharged by an explosive
fire 2) v.t. and i. (*fīr*) To discharge firearms
firm 1) adj. (*furm*) Solid, compact, not yielding to pressure, *firm flesh*; resolute, steadfast, not

easily swayed
firm 2) n. (*furm*) Association of two or more persons for the conduct of a business enterprise.
fist n. (*fist*) Hand clenched, as for striking
fit 1) n. and i. (*fit*) To be fit for, adapted to, in shape and size, *this coat fits me* put into place, *fit a window-pane into a frame*
fit 2) v.t. adj. (*fit*) Appropriate, suitable
fitter n. (*fit'er*) Person who fits, esp. a tailor who fits clothes, or mechanic who assembles or adjusts parts of machine
fizz v.i. and n. (*fiz*) Making a hissing sound
flabby adj. (*flăb'i*) Limp, hanging loose (esp. of flesh)
flag 1) n. and v.t. (*flăg*) Piece of bunting or similar cloth, usually having distinctive colours or design, and attached to pole etc. as emblem
flag 2) v.i. (*flăg*) To droop, weaken, lose energy; die out
flame 1) n. (*flām*) Luminous heat rising from burning object, burning
flame 2) v.i. (*flām*) To blaze, emit flames; to emit vivid glow as of flame, to blaze with colour (of garden etc.); to flush, blush, deeply, *her cheeks flamed*
flank n. and v.t. (*flăngk*) Fleshy part of body between ribs and hip; side of hill, building, army in formation etc. As v.t. to be at, guard, the side of (army etc.)
flannel n., adj., and v.t. and i. (*flăn'el*) Soft plain woollen cloth
flap 1) v.t. and i. (*flăp*) To move quickly up and down (as bird's wings)
flap 2) n. (*flăp*) piece of material hinged at one side to cover hole, pocket etc
flare 1) v.i. and t. (*flār*) To blaze up (of fire, also **flare up**)
flare 2) n. (*flār*) Bright fitful light; brief dazzling light used as signal, marker for bombing targets etc.; sudden fit of rage
flash 1) v.i. and t. (*flăsh*) To give sudden, momentary blaze of light
flash 2) n. (*flăsh*) Sudden momentary blaze of light; a very brief moment, *over in a flash*; sudden access of feeling, thought etc., *flash of hope*
flashlight intermittent light; lamp for signalling morse; electric torch; dazzling light lasting an instant, for photography
flask n. (*flahsk*) Small flattened bottle for wine, spirits etc
flat adj. (*flăt*) Horizontal, level
flatten v.t. and i. (*flăt'en*) To make flat
flatter v.t. (*flăt'er*) To praise falsely, insincerely, excessively; represent too favourably, *the portrait flatters her*
flavour n. and v.t. (*flā'ver*) Taste. As v.t. to give flavour to, season (dish etc.)
flaw n. and v.t. (*flaw*) A blemish, defect, crack
flax n. (*flăks*) Blue-flowered plant, *Linum*, the stalk yielding fibres for making linen, and the seeds yielding linseed oil; the fibres of this, esp. prepared for spinning
flea n. (*flē*) Small bloodsucking insect with powerful hop and discomforting bite
flee v.i. and t. (*flē*) pret. and p.p. fled (*fled*) To run away
fleece n. and v.t. (*flēs*) Woolly coat of sheep
fleet 1) n. (*flēt*) Number of vessels sailing together collection of vehicles (taxis, aircraft etc.) under one ownership
flesh 1) n. (*flesh*) The soft tissue, chiefly muscular, covering bones of animal bodies
flex 1) v.t. and i. (*fleks*) To bend
flex 2) n. (*fleks*) Flexible insulated wire to carry electric current
flexible adj. (*flek'sibl*) Pliable, easily bent this way and that
flicker v.i. and n. (*flik'er*) To flutter, quiver, waver
flight 1) n. (*flīt*) Act of flying, a journey through the air, *the flight from London to New York* number of creatures or things flying together, flock or volley, *flight of geese, of arrows*; continuous series of stairs
flight 2) n. (*flīt*) Act of fleeing, running away
flimsy adj. and n. (*flim'zi*) Light and frail
fling v.t. and i. (*fling*) To throw vigorously, hurl; move (part of body) hastily and impulsively
flip v.t. and i. and n. (*flip*) To flick over or upwards with quick jerk of thumb or finger
flipper n. (*flip'er*) Limb of animal (seal, penguin etc.) used for swimming
flit v.i. and n. (*flit*) To fly swiftly and lightly (of bats, moths etc.)
float 1) v.i. and t. (*flōt*) To rest on surface of liquid, *cork floats*

flipper
seal (top) and dolphin

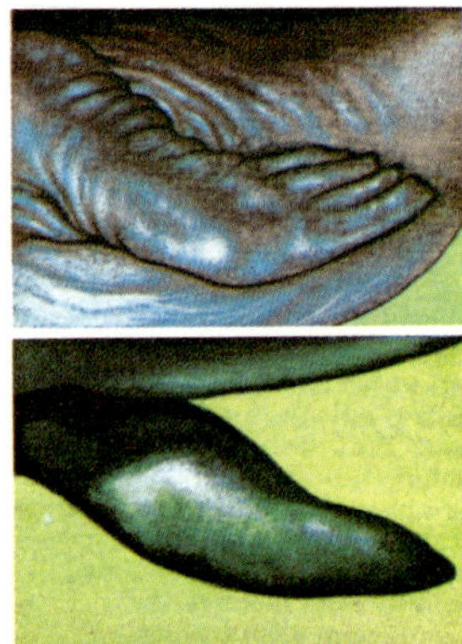

flute

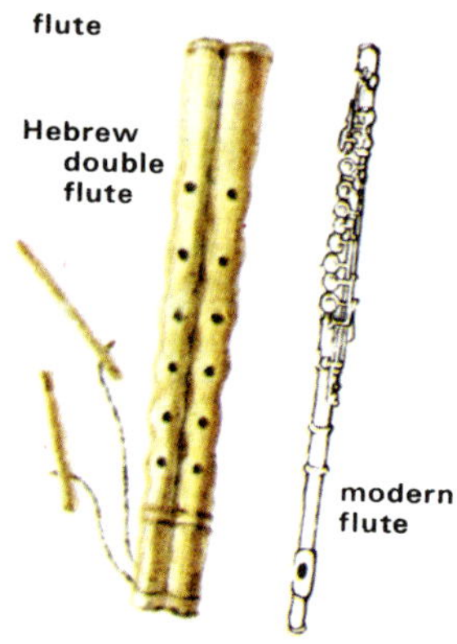

As v.t. to set (ship etc.) afloat on surface of water (comm.) to launch (a company, scheme, loan etc.)
float 2) n. (*flōt*) Thing that floats, platform on wheels for tableaux etc. in processions
flog v.t. and i. (*flog*) To whip
flood n. and v.t. and i. (*flud*) Large body of water covering usually dry land
As v.t. to cover with a flood
florist n. (*flo'rist*) Flowerseller or grower
flour n. and v.t. (*flow(r)*) Meal of grain (esp. wheat) ground to fine powder
flourish v.i. and t. (*flu'rish*) To grow vigorously (of plant) ; to prosper, thrive, be healthy, succeed (of person, business etc.) ; to be in full activity at a certain time (esp. of artists etc.)
flow v.i. (*flō*) To glide along (of water in stream etc.) move in steady stream (of crowds, traffic etc.) to hang loosely (of hair, drapery)
flower 1) n. (*flow'er*) (bot.) The reproductive organs of a seed-plant; (pop.) the showy part of plant from which fruit or seed is later developed
flower 2) v.i. and t. (*flow'er*) To bear a flower, blossom
fluid adj. and n. (*flōō'id*) Not solid (of liquid, viscous, gaseous substances) ; not rigid or set, changeable
n. a substance that flows and takes shape of vessel containing it

flute n. and v.i. and t. (*flōōt*) Musical wind-instrument consisting of wooden or metal pipe with holes stopped by keys or fingers and blow-hole near one end
flutter v.i. and t. and n. (*flut'er*) To flap wings quickly and nervously to throb faintly, unevenly (pulse) As n. act of fluttering, nervous and tremulous excitement
fly 1) n. (*flī*) One of many kinds of small two-winged insect
fly 2) v.i. and t. (*flī*) pret. flew (*flōō*) p.p. **flown** (*flōn*) To move through air with wings; travel through air in aircraft; to be borne up by airstream etc. (of kite etc.) ; to pass quickly through air, *arrow flew to its mark*
foal n. and v.i. and t. (*fōl*) Young of horse, ass etc. (**with, in, foal** pregnant (of mare)). As v.i. (of mare) to give birth (v.t. bear a foal)
foam n. and v.i. (*fōm*) Frothy mass of small bubbles formed on surface of liquid
foe n. (*fō*) Enemy
fog 1) n. and v.t. and i. (*fog*) Low-lying mass of dense watery vapour, smoke particles etc. resulting in visibility less than one kilometre
foil 1) n. and v.t. (*foil*) metal plate beaten very thin, *tin foil*
foil 2) v.t. and i. and n. (*foil*) To frustrate, baffle (attempts etc.)
foil 3) n. (*foil*) Light fencing sword with button or point
fold 1) v.t. and i. (*fōld*) To bend one part of flexible thing upon

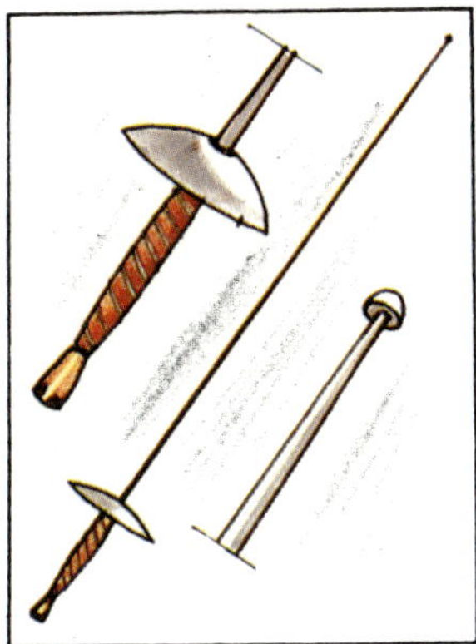
foil

font

another, *fold one's clothes* envelop, wrap up (thing in paper etc.) As v.i. to be capable of being folded (often with *up*)
fold 2) n. (*fōld*) Bend in flexible material
fold 3) n and v.t. (*fōld*) Pen, enclosure, for sheep
foliage n. (*fō'li ij*) Leaves
folk n. (*fōk*) People in general
follow v.t. and i. (*fol'ō*) To go or come after to engage in a certain profession etc., *to follow the sea* understand (argument etc.)
follower n. (*fol'ō er*) Disciple, adherent, supporter
following 1) n. (*fol'ōing*) Body of followers, *a large following*
folly n. (*fol'i*) Foolishness
fond adj. (*fond*) Loving, affectionate
fondle v.t. and i. (*fondl*) To caress, toy lovingly with
font n. (*font*) Receptacle for baptismal water
food n. (*fōōd*) Nutriment, that which is eaten for nourishment
fool 1) n. (*fōōl*) Silly, stupid person, without sense or wisdom; jester in medieval court or household
foot 1) n. (*fŏŏt*) pl. **feet** (*fēt*) Part of leg below ankle, on which man or animal stands or walks lower part, base (of mountain, column etc.) lineal measure of 12 inches
forbid v.t. (*fer bid'*), pret. **forbade** (*-băd*), p.p. **forbidden** (*-bidn*) To order not to do, refuse to allow
force 1) n. (*faws*) Power, strength, or exertion of this, *brute force, to use force* body of troops (often pl., **the Forces** army, navy, and air force)
ford n. and v.t. (*fawd*) Shallow place where river etc. may be crossed by wading
fore adj. and n. (*faw*(*r*)) Situated at the front. As n. (naut.) front part of
forecast v.t. and n. (*faw'kahst*) To calculate beforehand, estimate, predict (weather etc.). As n. estimate, prediction
forefather n. (*faw'fah ther*) Ancestor
foreign adj. (*fo'rin*) of, from, relating to, characteristic of, another country or other countries, *foreign goods, affairs, accent*
Hence: **foreigner** n. person of another nationality
foreman n. (*faw'man*) Spokesman of jury; in charge of gang of workmen
foresight n. (*faw'sīt*) Seeing what will happen in the future
forest n. and v.t. (*fo'rist*) Large tract of land mainly tree-covered
Hence: **forester** n. official in charge of, man working in, a forest
forfeit n., adj. and v.t. (*faw'fit*) Thing risked or lost through crime, As v.t. to lose, be deprived of, as penalty
forge 1) n. (*fawj*) Blacksmith's workshop, smithy; his furnace; any workshop or plant for heating and working metals
forge 2) v.t. and i. (*fawj*) To shape (metal) by heating and hammering to counterfeit, fabricate (esp. money, signature, document)

forge

forget v.t. and i. (*ferget'*) pret. **forgot** (*-got*) p.p. **forgotten** (*-gotn*) To lose remembrance of, fail to recall to mind

forgive v.t. and i. (*fer giv'*) pret. **forgave** (*-gāv*) p.p. **forgiven** (*-givn*) To pardon (person or offence), waive penalty (for offence) or cease to bear hard feelings (towards person); to remit, cancel (debt etc.)

fort n. (*fawt*) Fortified building

fortify v.t. and i. (*faw'ti fi*) To make strong or stronger; strengthen

fortnight n. (*fawt'nit*) Period of two weeks

fortress n. (*fawt'res*) Fortified town, camp etc

fortunate n. (*faw'chōō nat, faw'tū nat*) Lucky, enjoying, bringing or heralding luck

fortune n. (*faw'choon, faw'tūn*) Chance, luck

forward 1) adv. (*faw'wud*) Onward, towards the front

forward 2) v.t. (*faw'wud*) To help onward, promote (scheme etc.); to send (letter) on to further destination

fossil n. and adj. (*fosl*) Petrified remains of plant or animal, or cast of these, found in stratified rock

foster v.t. (*fos'ter*) To rear, bring up (child)

foul 1) adj. and adv. (*fowl*) Filthy

foul 2) n. (*fowl*) (naut.) breach of rules

foul 3) v.i. and t. (*fowl*) To become clogged, choked with filth, entangled; (sport) commit a foul

found v.t. and i. (*fownd*) To lay foundation of, begin constructing

foundation n. (*fown dā'shun*) Act of founding, establishing, setting up (city, institution etc.) base, part on which structure rests (often pl.)

founder n. (*fown'der*) Person who starts a firm, a school of thought etc

fountain n. (*fown'tin*) spout of water issuing from pipe

fowl n. and v.i. (*fowl*) Bird, esp. edible domestic kind

fox n. (*foks*) Dog-like animal with reddish fur and bushy tail

fracture n. and v.t. and i. (*frăk'cher*) Breakage, esp. of bone

fragile adj. (*frăj'il*) Easily broken delicate

fragment n. (*frăg'ment*) Part broken off

fragrant adj. (*frā'grant*) Sweet-smelling

frail adj. (*frāl*) Fragile, delicate

frame 1) v.t. and i. (*frām*) To to provide (picture) with frame (slang) to contrive that innocent person should appear guilty

frame 2) n. (*frām*) Structure designed to surround and support, skeleton of structure, building, vehicle etc. border of wood etc. for picture, window etc

frank adj. (*frăngk*) Free and open in manner

frantic adj. (*frăn'tik*) Violently excited, esp. with rage, grief, pain, anxiety etc

fraternal adj. (*fra tur'nal*) Of brothers; brotherly

fraternity n. (*fra tur'ni ti*) Brotherliness, being fraternal; an association of men with common interests, esp

fossil

fox

fraternize v.t. (*frăt'er niz*) To associate as brothers, make friends
fraud n. (*frawd*) Deceitfulness; wilful deception, false representation, for profit
freckle n. and v.t. and i. (*frekl*) Small brown blotch on skin
free 1) adj. (*frē*) not compelled by necessity, *free to do as you please* not busy, not occupied (of person or place)
costing nothing, gratis, *a free seat*
free 2) v.t. (*frē*) To liberate, set free (person, nation etc.)
freedom n. (*frē'dom*) State of being free
freeze v.i. and t. and n. (*frēz*) pret. **froze** (*frōz*) p.p. **frozen** (*frōzn*) (impers.) To be cold enough to turn water to ice, *it froze during the night*
preserve meat etc. by refrigeration
freight n. and v.t. (*frāt*) Hire of ship for transporting goods, or charge for this; the goods transported
frenzy n. and v.t. (*fren'zi*) Mental disturbance; violent rage, excitement etc
frequency n. (*frē'kwen si*) Regular or repeated occurrence, state of being frequent; (phys.) number of vibrations, waves, cycles per second
frequent 1) adj. (*frē kwent*) Oft repeated, *a frequent error*
frequent 2) v.t. (*fri kwent'*) To go to, visit, often (place, persons)
friar n. (*frī'er*) Member of religious order
friction n. (*frik'shun*) Rubbing of one thing against another
friend n. (*frend*) Person bound to another by ties of affection
fright n. and v.t. (*frīt*) Sudden fear, *give someone a fright, die of fright;* (colloq.) grotesque, unkempt, person or thing, *what a fright you look!*
frighten v.t. (*frīt'en*) To alarm, scare
frightful adj. (*frīt'fool*) Terrible, dreadful, shocking, *a frightful accident*
frigid adj. (*frij'id*) Very cold
frill n. and v.t. and i. (*fril*) Narrow gathered strip of material as edging
fringe n., adj. and v.t. (*frinj*) Ornamental border of loose threads, twists, tassels hair
brushed down on forehead and cut straight across: extreme outer part of something, *on the fringe of the city*
frisk v.i. and t. and n. (*frisk*) To caper, gambol sportively (as lambs etc.) As v.t. (slang) to
search person rapidly for gun, liquor etc
frog 1) n. (*frog*) Tailless and amphibian animal of genus *Rana*
frolic v.i. and n. (*frol'ik*) To gambol, play pranks, be merry
front 1) n. and adj. (*frunt*) Forehead, face (milit.) foremost rank, firing line area along shore, esp. a built-up promenade As adj. of, at, the front, *front row, front door*
frontier n. and adj. (*frun'tyer*) The part of the country bordering on another
frost n. and v.t. and i. (*frost*) Freezing, prevailing air temperature below 0°C. (32°F.), *3 degrees of frost*; frozen dew, vapour, on ground etc
frown v.i. and t. and n. (*frown*) To knit the brows in anger, displeasure, or concentration
fruit n. and v.i. (*froot*) Produce of tree or other plant, esp. that part containing the seeds (including nuts, berries etc.); esp. the edible produce of certain trees or bushes
fruiterer n. (*froo'ter er*) Dealer in fruit
fruitful adj. (*froot'ful*) Productive of much fruit, offspring or profit; yielding results, rewards, *a fruitful idea, career.* Hence
fruitless n. (*froot'les*) Not bearing fruit, esp. fig. (of efforts, toil etc.) useless, unprofitable, vain
(fruit + less)

fruity adj. (*froo'ti*) Of fruit, esp. tasting, smelling of fruit
fry 1) n. (*fri*) Young fish recently hatched
fry 2) v.t. and i. and n. (*fri*) To cook in boiling fat over fire
fuel n., and v.t. and i. (*fū'el*) Combustible material for fires (coal, oil, wood etc.) ; petrol for engine
fugitive adj. and n. (*fu'ji tiv*) Fleeing, running away, esp. from danger, prison etc. As n one who flees, esp. from danger, justice etc
fulfil v.t. (*fool fil'*) To accomplish, satisfy (hopes, expectations etc.) ; to carry out (duty, obligations etc.) ; to comply with (conditions)
full adj., n., v.t., and adv. (*fool*) Containing as much as it (space, receptacle) will hold, having reached the highest or utmost degree or state
fumble v.i. and t., and n. (*fumbl*) To use hands clumsily, grope *at, with* thing
fume n., and v.t. and i. (*fūm*) Pungent smoke or vapour As v.i. to give off smoke and fumes (chimney etc.) ; to be in a rage
fun n. (*fun*) Matter for laughter, amusement, or a good time generally, *tennis is great fun* (of persons) amusing
function n. and v.i. (*fungk'shun*) The activity proper to a person or thing, purpose, *a clock's function is to tell the time* a ceremony, formal meeting, or (more loosely) social gathering
fund n. and v.t. (*fund*) Store, stock, *a fund of good stories* ; sum of money, esp. set apart for some purpose ; (pl.) money, capital resources
funeral n. and adj. (*fū'ner al*) A burial of the dead with ceremonial rites
fungus n. (*fung'gus*) pl. **fungi** (*-gi, -ji*), **funguses** Mushroom, toadstool, etc
funnel n. and v.t. (*funl*) Tapering tube with wide mouth, for pouring liquid into small hole ; cylindrical chimney of steamship or locomotive
funny adj. (*fun'i*) Laughable, comical, amusing, *funny story, hat* ; odd, peculiar, queer, *a very funny way to behave*
fur n. and v.t. and i. (*fur*) The short soft hair forming the coat of

fungus

certain animals
prepared animal skin for use as coat, lining, trimming etc.; coating, deposit, of various kinds, as on tongue, in kettle etc
furious adj. (*fūr'i us*) Raging, full of fury; very angry
furnace n. and v.t. (*fur'nis*) Enclosed chamber for generating intense heat
furnish v.t. (*fur'nish*) To provide, equip *with*; also fig., *to furnish (with) information*; to fit up a house, esp. with movable furniture. Hence: **furnisher** n. esp. tradesman dealing in household furniture and fittings; **furnishings** n.pl
furniture n. (*fur'ni cher*) Articles of equipment, esp. movable ones of household use (tables, chairs etc.)
furrow n. and v.t. (*fu'rō*) Trench made by plough
further 1) adv. and adj. (*fur'ther*) To a greater distance or degree, *to go further, to enquire further*; in addition, *I'll further declare . . .* (also **furthermore**). As adj. farther, more distant, *the further side of the hill*; additional, *further enquiries*.
further 2) v.t. (*fur'ther*) To promote, help on, *to further one's career*
fury n. (*fūr'i*) Violent emotional agitation, esp. anger
fuse n. and v.i. (*fūz*) Tube, cord etc. filled with explosive or combustible matter for touching off bomb, blasting charge etc.; (elect.) piece of fusible metal, wire etc., inserted into electric circuit as safety device. As v.i. (of lights, electric circuit) to go out, be interrupted, when the fuse "blows" or melts
fuselage n. (*fū'zi lahzh, -lij*) Body of an aeroplane. (Fr., from Lat.
fuss n., and v.i. and t. (*fus*) Nervous excitement, bustle, bother, worry As v.i. to bustle nervously, make a fuss, worry over trifles. As v.t. to worry
future adj. and n. (*fū'cher*) Going to happen after the present, about to happen As n. the time yet to come, *in the future*

G

gable n. (*gābl*) Triangular upper part of an outside wall, between the sloping sides of the roof
gag 1) n. (*găg*) Something put into, or covering, a person's mouth to silence him
gag 2) v.t. and i. (*găg*) To put a gag into someone's mouth to silence them
gaiety n. (*gā'e ti*) State or quality of being gay, cheerfulness
gain 1) v.t. and i. (*gān*) To obtain, to acquire as an increase, addition, obtain as a profit, *the baby gained 3 lb. in weight, the shopkeeper gained £3 on the sale*; to reach, attain to, arrive at, *gain the summit of a mountain*; (of a watch etc.) to become fast, increase in rate
gait n. (*gāt*) Manner of walking
gala n. (*gah'la, gā'la*) Festivity, time of public merrymaking
Galaxy n. (*găl'ak si*) The Milky Way, a belt of stars extending across the heavens and too faint to be seen separately by the naked eye
gale n. (*gāl*) Strong, violent wind
gallant adj. (*găl'ant*) and n. (*găl ănt'*) Brave, daring, noble, *a gallant knight* showing special courtesy and deference to women
gallery n. (*găl'er i*) raised floor projecting from the walls of a building and supported on brackets or pillars, so as to command a view of the interior, *the gallery of a church*; (theatre) floor of this type, forming the uppermost and cheapest tier of seats; room or building for exhibition of works of art, *an art gallery*
gallon n. (*găl'on*) Measure of liquid
gallop 1) n. (*găl'op*) Fastest pace of horses etc.
gallop 2) v.i. and t. (*găl'op*) To go at a gallop
gallows n. (*găl'ōz*) Wooden framework of posts and crossbeam, on which criminals used to be hanged
gamble v.t. and i., and n. (*gămbl*) To play games of chance for money, esp. for high stakes; to speculate in financial transactions; (fig.) to take risks for possible advantage
As n., the act of gambling; any risky undertaking where there is a chance of advantage
gambol n. and v.i. (*găm'bol*) A skipping about in frolic, esp. of young lambs and children
game 1) n. (*gām*) Sport, amusement, play athletic contests, *the Olympic games*; apparatus etc. needed for a game, *this is the*

department for the sale of children's games; scheme, undertaking; trick, dodge, *so that's your little game!*; wild animals or birds hunted for food or sport, to hunt game; their flesh
game 2) adj. (*gām*) Plucky, courageous; spirited, eager, willing, *I'm game to try it*
gander n. (*găn'der*) The male of the goose
gang n. and v.i. (*găng*) Group, band, set of persons associated or working together, *a gang of road-workers*; group of persons organized for a criminal purpose
gangster n. (*găng'ster*) Member of a gang of criminals
gangway n. and inter. (*găng'wā*) Passage between rows of seats, as in a theatre etc., *please pass down the gangway*; movable bridge from a ship's side to land
gaol, jail n. and v.t. (*jāl*) A prison
v.t., to put in gaol, imprison Hence:
gaoler, jailer n. man in charge of a gaol or of those in it; one responsible for keeping another person in custody
gap n. and v.i. (*găp*) Hole or opening in a hedge, fence, etc
gape 1) v.i. (*gāp*) To yawn, open the mouth wide; stare open-mouthed
gape 2) n. (*gāp*) The act of gaping; a yawn
garage n. and v.t. (*gă'rahzh, gă'rij*) Building in which vehicles may be housed, *this house has an attached garage*; commercial establishment for the storage, repair, and sale of vehicles, and at which petrol etc. may be obtained. As v.t. to put (a motor-car) into a garage
garbage n. (*gah(r)'bij*) Refuse, offal; waste matter
garden 1) n. (*gah(r)dn*) Piece of ground, usually adjoining a house, for growing flowers, vegetables, fruit etc., and often laid out with a lawn and paths; (pl.) park or enclosure, planted with trees, flowers, lawns etc., for the enjoyment and recreation of the public
garden 2) v.i. (*gah(r)dn*) To work in, cultivate a garden
gargle 1) v.i. and t. (*gah(r)gl*) To wash the throat with liquid, which is agitated by a stream of breath
gargle 2) n. (*gah(r)gl*) The act of gargling; a medicated liquid used for this purpose

garlic

garland n. and v.t. (*gah(r)'land*) Wreath or circle of flowers or leaves worn or hung on an object for decoration
garlic n. (*gah(r)'lik*) Perennial plant allied to the onion, *Allium sativum*, with strong taste and smell, used in cooking.
garment n. (*gah(r)'ment*) Article of clothing
garnish v.t. and n. (*gah(r)'nish*) To decorate
garret n. (*gă'ret*) Room immediately below the roof of a house, esp. one that is small and wretched; an attic. (OFr. *garite* watchtower)
garrison 1) n. (*gă'ri son*) Body of troops stationed in a town or fortress
garrison 2) v.t. (*gă'ri son*) To provide with a garrison; to occupy as a garrison; to send (troops etc.) as garrison
garter n. (*gah(r)'ter*) Band, usually elastic, worn round leg to keep stocking up
gas 1) n. (*găs*) State of matter in which a substance is vaporous, and has the property of indefinite expansion; in popular usage, the 'town gas' used for industrial and domestic heating
gas 2) v.t. and i. (*găs*) To poison by gas-fumes
gash n. and v.t. (*găsh*) Long, deep cut, slash
gasp v.i. and t. (*gahsp*) To struggle for breath, breathe through the mouth rapidly and convulsively; to catch the breath in fear or astonishment

gate n. (*gāt*) Hinged or sliding structure, either solid or with open framework, that can close the entrance to an enclosure; a gateway
gather v.t. and i. (*gă'ther*) To bring together, collect to pick, pluck, *gather flowers*; to acquire information, *I could gather little from what he said*
As v.i., to assemble, congregate
gauge 1) n. (*gāj*) A standard measure, esp. the distance between inside edges of rails of a railway an instrument for regulating or measuring dimensions, pressure, volume etc
gauge 2) v.t. (*gāj*) To measure accurately, *gauge the rainfall*; to estimate, appraise, *gauge a person's character*
gaunt adj. (*gawnt*) Thin, lean, haggard; (of places) austere, forbidding
gay adj. (*gā*) Light-hearted, cheerful, full of fun
gaze 1) v.i. (*gāz*) To look steadily, fixedly, *he gazed at the scene for several minutes*
gaze 2) n. (*gāz*) Long, steady look
gazette n. (*ga zet'*) News-sheet, periodical record or journal of current events; official publication containing lists of public appointments etc
gear n. (*gēr*) Any mechanical system of moving parts designed to transmit motion mechanism built for a particular purpose equipment in general
gelignite n. (*jel'ig nīt*) High explosive used for blasting
gem n. and v.t. (*jem*) Precious stone anything of great value, or much prized
gender n. (*jen'der*) Grammatical classification of nouns, pronouns, and the adjectives associated with them, sometimes corresponding to that of sex in nature
general 1) adj. (*jen'er al*) Not confined to a particular section, aspect, or part; universal, relating to all or many persons not specific, not defined in detail, *a general statement*
general 2) n. (*jen'er al*) (milit.) Officer next in rank below a field-marshal
generally adv. (*jen'er al i*) Usually, as a general rule
generation n. (*jen er ā'shun*) The persons of approximately the same age, living at the same time, *the rising generation*; period in which they live; period of time, roughly thirty years, generally regarded as a stage in the line of descent, *a generation ago*
generator n. (*jen'er ā tor*) Machine for converting mechanical energy into electrical energy, or for generating gas, steam etc
genial adj. (*jē'ni al*) Kindly
genius n. (*jē'ni us*) extraordinary intellectual endowment, person possessing this, *Mozart showed his musical genius at an early age*
gentle adj. (*jentl*) not rough or boisterous
geography n. (*jē og'ra fi*) Study of the earth's surface, its physical features, divisions, population, races, climate, products etc
geology n. (*jē ol'o ji*) Study of the history of the earth's crust, the arrangement, composition, and origins of its rocks, and the processes of evolution of its structure
geometry n. (*jē om'et ri*) Branch of mathematics concerned with properties of points, lines, surfaces, and solids
gesture n. (*jes'cher*) Movement of hand or arm to express an idea, feeling etc., or to emphasize what is being said
get v.t. and i. (*get*) pret. and p.p. **got** (U.S. p.p. often **gotten**) To obtain possession of, acquire, procure, *you ought to get a new raincoat*; to receive, *I get a letter from him once a week*; to succeed in doing something or bringing something about, *I got the lawn mowed at last* to arrive at, *to get home*
geyser n. (*gā zer, gī zer*) Hot spring from which column of hot water and steam is explosively discharged at intervals
ghost n. (*gōst*) The spirit of a dead person appearing before the living in visible form, *do you believe in ghosts?*
giant 1) n. (*jī'ant*) Fabulous being in human form, very tall and large
giant 2) adj. (*jī'ant*) Of extraordinary size or strength
giddy adj. (*gi'di*) Having the feeling of vertigo, the impression that stationary objects are reeling about
gift n. (*gift*) Something given, *a birthday gift*; natural endowment or talent, *have a gift*

for music
giggle v.i. and n. (*gigl*) To laugh in a foolish, nervous manner
gild v.t. (*gild*) To cover with gold leaf, gold paint, or similar substance
gilt n. (*gilt*) Gold leaf, gold paint, or similar substance used for gilding
gimmick n. (*gim'ik*) (colloq.) Device, esp. a new and showy one
gin n. (*jin*) A colourless spirit drink distilled from grain or malt and then further distilled with aromatic substances such as juniper, orris, almonds etc
ginger n. and adj. (*jin'jer*) Aromatic tropical plant; the hot-tasting root of this plant, used in cooking and medicine
gipsy, gypsy n. and adj. (*jip'si*) Member of a nomadic race of Indian origin, now living in many parts of Europe, Asia etc
giraffe n. (*jirăf'*) African hooved ruminant with long neck and legs and spotted skin
girder n. (*ger'der*) Beam, usually of steel, bridging an open space, esp. when supporting the upper floor of a building or the superstructure of a bridge, etc
girdle n. (*gerdl*) Belt, cord, or band used to gird the waist and keep clothes in position
thing which encircles like a girdle
girl n. (*gerl*) Female child
give v.t. and i. (*giv*) pret. **gave** (*gāv*), p.p. **given** (*giv'n*) To convey to the possession of another without requiring any exchange to transfer something in return or exchange for something else, *I gave a lot of money for that coat* to break down under pressure, *he felt the branch give beneath his feet*
glacier n. (*glă'si er*) A river of ice, that moves gradually downhill
glad adj. (*glăd*) Happy; pleased, satisfied, *I'm glad I didn't go*; willing, *glad to help*; affording pleasure, *glad tidings*
glamour n. (*glăm'er*) Enchantment, charm; feeling of delight and fascination associated with something or someone, *the glamour of this festive occasion*
glance 1) v.i. and t. (*glahns*) To take a quick look (at, over, through), *glance out of the window*; strike obliquely so as to be deflected, *the arrow glanced off his armour*; (of light) to be reflected from, flash; (of bright objects) to reflect light, flash, *the lake glanced in the sunlight*
glare v.i. (*glār*) To give out a blinding, dazzling light; to stare angrily or fiercely
gleam n. (*glēm*)
beam or flash of light
glee n. (*glē*) Exultant happiness, gay laughter; (mus.) part-song for three or more voices, usually unaccompanied
glen n. (*glen*) Narrow valley
glide v.i. (*glīd*) To move along smoothly as though sliding
Hence: **glider** n. heavier-than-air aircraft not powered by an engine of its own; **gliding** n. sport of flying in gliders

giraffe

glider

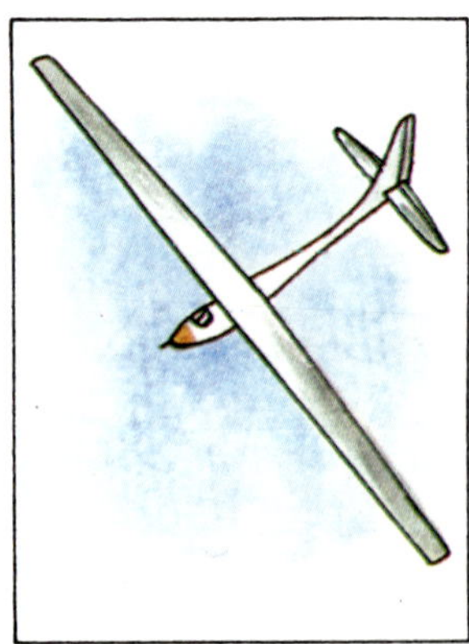

glimmer 1) v.i. (*glim'er*) To flicker, shine feebly and fitfully
glimmer 2) n. (*glim'er*) Fitful gleam, feeble light
glimpse v.t. and n. (*glimps*) To catch a brief sight of. As n., a fleeting impression, brief, imperfect view
glisten v.i. and n. (*glisn*) To glitter, reflect light brightly, sparkle
glitter v.i. and n. (*gli'ter*) To sparkle with light, shine brightly
globe n. (*glōb*) A sphere, ball; the Earth; spherical model of the Earth or the constellations, with map or chart on it
gloom n. (*glōōm*) Semi-darkness, obscurity, *the gloom of the dungeon*; (fig.) depression of spirits
glory 1) n. (*glaw'ri*) Splendour, radiance
glory 2) v.i. (*glaw'ri*) To exult, rejoice in, *glory in one's strength*
gloss n. and v.t. (*glos*) Smooth sheen, bright, reflecting surface
glove n. and v.t. (*gluv*) Covering for the hand and fingers, with separate compartments for each finger and for the thumb
glow v.i. (*glō*) To be bright with intense heat but without flame or smoke to feel, look, warm and flushed from exercise or emotion, *to glow with enthusiasm*
glue 1) n. (*glōō*) Sticky substance obtained from bones, gelatine, or other sources, and used as an adhesive agent to join surfaces
glue 2) v.t. (*glōō*) To coat with glue, stick together with glue
glum adj. (*glum*) Depressed
gnash v.t. (*năsh*) To grind the teeth together in rage etc.
gnat n. (*năt*) Any of the small two-winged insects of the family *Culex*
gnaw v.t. and i. (*naw*) To wear away by biting or scraping with the teeth, *a dog gnawing at a bone*
gnome n. (*nōm*) Mythical dwarfish sprite, living underground and usually represented as guarding buried treasure
go 1) v.i. (*gō*) pret. **went** (*went*), p.p. **gone** (*gon*) To move, walk, proceed, *I shall go by car*; to depart from, *it is time for me to go*; to disappear, be eliminated, *that paragraph will have to go*; to work properly, function, *the engine is going well now*
go 2) n. (*gō*) (colloq.) Turn, *let's have a go*

gnat

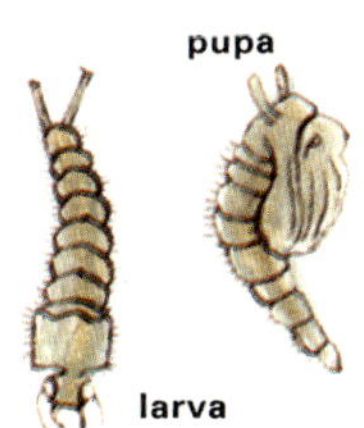

goal n. (*gōl*) Point marking the end of a race; two posts between which the ball has to be driven in various team-games in order to score; point made by doing this; destination, object of ambition or efforts, *the goal of one's dreams*; **goal-keeper** player whose object is to keep the ball out of goal
gobble v.t. and i. (*gobl*) To eat greedily, noisily, and fast
goblet n. (*gob'let*) Drinking vessel with a stem and base, and no handles
goblin n. (*gob'lin*) Malicious, grotesque sprite, a demon
god n. (*god*) Deity, divinity, supernatural being regarded as controlling an aspect of nature or of human activity, and worshipped as such; (with cap.) Creator of the Universe, the Almighty

goblet

goggle v.i. and n. (*gogl*) To open the eyes widely and stare, *he goggled at her in amazement.* As n., wide-eyed stare of amazement or horror; **goggles** spectacles with guards against dust etc.
gold n. (*gōld*) Precious yellow, heavy metallic element; objects of gold, *he collects gold and silver*
golden adj. (*gōld'en*) Made of gold, resembling gold in colour or
golf n. and v.i. (*gōlf*) Game in which a ball has to be placed successively into 9 or 18 holes along a specially laid-out course or 'links', by striking with golf clubs
good 1) adj. (*good*) Of superior quality, excellent of its kind, having the right or desired qualities, *a good knife*; pleasant, enjoyable morally excellent, virtuous, pious, *a good man*; well-behaved, *be a good boy*
good 2) n. (*good*)
(pl.) wealth, property
goose n. (*goos*) pl. **geese** (*gēs*) Large web-footed bird of the family *Anatidae*
gorge 1) n. (*gawj*) Throat; steep-sided, narrow valley
gorge 2) v.i. and t. and n. (*gawj*) To eat greedily
gorgeous adj. (*gaw'jus*) Richly magnificent, imposing, splendid
gorilla n. (*go ril'a*) Largest of anthropoid apes, found in Central Africa
gospel n. (*gos'pel*) One of the first four books of the New Testament, containing accounts of the life and teachings of Christ; the teachings of Christ, Christianity; principle or set of beliefs strongly held and acted on
govern v.t. and i. (*guv'ern*) To direct, control, have authority over, esp. the public affairs of a state, city etc.
government n. (*guv'ern ment*) Act or power of governing, *the government was in the hands of a dictator*; (with capital letter) the governing machinery or body of a country
governor n. (*guv'er nor*) One who governs, esp. the province or colony of a state
gown n. and v.t. (*gown*) A loose, flowing garment; one-piece woman's dress
grab v.t. and i. (*grăb*) To snatch, clutch, seize suddenly and forcefully, *the boy grabbed a sweet and ran off*
grace n. (*grās*) Pleasing quality, elegance,
smoothness of movement,
thanksgiving at mealtimes
(with capital letter) title used when speaking of or to a duke, duchess, or archbishop, *His (Her, Your) Grace*
graceful adj. (*grās'fool*) Having or showing grace, *a graceful dancer*
grade 1) n. (*grād*) Step, stage, degree (in rank, quality, value, proficiency etc.), *a high grade of potatoes*; mark, rating given to a student, *the teacher gave him a high grade for his work*
grade 2) v.t. (*grād*) To put into grades, classify
gradient n. (*grā'di ent*) Degree of slope, *a gradient of one in six*
gradual adj. (*grăd'ū al, grăj'ū al*) Proceeding, happening, slowly, by degrees
graduate n. (*grăd'ū at*) One who has taken a degree in a university
grain n. (*grān*) Small, hard seed of plant; cereal, produce, grain imports; a small, round body, *grain of sand*; (fig.) tiny amount, *a grain of sense*; smallest unit of weight; arrangement of fibres or particles in timber, leather etc.
grammar n. (*grăm'er*) Study of the forms of a language and its analysis
gramophone n. (*grăm'o fōn*) Machine reproducing sounds recorded on flat discs, by means of a needle connected to a vibrating plate
grand adj. (*grănd*) Splendid, magnificent main, most important, *the grand staircase*; (colloq.) very enjoyable, extremely good, *I had a grand time*
grape n. (*grāp*) Fruit of the vine
graph n. (*grăf, grahf*) Diagram expressing mathematical relationships by means of lines and curves
grasp v.t. and i. (*grahsp*) To grip firmly, clutch, *he grasped the lifebelt*; (fig.) comprehend, *he grasped my meaning*
grate 1) v.t. and i. (*grāt*) To produce a harsh, discordant noise by the rough friction of two surfaces
grate 2) n. (*grāt*) Frame of metal bars, esp. one used in a fireplace for holding fuel
grateful adj. (*grāt'fool*) Thankful, feeling or expressing gratitude

grape

gratitude n. (*grǎ'ti tūd*) Thankfulness.
grave n. (*grāv*) Hole dug in the ground to contain a corpse
graze 1) v.t. and i. (*grāz*) To feed on growing grass
graze 2) v.t. (*grāz*) To touch, rub, or scrape lightly during passage; to cause a graze in, *graze the skin*
grease n. and v.t. (*grēs*) Soft animal fat
greasy adj. (*grē'si, grē'zi*) Coated with grease, *greasy fingers*; containing grease, *a greasy substance*
great adj. (*grāt*) Above the average in size, degree, amount, number, *a great city*
greed n. (*grēd*) Excessive desire to obtain.
greet v.t. (*grēt*) To address, salute or hail in welcome
grenade n. (*gren ād'*) Small bomb thrown by hand or projected by a rifle
grid n. (*grid*) (elect.) national network of transmission lines interlinking power stations; (surveying) network of lines imposed on a map for purposes of reference
grief n. (*grēf*) Deep sorrow, woe
grievance n. (*grē'vans*) Real or imaginary ground of complaint
grieve v.t. and i. (*grēv*) Cause grief to; feel grief
grim adj. (*grim*) Stern, forbidding.
grime n. and v.t. (*grīm*) Dirt, deposited on a surface
grin v.i. and t. and n. (*grin*) To smile broadly, showing the teeth
grind 1) v.t. and i. (*grīnd*) To reduce to powder or fragments by friction and pressure, *grind coffee*; to polish, sharpen, roughen, by friction, *grind a lens*
grindstone n. (*grīnd'stōn*) Disc of stone revolving on an axle, for grinding or polishing; **keep one's nose to the grindstone** work hard with no rest
grip v.t. and i. (*grip*) To clutch firmly, *he gripped the steering-*
grit n. and v.t. (*grit*) Small fragments of stone, gravel etc
grizzly n. (*griz'li*) Large, fierce N. American bear
groan v.i. and t. (*grōn*) To utter a deep, moaning sound of pain, sorrow, or distress; to creak, *the beams groaned under his weight*
grocer n. (*gro'ser*) Dealer in dry stores and household requirements. Hence: **grocery** n. grocer's trade; (pl.) things sold by a grocer
groom n. and v.t. (*groōm*) Servant in charge of horses bridegroom. As v.t., to rub down, brush, and clean a horse
groove n. and v.t. (*groōv*) Long narrow channel cut in the surface of wood etc.
ground 1) n. (*grownd*) Earth, land, *fertile ground*; surface of the earth, *fall to the ground*; piece of land, esp. one set aside for a particular purpose, *the cricket ground* (often pl.) foundation, reason, *have you any grounds for your statement?*
ground 2) v.t. and i. (*grownd*) To touch ground; place on the ground
groundless adj. (*grownd'les*) Unfounded, without good reason
group n. and v.t. and i. (*groōp*) Collection or assemblage of objects or persons gathered or placed together, *a group of cows* As v.t. and i., to form or gather into a group or groups
grouse n. (*grows*) pl. **grouse** One of several kinds of wild fowl
grow v.i. and t. (*grō*) To develop, increase in size, weight, amount, length etc
growl v.i. and t. and n. (*growl*) To utter a deep, menacing rumble, *the dog growled at the intruder*; to speak in a growling manner, *he growled (out) an answer*
grudge v.t. and n. (*gruj*) To resent, be unwilling to allow or give, *grudge paying a high price* n., feeling of resentment, envy, ill-will, *he still bears me a grudge*
gruesome adj. (*groō'sum*) Inspiring horror and disgust

gruff adj. (*gruf*) (Of the voice or manner) rough, surly
grumble v.i. and t. and n. (*grumbl*) To mutter angrily, rumble; to complain, express discontent
guarantee n. (*gă ran tē'*) Pledge, promise, that certain conditions agreed to in a transaction will be fulfilled; something given as security for one who gives or receives a guaranty or surety
guard 1) n. (*gah(r)d*) sentry or body of men keeping watch against attack official in charge of a railway train part of an object designed to protect against danger, *guard of a sword*
guard 2) v.t. and i. (*gah(r)d*) To protect, keep watch over
guardian n. (*gah(r)'di an*) One who guards
guer(r)illa n. and adj. (*ger il'a*) Form of war waged by armed bands making sporadic attacks and raids; one engaged in such warfare
guess v.t. and i. (*ges*) To form a judgement without real evidence
guest n. (*gest*) Person entertained in another's house, either to a meal or to stay; lodger paying for accommodation at an inn etc
guide 1) v.t. (*gid*) To show a person the way
guide 2) n. (*gid*) Person who shows another the way; one who conducts visitors or sightseers
guilt n. (*gilt*) Fact, state, or consciousness of having done wrong
guilty adj. (*gil'ti*) Having done wrong
gull n. (*gul*) Member of group of long-winged, web-footed sea-birds
gullet n. (*gul'et*) Passage from mouth to stomach
gully n. (*gul'i*) Channel worn by water; artificial channel for water, gutter
gulp v.t. and i. and n. (*gulp*) To swallow noisily and quickly
gum 1) n. (*gum*) Thick tissue masses in the jaws, in which the teeth are set
gum 2) n. (*gum*) One of various sticky plant products which swell or dissolve in water; preparation of such substance for use as adhesive
gun n. (*gun*) Any firearm that sends missiles from a metal tube
gurgle v.i. and n. (*gurgl*) To make a bubbling sound, as of water flowing over stones
gush v.i. and n. (*gush*) To flood out suddenly
gust n. (*gust*) Sudden brief blast of wind
gutter n. (*gut'er*) Channel round eaves of a building or along side of a road, for carrying away surface waters
gymkhana n. (*jim kah'na*) Public display of riding or athletics
gymnasium n. (*jim nā'zi um*) Hall equipped for performing gymnastics
gymnast n. (*jim'năst*) Expert in gymnastics. (As above)
gymnastic adj. and n. (*jim năs'tik*) Of gymnastics, bodily training. As n., (usually pl.) art and practice of promoting a healthy body through physical exercises

H

habit n. (*hăb'it*) Settled tendency or practice
habitat n. (*hăb'i tăt*) Natural environment of plant or animal
hack v.t. and i. (*hăk*) To chop, cut, as with axe; gash, cut clumsily
haddock n. (*hăd'ok*) An edible sea-fish allied to cod
haemorrhage, hemorrhage n. (*hem'er ij*) (med.) Bleeding
haggard adj. and n. (*hăg'erd*) Drawn, gaunt with weariness (of face)
hail 1) n. and v.i. and t. (*hāl*) Frozen rain; a shower of this v.i. (impersonal) to shower down hail, *it is hailing*
hail 2) inter. (*hāl*) Expression of greeting
hail 3) v.t. and i. and n. (*hāl*) To greet, salute **to hail from** come from (point of origin, home etc.)
half n., adj. and adv. (*hahf*) pl. of n. **halves** (*hahvz*) One of two equal parts into which a thing may be divided
halibut n. (*hăl'i but*) An edible fish, largest of the flatfishes
hall n. (*hawl*) corridor, into which an entrance opens, *front hall*; mansion, large country house; large public building for administration etc., *Town Hall*; large room etc. for social functions, assembly etc., *village hall*
hallucination n. (*ha lū si nā'shun*)

Perception of something not really there, illusion
halo n. (*hā'lō*) Ring of light round sun or moon symbolizing this round head of saint etc
halt n and v.i. and t. (*hawlt*) Temporary stoppage (of work, movement etc.) to make a halt, stop (marching etc.). As v.t. to call (troops etc.) to a halt
halve v.t. (*hahv*) To divide into halves; reduce by half; share equally *with* another
ham n. (*hăm*) Inner part or back of thigh; pig's thigh salted and smoked; portion of this to eat
hamlet n. (*hăm'let*) Small village
hammer 1) n. (*hăm'er*) Metal-headed tool for striking, beating driving in with repeated blows
hammer 2) v.t. and i. (*hăm'er*) To strike, beat, drive in, with or as with a hammer
hammock n. (*hăm'ok*) Hanging bed of net or canvas slung on cords from beams, trees etc
hamper 1) n. (*hăm'per*) Large lidded basket esp. for food
hamper 2) v.t. and n. (*hăm'per*) To impede, obstruct (materially and otherwise)
hamster n. (*hăm'ster*) Large rat-like rodent with two cheek-pouches for hoarding grain
hand 1) n. (*hănd*) End part of human arm, below wrist, comprising palm and fingers; corresponding part of animal, esp. monkey handwriting, signature, *he writes a fine hand, as witness the hand of . . .*; moving indicator on dial of clock or watch; total of cards dealt to one player
hand 2) v.t. (*hănd*) To pass, transfer, something with the hand
handicap n. and v.t. (*hăn'di kăp*) Disadvantage imposed on competitor (horse, athlete etc.); race in which handicaps are imposed. As v.t. to impose a handicap on. Hence: **handicapped** adj. also fig., physically disabled, mentally retarded
handle 1) n. (*hăndl*) Part of tool, utensil, made to hold it by
handle 2) v.t. (*hăndl*) To touch, feel, move, wield, with the hands; to control, manage, with the hands (also fig., control in any sense); (comm.) to deal in (a commodity)
handsome adj. (*hăn'sum*) Good-looking, fine in form etc. (of persons or things)
hang v.t. and i. (*hăng*) pret. and p.p. **hung** (*hung*) or **hanged** (*hangd*) (see below) To fasten thing to, suspend it from, a point situated above it, *hang a hat on a peg, a picture on a hook* to execute by hanging by the neck (pret. and p.p. **hanged)**
hangar n. (*hăng'er*) Large shed for housing aircraft. (Fr., 'shed')
hanger n. (*hăng'er*) thing from which object is hung, *clothes-hanger*
happen v.i. (*hăp'en*) To come to pass, befall, take place (of events)
happy adj. (*hăp'i*) Joyful, contented, cheerful (of persons)
harass v.t. (*hă'ras*) To vex, trouble, by repeated attacks
harbour n and v.t and i. (*hah'ber*) Natural or artificial shelter for ships, port, haven; shelter, refuge. As v.t. to give shelter to
hard adj., adv. and n. (*hahd*) Firm to touch, unyielding, requiring vigour, *hard work* difficult to imagine, understand, solve etc., *a hard problem, question*
harden v.t. and i. (*hah'den*) To make or become hard
hardship n. (*hahd'ship*) Hard conditions of living,
hardware n. (*hahd'wār*) Ironmongery, pots and pans etc
hardy adj. (*hah'di*) Tough, capable of endurance; bold
harm n. and v.t. (*hahm*) Injury, damage. As v.t. to do injury to
harmonica n. (*hah mon'i ka*) Musical instrument,
harmonious adj. (*hah mō'ni us*) Producing harmony,
harmony n. (*hah'mon i*) Just proportion between parts, producing an agreeable whole
harness n. and v.t. (*hah'nes*) Driving or dragging gear for horse
harp n. and v.i. (*hahp*) Musical instrument consisting of strings stretched in triangular frame, these being plucked with the fingers
harpoon n. and v.t. (*hah pōōn'*) Barbed spear with rope attached, used to catch whales; smaller version used by underwater fishermen
harsh adj. (*hahsh*) Rough, coarse to touch, hear, taste or see, severe, *harsh punishment*
harvest n. and v.t. and i. (*hah'vist*) The gathering in of crops (esp. grain); season when this is done As v.t. to gather in a crop; to store it. As v.i. to gather crops
harvester n. (*hah'vis ter*) Person working to gather crop; machine

for cutting and binding crop
hatch 1) n. (*hăch*) Movable covering over opening
hatch 2) v.t. and i. and n. (*hăch*) To produce young from eggs, to plan and develop secretly, *to hatch a plot*. As v.i. (of birds, fish etc.) to emerge from the egg
hatchet n. (*hăch'it*) Light axe
hate n. and v.t. (*hāt*) Intense loathing
haughty adj. (*haw'ti*) Insolently proud, arrogant
haul v.t. and i. and n. (*hawl*) To pull, drag (*along, up* etc.) with effort As n act of hauling; distance thing is hauled, *a long haul*; a catch of fish; (fig.) booty, amount acquired, *a good haul*
haunt v.t. and i. and n. (*hawnt*) To visit (place or person) frequently or too frequently; also of thoughts, *fear haunts him*; often of ghosts, spirits, to appear in (house etc.) or to (person). As n. a place often visited, a resort, *one of my old haunts*
have v.t. and auxil. (*hăv*) pret. and p.p. **had** (*hăd*) To possess, own, *I have a car*; to possess the services, affection, enjoyment of, *I have two servants, I have a wife*; to possess as an accessory, feature, quality, *my house has six rooms, I have a long nose and a woolly mind*; to retain, entertain, in the mind, *I have an idea*; to experience, *to have fun, to have a headache*; to take, consume, *to have lunch*; expressing obligation, *I have to go*; to cause (in the construction *to have something done*) As auxil, used with p.p. of verb to form perfect tenses (*I have done, had done, shall have done*)
haversack n. (*hăv'er săk*) Soldier's, traveller's, canvas bag for provisions etc., carried slung on back or at side
havoc n. (*hăv'ok*) Devastation, destruction, chaos
hay n. and v.t. and i. (*hā*) Cut grass dried for fodder
hazard n. and v.t. (*hăz'erd*) Chance, risk; (a) danger
haze n. and v.t. and i. (*hāz*) Faint obscurity of the atmosphere, as on very hot day
head 1) n. (*hed*) Part of body of man or animal that contains the brain, mouth, and sense organs; thing resembling this, *head of a pin* topmost or foremost part of, *head of a flower, of a ladder, at the head of his troops*; an individual, esp. member of a group, *a shilling a head* (also of cattle, *twenty head of cattle*); side of coin bearing ruler's head (often pl., *heads or tails*); chief position, *at the head of the government, of the table*, intelligence, aptitude, *a head for business*
head 2) v.t. and i. (*hed*) To lead, be at the head of,
health n. (*helth*) Soundness of body or mind, freedom from disease, injury etc
heap n. and v.t. (*hēp*) An accumulation of things one upon the other, a pile
hear v.t. and i. (*hēr*) pret. and p.p. **heard** (*hurd*) To perceive sound with the ear; be able to do this, not be deaf, *I can't hear a word*; to listen to, attend to, *to hear a concert*; to learn, be told, *to hear a rumour, the truth*
hearing n. (*hēr'ing*) Faculty of perceiving sound with the ear
hearse n. (*hurse*) Vehicle for carrying corpse to burial
heart n. (*haht*) Organ of body that pumps blood through circulation; (fig.) this considered as seat of the emotions etc., *his heart is broken*; courage, ardour, *to take heart, in good heart*; the centre, core of anything thing like heart in shape, esp. conventional figure representing this, as on playing cards
hearth n. (*hahth*) Floor of fireplace, furnace etc
heat 1) n. (*hēt*) warmth, high temperature, the reverse of *cold*, or the perception of this
heat 2) v.t. and i. (*hēt*) To make (v.i. become) hot
Hence: **heater** n. apparatus for heating house, car etc
heath n. (*hēth*) Stretch of open, uncultivated land
heave v.t. and i. and n. (*hēv*) in naut. senses only, pret. and p.p. **hove** (*hōv*) To lift, swing, a heavy thing (axe, sack etc.); to drag, shift, throw, with effort
heavy adj. and adv. (*hev'i*) Having great weight
hectare n. (*hek'tār*) Metrical measure of 100 ares (2·471 acres)
hedge n. (*hej*) Fence of closely planted bushes or small trees
hedgehog n. (*hej'hog*) A British insect-eating mammal with body covered with sharp defensive quills
heed v.t. and i. and n. (*hēd*) To pay attention, notice, have care of

heel 1) n. (*hēl*) Back part of foot below ankle
heel 2) v.t. and i. (*hēl*) To put heel on (shoe)
heel 3) v.i. and t. and n. (*hēl*) To tilt, lean to one side, list, esp. of ship
heifer n. (*hef'er*) Young cow not yet having calved
height n. (*hīt*) Measurement from base to top (of tree, building etc.); distance above ground, sea-level etc. (of aircraft, mountain-peak etc.); high place, mountain-top
heir n. (*ār*) Person succeeding or entitled to succeed to another's property, either by right of blood (*heir-at-law, legal heir*) or by will
heiress n. female heir
heirloom n. (*ār'lōōm*) something that has been in the family for generations
helicopter n. (*hel'i kop ter*) Aircraft rising vertically and sustained by means of screw revolving on vertical axis above it
hell n. (*hel*) Abode of the dead,
helm n. (*helm*) Tiller, wheel, or whole steering gear of ship
helmsman steersman of ship
helmet n. (*helmet*) Protective armour for head
help v.t. and i. and n. (*help*) To aid, assist
hem n. and v.t. (*hem*) Edge of cloth turned back and sewn down
hen n. (*hen*) Female of domestic fowl; female of any bird
herald n. and v.t. (*he'rald*) Official who makes public announcements etc. (loosely) person announcing anything, bringing news etc.; a forerunner (lit. and fig.), *the crocus, herald of spring.* As v.t. to announce
herd 1) n. (*hurd*) Group of large animals feeding and moving together (of cattle, deer etc.)
here adv. and n. (*hēr*) In this place, *I sit here and write*
herd 2) v.t. and i. (*hurd*) To gather into a herd
hermit n. (*hur'mit*) Person living in seclusion, devoted to meditation and prayer
hero n. (*hēr'ō*) pl. **heroes** great warrior, outstandingly brave man (Nelson etc.); chief male character in story, novel etc
herring n. (*he'ring*) A much-eaten marine fish
hesitate v.i. (*hez'i tāt*) To be indecisive, falter, in speech or action
hibernate v.i. (*hī'ber nāt*) To pass the winter in sleep
hide v.t. and i. and n. (*hīd*) pret. **hid**, p.p. **hidden**. To conceal, put or keep out of sight
hideout n. (*hīd'owt*) Safe hiding-place
hieroglyph n. (*hir'o glif*) A character in ancient Egyptian picture writing, hence in any such writing
high adj., adv., and n. (*hī*) Lofty, elevated, extending upwards to a great (or specified) extent, *a high mountain; six inches high*; (of persons etc.) exalted, of important status, *high office*; chief, main, *high altar* (of sounds) acute in pitch, *a high note*
(of food) beginning to decay
hike v.i. and n. (*hīk*) To tramp, go on country walk. As n. such an excursion; **hitch-hike** travel by getting lifts in cars
hill n. and v.t. (*hil*) A natural elevation of earth's surface, smaller than a mountain; an artificial mound, *ant-hill, mole-hill*
hilt n. and v.t. (*hilt*) Handle of sword or dagger
hind 1) n. (*hīnd*) Female of (esp. red) deer

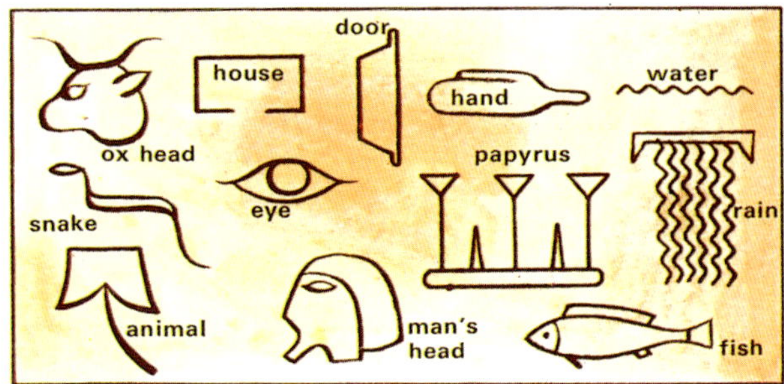

hieroglyphs – Egyptian

hind 2) adj. (*hind*) Rear
hinder v.t. (*hin'der*) To prevent
hindmost adj. (*hind'most*) Furthest behind
hindrance n (*hin'drans*) Act of hindering; an obstacle
hindsight n. (*hind'sit*) Wisdom after the event
hinge n. and v.t. and i. (*hinj*) Joint, usually of metal, on which door, window etc. hangs and swings
v.t. to fasten or connect with hinge. As v.i. to swing on a hinge; (fig.) to turn, depend, on, *the whole plot hinged on one tiny clue*
hint n. and v.t. and i. (*hint*) A slight indication, suggestion
hip n. (*hip*) Projection made by side of pelvis and upper end of thigh-bone
hippopotamus n. (*hip o pot'a mus*) pl. **-muses, -mi** (*-mi*) Large African mammal related to pig and given to wallowing in water etc
hire n. and v.t. (*hir*) Payment for temporary use of thing or services of person As v.t. to obtain such use or services; to lend (*out*) the same
historian n. (*his taw'ri an*) Writer of, one learned in, history
historic adj. (*his to'rik*) Of history, *historic times*; (now esp.) important in history, *an historic event, moment*
history n. (*his'ter i*) the whole course of past events, the sum of human affairs
hit 1) v.t. and i. (*hit*) To strike, knock, a thing aimed at, (target, nail on the head etc.)
hit 2) n. (*hit*) A blow, stroke, esp. when it hits its mark
hive n. and v.t. and i. (*hiv*) Special box-like house for bees
hoard n. and v.t. (*hawd*) Secret store, As v.t. to amass store up (esp. food).
hoarding n. (*haw'ding*) Tall fence of boards screening off building site etc., such a fence for displaying posters
hoax v.t. and n. (*hōks*) To deceive, trick, play practical joke on
hobby n. (*hob'i*) Favourite occupation of one's leisure time
hoe n. and v.t. and i. (*hō*) Tool for weeding and loosening earth
hoist v.t. and n. (*hoist*) To raise, pull up, esp. by means of tackle, a crane etc., *to hoist a flag, hoist a load aboard*
hold 1) v.t. and i. (*hōld*) pret. and p.p. **held** (*held*) To have and retain, esp. in the hand; embrace, *hold me tight*; to keep (oneself or part of body) in a certain posture, *he held himself like a soldier*; to support, bear the weight of; to possess, own (shares in company, title to land etc.); (milit.) keep possession of (place), defend successfully, *Horatio held the bridge*; to contain, *the jar holds a pint*; have (ideas) in mind, retain in memory; consider, have an opinion of, *I hold him to be a liar, he holds life cheap*; control, restrain, keep in certain position, *held prisoner, held at bay*; make person keep *to* promise etc.; attract (attention), engross (person, thoughts), *the sermon held me spell-bound*; organize, take part in (meeting etc.). As v.i. to withstand strain, *what a crowd! I hope the floor holds*; remain valid, *my word still holds* (also *holds good*); (esp. of weather) to last, *a picnic tomorrow if the weather holds*
hold 2) n. (*hōld*) Grasp, grip,
hold 3) n. (*hōld*) Storage space below ship's deck
holder n. (*hōl'der*) Person or thing that holds
holiday n. (*hol'i dā*) day of not working, day off, *Bank holiday*; period of rest from work or school (usually pl.), *the summer holidays*
hollow 1) adj., n., and adv. (*hol'ō*) Having a cavity, not solid, *hollow tree, tooth*
hollow 2) v.t. (*hol'ō*) To make hollow, scoop *out* the inside of
holocaust n. (*hol'ō kawst*) Sacrifice entirely consumed by fire; (fig.) massacre, wholesale slaughter
holster n. (*hōl'ster*) Leather pistol-holder on belt
holy adj. and n. (*hō'li*) Sacred, of or dedicated to God or gods
home n., adj., and adv. (*hōm*) Place (house, town, country) where one lives or feels one belongs, *no place like home, to feel at home*; natural habitat, *the home of the condor is in the Andes*; institution for the aged, infirm, orphaned etc. or insane, *a rest home*; (in certain games) base, goal. As adj. of one's home or native place; coming from, produced at, home, *home cooking*, (of a country) internal, *home*

affairs as opposed to *foreign*. As adv. towards home, *to go home*
honest adj. (*on'ist*) Trustworthy, upright in character, not given esp. to lying and stealing
honey n. and adj. (*hun'i*) The sweet, yellow, sticky stuff that bees make from nectar of flowers
honeymoon n. and v.i. (*hun'i mōōn*) Holiday for newly-married couple
honour 1) n. (*on'er*) A complex virtue compounded of truthfulness, purity, courage, loyalty and integrity
honour 2) v.t. (*on'er*) To feel, show, high respect to
honourable adj. (*on'er abl*) Worthy to be honoured (of person, conduct)
hook 1) n. (*hōōk*) Piece of metal etc. bent in form of letter J, for hanging things on, fastening etc.
hook 2) v.t. and i. (*hōōk*) To seize, hold, with a hook
hooligan n. (*hōō'li gan*) Rough rowdy, street-lad, member of gang of roughs etc. Hence: **hooliganism** n
hoop n. and v.t. (*hōōp*) Ring of metal, wood etc
hoot v.i. and t. and n. (*hōōt*) To make a sound like *hoot*, as cry of derision; (of owl) to utter cry; to sound a motor horn, fog-horn, siren on ship etc
hop v.i. and t. and n. (*hop*) To jump, make series of jumps, on one foot only
hope n. and v.i. (*hōp*) State of mind combining desire with expectation, in which one believes one's desires will be realized
hopeful adj. and n. (*hōp'ful*) Full of hope
hopeless adj. (*hōp'les*) Feeling no hope, despairing; giving no reason for hope, *a hopeless cause*
horizon n. (*ho ri'zon*) Line at which earth and sky seem to meet
horizontal adj. and n. (*ho ri zon'tal*) Parallel to the horizon, flat, level (opposed to *vertical*)
horn n. (*hawn*) Hard projection, usually curved and pointed, on the heads of cattle and other animals; the hard substance of which this is made musical wind instrument once made of horn, now of metal, *hunting-horn, French-horn*
horoscope n. (*ho'ro skōp*) Calculation of position of stars and planets at a certain moment, esp. at person's birth with a view to predicting his future
horrible adj. (*ho'ribl*) Causing or liable to cause horror; dreadful, shocking
horrid adj. (*ho'rid*) Liable to provoke horror, frightful, very disgusting
horrify v.t. (*ho'ri fi*) To fill with horror
horror n. (*ho'rer*) Powerful feeling of disgust and fear, such as to cause shuddering; thing that provokes this, *the horrors of war*
horse n. (*haws*) Large hoofed quadruped used for riding and as beast of burden frame for hanging clothes on etc., *clothes-horse;* apparatus for gymnastic exercises, vaulting over etc
horticulture n. (*haw'ti kul cher*) Art of gardening
hose n. (*hōz*) Long tube of rubber etc. for conveying water for fire-fighting, watering plants etc
hosier n. (*hō'zher*) Dealer in socks and knitted goods. Hence: **hosiery** n. his goods or trade
hospital n. (*hos'pit al*) Building where patients are treated for and nursed through physical or mental illness
hospitality n. (*hos pi tăl'i ti*) Generous entertainment of guests
host 1) n. (*hōst*) Army, vast force (archaic); crowd, large number (often pl.), *hosts of friends*
host 2) n. (*hōst*) Person who receives guests; innkeeper
hostage n. (*hos'tij*) Person handed over (esp. to enemy after hostilities) as pledge of good faith; (fig.) a security
hostel n. (*hos'tel*) Hall, boarding-house, for students, nurses, or other particular group, esp. (as **Youth Hostel**) run on non-commercial basis
hostess n. (*hōs'tes*) Woman host;
hostile adj. (*hos'til*) Of an enemy, *a hostile army*; unfriendly
hotel n. ((*h*)*ō tel'*) Large inn, establishment letting rooms by the night
hound 1) n. (*hownd*) Dog, esp. for hunting
hound 2) v.t. (*hownd*) To pursue, hunt; pursue (person) mercilessly
hour n. (*owr*) A twenty-fourth part of the day, 60 minutes
house n. (*hows*) pl. **houses** (*how'ziz*) Building designed for human dwelling theatre audience
hover v.i. and n. (*hov'er*) To hang in the air without forward motion
hovercraft n. (*hov'er krahft*) Vessel designed to travel on cushion of air just above surface of water etc
howl v.i. and t. and n. (*howl*) To utter long-drawn-out cry
huddle v.t. and i. and n. (*hudl*)

As v.i. to gather *together* for warmth
hue 1) n. (*hū*) Shade or tint of a colour
hug v.t. and n. (*hug*) To squeeze (person etc.) tightly in one's arms
huge adj. (*hūj*) Enormous, great
hull 1) n. and v.t. (*hul*) Seed-pod, shell (of vegetable, fruit etc.); covering. As v.t. to remove hull of, to pod
hull 2) n. and v.t. (*hul*) Body of ship
hum v.i. and t. and n. (*hum*) To make a prolonged voiced nasal sound, keeping the lips shut; to make the buzzing sound of a bee, machine etc.; (fig.) be very active (of business etc.), *to make things hum* As v.t. sing (tune) with closed lips. As n. the sound produced by humming
human adj. and n. (*hū'man*) Of, belonging to, mankind, *human nature*; consisting of men (women and children)
humble adj. and v.t. (*humbl*) Meek, modest, unassuming
humid adj. (*hū'mid*) Damp, moist (often, of atmosphere)
humour 1) n. (*hū'mer, ū'mer*) State of mind, mood, *in a good humour*; fun, joking, comicality, comic imagination, *a book full of humour*; ability to enjoy this
humour 2) v.t. (*hū'mer*) To indulge the whims of (difficult person); to make happier by indulgence or tact
hump n. and v.t. (*hump*) Lump
hunch n. and v.t. (*hunch*) Hump on the back (thus, **hunchback** n.; **hunchbacked** adj.)
(U.S. slang) a notion, an intuition, *I've a hunch that he won't come*
hunger n. and v.i. (*hung'ger*) The pain, discomfort, weakness etc. caused by lack of food; a craving for food; any strong desire, *hunger for knowledge*. **hunger-strike** refusal to eat as method of protest
hungry adj. (*hung'gri*) Lacking food, starving
hunt v.t. and i. (*hunt*) To pursue (animals) for sport or food to search *for, we hunted high and low for it*
huntsman n. (*hunts'man*) Person who hunts; man in charge of pack of hounds
hurdle n. and v.t. and i. (*hurdl*) Light oblong wooden framework used to make temporary fence, sheep pen etc. light frame (usually metal) with wooden crossbar as obstacle in race
hurl v.t. and i. and n. (*hurl*) To throw with great force
hurricane n. (*hu'ri kan*) Tropical cyclonic storm with very violent winds
hurry 1) n. (*hu'ri*) Bustle, undue haste
hurry 2) v.t. and i. (*hu'ri*) to do with undue haste, *don't hurry the job*. As v.i. to move, act, in haste or more haste, *if you don't hurry we'll be late*
hurt 1) v.t. and i. (*hurt*) pret. and p.p. **hurt** To cause pain or injury to
hurt 2) n. (*hurt*) Pain, damage, injury
husband 1) n. (*huz'band*) Man married to a (specific) woman
husband 2) v.t. (*huz'band*) To manage with economy, *to husband one's resources*; (archaic) to cultivate (ground, crops). Hence: **husbandman** n. farmer; **husbandry** n. good management; farming
hush v.t. and i. and n. (*hush*) To make (v.i. to become) silent or calm
husk n. and v.t. (*husk*) Dry outer covering of some seeds and fruits
husky 1) adj. (*hus'ki*) (of voice) rough hoarse; (of persons) rough and tough
husky 2) n. (*hus'ki*) Eskimo dog.
hustle v.t. and i. and n. (*husl*) To jostle, shove
hut n. and v.t. and i. (*hut*) Small building, cabin, shelter
hutch n. and v.t. (*huch*) Cage, esp. wooden with wire netting in front, for rabbits
hydrant n. (*hi'drant*) Pipe (esp. in street) from water-main to which a hose can be attached
hydraulic adj. and n. (*hi draw'lik*) Pertaining to water flowing through a pipe etc.; operated by water or other liquid, *hydraulic brake, lift*
hydrogen n. (*hi'dro gen*) A highly inflammable gas, the chemical element H
hygiene n. (*hi'jēn*) The principles of private and public health
hymn n. and v.t. and i. (*him*) Solemn song of praise to God or gods
hyphen n. and v.t. (*hi'fen*) Short dash (-) connecting words or syllables of broken words
hypnosis n. (*hip nō'sis*) Artificially induced state like sleep
hypnotism n. (*hip'no tizm*) Artificially induced sleep in which person remains open to external influence and suggestion; the practice of inducing this
Hence: **hypnotist** n.; **hypnotize**
hypocrisy n. (*hi pok'ra si*) Pretence
hypocrite n. (*hip'o krit*) Person who practises hypocrisy
hypodermic adj. and n. (*hi po dur'*

mik) Beneath the skin; of, applied to, part of body under the skin, *hypodermic syringe, injection.* As n. drug injected under skin; such an injection; syringe for this

I

ice n. (*is*) Frozen water; kind of sweet made from frozen water, cream, etc., ice cream
idea n. (*i dē'a*) plan, scheme, purpose
ideal adj. (*i dē'al*) Satisfying or typifying one's idea of what is perfect, *an ideal holiday*
identical adj. (*iden'tikal*) The same; alike in every way
idiot n. (*i'di ot*) Person in severest grade of feeble-mindedness from birth
idle 1) adj. (*idl*) Doing no work
idle 2) v.i. and t. (*idl*) To remain idle, waste time, *idle about* (of an engine) to run slowly
idol n. (*i'dol*) Image of a god, worshipped as such; a false god; person or thing extravagantly admired or adored, *a popular idol*
if conj. (*if*) Supposing that, provided that, *I shall go if I am ready in time*; even though, although, *she will buy it, if it leaves her penniless*; whether, *she asked if you were at home*
igloo n. (*ig'lōō*) Dome-shaped hut made of blocks of snow
ignite v.t. and i. (*ig nit'*) To set on fire; take fire
ignorance n. (*ig'nor ans*) Lack of knowledge, experience, or education Hence: **ignorant** adj. (*ig'norant*)
ignore v.t. (*ig naw(r)'*) Take no notice of, disregard
ill 1) adj. (*il*) Sick, ailing, *ill health*
ill 2) adv. (*il*) Sick, ailing, *to feel ill*; badly, not well, *to behave ill*
illegal adj. (*i lēg'al*) Unlawful.
illegible adj. (*i lej'ibl*) Difficult or impossible to read
illiterate adj. and n. (*i lit'er at*) unable to read or write
illness n. (*il'nes*) State of being ill; specific form or occasion of disease or sickness, *a serious illness*
illuminate v.t. (*i lūm'i nāt*) To give light to,Hence: **illumination** n. (*i lūm i nā'shun*) illuminating or being illuminated; (usually pl.) display of bright lights etc. for festive occasion; decorations in a manuscript
illusion n. (*i lū'zhun*) A false interpretation of something perceived through the senses
illustrate v.t. (*il'us trāt*) To make clear by examples etc.; provide with pictures and drawings, *a well-illustrated book.* Hence: **illustration** n. (*il us trā'shun*) example; picture in a book etc
imaginary adj. (*i mǎj'i na ri*) Unreal, existing only in imagination
imagination n. (*i mǎj i nā'shun*) Faculty of forming images in the mind
imaginative adj. (*i mǎj'i na tiv*) Of, possessing, showing, using imagination, *imaginative writers*
imitate v.t. (*im'i tāt*) To copy the behaviour of; follow the example of
immediate adj. (*i mēd'i at*) With nothing coming between; instant, following directly Hence: **immediately** adv. at once, without delay
immense adj. (*imens'*) Very large, vast
immigrate v.i. (*im'i grāt*) To enter a foreign country as a settler and not a visitor. Hence: **immigrant** n. one who immigrates; **immigration** n. (*i mi grā'shun*) immigrating; instance of this
immortal adj. and n. (*i mor'tal*) Living for ever
impact n. and v.t. (*im'pǎkt*) Collision, striking against
impassable adj. (*im pah'sabl*) Impossible to pass over, *an impassable road*
impatience n. (*im pa'shens*) Inability to endure delay, restraint, etc.; intolerance. Hence: **impatient** adj
imperfect adj. and n. (*im per'fekt*) Not perfect, defective
imperial adj. and n. (*im pēr'i al*) Of an empire or emperor
imperialism n. (*im pēr'i al izm*) Belief in the value of dependencies and dominions to a state; policy of increasing these whenever possible.
impersonate v.t. (*im per'son āt*) To pretend to be someone else
impertinent adj. (*im per'tin ent*) impudent.
implement v.t. (*im'pli ment*) To accomplish, put into effect; to fulfil contract, promise etc
import 1) v.t. (*im pawt'*) To bring in, esp. (goods) into a country from abroad
import 2) n. (*im'pawt*) That which is imported(pl.) goods imported into a country
impossible adj. (*im pos'ibl*) Not possible
impress v.t. (*im pres'*) To mark by use of pressure, imprint; to fix firmly in the mind, *he impressed on us the need for speed*; to affect strongly

evoke a vivid impression, *his work impressed me enormously*
imprison v.t. (*im priz'on*) To confine in a prison, be shut up
improve v.t. and i. (*im prōōv'*) To make better, increase the value of; to become better
in prep. (*in*) Inside of, within, *in the house*; held by, partly enclosed or surrounded by, *a flower in a pot*; used to express place, *in the country*; physical surroundings, *in the rain*; state or condition, *in good health*; action, *engaged in digging*; relation to time during, *in the spring*; within the space of, at the end of, *I shall return in a week*; direction or motion of activity, *dip a pen in ink*; dress etc., *in uniform*; expressing inclusion, *seven days in a week*; ratio, *gradient of one in five*; degree or extent, *in small amounts*; limitation to a particular part, amount, quality, capacity etc. *they vary in colour (strength etc.)*; indicating occupation, membership of, *in the Army*; method of expression, *written in pencil*; method of arrangement, *in groups*; having regard to, *in that case*; by way of, *speak in reply*
inaccessible adj. (*in ăk ses'ibl*) Out-of-the-way, hard to approach
incense 1) n. (*in'sens*) Fragrant smoke from burning aromatic herbs, spices etc
incense 2) v.t. (*in sens'*) To enrage, make furious. Hence: **incensed** adj.
inch n. (*inch*) One-twelfth of a foot; small amount, distance
incident n. (*in'si dent*) Something that happens, an event
incinerate v.t. (*in sin'er āt*) To burn to ashes
incline 1) v.t. and i. (*in klīn'*) To cause to slope, slant
be or feel inclined to tend in feeling, thought etc., *be inclined to think*; be disposed to, *be inclined to eat too much*
incline 2) n. (*in'klīn*) Slope, slant,
include v.t. (*in klōōd'*) To comprise, contain as a part of the whole
inclusive adj. (*in klōō'siv*) Including
income n. (*in'kum*) Money periodically received as salary, rent, profit etc
increase 1) v.t. and i. (*in krēs'*) To make greater, extend. As v.i., to grow larger, greater, more numerous, *the population*
increase 2) n. (*in'krēs*) Growth, enlargement
indeed 1) adv. (*in dēd'*) In reality, in truth; giving emphasis, *very warm indeed*
independent adj. (*in di pen'dent*) Not dependent on or controlled by another, not having to rely on others
index n. (*in'deks*) (pl. **indices** (*in'di sēz*) That which indicates, points out, esp. a pointer on an instrument for indicating measurement etc.; alphabetical list of words, topics etc. in a book; (fig.) an indication, guide; the forefinger
indicate v.t. (*in'di kāt*) To point to, point out, make known
indicator n. (*in'di kā tor*) What or who indicates: esp. pointer on an instrument denoting measurement of some kind; mechanical device used on motor vehicle to indicate direction in which the vehicle is about to turn
individual n. (*in di vid'ū al*) Single member of a class or group of persons, animals, things etc
indoors adv. (*in dawz'*) Inside a building; in a building, in the house
industry n. (*in'dus tri*) specific branch of trade or manufacture, *the agricultural, shipping industry*
infant n. and adj. (*in'fant*) Young child
infantry n. (*in'fan tri*) Foot-soldiers
infect v.t. (*in fekt'*) To convey living, disease-bearing micro-organisms into
infinite adj. (*in'fin it*) Boundless, unlimited
infirm adj. (*in ferm'*) Physically weak, feeble, esp. through old age
infirmary n. (*in fer'ma ri*) Old-fashioned name for hospital
inflame v.t. and i. (*in flām'*) To render hot, red, angry, *an inflamed eye*; (fig.) rouse passion, anger, etc
inflammable adj. (*in flăm'abl*) Flammable, easily set on fire
inflammation n. (*in fla mā'shun*) Act or process of inflaming; hot and swollen condition of living tissue, due to injury or infection
inflate v.t. and i. (*inflāt'*) To cause to swell, distend with air or gas; (econ.) to cause a rise in prices Hence: **inflation** n. (*in flā'shun*) inflating or being inflated; rise in prices caused by decrease in value of money
inflict v.t. (*in flikt'*) To strike, cause to undergo, *inflict pain*; impose, *inflict a penalty*
influence 1) n. (*in'flōō ens*) Effect produced, esp. on the mind or body by any external power of producing such an effect
influence 2) v.t. (*in'flōō ens*) To

exert influence upon, persuade by one's influence
inform v.t. and i. (*in fawm'*) part knowledge to, *inform someone of something*
information n. (*in faw mā'shun*) Informing or being informed; something told
informer n. (*in faw'mer*) One who informs, esp. one who brings accusations against another
ingot n. (*ing'got*) Bar or lump of metal, esp. gold or silver
ingredient n. (*in grē'di ent*) A component part, what goes to make up a compound or mixture
inhabit v.t. (*in hăb'it*) To dwell in, live in; occupy
initial 1) adj. (*in ish'al*) Of, at, the beginning, *initial stages*
initial 2) n. (*in ish'al*) Initial letter, esp. (pl.) first letters of a person's names
initial 3) v.t. (*in ish'al*) To mark, sign with one's initials. (As above)
initiate v.t. (*in ish'i āt*) To begin
inject v.t. (*in jekt'*) To drive in (fluid etc.) by pressure; to fill by injection. Hence: **injection** n. (*in jek'shun*) injecting; instance of this; liquid etc. that is injected
injure v.t. (*in'jer*) To harm, offend, damage, Hence: **injured** adj. wronged; hurt
ink n. (*ingk*) Black or coloured fluid used in writing
inlet n. (*in'let*) Recess, creek etc. in a coast-line; way in; something let in, inserted
inn n. (*in*) House providing food, drink and accommodation for travellers
inner adj. (*in'er*) Inside, interior
innings n. (*in'ingz*) (cricket) The turn of a particular player or side to bat
innocent 1) adj. (*in'ō sent*) Blameless, not guilty; harmless
inoculate v.t. (*in ok'ū lāt*) (med.) To inject into a person vaccine containing infected material or bacteria to secure protection from a particular disease. Hence: **inoculation** n. (*in ok ū lā'shun*) inoculating or being inoculated; instance of this
inquisitive adj. (*in kwi'zi tiv*) Curious
insane adj. (*in sān'*) Mentally disordered
insect n. (*in'sekt*) (popularly) any small creeping or flying animal. Hence: **insecticide** n. (*in sek'ti sīd*) substance for killing insects
insert v.t. (*in sūrt'*) To put, place into something else
insist v.i. and t. (*in sist'*) (With on, upon) To persist in, urge with emphasis
insolent adj. (*in'so lent*) Haughtily contemptuous, insulting
insomnia n. (*in som'ni a*) Inability to sleep; sleeplessness
inspect v.t. (*in spekt'*) To examine carefully, esp. as an official inspector
inspector n. (*in spek'tor*) One who inspects
inspire v.t. (*in spīr'*) To draw air into the lungs; to fill with creative power
install v.t. (*in stawl'*) To establish, settle, *installed in a seat*; place, prepare for use, *install a washing-machine*. Hence: **installation** n. (*in sta lā'shun*) installing or being installed; something that is installed
instalment n. (*in stawl'ment*) Part of a whole supplied periodically until complete, esp. a publication or story appearing in parts, *another instalment next week*, sum of money paid as one of a series of payments
instance n. (*in'stans*) Single example, occurrence, illustrative fact
instant 1) adj. (*in'stant*) Immediate, without delay
instant 2) n. (*in'stant*) Precise point of time
instead adv. (*in sted'*) In place (of)
instep n. (*in'step*) Upper surface of human foot between toes and ankle
instruct v.t. (*in struckt'*) To teach, impart information or knowledge to
instrument n. (*in'strōō ment*) Thing by means of which something is done, esp. a tool, implement, used for scientific purposes, *surgical*
insulate v.t. (*in'sū lāt*) (phys. and elect.) cut off from heat, sound, or elect. by covering with a non-conducting substance
insult n. and v.t. (*in'sult*) Word or act tending to humiliate or offend another
intelligence n. (*in tel'i jens*) The relating activity of mind; mental ability, quickness of understanding; sagacity; information, news
intelligent adj. (*in tel'i jent*) Having, showing, intelligence
intelligible adj. (*in tel'i jibl*) Capable of being easily understood, clear in meaning
intercept v.t. (*in ter sept'*) To seize, stop, person or object between starting-point and destination
interest 1) n. (*in'ter est*) State of wanting to know and learn about something

interest 2) v.t. (*in'ter est*) To awaken interest in, engage the attention
interfere v.i. (*in ter fēr'*) (of persons) To intervene, esp. without right or invitation, meddle
interior adj. and n. (*in tēr'i or*) Placed, existing, on the inside, internal
internal adj. (*in tur'nal*) Of or in the inside
international adj. and n. (*in ter năsh'un al*) Of, affecting, carried on between, representing, different nations
interpret v.t. and i. (*in tur'pret*) To explain, show the meaning of **interpreter** n. one who translates orally from one language to another; **interpretation** n. (*in tur pre tā'shun*) explanation or meaning; translation
interrupt v.t. and i. (*in ter upt'*) To break in upon
interval n. (*in'ter val*) Intervening space; extent of separation or difference; intervening period between two fixed periods; pause between two acts of a play
intervene v.i. (*in ter vēn'*) To take place, occur, lie, between; prevent, *I shall come if nothing intervenes*; interfere, *he intervened in the dispute*
intimate 1) adj. (*in'tim at*) Inward, deep-seated, *one's intimate feelings*; closely associated, *intimate friends*; private, personal
Hence: **intimately** adv.; **intimacy** n. (*in tim'a si*) state of being intimate. (Lat. *intimus* innermost)
intimate 2) v.t. (*in'ti māt*) To make known, declare
intimidate v.t. (*in tim'i dāt*) To frighten, terrorize,
invade v.t. (*in vād'*) To enter a country with a hostile army
invalid 1) adj. and n. (*in'va lid*) Weak, disabled, by illness or injury; suitable for invalid persons, *invalid chair.* As n., sickly person
invalid 2) v.t. (*in'va lid*) To make into an invalid; **invalid out** remove from active service on account of ill health
invalid 3) adj. (*in văl'id*) Not valid
invasion n. (*in vā'zhun*) Invading or being invaded; instance of this
invent v.t. (*in vent'*) To originate; construct, use, or devise something for the first time
investigate v.t. (*in ves'ti gāt*) To examine, enquire into. Hence: **investigator** n. one who investigates; **investigation** n. (*in ves ti gā'shun*) act of investigating; enquiry
invite v.t. (*in vīt'*) To request some-one politely to do something, be present at a social gathering etc
invoke v.t. (*in vōk'*) To call upon, summon aid from, *invoke the law*; beg for solemnly; conjure up (spirits etc.)
iron 1) n. (*ī'un*) Metallic element, most widely used of all metals, symbol Fe
iron 2) adj. (*ī'un*) Made of iron; (fig.) like iron, firm
iron 3) v.t. (*ī'un*) To smoothe linen etc. with a heated iron; to fetter; **iron out** smoothe away
ironing-board board on which clothes are spread for ironing
irrigate v.t. (*i'ri gāt*) To supply land with water, esp. through artificial canal etc
irritate v.t. (*i'ri tāt*) To annoy, anger exasperate
island n. (*ī'land*) Piece of land entirely surrounded by water
isthmus n. (*isth'mus*) Neck of land linking two larger bodies of land
item n. and adv. (*ī'tem*) Particular article in list or account; piece of news
ivory n. (*ī'vor i*) Hard white substance forming tusks of elephant etc.; whitish colour; (pl., colloq.) things made of ivory, esp. piano-keys; (attrib.) made of ivory. (OFr. *ivurie* from Lat. *ebur*)
ivy n. (*ī'vi*) Evergreen climbing shrub

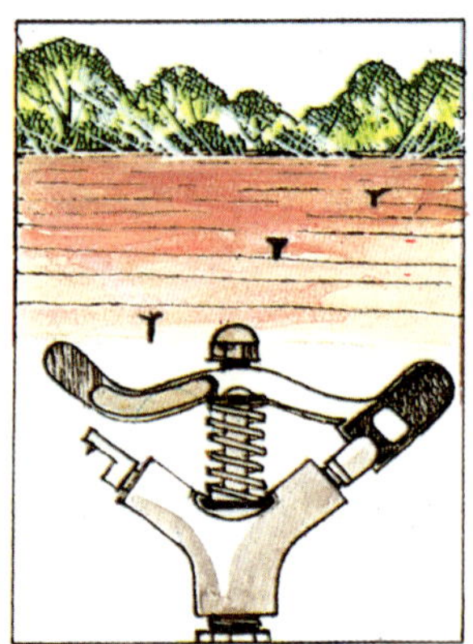

irrigation

isthmus

jaguar

J

jacket n. (*jăk'et*) Short, sleeved coat; any outer coat or covering
jaguar n. (*jag'ū ar*) Large carnivorous animal of the cat family
jam 1) v.t. and i. (*jăm*) To press, crowd, squeeze tightly into a constricted space
jam 2) n. (*jăm*) Number of persons or things wedged together so that movement is difficult, *a traffic jam*
jam 3) n. (*jăm*) Preserve of fruit boiled with sugar and poured into jars, pots etc. where it becomes firm
jangle v.t. and i and n. (*jăng'gl*) To make a discordant noise, esp. with bells
jar 1) n. (*jah(r)*) Harsh sound; shock, vibration caused by collision of two bodies
jar 2) n. (*jah(r)*) Deep vessel of glass, stone, or earthenware, usually cylindrical, without a spout
jaunt n. and v.i. (*jawnt*) Pleasure-trip, excursion
javelin n. (*jă've lin*) Light spear for throwing
jaw n. (*jaw*) One of the two bones forming the framework of the mouth
jealous adj. (*je'lus*) Envious, feeling ill-will because of the better fortune etc. of others
jeep n. (*jēp*) Small high-powered utility motor vehicle, originally military, useful on rough ground
jeer v.i. and n. (*jēr*) To mock, speak derisively
jelly n. and v.t. and i. (*je'li*) Soft wobbly semi-transparent substance
jerk n. and v.t. and i. (*jerk*) Sudden sharp movement; sudden, quick pull or tug
jersey n. (*jer'zi*) Close-fitting knitted garment reaching from neck to waist
jest n. (*jest*) Joke;
jetty n. (*jet'i*) Structure built out into the water as breakwater; landing-pier
jewel n. and v.t. (*jōō'el*) Precious stone, gem Hence: **jeweller** n. one who deals in or sets jewels; **jewellery** n. jewels collectively; ornaments set with jewels
jig n. and v.i. and t. (*jig*) Quick lively dance, or music for such a dance
jingle n. and v.t. and i. (*jing'gl*) Metallic ringing or tinkling sound, esp. of bells; series of words or simple verse with frequent repetition of sounds
job n. (*job*) Piece of work, something to be done, *to do a job well*; occupation, profession, employment, *give someone a job*
jockey n. and v.t. and i. (*jok'i*) Professional race-horse rider
join v.t. and i. and n. (*join*) To fasten together, attach; to combine, unite into a whole; to be united
joiner n. (*joi'ner*) One who works timber to form the finishings of a building, as distinct from a carpenter. Hence: **joinery** n. the work of a joiner; woodwork, furniture etc., made by a joiner
joint n. (*joint*) Place, line, or surface where two things are joined
joke n. (*jōk*) Something said or done to cause amusement
jot v.t. (*jot*) to make a written note of. Hence: **jotter** n. notebook
journal n. (*jur'nal*) Daily record of events, esp. private; daily newspaper; any periodical publication

journalism n. (*jur na lizm'*) profession of a journalist; **journalist** n. one who writes for or edits a journal
journey n. and v.i. (*jur'ni*) Expedition, esp. to a distant place
joy n. (*joi*) Gladness, delight
jubilee n. (*jōō bi lē'*) 50th anniversary of some event, esp. a coronation or wedding
judge 1) n. (*juj*) Officer of the Crown appointed to preside over a court of justice, and to hear and decide cases
judge 2) v.t. and i. (*juj*) To hear, try a case in a law-court; to pronounce judgement
judo n. (*jōō'dō*) Japanese art of wrestling and self-defence. (Jap.)
jug n. (*jug*) Any deep pouring vessel, with handle
juice n. (*jōōs*) Fluid part of animal or vegetable tissue, *lemon juice*
jumble v.t. and i. and n. (*jumbl*) To mix, confuse, put unrelated things together
jump v.i. and t. (*jump*) To propel oneself quickly upwards or forwards from the ground by use of muscular energy, to leap, bound
junction n. (*jungk'shun*) Act or process of joining; point, line, at which two things join, esp. railway station where two or more branches of railway meet
jungle n. (*jungl*) Uncultivated land overgrown with dense vegetation, esp. in tropical lands
junior adj. and n. (*jōō'ni or*) Younger
juror n. (*jōō'ror*) Member of jury
just 1) adj. (*just*) Fair, equitable; well-grounded, reasonable
just 2) adv. (*just*) Exactly, *just right*; nearly, barely, *only just enough*; at that precise moment, *just then*; a short time before
jut v.i. and n. (*jut*) To project, protrude
juvenile adj. and n. (*jōō've nil*) Young, youthful

K

kaleidoscope n. (*ka lī'da skōp*) Tube with eyehole at one end, and containing reflectors and bits of coloured glass which form patterns as the tube is turned or shaken
keel n. and v.t. (*kēl*) Lowest longitudinal timber or set of plates upon which a ship's framework is built
keep v.t. and i. (*kēp*) pret. and p.p. **kept** (*kept*) To retain, preserve; to hold, retain, in hand etc
keg n. (*keg*) Small barrel
kennel n. and v.t. and i. (*kenl*) Small hut for dog
kerb n. (*kurb*) Stone edge of pavement in a street
kernel n. (*kurnl*) Seed of a fruit, esp. softer part within hard shell of
kettle n. (*ketl*) Metal vessel with spout and handle, used for boiling water
key n. (*kē*) Metal instrument with one end shaped to fit the wards of a lock, and moving the bolt of this back and forth (fig.) explanation, solution, of mystery, problem, puzzle etc.; literal translation of foreign text; (mus.) system of related notes based on one particular note, *the key of C major* thing like a key in shape or function, esp. for winding clock, tightening screws, opening tin cans etc.
lever on musical instrument, pressed with finger to produce or modify sound; knob pressed similarly for working typewriter
kick v.t. and i. (*kik*) To strike with the foot (ball, person etc.)
kid 1) n. and v.i. (*kid*) The young of a goat
kid 2) v.t. and i. and n. (*kid*) (slang) To hoax, swindle; delude, take in; tease. As n. a hoax
kidnap v.t. (*kid'năp*) To steal a child; to carry (person) off by force. Hence: **kidnapper** n.
kill v.t. and i. (*kil*) To put to death, slay, deprive of life
kiln n. (*kiln*) Furnace or oven for drying (hops etc.), burning (lime), baking (bricks etc.)
kilo- pref. A thousand, in compounds as: a **kilogram(me)** thousand grammes (about 2.2 lb.) **kilolitre** a thousand litres; **kilometre** a thousand metres (about five-eighths of a mile); **kilowatt** (elect.) a thousand watts
kilt v.t. and n. (*kilt*) To tuck up (skirt etc.); to fold in vertical pleats. As n. pleated skirt, usually of tartan cloth, worn by Highlanders
kin n. (*kin*) Family, persons connected by blood or descent; relatives in general
kind 1) n. (*kīnd*) Sort, variety, type
kind 2) adj. (*kīnd*) Benevolent by nature, disposed to do good to others, considerate.
kindergarten n. (*kin'der gah ten*)

School for the very young
kindle v.t. and i. (*kindl*) To set light to, start
king 1) n. and v.i. and t. (*king*) Male sovereign ruler of a state
kingdom n. (*king'dum*) A State having a king (or queen), *the United Kingdom*; territory ruled by a king
kingfisher n. (*king'fish er*) Bird of genus *Alcedo*, having long beak and brilliant plumage, frequenting rivers and feeding on fish
kipper n. and v.t. (*kip'er*) fish (esp. herring) dried, smoked, and salted
kiss 1) n. (*kis*) Caress of the lips upon lips, cheek etc. as sign of affection
kiss 2) v.t. (*kis*) To give kiss to
kit n. and v.i. (*kit*) equipment generally, esp. workman's tools, equipment for special purpose (often sport)
kitchen n. (*kich'en*) Room specially equipped for cooking food
kite n. (*kit*) Bird of prey of hawk family, with long forked tail, long wings toy consisting of paper etc. stretched on light frame, which soars on the wind controlled by a long string
kitten n. and v.i. (*kitn*) Young cat
knapsack n. (*năp'săk*) Canvas or leather bag for food, clothing etc., slung over shoulder or worn on the back esp. when travelling on foot
knave n. (*nāv*) Rogue, rascal, man without principles; (cards) lowest court card, between ten and queen
knead v.t. (*nēd*) To work (esp. dough or clay) by squeezing and pressing with the hands
knee n. (*nē*) Joint between thigh and lower leg in man; corresponding part in animals
knell n. and v.i. and t. (*nel*) Sound of church bell tolling, esp. at death or funeral
knife n. and v.t. (*nif*) Cutting instrument consisting of long blade sharpened (usually) on one edge, fixed in handle either rigidly or on hinge, *bread knife*, *pocket knife*
knit v.t. and i. (*nit*) pret. and p.p. **knitted** or **knit**. To make (woven material or garment) of a series of interlocking loops and knots of wool, yarn etc
knock v.t. and i. (*nok*) To strike, rap, deliver sharp blow to (head, ball, *at* door etc.)
knot n. (*not*) Intertwining of ends of rope, string etc. to join them together
(naut.) unit of measurement of ship's speed

kingfisher

know v.t. and i. and n. (*nō*) pret. **knew** (*nū*) p.p. **known** (*nōn*) To be aware of, familiar with, possess in the mind as knowledge or information
knuckle n. and v.t. and i. (*nukl*) Finger-joint, esp. at base of finger

L

label n. and v.t. (*lā'bel*) Piece of paper, card, linen etc. for attachment to object, to show identity, destination, etc
laboratory n. (*la bor'a ter i*) Room or building used for experimental work in sciences, or for manufacturing chemicals etc
labour n. (*lā'ber*) Work, mental or bodily
Labour Party, one of two chief parties in Britain
labyrinth n. (*lă'bi rinth*) Complex arrangement of paths, passages etc. hard to negotiate without help; a maze
lace n. and v.t. and i. (*lās*) Cord or leather strip threaded through eyelets or hooks to draw together edges in stays, shoes etc.; delicate ornamental network of threads formed into patterns by looping, knotting, plaiting, or twisting
lacquer n. and v.t. (*lăk'er*) Kinds of varnish used to give hard bright coating to metal, esp. brass; varnish used on wood, esp. Japanese lacquer; articles coated with this. As v.t., to coat with lacquer
lad n. (*lăd*) Boy, youth

ladder n. and v.i. (*lăd'er*) Two lengths of wood, metal or rope, connected by cross-pieces or rungs to serve as means of ascending walls etc
ladle n. and v.t. (*lā'dl*) Large, deep spoon for dipping out liquids
lady n. (*lā'di*) Woman of upper classes, or fitted by manners to belong to them; (courteously) any woman
lag 1) v.i. and n. (*lăg*) To go too slow, fall behind
lag 2) v.t. and n. To cover water-pipes, cisterns etc. with non-conductive material to prevent freezing of water or waste of heat
lager n. (*lah'ger*) Kind of light beer
lagoon n. (*la gōōn'*) Salt-water lake separated from the sea by incomplete obstacle such as sandbank or coral reef
lair n. (*lār*) Den, resting place of a wild animal
lake n. (*lāk*) Large area of water surrounded by land; **the**
lamb n. and v.t. (*lăm*) Young of sheep
lame adj. and v.t. (*lām*) Limping, unable to walk normally owing to injury or defect
lament n. and v.t. and i. (*la ment'*) Expression of grief; song or poem expressing grief
lamp n. (*lămp*) Apparatus for giving light, from oil, gas, electricity etc
lance n. and v.t. (*lahns*) Weapon with long shaft and pointed metal head used by horsemen; similar weapon for spearing fish
land n. (*lănd*) Solid surface of earth, as contrasted with water surface; ground, earth used for farming, *he works on the land*
a country and its people, *my native land*
lane n. (*lān*) Narrow road, esp. in the country
language n. (*lăng'gwij*) System of articulate sounds and sound combinations used as a means of communication, esp. by a particular nation, people, or race
lantern n. (*lăn'tern*) Portable case, usually metal and glass, protecting light from wind etc.; light-chamber of lighthouse
lap 1) n. (*lăp*) Flap, fold; front of person's body from waist to knees, when sitting
circuit of a race-track
lap 2) v.i. and t. (*lăp*) To drink by licking up with the tongue

lapse n. and v.i. (*lăps*) Interval, passing away of time; slip of pen, tongue, or memory
larceny n. (*lah(r)'se ni*) Stealing, theft
lard n. and v.t. (*lah(r)d*) Refined fat of the pig
larder n. (*lah(r)d'er*) Cupboard or room where foods are stored
large adj. (*lah(r)j*) Big, bulky; taking up much space
larva n. (*lah(r)'va*) (entom.) mature form of any animal such as tadpole
larynx n. (*lă'rinks*) (anat.) Upper part of windpipe containing the vocal cords. Hence: **laryngitis** n., inflammation of the larynx
lash n. and v.t. and i. (*lăsh*) Thong, esp. of a whip, with which a stroke is given; blow or stroke so given; an eyelash
lass n. (*lăs*) Young girl
lasso n. and v.t. (*lăs ōō'*) Long rope with running noose at one end for catching horses or cattle. As v.t., thus to catch
last adj., adv., and n. (*lahst*) Coming after all others in place or time, at the end of a series; only remaining, *that was my last hope*
latch n. and v.t. and i. (*lăch*) Simple fastening for door, gate, or windows
late adj. and adv. (*lāt*) After the expected or agreed time, *you are ten minutes late*; far on in the day, season or period; backward, after the normal season; former, having recently ended, *the late Government*; no longer living, *my late uncle*

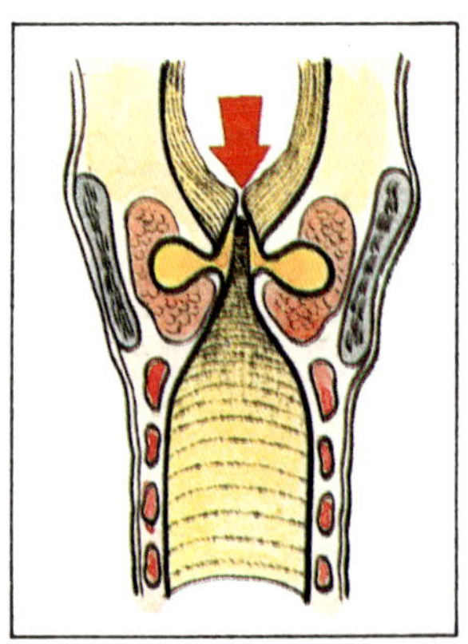

larynx

lathe n. (*lāth*) Machine for holding or turning wood or metal while being shaped

lather n. and v.t. and i. (*lah'then lă'ther*) Mass of white froth from soap and water

latitude n. (*lăt'i tūd*) Distance from the equator measured in degrees

latter adj. (*lă'ter*) Later, recent; further removed in time from the beginning, *the latter half of the week*; second of two (contrasted with 'former')

laugh v.i. and t. (*lahf*) To make inarticulate sounds, usually accompanied by movements of the face and body, expressing amusement or happiness

launch v.t. and i. (*lawnch*) To set a ship, esp. a new one, afloat; to throw, *he launched his spear*; to strike, aim (a blow etc.); to send into space (missile etc.); to initiate

launder v.t. and i. (*lawn'der*) To wash and press clothes or linen

laundry n. place where clothes and linen are laundered; things sent to or from a laundry; **launderette** laundry at which public waits while clothes are washed and dried in automatic machines

lava n. (*lah'va*) Matter flowing in molten state from a volcano

law n. (*law*) Rule made by authority for regulation of action and conduct in a community

lawn n. (*lawn*) Area of grass kept closely cut, esp. in gardens and parks

lay v.t. and i. (*lā*) p.t. and p.p. **laid** (*lād*) To put down in a particular place or position; place or arrange ready for use, *lay the table* produce (of birds and insects), *lay eggs*; propose odds for a wager, *lay heavy odds*

layer n. and v.t. (*lā'er*) One thickness of a substance lying upon another

lazy adj. (*lā'zi*) Unwilling to work; doing little work

lead 1) n. (*led*) (chem.) Element, symbol Pb; soft, heavy bluish-grey metal

lead 2) v.t. and i. (*lēd*) p.t. and p.p. **led** (*led*) To conduct, direct by going in front; conduct by the hand; act as head, controller; to influence, persuade to do something, *I led him to believe that*

league n. and v.t. and i. (*lēg*) A compact or alliance between persons or nations for their common welfare

leak n. and v.t. and i. (*lēk*) Hole, crack etc. in a container or vessel which allows liquid etc. to pass in or out

lean 1) adj. and n. (*lēn*) Thin

lean 2) v.i. and t. (*lēn*) To deviate from the perpendicular, incline

leap v.i. and t. and n. (*lēp*) p.p. and p.t. **leapt** (*lept*) To spring into the air, jump

learn v.t. and i. (*lurn*) To gain knowledge of, develop skill in, by practice, study, or being taught

leash n. and v.t. (*lēsh*) Thong, strap etc. for controlling a dog

leather n. (*le'ther*) Skin of animals preserved and toughened by tanning

ledge n. (*lej*) A narrow shelf; a projection from a cliff or other upright surface

ledger n. (*lej'er*) Book in which business accounts are kept

leg n. and v.i. (*leg*) One limb of animal or person used for support and walking, esp. part of human body from hip to ankle

legacy n. (*leg'a si*) A bequest left by will

legal adj. (*lē'gal*) Connected with, relating to, according to law

legend n. (*lej'end*) Orig., account of a saint's life; traditional story, esp. one of oral origin and doubtful truth

legible adj. (*lej'ibl*) What can be read easily

legislate v.i. (*lej'is lāt*) To make laws

leisure n. (*le'zher*) Freedom from occupation; time free from employment

lemon n. and adj. (*lem'on*) *Citrus limonum*, tree bearing yellow fruit with acid juice; its fruit

lend v.t. (*lend*) p.p. and p.t. **lent** (*lent*) To transfer to a person for a limited period

length n. (*length*) Measurement from end to end, *length of a field*

lenient adj. (*lē'ni ent*) Not severe, mild (esp. in punishments)

lens n. (*lenz*) Piece of glass or glasslike substance with one or both surfaces curved, and used in eye-glasses, cameras etc. to affect the rays of light and modify vision

less adj., adv., n. and prep. (*les*) Smaller in size and amount

lesson n. (*les'on*) Something learnt or taught; piece of instruction given or received

lest conj. (*lest*) For fear that; in

order that . . . not; in case, *take heed lest ye fall.* to give temporary use of in return for rent, esp. a house; to allow, permit

lethal adj. (*lē'thal*) Causing death

letter n. and v.t. (*let'er*) Written or engraved symbol representing a speech sound, message, greeting etc. sent from one person to another

lettuce n. (*let'is*) Garden plant with green leaves used in salads

level n., adj., adv., and v.t. and i. (*lev'el*) A horizontal even surface or plane; a flat area of ground

levy v.t. and i. and n. (*lev'i*) To impose, collect by force or authority, esp. taxes or an army

liable adj. (*lī'a bl*) Responsible in law apt, inclined to, *liable to make mistakes*

liberal adj. and n. (*lib'er al*) Giving freely, generous; ample

liberty n. (*lib'er ti*) State of being free, esp. from control by others

library n. (*lī'brer i*) A collection of books; the room or building in which they are kept

licence n. (*lī'sens*) Permission from an authority to do something; statement in writing of such permission

license v.t. (*lī'sens*) To authorize, grant a licence for something

lieutenant n. (*lef ten'ant*, U.S. *lōō ten'ant*) Deputy, substitute; (milit.) rank of officer immediately below captain; (nav.) rank of a junior officer

life n. (*līf*) Condition of organic matter in which it is capable of performing its natural functions of growth, food absorption etc

lightning n. (*līt'ning*) (meteor.) Flash of bright light produced by the spark marking the discharge of an electrified thunder cloud

like 1) adj., adv., prep., and n. (*līk*) Resembling; having the same or similar qualities, quantities etc.; characteristic of, *that's just like you*

like 2) v.t. (*līk*) To be pleased by, attracted to, fond of; have a taste for

likely adj. and adv. (*līk'li*) Such as might reasonably be expected

limb n. (*lim*) A jointed appendage as arm, wing; branch of a tree

lime 1) n. and v.t. (*līm*) White substance, calcium oxide, obtained by heating limestone

lime 2) n. (*līm*) Tree, *Citrus medica*; its fruit

lettuce

limit n. and v.t. (*lim'it*) Extreme edge, boundary, terminus; the utmost possible; restriction

limp 1) adj. (*limp*) not stiff or firm, *the book has a limp cover*; (fig.) lacking energy

limp 2) v.i. and n. (*limp*) To walk lamely or unevenly

line n. (*līn*) String, cord, *fishing line*; thread-like mark made on a surface; thread-like furrow on the face, hands etc.; mark on the ground indicating limit etc., esp. in games; row of persons or things; row of words, figures etc. written across or down a page; railway; single track of railway lines, *the up line*; system of transport under one management, *a steamship line*; contour, outline, *the clean lines of the new church*

linen n. and adj. (*lin'en*) Cloth made of flax; articles or garments made of this, esp. shirts, bed-sheets etc

linguist n. (*ling'gwist*) Person skilled in foreign languages

link n. and v.t. and i. (*ling'k*) One ring or loop of a chain; (fig.) person or thing forming a connection between others

lion n. (*lī'on*) Large, powerful wild cat

lip n. (*lip*) The upper or lower fleshy edge of the mouth; edge, rim of hollow container or opening

liquid adj. and n. (*lik'wid*) Fluid, flowing

liquor n. (*lik'er*) Liquid substance, esp. alcoholic

liquorice n. (*lik'er is*) The plant *Glycyrrhiza glabra*, from the root of which comes a black substance used in sweets

lion

listen v.i. (*lis'en*) To direct the hearing upon
literature n. (*lit'er a cher*) Written works in general
litter n. (*lit'er*) Couch or bed slung between shafts for carrying; kind of stretcher; straw, hay etc. used as bedding for animals; all the young of certain animals at one birth; odds and ends, rubbish
little adj. (*lit'l*) Small in height, size, quantity, extent
live 1) v.i. and t. (*liv*) To be alive, exercise the functions of a living organism
live 2) adj. (*liv*) Having life, *a live fish*; (of fire etc.) still alight; (elect.) circuit or conductor which is electrified or potentially so

liquorice

load 1) n. (*lōd*) That which is carried, esp. a heavy weight
load 2) v.t. and i. (*lōd*) To put a load on or in
the charge in a firearm
loaf n. (*lōf*) A mass of bread of specific size, shape, and weight
loathe v.t. (*lōth*) To abhor, detest
lobby 1) n. (*lob'i*) Hall, ante-room, waiting-room
lobby 2) v.t. and i. (*lob'i*) To try to influence the members of a law-making body to support a particular measure or programme
lobe n. (*lōb*) Rounded or flap-like projection, esp. lower end of the ear
local adj. (*lō'kl*) Of a particular place or district
lock n. (*lok*) Appliance or mechanism for closing doors, box-lids etc. by the operation of a bolt through the turning of a key; mechanism by which a gun is fired; a grapple in wrestling; enclosed section on a river or canal where the water-level changes, having gates with sluices at both ends so that vessels may be transferred from one level to the other
locomotion n. (*lō kō mō'shun*) Act, process, or power of moving from place to place
locomotive adj. and n. (*lō'kō mō tiv*) Having the power of locomotion; an engine, esp. one driven by steam or oil or electricity, for hauling carriages and trucks on a railway
locust n. (*lō'kust*) Large insect allied to the grasshopper, which migrates in swarms and destroys crops and vegetation

lock

lodge 1) n. (*loj*) Dwelling, esp. a small house at the entrance to the grounds of a larger house; porter's rooms at the entrance to a college, block of flats etc
lodge 2) v.i. and t. (*loj*) To reside temporarily, *I was lodged over a shop*; to house, give lodging to
loft n. (*loft*) Room immediately below the roof of a building
logic n. (*loj'ik*) Science of reasoning
loiter v.i. and t. (*loi'ter*) To linger, be slow in moving
lonely adj. (*lōn'li*) Solitary
longitude n. (*lon'ji tūd*) Distance west or east in degrees from a given meridian, esp. that of Greenwich
loom 1) n. (*lōōm*) A machine for weaving cloth
loom 2) v.i. (*lōōm*) To appear gradually and indistinctly, esp. through fog or clouds
loop n. (*lōōp*) Fold formed in a string etc. by doubling it and crossing the ends so as to leave a circular opening; any similar shape
loose 1) adj. (*lōōs*) Free, not under restraint, *the tiger got loose from the zoo*; slack, not close-fitting, *a loose collar*
loose 2) v.t. (*lōōs*) To make free or loose, unfasten
loosen v.t. and i. (*lōōs'en*) To make or become loose or looser
loot n. and v.t. and i. (*lōōt*) Plunder, spoils of war
lose v.t. and i. (*lōōz*) pret. and p.p. **lost** (*lost*) To mislay, be deprived of possession of, through accident, carelessness etc
loss n. (*los*) Act or fact of losing, *loss of a limb*; amount lost, what is lost
lotion n. (*lō'shun*) Medicinal liquid for use on the skin
loud adj. and adv. (*lowd*) Characterized by considerable noise
lounge 1) v.i. (*lownj*) To sit, stand about in a lazy way
lounge 2) n. (*lownj*) Act of lounging; room etc. furnished with comfortable chairs for lounging
love 1) n. (*luv*) Intense attraction towards someone or something; affection, tender devotion
love 2) v.t. and i. To feel love for, have a strong affection for in, *love one's work*. As v.i., to have the feeling of love. (As above)
lovely adj. (*luv'li*) Beautiful, charming, delightful, *a lovely scene*
lover n. (*luv'er*) One who is fond of, or enjoys something, *a lover of good food*; a sweetheart
loving adj. (*luv'ing*) Feeling or showing love, *a loving friend*
low 1) v.i. and n. (*lō*) To utter the characteristic cry of a cow
low 2) adj. (*lō*) Not high, not extending far upwards from a surface, *a low wall*; below the normal height, *the river is low*; (of sounds) not loud, *a low whisper*
loyal adj. (*loi'al*) Faithful, true
lubricate v.t. and i. (*lōō'bri kāt*) To make slippery or smooth, esp. by putting oil or grease into machine parts etc
luck n. (*luk*) Chance; fortune (good or bad)
lucky adj. (*luk'i*) Having good luck, fortunate
lull v.t. and i. and n. (*lul*) To quiet, soothe, calm down
lumber n. (*lum'ber*) Miscellaneous useless or unwanted articles stored away; rubbish; sawn wood of all types; **lumber-jack** man who fells trees, or saws and transports lumber
luminous adj. (*lū'min us*) Radiating light; bright, glowing
lump 1) n. (*lump*) A mass, usually shapeless, *a lump of clay*; bump or swelling
lunatic n. and adj. (*lōōn'a tik*) Madman
lunch n. and v.i. and t. (*lunch*) Mid-day meal
lurch 1) n. and v.i. (*lurch*) A sudden unsteady sideways stagger
lurk v.i. (*lurk*) To lie furtively hidden; lie in wait
luscious adj. (*lush'us*) Appealing strongly to taste and smell; rich in taste, fragrance etc
lustre n. (*lust'er*) Brilliance, gloss
luxury n. (*luk'zū ri*) State of life characterized by great ease and comfort, *to live in luxury*; something giving pleasure, but not essential, esp. something expensive, *he cannot afford many luxuries*
lynch v.t. (*linch*) To put to death without a legal trial, esp. by mob action
lyric n. (*li'rik*) A lyrical poem; words for a song

M

macadam n. (*ma kăd'am*) A road-surfacing material made from broken stones and gravel
macaroni n. (*măk a rō'ni*) Wheat-flour paste made in the form of long tubes and cooked as food

macaroon n. (*măk a rōōn'*) Small, flat, sweet cake made from ground almonds
mace 1) n. (*mās*) Heavy iron club with a spiked head; symbol of authority similarly shaped, and carried before Speaker of House of Commons, civic dignitaries etc
mace 2) n. (*mās*) A spice obtained from nutmeg
machine n. (*ma shēn'*) apparatus consisting of interconnecting parts, which by their motion transform power into work, *a sewing-machine* who makes, operates, or controls a machine
mackintosh n. (*măk'in tosh*) A rainproof coat made of cloth coated with rubber
mad adj. (*măd*) Insane, out of one's mind
magazine n. (*măg a zēn'*) Store for ammunition, equipment etc.; storehouse for explosives; chamber holding cartridges in a repeating rifle; place for film in a camera; periodical publication containing articles, stories etc. by various writers
magic n. (*măj'ik*) Power of controlling events by the use or pretended use of superhuman forces
magistrate n. (*măj'is trāt*) Civil official with administrative and judicial functions
magnet n. (*măg'net*) A mass of iron or other material which has the property of attracting or repelling other masses of iron
magnificent adj. (*măg nif'i sent*) Noble, splendid; outstanding in quality, generosity etc
magnify v.t. (*măg'ni fi*) To increase the apparent size of, esp. by means of a lens
mahogany n. (*ma hog'a ni*) Wood of a tropical American tree that takes high polish; this tree; reddish brown colour of this wood
maid n. (*mād*) Girl; female servant; (old use) unmarried woman
maiden 1) n. (*mā'dn*) Girl; young unmarried woman
maiden 2) adj. (*mā'dn*) Unmarried; (fig.) unblemished, experienced or done for the first time; **maiden over** (cricket) an over in which no runs are made
mail 1) n. (*māl*) Body armour of metal rings or plates
mail 2) n. (*māl*) Bag, sack, for conveying letters etc. by post; letters so conveyed; a postal collection or delivery, *the mail is late this morning*; postal system for conveying letters, *I sent my letter by air mail*
maintain v.t. (*mān tān'*) To continue, keep up, *maintain a position*; to support, *maintain a dependent relative*; retain, preserve, *maintain an open mind*; keep in good repair, *maintain the roads*; assert as true, *maintain that one is innocent*
majesty n. (*măj'es ti*) Stateliness, dignity, royal power; title used in addressing or referring to a sovereign, *Your Majesty*
major 1) n. (*mā'jer*) Army officer between captain and lieutenant-colonel in rank
major 2) adj. (*mā jer*) Greater or more important of two parts, groups etc
make v.t. and i. (*māk*) (pret. and p.p. **made** (*mād*) To construct, put together, form, build up, *to make bricks*; cause to happen, appear, develop, *to make good teeth by drinking milk*; to get ready for use, prepare, *make tea*; to perform, carry out, *make war*; to achieve, gain, acquire, earn, *make a profit*; to constitute, result in, prove to be, *he will make a good master*; to add up to, *two and two make four*; to reckon, calculate, *what time do you make it?*; to compel, coerce, *I can't make you do it if you don't want to*; to cause to happen, lead to do, *make someone understand*; to appoint, constitute, *make a man a judge*; to reach, arrive at, be able to reach, *shall we make the station in time?*; to create, compose, devise, *make a plan*; to produce, be the cause of; cause to become, *a good book makes him happy*
malady n. (*măl'a di*) A disease, ailment
malice n. (*măl'is*) Ill-will, desire to harm others
malignant adj. (*ma lig'nant*) Evilly disposed, showing a desire to harm, *his malignant expression frightened me*; (med.) likely to go from bad to worse, esp. cancerous, *a malignant growth*
mallet n. (*măl'et*) Hammer with a wooden head
malnutrition n. (*mal nu tri'shun*) Inadequate nutrition
mammal n. (*măm'al*) Any of the class Mammalia, warm-blooded vertebrates with mammary glands for suckling their young
mammoth n. and adj. (*măm'oth*) Species of large elephant with long hairy coat, now extinct. As

mammoth

adj., enormous, immense
manage v.t. and i. (*măn'ij*) To control, guide with the hands, *manage a boat*; to control the behaviour of, *manage a difficult child*; control, direct the working of, *manage a business*; deal with, *can you manage it alone?*
manager n. (*man'ij er*) One who manages, esp. a business or other enterprise
mane n. (*mān*) Long hair on the neck of an animal
manger n. (*mān'jer*) An eating trough for cattle.
mangle 1) n. and v.t. (*măngl*) Machine with rollers for pressing the water out of washed clothing etc
mangle 2) v.t. (*măngl*) To cut roughly, tear, damage badly.
mania n. (*mā'ni a*) Mental disorder manifesting itself in high uncontrolled excitement
manicure n. and v.t. (*măn'i kūr*) Treatment, care, of hands and nails. As v.t., to give treatment to hands and nails. Hence: **manicurist** n. one who practises manicure as a profession
manifest adj. (*măn'i fest*) Clear, obvious, *that is a manifest truth*
manifesto n. (*măn i fes'tō*) Public statement of principles and policy by a ruler or person or party
manipulate v.t. (*man ip'ū lāt*) To work, operate, fashion with the hands; to handle skilfully, influence
manner n. (*măn'er*) Way, method mode in which a thing is done or happens, *he did it in a slovenly manner*; personal bearing, behaviour
manoeuvre 1) n. (*ma nōō' ver*) Planned movement of troops or warships
mantle n. (*măntl*) Loose, sleeveless garment, a cloak; (fig.) covering, *a mantle of snow lay on the hills*
manual adj. and n. (*măn'ū al*) Of, done with, the hands, *manual labour*. As n., textbook or handbook
manufacture n. and v.t. (*măn ū fak'cher*) The making of goods by hand or machinery, esp. on a large scale
manure n. and v.t. (*ma nūr'*) Fertilizer spread on the ground
manuscript n. and adj. (*măn'ū skript*) Text, document, written by hand, esp. (modern) author's original draft
map 1) n. (*măp*) Plane representation of part of the earth's surface; representation of the sky, showing stars etc
map 2) v.t. (*măp*) Make a map of, show on a map
march v.i. and t. (*mahch*) To walk in regular, measured steps, as
mare n. (*mār*) Female horse or donkey
margarine n. (*mah ger ēn'*, *mah jer ēn'*), **marge** (*mahj*). Butter substitute made usually from vegetable fats
margin n. (*mah'jin*) Edge, border, limit; space round printed or written matter on a page; extra amount beyond what is necessary
marine adj. (*ma rēn'*) Of, found in, connected with the sea, *marine animals*; of shipping and sea-trade, *marine insurance*; of soldiers serving in the navy, *marine corps*
mariner n. (*mă'rin er*) Sailor, seaman
maritime adj. (*mă'ri tīm*) Connected with the sea or navigation
mark 1) n. (*mahk*) Line, spot etc. that breaks or destroys the normal appearance of a surface; blemish, stain, *what is that mark on your shirt?*; distinguishing feature, *birth-mark*
mark 2) v.t. (*mahk*) To put or leave a mark on
mark 3) n. (*mahk*) Unit of German currency
market n. (*mah'ket*) Public meeting for buying and selling

goods; place where, or time during which, this is done
marriage n. (*măr'ij*) Legal, religious, union of a man and woman as husband and wife; state of being married; wedding ceremony, *it was a civil marriage*
marsh n. (*mahsh*) Area of soft, very damp land, generally water-logged; bog, swamp
marsupial adj. and n. (*mah su' pi al*) Of the order of mammals in which the young are born immature and are carried in a pouch
martial adj. (*mah'shal*) Of, relating to, fitted for, war
martyr n. and v.t. (*mah'ter*) One who suffers or dies for the sake of a cause or principle
marvel n. (*mah'vel*) Wonderful thing; thing causing amazement
marzipan n. (*mah'zi păn*) Thick paste of ground almonds, sugar etc. made into sweetmeats or used to cover cakes before icing
mascara n. (*măs kah'ra*) Cosmetic preparation for colouring the eyelashes
mascot n. (*măs'kot*) Person or thing believed to bring good fortune
masculine adj. (*măs'cū lin*) Of the male sex
mask n. (*mahsk*) Covering for the face or part of it
mason n. (*mā'son*) Worker in stone
mass n. (*măs*) Coherent lump of matter with no regular shape
mass v.t. and i. (*măs*) To gather or collect together in a mass, to concentrate, *mass troops*
massacre n. and v.t. (*măs'ak er*) Wholesale slaughter, esp. of persons. As v.t., to put to death by massacre
massage n. and v.t. (*măs'ahzh*) Remedial treatment by manipulating, rubbing, and kneading parts of the body
mast n. (*mahst*) Upright support for sails and yards of a ship, or for television aerials, flags etc
master n. (*mah'ster*) Man having authority over others
mat n. (*măt*) Piece of coarse material used as a floor-covering
matador n. (*măt'a daw(r)*) Man who kills the bull in a Spanish bullfight
match 1) n. (*măch*) Contest of skill or strength, game between opposing sides, *a cricket match*
match 2) v.t. and i. (*măch*) To put one person into conflict with another; be equal to, *her courage matched his own*
match 3) n. (*măch*) Short piece of wood etc. tipped with material ignited by friction
mate n. (*māt*) Companion, work-fellow; friendly form of address; husband or wife; one of a pair in birds or animals
material n. (*ma tēr'i al*) The stuff of which something is or can be made or done, *raw materials*
maternal adj. (*ma ter'nal*) Of or like a mother
mathematics n. (*măth i mat'iks*) Science of the properties and relations of quantities and numbers
matinée n. (*măt'i nā*) Afternoon performance at theatre, cinema
matter n. (*mă'ter*) Substance of which physical objects are made
mattress n. (*măt'res*) Container stuffed with feathers, wool, or other material and used to lie on
mature adj. (*ma tūr'*) Ripe; fully developed
maximum n. (pl. **maxima**) and adj. (*măk'si mum*) Greatest quantity, size, etc.; highest point, degree
may auxil. v. (*mā*) Expressing possibility, *it may be so*; uncertainty, *what may that be?*; permissibility, *you may come if you wish*; wish, hope, *may you both be happy!*
mayor n. (*mār*) Head of a municipal corporation
maze n. (*māz*) Complex of winding and enclosed paths designed to puzzle those who walk in them
meadow n. (*me'dō*) Grass field, esp. one mown for hay
mean v.t. and i. (*mēn*) To convey, signify, imply, *what do these words mean?*; intend, have as an aim, *he means mischief*
meander v.i. and n. (*mē ăn'der*) (Of streams) to wind slowly about
measure 1) n. (*mezh'er*) Size, extent, quantity, weight, etc. in terms of some unit
measure 2) v.t. and i. (*mezh'er*) To find the quantity, dimensions, of, *measure a piece of ground*
meat n. (*mēt*) Edible flesh of animals
mechanic n. (*mi kăn'ik*) Skilled worker, esp. one who makes or uses machinery
medal n. (*med'al*) Metal disk with design and inscription, given as

an award or prize
meddle v.i. (*medl*) To interfere with
mediate v.i. and t. (*mē'di āt*) To act as intermediary, intervening agent
medicine n. (*med'i sin*) Art and science of preventing and curing disease
mediocre adj. (*mē di ō'ker*) Neither good nor bad, average
meditate v.t. and i. (*med'i tāt*) To contemplate; plan, *meditate revenge*; ponder, engage in contemplation
meet v.t. and i. (*mēt*) To come face to face with, *meet someone in the street*; come into the company of; make the acquaintance of
megaphone n. (*meg'a fōn*) Large speaking-trumpet for carrying the voice over a distance
melancholy n. and adj. (*mel'an kol i*) Sadness
melody n. (*mel'o di*) Sequence of pleasant musical sounds, esp. an air, tune, in music
memory n. (*mem'o ri*) Faculty of retaining and recalling to the mind past experiences
menace n. and v.t. (*men'as*) Threat. As v.t., to threaten
menagerie n. (*me nǎj'e ri*) Collection of wild animals in cages etc
mend v.t. and i. and n. (*mend*) To repair, put right
mention n. and v.t. (*men'shun*) Act of mentioning or speaking of, *to make mention of*; brief reference to, *there was only a bare mention of him*. As v.t., to refer to, speak of
menu n. (*men'yōō*) Bill of fare, list of courses or dishes; the meal itself
merchandise n. (*mer'chan dīz*) Goods, wares, bought or sold
merchant n. (*mer'chant*) Wholesale trader, esp. with foreign countries
mercy n. (*mer'si*) Compassion, forbearance, leniency
merge v.t. and i. (*murj*) To cause to be, become, absorbed by another
merit n. and v.t. (*me'rit*) Fact or quality of deserving reward
mermaid n. (*mur'mād*) Fabulous sea-creature with head and body of a beautiful woman, and tail of a fish
merry adj. (*me'ri*) Happy, cheerful, jolly, *a merry laugh*
mess n. (*mes*) State of confusion, disorder, dirt etc
message n. (*mes'ij*) Written or spoken communication sent by one person to another through an intermediary
messenger n. (*mes'en jer*) One who carries a message.
meteor n. (*mē'tē or*) Shooting star
meteorite n. (*mē'tē o rit*) Meteor that reaches the earth's surface
meter n. (*mē'ter*) Machine for measuring quantity, volume, time, etc., *a gas-meter, parking-meter*
method n. (*me'thod*) Manner, way of doing something
metre 1) n. (*mē'ter*) Poetical rhythm
metre 2) n. (*me'ter*) Unit of length in metric system, 39.37 inches. (As above)
metric adj. (*met'rik*) Measuring by metres; **metric system** decimal system of weights and measures based on the metre, gramme, and litre
mew v.i. and n. (*mū*) To utter the characteristic cry of a cat
micro- pref. (*mī'krō*) Very small, minute
microbe n. (*mī'krōb*) Popular name for bacteria which can be seen only with the aid of a microscope
microphone n. (*mī'krō fōn*) Instrument for converting sound wave-forms into electrical energy, as in the transmitter of the telephone
microscope n. (*mī'krō skōp*) Optical instrument used for obtain-

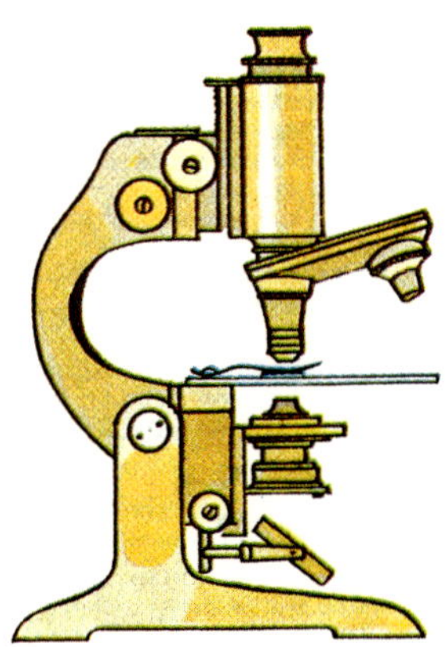

microscope

ing magnified images
midget n. (*mi'jet*) Very small person; dwarf
midnight n. (*mid'nit*) Twelve o' clock in the middle of the night
might n. (*mīt*) Power, strength, force
migraine n. (*mi'grān*) Severe headache
migrate v.i. (*mi'grāt*) To move from one habitation, region etc. to another, esp. to leave one's own country in order to settle abroad; (of birds and fishes) to go periodically from one region to another in search of milder climate for breeding, etc
mild adj. (*mild*) Gentle, kind, not severe
mile n. (*mil*) Measure of distance, 1760 yards
military adj. and n. (*mil'i ta ri*) Of, for, by, soldiers or the army
million n. and adj. (*mil'yun*) A thousand thousands Hence: **millionaire** n. person whose wealth amounts to a million pounds, dollars etc
mimic v.t. (*mim'ik*) To copy, imitate
mince v.t. and i. (*mins*) To cut, chop (meat etc.) into small pieces
mine 1) poss. adj. (*mīn*) Of or belonging to me, *that book is mine*
mine 2) n. (*mīn*) Shaft, passage dug in the earth to extract coal, mineral ores etc
miner n. (*mi'ner*) One who works in a mine underground
mingle v.t. and i. (*ming'gl*) To mix, blend
minimum n. (*min'i mum*) pl. **minima** Smallest, least possible quantity or amount
minor adj. (*mi'nor*) Less, not so important
minstrel n. (*min'strel*) (hist.) Professional entertainer, esp. one who recited or sang poetry, played the harp, etc
mint 1) n. (*mint*) Aromatic herb
mint 2) n. (*mint*) Place where money is officially coined and stamped
minus adj. and n. (*mi'nus*) Less
minute 1) n. (*min'it*) The sixtieth part of an hour or degree, 60 seconds; a moment
minute 2) adj. (*mi nūt'*) Very small, *a minute amount*
miracle n. (*mi'rakl*) Act or event that apparently cannot be explained by the laws of nature and is therefore believed to be due to supernatural agency
mirage n. (*mi rahzh'*) Optical illusion caused by atmospheric conditions
mirror n. and v.t. (*mi'ror*) A looking-glass
mischief n. (*mis'chif*) Harm, injury, *do someone a mischief*
miser n. (*mi'zer*) One who hoards wealth for the sake of hoarding
miserable adj. (*miz'er abl*) Unhappy
misfortune n. (*mis faw'tūn*) Bad luck
mislead v.t. (*mis lēd'*) To lead astray, cause to act or judge wrongly, deceive
mission n. (*mish'un*) A sending, esp. the sending out of representatives to a foreign country for a specific purpose
mist n. and v.t. and i. (*mist*) Visible water vapour in the air
mistake 1) v.t. (*mis tāk'*) To misunderstand, misinterpret
mistake 2) n. (*mis tāk'*) Error, blunder
mix v.t. and i. (*miks*) To mingle together
moan n. and v.t. and i. (*mōn*) Low, drawn-out cry of pain or sorrow
moat n. (*mōt*) Water-filled ditch round a castle etc. as a defence
mob n. and v.t. and i. (*mob*) Disorderly crowd, rabble
mobile adj. and n. (*mō'bil*) Movable, moving easily
mock 1) v.t. and i. (*mok*) To scorn, ridicule
mock 2) adj. (*mok*) Sham, counterfeit, imitation
model n. (*mod'el*) Small-scale copy of something someone who poses for an artist; a mannequin
modern adj. and n. (*mod'ern*) Of, characteristic of, the present
modest adj. (*mod'est*) Moderate *modest hopes*; having a moderate opinion of one's capabilities and merits, *modest behaviour*
moist adj. (*moist*) Damp
mole 1) n. (*mōl*) Small dark spot or blemish on the skin. (OE *mal*)
mole 2) Small burrowing mammal
molecule n. (*mol'e kūl*) (chem.) The smallest particle of a substance that is capable of independent existence
molest v.t. (*mo lest'*) To pester, interfere with
moment n. (*mō'ment*) A brief space of time, *wait a moment*
monarch n. (*mon'ak*) Supreme ruler

mole

monastery n. (*mon'as tri*) The abode of a community of monks
money n. (*mun'i*) pl. **moneys, monies** (*mun'iz*) Coin used as a medium of exchange wealth, property, *to lose all one's money*
mongrel n. and adj. (*mung'grel*) Dog of mixed breed
monitor n. and v.t. and i. (*mon'i tor*) One who warns, checks, or instructs, esp. a school-boy given special disciplinary powers
monk n. (*mungk*) Member of a religious order of men living in a community apart from the normal world
monkey n. (*mung'ki*) Mammal of the order of Primates, esp. a tailed member of this order
monster n. (*mon'ster*) Legendary beast, often part human and part animal
monstrous adj. (*mon'strus*) Enormous; abnormal, unnatural
month n. (*munth*) One of the 12 divisions of a year
monument n. (*mon'ū ment*) Memorial; something erected to commemorate some event or person
mood n. (*mōōd*) Temporary state of mind or feelings
moon n. (*mōōn*) Satellite revolving round the Earth
moor 1) n. (*mōōr*) Open stretch of waste ground overgrown with heather, and marshy or peaty in parts
moor 2) v.t. (*mōōr*) To fasten a boat to shore
moral adj. (*mo'ral*) Of the principles of right and wrong in matters of conduct
morale n. (*mo rahl'*) Mental state or condition, esp. of troops.
morbid adj. (*maw'bid*) unhealthy; depressed; tending to dwell on depressing things
more 1) adj. (*maw(r)*) Greater in number, size, amount
more 2) adv. (*maw(r)*) In greater quantity, to a greater degree
morning n. (*maw'ning*) The early part of the day from midnight to noon
morose adj. (*mo rōs'*) Sullen, surly, gloomy
mortal adj. and n. (*maw'tal*) Liable to die
mortar 1) n. and v.t. (*maw'tar*) Mixture of sand, lime, and water used for jointing in masonry or brickwork
mortar 2) n. (*maw'tar*) Bowl made of metal, stone, or hard porcelain, in which solids are ground up by a pestle; short gun for firing shells at a high angle
mortgage n. and v.t. (*maw'gij*) (law) Temporary conveyance of property by the owner as security for a loan
mosquito n. (*mos kē'tō*) pl. **mosquitoes**. One of several species of gnats of the family *Culicidae*, the females of which suck the blood of animals
most adj., n., and adv. (*mōst*) Greatest in number, quantity, or degree, *have the most money*
mother n. (*mu'ther*) A female parent; head of a convent
motion n. (*mō'shun*) Act or process of changing position or place
motive n. and adj. (*mō'tiv*) What causes and influences an action
motor n. (*mō'tor*) That which imparts motion, esp. mechanical motion
motorway road designed for use solely by motor vehicles, without intersections. Hence: **motorist** n. one who drives or travels in a motor-car
mould 1) n. (*mōld*) (bot.) Any of numerous small fungi appearing on bread, cheese etc. when kept in the damp, as a woolly or furry growth
mould 2) n. (*mōld*) Soft, fine earth
mould 3) n. (*mōld*) Receptacle, matrix, within which soft or molten materials may be cast and shaped in the required form; something
mound n. (*mownd*) Heap of earth, stones etc
mount v.t. and i. (*mownt*) To climb, ascend, *mount the stairs*; set in a fixed position or secure holder, *mount jewels in a setting*;

stuff and set up the skin of an animal; provide with a horse or horses
mourn v.t. and i. (*mawn*) To feel or express grief or regret
moustache n. (*mōōs tahsh'*) Hair grown on the upper lip
mouth n. (*mowth*) Opening in the head of animals and humans, through which food is taken
move v.t. and i. (*mōōv*) To change the position of
movement n. (*mōōv'ment*) Act, process, fact of moving or being moved
mow v.t. and i. (*mō*) To cut down grass etc. with scythe or mechanical mower
muddle v.t. and i. (*mudl*) To bewilder, confuse, bungle
mule n. (*mūl*) Offspring of a mare by a male ass
multiply v.t. and i. (*mul'ti pli*) To increase in number; make more numerous; (math.) add a number to itself a specified number of times
multitude n. (*mul'ti tūd*) Greatness of number, *as the stars in their multitude*; a great number, esp. a crowd, assembly of people
mumble v.t. and i. and n. (*mumbl*) To speak, utter (words etc.) indistinctly
mummy n. (*mum'i*) Body of a human being or animal preserved from decay by embalming, esp. one so preserved by the ancient Egyptians
munch v.t. and i. (*munch*) To chew food with much movement of the jaws

mummy

municipal adj. (*mū nis'i pal*) Of the government of a borough, city, or town
munition n. and v.t. (*mū nish'un*) (Usually pl.) military supplies, esp. shells and ammunition for guns and rifles
murder n. (*mur'der*) (law) Felonious killing of a human being with premeditated malice
murky adj. (*mur'ki*) Dark, gloomy
murmur n. (*mur'mur*) Low, continuous, indistinct sound, esp. of subdued talk
museum n. (*mū zē'um*) Institution for the collection, preservation, and exhibition of objects of cultural, historical, and scientific interest; the collections themselves; building in which the collections are housed
mushroom n. and v.i. (*mush' rōōm*) Any variety of edible fungus.
music n. (*mū'zik*) Art of making pleasing combinations of sounds or tones in rhythmical and harmonic form
musket n. (*mus'ket*) An early form of hand firearm
muslin n. (*muz'lin*) Light-weight, soft, cotton cloth of open texture
must aux. vb. (*must*) Used to express necessity, *one must eat to live*; obligation, *you must do as I tell you*; certainty or extreme likelihood, *you must be hungry by now*; what is desirable or advisable, *I must ask you not to do that*
mustard n. (*mus'tard*) (bot.) A yellow-flowered plant, genus *Sinapis*; hot, spicy powder made from the ground seeds of the mustard plant
muster n. and v.t. and i. (*mus'ter*) An assembly of troops for parade
mute adj. and n. (*mūt*) Silent, not making a sound, *he stood in mute astonishment*; not capable of speaking, dumb
mutilate v.t. (*mū'ti lāt*) To maim, cripple
mutiny n. and v.i. (*mū'ti ni*) Rebellion against lawful authority
mutter v.i. and t. and n. (*mut'er*) To speak, utter sounds or words, below one's breath and indistinctly
mutton n. (*mut'on*) Flesh of the sheep, as used for food
muzzle n. and v.t. (*muzl*) Projecting nose and mouth of an animal; cage-like guard fastened over head and muzzle of animal to prevent it biting etc.; mouth or opening of anything, esp. a firearm
mystery n. (*mis'ter i*) Something

of which the cause, origin, motive etc. is hidden or inexplicable, *it remains an unsolved mystery*
myth n. (*mith*) Traditional story embodying ancient religious beliefs and interpretations of natural events

N

nag v.t. and i. and n. (*năg*) To scold continually
nail 1) n. (*nāl*) Horny substance covering outer tip of fingers and upper tips of toes; claw or talon of animal
metal spoke with flat head, used for fastening things together
nail 2) v.t. (*nāl*) To fasten together, fix, by means of nails
naked adj. (*nā'kid*) With no clothes on
napkin n. (*năp'kin*) Small linen cloth for protecting clothes while one is eating
narrow adj. and n., v.t. and i. (*nă'rō*) Of little width in comparison to length, *a narrow road*
nasty adj. (*nah'sti*) Offensive to the senses, esp. taste or smell, disgusting
nation n. (*nā'shun*) Race or people (usually) living in one country, and sharing common government, history, and feeling themselves to be of one group
natural adj. and n. (*năch'(e) ral*) Of, connected with, arising from, nature or the external physical world, *natural forces*
naturalist n. (*năch'(e)ra list*) Student of nature, esp. of animals, plants etc
nature n. (*nā'cher*) All the forces, processes etc. that go to produce the phenomena of the material world
navigate v.t. and i. (*năv'i gāt*) To sail a ship, esp. to direct its course. Hence: **navigator** n. one who directs course of ship, aircraft etc
navy n. (*nā'vi*) The warships of a state
neat adj. (*nēt*) Tidy, trim (of dress, room, personal appearance etc.)
necessary adj. and n. (*nes'es er i*) fulfilling an essential function
neck n. (*nek*) Part of body connecting head and shoulders; thing of similar (i.e. narrow) shape or similar function, *neck of a bottle a neck of land*
nectar n. (*nek'ter*) The mythological drink of the Greek gods; thus, any very sweet or delicious drink
need 1) n. (*nēd*) Circumstances in which there is some deficiency, lack, want, necessity
need 2) v.t. and i. (*nēd*) To require, be in need of, lack (a necessity), *we all need food*
negative adj. (*neg'a tiv*) Expressing or implying denial, saying no to, refusing
neglect v.t. and n. (*ni glekt'*) To give no attention to, leave uncared for, disregard (person, duty, study, object etc.)
negotiate v.t. and i. (*ne gō'shi āt*) To arrange some business (commercial, political etc.) by discussion, bargaining etc
neigh v.i. and n. (*nā*) To utter the cry of a horse. As n. this cry. (OE
neighbour n. and v.t. and i. (*nā'ber*) Person who lives near or next door to another
neither adj., pron., adv., and conj. (*nī'ther*) Not the one nor the other of two alternatives
nephew n. (*nev'ū*) The son of one's brother or sister
nerve n. and v.t. (*nurv*) (anat.) Fibre or bundle of fibres in the body, which transmit sensations to brain
nest n. and v.i. and t. (*nest*) Structure made, or place chosen, by bird to lay eggs and rear young
net n. and v.t. and i. (*net*) Openwork fabric of twine etc. knotted where threads cross; piece of this for catching fish
neutral adj. and n. (*nū'tral*) Not taking either side in war, dispute etc
never adv. (*nev'er*) At no time, *I have never met him*
new adj. and adv. (*nū*) Not in existence before, now coming into existence for the first time, *a new book idea*; recently discovered or known
news n. (*nūz*) New information, report of recent events
nibble v.t. and i. and n. (*nibl*) To bite (at) with small bites,
nice adj. (*nīs*) (in most common use) pleasant, agreeable, kind, charming etc
niche n. and v.t. (*nich, nēsh*) Shallow recess in wall for statue or other ornament
nick n. and v.t. (*nik*) Small cut, slit, or notch
nickname n. and v.t. (*nik'nām*) Additional name given in affection or derision
niece n. (*nēs*) A daughter of one's

brother or sister
night n. (*nīt*) The time between sunset and sunrise
nimble adj. (*nimbl*) Quick, agile,
nip v.t. and i. and n. (*nip*) To pinch, bite, sharply with fingers, tweezers etc
noble adj. and n. (*nōbl*) Having or expressing lofty sentiments and ideals
nobody n. (*nō'bod i*) No person, not any one, *I saw nobody there*; insignificant or obscure person, *they are mere nobodies*
nod v.i. and t. and n. (*nod*) To make a short sharp downward and forward movement of the head, as greeting or sign of assent, understanding, command etc
nomad n. and adj. (*nō'măd*) Member of tribe wandering from place to place
nominate v.t. (*nom'in āt*) To propose (candidate) for election
none pron., adj., and adv. (*nun*) Not one, not any, no one, *none of us knows, we found none*
nonsense n. (*non'sens*) Absurd, meaningless word or words
noon n. (*nōōn*) Midday, 12 o'clock in the day
nose n. (*nōz*) The projecting feature of the human face, placed above the mouth, and being the external part of the organs of smell
nostalgia n. (*nos tăl'ja*) Homesickness; (loosely) intense longing for a past time or place associated with it
nostril n. (*nos'tril*) One of the two openings in the nose that admit air
not adv. (*not*) Particle expressing negation, denial, refusal, *I do not see, I have not seen, I have not been told*
notable adj. and n. (*nōt'abl*) ' Worthy of notice, remarkable, considerable
notch n. and v.t. (*noch*) A V-shaped cut in wood or other material
nothing n. and adv. (*nuth'ing*) Not anything, nought; something of almost no importance (*a mere nothing*); esp. in comparison, *my trouble is nothing to yours*
notice 1) n. (*nō'tis*) Observation, attention, *brought to my notice*; indication of an intention or action, intimation, warning, instructions
notice 2) v.t. (*nō'tis*) To observe, pay attention to, mark
notify v.t. (*nōt'i fī*) To make known, announce (fact etc.); to inform, give notice to (person)
notion n. (*nō'shun*) Idea
notorious adj. (*nō taw'ri us*) Well known
nought n. (*nawt*) Nothing; the figure or symbol O, zero
noun n. (*nown*) (gram.) A word used as the name of anything
nourish v.t. (*nu'rish*) To feed, sustain by (good) food
novel 1) adj. (*nov'el*) New, unfamiliar, unusual
novel 2) n. (*nov'el*) Prose narrative long enough to fill one or more volumes, generally dealing with a group of characters and the successive events of their lives
novelty n. (*nov'el ti*) Quality of being novel, newness
now adv., conj., and n. (*now*) At the present time, at this moment
nowadays adv. (*now'a dāz*) At the present time, in this modern age
nowhere adv. (*nō'war*) In no place, not anywhere
nozzle n. (*nozl*) Spout, mouthpiece (of hose etc.)
nuclear adj. (*nū'kli er*) Of a nucleus; atomic, involving the splitting of atoms, *nuclear bomb, warfare, research, radiation*
nucleus n. (*nūk'li us*) pl. **nuclei** (*nūk'li i*) Central core or kernel about which matter gathers
nude adj. and n. (*nūd*) Naked, bare, unclothed
nudge v.t. and n. (*nuj*) To push gently with the elbow
nugget n. (*nug'it*) Lump of metal, esp. of native gold
nuisance n. (*nū'sans*) Thing or person or event that causes injury, hindrance, annoyance etc., *commit*
numb adj. and v.t. (*num*) Lacking the sense of touch, deadened, insensitive

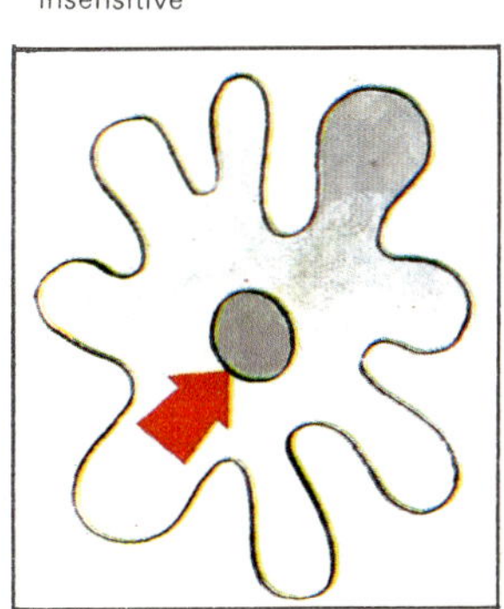

nucleus

number 1) n. (*num'ber*) Total, sum, a mathematical total, the symbol for this (as *9*) a collection or company, *he showed me a number of books, a number of readers complained* (also pl. **numbers**, i.e. many); single issue of a periodical publication, *the summer number*; piece of music, item, song; (pl.) numerical superiority, *by sheer weight of numbers*; (gram.) that form of a word which shows whether it refers to one, two, or many, *singular, dual, plural, number*; (poet.) lines, verses
number 2) v.t. (*num'ber*) To count, reckon the number of
numerous adj. (*nū'mer us*) Consisting of a great number
nun n. (*nun*) Woman living in religious community
nurse n. (*nurs*) Woman who looks after young children person (usually woman) trained to look after the sick
nursery n. (*nurs'ri*) Room or rooms set aside for children
nut n. and v.i. (*nut*) The hard-shelled fruit of certain plants, small block of metal with hole into which a bolt is screwed
nutrition n. (*nū trishn'*) food, nourishment. Hence: **nutritious** adj. nourishing, beneficial as food, sustaining, promoting growth

O

oar n. (*aw(r)*) Implement for propelling a boat, consisting of a long pole with a flat blade at one end

nun

oasis n. (*o ā'sis*) Fertile place in a sandy desert
oat n. (*ōt*) (bot., usually in pl.) Cereal, *Avena sativa*, or its grain, used as food
oath n. (*ōth*) Solemn, binding undertaking with an appeal to God or some sacred object or person as sanction and witness
obey v.t. and i. (*ō bā'*) To carry out the commands or wishes of
object 1) n. (*ob'jekt*) Something visible and tangible, a material thing
object 2) v.i. and t. (*ob jekt'*) To oppose, disapprove of
oblige v.t. (*o blīj'*) To require, constrain, compel, *the law obliges dog-owners to purchase a licence*
oblivion n. (*o bliv'i on*) Act of forgetting; state of being forgotten
oblong n. and adj. (*ob'long*) Rectangular figure having two opposite and equal sides greater than the other two
obscene adj. (*ob sēn'*) Morally offensive, indecent
obscure adj. (*ob skūr'*) Dim, lacking light; not clearly seen, indistinct; not easy to find, *an obscure reference*; not clear in meaning, *an obscure style*; hard to understand, *his part in the plot remains obscure*
observatory n. (*ob zer'va to ri*) Building equipped for observing natural, esp. astronomical, phenomena
observe v.t. and i. (*ob zerv'*) To keep, pay attention to, *observe the rules*; watch, consider attentively; remark, comment
obstacle n. (*ob'stakl*) Hindrance, impediment preventing progress,
obstinate adj. (*ob'sti nat*) Stubborn
obtain v.t. and i. (*ob tān'*) To get, acquire, receive, *obtain a prize*
obvious adj. (*ob'vi us*) Easily perceived or understood
occasion n. and v.t. (*o kā'zhun*) Point in time at which a certain event or action takes place
occasional adj. (*o kā'zhun al*) Occurring or appearing from time to time
occupy v.t. (*ok'ū pi*) To take and retain possession of dwell in, have for one's use hold, *Mr Brown occupies an important position*; to busy (oneself); **be occupied with** be busy with. (Lat. *occupare* to take hold of)
occur v.i. (*o ker'*) To happen

ocean n. (*ō'shun*) The open sea, the whole body of salt water; one of the main divisions of this, *the Pacific Ocean*
octave n. (*ok'tāv*) The eighth full tone above or below any note
oculist n. (*ok'ū list*) Specialist in diseases of the eye
odd adj. (*od*) Not even, not divisible by two
offal n. (*of'al*) What is discarded as useless
offence n. (*o fens'*) Wrongdoing, misdemeanour
offend v.i. and t. (*o fend'*) To do wrong, commit an offence
Hence: **offender** n. one who offends, esp. by breaking a law
offensive adj. and n. (*o fen'siv*) Causing offence
offer 1) v.t. and i. (*of'er*) To bring or put forward, proffer, present, tender, *to offer assistance*
offer 2) n. (*of'er*) Proposal, statement of willingness to do or give something, *an offer of help*
office n. (*of'is*) Function, duty, service, *the office of host*; position involving certain specific functions and duties, *judicial office*; public or state department, *the Home Office*; place, building, rooms, where business is transacted
officer n. (*of'i ser*) One who holds an office or position of authority
officiate v.i. (*o fish'i āt*) To perform the duties of an office
officious adj. (*o fish'us*) Too eager to help, meddlesome
often adv. (*of'en*) Many times, repeatedly
ogre n. (*ō'ger*) Ugly, man-eating giant in fairy-tales
oil n. (*oil*) General term for a group of greasy, fatty, flammable substances
ointment n. (*oint'ment*) Oily compound used for medicinal purposes
old adj. (*ōld*) Aged, not young
omit v.t. (*ō mit'*) To fail to do, *he omitted to tell me*; fail to include, *you may omit this chapter*
omnibus n. and adj. (*om'ni bus*) Former name for bus
once adv. (*wuns*) On one single occasion only, *you are born only once*; at one time, formerly, *he once lived here*
onion n. (*un'yun*) (bot.) Hardy bulbous plant *Allium cepa*; its edible bulb, used as a vegetable and as a flavouring in cooking
onlooker n. (*on'lo͝ok er*) Spectator, looker-on.
only adj., adv., and conj. (*on'li*) Single, sole, *an only child*
onward adj. and adv. (*on'ward*) Moving forward, advancing
opaque adj. (*o pāk'*) Not allowing light to pass through; not transparent; obscure; stupid
open adj. (*ō'pen*) Not shut or closed, allowing entrance or exit, *an open door*; not enclosed or fenced in, *an open field*; not covered in or over, *an open sewer*; free from restrictions, available to all, *an open port, a career open to talent*
opera n. (*op'e ra*) Drama set to music, in which the words are sung
operate v.t. and i. (*op'e rāt*) To perform a certain function or task, (surg.) perform a surgical operation
opinion n. (*o pin'yun*) Belief or judgement not founded on absolute conviction or knowledge, *political opinions*; estimate; judgement or feeling concerning persons or things, *have a high opinion of someone*; expert or professional judgement, *consult a medical opinion*
opportunity n. (*op or tū'ni ti*) Favourable time or chance for doing something
oppose v.t. (*o pōz'*) To offer opposition to, resist
opposite adj. and n. (*op'ō zit*) Facing, fronting, situated over against, *opposite sides of a street*
oppress v.t. (*o pres'*) To crush down, treat unjustly and cruelly
optician n. (*op tish'un*) One who tests eyes and makes and sells optical instruments
optimism n. (*op'ti mizm*) tendency to look on the bright side of things.
Hence: **optimist** n. (*op'ti mist*) one who looks on the bright side of things
option n. (*op'shun*) The right, liberty, power of choosing
oracle n. (*o'rakl*) Answer given by ancient Greek priest to inquiries about the future etc
orange n. and adj. (*o'ranj*) An evergreen tree, *Citrus aurantium*; the fruit of this tree; colour resembling that of the orange fruit
orate v.i. (*o rāt'*) To make long speeches
orbit n. and v.i. (*aw'bit*) Path of a heavenly body about another
orchard n. (*aw'chard*) Enclosure for a plantation of fruit trees
orchestra n. (*aw'kes tra*)

group of musicians
order n. (*aw'der*) Way in which things are arranged or placed in relation to one another
ordinary adj. (*aw'di na ri*) According to customary or regular usage; normal
ore n. (*aw(r)*) Mineral from which metal may be extracted
organ n. (*aw'gan*) (bot., zoo.) Part of the body adapted to the performance of a particular function
musical instrument consisting of pipes that produce sound when blown by compressed air, and operated by keys pressed by the fingers and pedals operated by the feet
organism n. (*aw'ga nizm*) (biol.) Living animal or plant
organize v.t. (*aw'ga niz*) To make give systematic form to
origin n. (*o'ri jin*) Starting point
original adj. and n. (*o rij'i nal*) Of the beginning, earliest, *an original edition*; newly created or invented, not copied, *an original design*
ornament n. and v.t. (*aw'na ment*) decorative object, *the ornaments on a mantelpiece*
orphan n., adj., and v.t. (*aw'fan*) Child who has lost one or both parents
other adj. and pron. (*u'ther*) Different, distinct from, alternative to
otter n. (*ot'er*) Furry aquatic mammal with webbed feet
ought auxil. v. (*awt*) Expressing duty obligation

otter

ounce n. (*owns*) Unit of weight, one-sixteenth of a pound
outcast n. and adj. (*owt'kahst*) One exiled from society
outing n. (*ow'ting*) Excursion, pleasure trip, holiday away from home
outline n. and v.t. (*owt'līn*) Boundary line(s) of a figure; outer line of a drawing showing the shape of the whole
outlook n. (*owt'lo͝ok*) Place from which a view is seen or watch is kept
outrage n. and v.t. (*owt'rāj*) Act of violence against person, property, or public feeling
outside adv., prep., adj., and n. (*owt sīd'*) Externally, on the surface, *to decorate a house outside*; in the open air, beyond, *put this chair outside* (a room etc.)
outsider n. (*owt sī'der*) One who is not a member of a social or other group, community etc
oval adj. and n. (*ō'val*) Egg-shaped
oven n. (*o'ven*) Enclosed receptacle that can be heated for cooking food; small furnace or kiln used in chemistry etc
overall 1) n. (*ō'ver awl*) Loose outer garment put on over other clothes
overall 2) adv. (*ō'ver all*) Over the whole length or area; including everything
overboard adv. (*ō'ver bawd*) Over the side of a ship into the water
overcast adj. (*o'ver kahst*) Cloudy
overcoat n. (*ō'ver kōt*) A coat worn over another, top-coat
overdue adj. (*ō ver dū'*) Behind its due time
overflow v.t. and i. and n. (*ō ver flō'*) To flow over banks or other limits owing to excess; to flood
overhang v.t and i. and n. (*ō'ver hăng*) To hang , jut out, over
overhaul v.t. and n. (*ō ver hawl'*) To examine the condition of thoroughly, make a thorough investigation of
overhear v.t. (*ō ver hēr'*) To hear without the speaker knowing
overrule v.t. (*o ver ro͞ol'*) To set aside another's ruling by superior authority
oversight n. (*ō'ver sit*) failure to notice or do something
overtime adv. and n. (*ō'ver tīm*) Beyond the normal working hours, *work overtime*

overwhelm v.t. (*ō ver welm'*) To pour down over; crush by superior force or numbers
owe v.t. and i. (*ō*) To be indebted (to someone for something)
owl n. (*owl*) One of the family *Strigidae* of nocturnal birds of prey, with large head and eyes and hooked beak
own v.t. (*ōn*) To possess, have legal title to, *own a house*; acknowledge as one's own, *own a child*; admit, *own the force of an argument*; confess, *own one's faults*
oxygen n. (*ok'si jen*) Non-metallic element, symbol O, a colourless, odourless gas, essential to life, that exists free in the atmosphere

owl. a) snowy owl, b) elf owl, c) hawk owl

P
pace n. (*pās*) A single step in walking or running, a stride, *one* speed, rate, of walking, running
pacifism n. (*păs'i fi zm*) The belief that violence, esp. war, is evil and must be abolished
pacify v.t. (*păs'i fi*) To appease (person, anger etc.), make peaceful
pack v.t. and i. (*păk*) To put (together) in bundle, box, trunk etc. for travel or storage
package n. (*păk'ij*) Parcel, bundle of packed things
packet n. (*păk'it*) Small parcel
pact n. (*păkt*) Agreement, between two or more parties
pad n. and v.t. (*păd*) Thing stuffed with soft material and used to protect, fill out etc
paddle 1) n. (*pădl*) Short oar with broad rounded blade, used in canoes
paddle 2) v.i. (*pădl*) To walk, dabble feet in, shallow water
page 1) n. and v.t. (*pāj*) Boy servant, messenger etc
page 2) n. and v.t. (*pāj*) One side of a leaf of paper in a book etc
pagoda n. (*pa gō'da*) Far-eastern sacred tower
pail n. (*pāl*) Round open-topped vessel, cylindrical or slightly tapering, for carrying liquid, a bucket
pain n. (*pān*) Suffering of body or mind
paint n. (*pānt*) Colouring matter, pigment mixed with water, oil etc. and used to colour a surface
pair n. (*pār*) Set of two things usually found together
palace n. (*păl'as*) Residence of royalty or bishop
palate n. (*păl'at*) Roof of the mouth
pale 1) n. (*pāl*) Pointed stake used for fence or boundary
pale 2) adj. and v.i. and t. (*pāl*) Whitish, pallid, lacking colour
palm 1) n. (*pahm*) Inner part of hand between wrist and fingers
palm 2) n. (*pahm*) One of a large family of trees with branchless trunk topped with a tuft of huge leaves
palmist n. (*pahm'ist*) One who claims to tell fortunes from the lines on one's palm

panda

parchment

pan n. (*păn*) Broad, flat cooking-vessel of metal or earthenware
panda n. (*păn'da*) Giant panda a rare Tibetan bear with cream and black fur
panel n. (*pănl*) Rectangular piece of wood in door, wall etc
panic n., adj., and v.i. and t. (*păn'ik*) Sudden, violent, uncontrollable terror
pant v.i. and t., and n. (*pănt*) To gasp for breath
pantry n. (*păn'tri*) Small room where plate, china etc. are kept and cleaned
paper n. (*pā'per*) Substance made from pulped fibres of wood, rags etc., and used for writing, drawing, wrapping, bags, lining walls etc.; a newspaper
papier mâché n. (*pap'yā mash'ā*) Moulded pulp of paper, used for trays, boxes etc
parable n. (*pă'rabl*) Short allegory, story embodying a moral or lesson
parachute n. (*pă'ra shōōt*) Apparatus opening like huge umbrella, for checking the fall of persons etc. descending from aircraft
paradise n. (*pă'ra dis*) Garden of Eden; heaven; any perfect, delightful place or state
paragraph n. and v.t. (*pă'ra grahf*) Distinct short section in book etc
parallel adj. (*pă'ra lel*) Continuously equidistant (of lines), in the same plane but never meeting
parasite n. (*pă'ra sit*) (biol.) plant or animal living within or upon another and drawing its nutriment from it
paratroops n.pl. (*pă'ra trōōps*) Troops trained to drop into battle area by parachute
parcel n. and adv. (*pah'sel*) Small package, goods wrapped up to form such
parch v.t. and i. (*pahch*) To make very dry or thirsty
parchment n. (*pahch'ment*) Skin of sheep, goat etc. prepared as writing material
pardon n. (*pah'don*) Forgiveness
pare v.t. (*pār*) To trim, shave
parent n. (*pār'ent*) Father or mother
parish n. (*pă'rish*) Subdivision of a county or diocese
park n. (*pahk*) (hist.) area in town laid out for public enjoyment and recreation

parka

parka n. (*pakh'ah*) Fur jacket with a hood worn by Eskimos
Parliament n. (*pah'la ment*) Deliberative and legislative assembly of a country
parsley n. (*pahs'li*) A green herb with crinkled leaves, used in cookery, on salads etc
particle n. (*pah'tikl*) Minute fragment of matter
particular adj. and n. (*pa tik'ū ler*) Relating to one thing etc. as distinct from others, individual, *this particular case*
partner n. and v.t. (*paht'ner*) One who shares *with* another, *of* or *in* a thing; one associated with other(s) in business enterprise etc
party n. (*pah'ti*) Body of persons united in opinion, interests etc.; a political faction; one of those concerned in a contract, lawsuit etc., *third party, the offended party*; a social gathering, *dinner*
pass v.i. and t. (*pahs*) To move onward, *pass along, over, on* etc.; to go by, overtake, go beyond, *I saw her pass*; (of time) elapse
pass n. (*pahs*) Narrow passage through mountains
passenger n. (*păs'in jer*) Traveller in ship or train, aircraft, car etc
passion n. (*păsh'on*) Strong emotion
passport n. (*pahs'pawt*) Document issued to citizen of a country allowing him to travel abroad
password n. (*pahs'wurd*) Secret word that must be spoken to gain admittance
past 1) adj. and n. (*pahst*) Over and gone, finished
past 2) prep. and adv. (*pahst*) Beyond in time or place
pasta n. (*pas'ta*) Flour paste or dough used in Italian cooking; any food (macaroni, spaghetti, etc.) made of this
pasteurize v.t. (*pahs'tūr iz*) To sterilize (esp. milk) by heating
pastime n. (*pahs'tīm*) Recreation, amusement; game
pasture n. and v.i. and t. (*pahs'cher*) Grass etc. as cattle-food; land on which cattle are grazed
pat n. (*păt*) Light tap or slap of the hand
patch n. (*păch*) Piece of material sewn on another to cover hole etc
patent 1) adj. (*pā'tent*, (law) *păt'ent*) Plain, obvious, *this is patent madness*
patent 2) n. (*pā'tent, păt'ent*) official grant of exclusive rights or privilege to make or market some commodity, device etc., *he took out a patent for his new tin-opener*
path n. (*pahth*; pl. *pah*thz) Footway; way made by treading of (human or animal) feet
pathetic adj. (*pa thet'ik*) Evoking pity, sadness, sympathy
patience n. (*pā'shens*) Calm endurance of pain, adversity etc
patient adj. and n. (*pā'shent*) Having, showing, patience As n. person undergoing medical treatment
patriot n. (*păt'ri ot, pā'tri ot*) One who loves, champions, defends, his country
patron n. (*pā'tron*) Person who protects, encourages, supports (person, art, artist, cause etc.); a regular customer
patronize v.t. (*păt'ro niz*) To support, encourage, as patron; give one's regular custom to (shop etc.); to treat (other person) condescendingly
pauper n. (*paw'per*) Person without money
pause n. and v.i. (*pawz*) Interval of inaction in writing, speech, action etc., due to hesitation, or for emphasis, or for rest, reflection etc
pave v.t. (*pāv*) To cover surface of (ground etc.) with flat stones, bricks etc. to form pavement
pavement n. (*pāv'ment*) Paved footpath, esp. by side of road
paw n., and v.t. and i. (*paw*) Foot of an animal, with claws or nails
pawn n. and v.t. (*pawn*) Pledge, esp. thing given as security on loan etc.; state of being pledged, *in pawn*. As v.t. to deposit as pledge with a pawnbroker, *I pawned my camera*; to **pawnbroker** moneylender who accepts personal property as security (thus, **pawnbroking** his business)
pay v.t. and i. (*pā*) pret. and p.p. **paid** (*pād*) To give (person) money for services, goods etc. or in discharge of a debt
peace n. (*pēs*) Freedom from, cessation from, warfare, hostility, strife
peach n. (*pēch*) Large roundish fruit of *Prunus persica* with yellow downy skin, sweet juicy yellow pulp, and large stone; the tree bearing this
peacock n. and v.i. (*pē'kok*) Male bird of genus *Pavo*, with brilliant

peacock

iridescent plumage and a tail that it can raise and spread out fanwise
peak n. (*pēk*) Top of anything
pear n. (*pār*) A juicy fruit with slightly granular flesh, egg-shaped but drawn-out towards the stalk; the tree which bears this
peasant n. (*pez'ant*) Countryman, farm labourer, esp. one cultivating small piece of land primarily for family subsistence
pebble n. (*pebl*) Small stone rounded smooth by action of water
peck v.t. and i., and n. (*pek*) To strike or bite with the beak
peculiar adj. and n. (*pe kū'li er*) Belonging exclusively to one individual, place, language etc. queer, *a peculiar sight*
pedal n., and v.t. and i. (*pedl*) Part of machine or instrument worked by the foot
pedestrian adj. and n. (*pe des'tri an*) As n. person on foot, walker; **pedestrian crossing** place marked across street where pedestrians take precedence over traffic; **pedestrian precinct** district in town closed to traffic and reserved for pedestrians
pedlar n. (*ped'ler*) Travelling salesman carrying pack of small wares from door to door
peel v.t. and i., and n. (*pēl*) To strip the skin or rind off, *to peel an orange*
peer 1) n. (*pēr*) Person or thing of equal rank or merit
peer 2) v.i. (*pēr*) To look closely, narrowly (*at, into* etc.)
peg n. (*peg*) Wooden or metal pin, usually tapering, used to fasten pieces of framework etc
pellet n. (*pel'it*) Small ball of paper, bread etc
pelt 1) n. (*pelt*) Skin or coat of an animal
pelt 2) v.t. and i., and n. (*pelt*) To attack with missiles, *pelted me with stones* (also fig. of questions etc.)
pen 1) n. and v.t. (*pen*) Small enclosure for animals, *sheep pen.* As v.t. to put in a pen, enclose
pen 2) n. and v.t. (*pen*) writing instrument with metal nib in handle
penal adj. (*pē'nal*) Of punishment, esp. legal, *penal code*; liable
penalty n. (*pen'al ti*) Legal punishment, esp. a fine, *minimum penalty* £5
pendulum n. (*pen'dū lum*) A body suspended from a point so as to be able to swing freely, esp. swinging weight regulating a clock's movements
penetrate v.t. and i. (*pen'i trāt*) To pierce and enter; to force one's way into or through (crowd, thicket etc.); (of light) get through, be visible, *no smallest ray penetrated the gloom*
penguin n. (*pen'gwin, peng'-*) Flightless sea-bird having wings developed into paddles, found in Antarctic regions
peninsula n. (*pen in'sū la*) Piece of land almost surrounded by water
penitent adj. and n. (*pen'i tent*) Contrite, repentant
pension n. and v.t. (*pen'shun*) Fixed regular payment made when recipient reaches certain age, or retires from service etc
pensioner n. (*pen'shun er*) One who receives a pension
people n. and v.t. (*pēpl*) Whole body of persons forming a congregation, community, nation, or group of nations
perch 1) n. (*purch*) Edible fresh-water fish
perch 2) n. (*purch*) Horizontal bar etc. for birds to rest on
perennial adj. and n. (*pe ren'i al*) Lasting (of stream, flowing) through all seasons of the year; lasting for years or for ever
perfect adj. (*pur'fekt*) Complete in all its parts, without fault or blemish, *a perfect specimen*
perfection n. (*per fek'shun*) Act of making, state of being, perfect
perforate v.t. and i. (*pur'fer āt*) To pierce, make a hole or holes in
perform v.t. and i. (*per fawm'*) To do, accomplish, carry out (task, play, operation etc.)

perch

performance n. (*per faw'mans*) public exhibition of play, music etc.
perfume n. (*pur'fūm*) Odour, aroma, esp. sweet and pleasant one; a sweet-smelling liquid for enhancing one's personal odour
perhaps adv. (*per hăps'*) Possibly, it may be (expressing all shades from barest possibility to virtual certainty)
peril n. and v.t. (*pe'ril*) Danger, risk, exposure to injury, harm or destruction
period n. (*pēr'i od*) any portion of time, either definite (*during this period*) or indefinite (*absent for long periods*)
periodic adj. (*pēri od'ik*) Recurring at (usually regular) intervals
Hence: **periodical** adj. and n. (as n. a magazine or journal published at regular intervals)
periphery n. (*pe rif'er i*) Perimeter, boundary line, esp. of circle; the outside, outer part (also fig.)
periscope n. (*pe'ri skōp*) Apparatus using mirrors and lenses to deflect line of vision and enable one to see over parapet in trench, or above water from a submerged submarine etc
perish v.i. (*pe'rish*) To die, come to an end,
Hence: **perishable** adj. and n. liable to perish, *perishable goods* (foodstuffs etc.) (also **perishables**)
permanent n. (*pur'ma nent*) Lasting, unchanging
permit 1) v.t. and i. (*per mit'*) To allow, give leave, *permit me to say*
permit 2) n. (*pur'mit*) Document giving official permission for something to be done, a licence
perpetual adj. (*per pet'chōō al*) Everlasting, eternal; ceaseless, continuous
perplex v.t. (*per pleks'*) To puzzle, baffle
persevere v.i. (*pur se vēr'*) To persist with dogged determination, in spite of all obstacles
persist v.i. (*per sist'*) To continue steadily or obstinately on a course, in doing something etc., esp. in spite of difficulties, objections
personal adj. (*pur'son al*) Of, characteristic of, belonging to, private to, a particular human individual
personality n. (*pur son ăl'i ti*) Quality of being a person; personal identity, existence as an individual person; qualities of mind and temperament that make up a person's character
personnel n. (*pur son el'*) Staff of persons employed, esp. in public institution, shop, armed forces etc
perspire v.i. and t. (*per spir'*) To exude moisture through the pores of the skin, to sweat
persuade v.t. (*per swād'*) To induce (person etc.) to believe something, do something etc. by reason, to convince, *I persuaded him that it was true*
pest n. (*pest*) Troublesome, harmful, person, animal etc
pester v.t. (*pes'ter*) To trouble, annoy persistently,
pet n. and v.t. (*pet*) Tame animal reared and kept as companion and object of affection
petition n., and v.t. and i. (*pe tishn'*) Humble request, earnest entreaty, esp. formally presented to sovereign, government etc
petticoat n. (*pet'i kōt*) Woman's underskirt
petty adj. (*pet'i*) Trivial, small in amount or importance
pew n. (*pū*) Long backed bench for congregation in church
phantom n. (*făn'tom*) Apparition, spectre; a vision *of* something
pharmacist n. (*fah'ma sist*) Person skilled or engaged in pharmacy, a chemist
pharmacy n. (*fah'ma si*) Study or practice of preparing and dispensing drugs as medicine; chemist's
pheasant n. (*fez'ant*) Game-bird,
philosophy n. (*fi los'o fi*) The study of ultimate reality, the general causes of things, thought, behaviour etc

phone n., and v.t. and i. (*fōn*) Short for telephone
phosphorus n. (*fos'forus*) (chem.) The non-metallic element denoted by P, a waxy yellowish highly flammable substance appearing luminous in the dark
photocopy (*fō to kop'i*) n. and v.t. Copy reproduced by photographic device; as v.t. to make such a copy. Hence **photocopier** n. machine that makes such copies
photograph n., and v.t. and i. (*fō'to grahf*) Picture produced by action of light on chemically sensitized film or glass plate; a print made from this on emulsified paper. As v.t. to take a photograph
phrase n. and v.t. (*frāz*) Group of words forming part of a sentence
physical adj. (*fiz'ikl*) Of, connected with, matter or material things, *physical force*
physician n. (*fi zishn'*) Medical doctor; in hospitals, doctor who diagnoses and treats, but does not operate (contrasted with *surgeon*)
physicist n. (*fiz'i sist*) Student of physics; one who aims to explain everything on physical basis
physics n. (*fiz'iks*) The science dealing with the properties of matter and energy, and the effects of forces upon matter
physique n. (*fi zēk'*) Bodily structure, physical development, build
piano n. (*pyăn'ō*) Musical instrument with keyboard, the keys activating hammers that strike metal strings stretched on a harp-like structure
pick 1) n. (*pik*) Tool with long wooden handle and long curved head with point at one end and chisel edge at the other, for breaking ground etc
pick 2) v.t. and i. (*pik*) To break (ground etc.) with a pick, make or dig (hole etc.) with pick; pluck with fingers so as to detach etc.; **on** choose (one person) as object of reproach etc., *why always pick on me?*; **pick out** select; distinguish, make out (face in crowd, meaning etc.)
pickle n. and v.t. (*pik'l*) Brine, vinegar etc. in which meat, vegetables etc. are preserved
picnic n. and v.i. (*pik'nik*) Outdoor excursion including meal in open air
picture n. and v.t. (*pik'cher*) A painting, drawing, photograph etc.; likeness, pictorial image, of a specific person or thing
pie n. (*pī*) Meat, fruit etc. covered with pastry and baked in a deep dish
piece n. (*pēs*) A bit or part or component of a whole

pigeons – top to bottom: wood pigeon, bleeding-heart pigeon, passenger pigeon and blue-crowned pigeon

pier n. (*pēr*) structure projecting into the sea and used as landing-stage, or promenade and place of amusement
pierce v.t. and i. (*pērs*) (Of sharp point or missile) to go into or through, penetrate, make a hole in
pigeon n. (*pij'in*) Wild or tame bird of dove family
pigment n. (*pig'ment*) Substance used for colouring; paint; dye; natural colouring matter of a plant or animal
pike 1) n. (*pīk*) Long wooden shaft with iron or steel head, formerly used by foot-soldiers
pike 2) n. (*pīk*) Large, voracious freshwater fish
pile n. (*pīl*) Heap, collection of things stacked one upon another
pilfer v.t. and i. (*pil'fer*) To steal in small quantities
pilgrim n. (*pil'grim*) Person who makes a journey to shrine or holy place from religious motives. Hence: **pilgrimage** n. journey of a pilgrim
pill n. (*pil*) Small ball or disc of medicinal drugs for swallowing whole
pillar n. (*pil'er*) Column of stone, wood, etc. used in architecture as support or ornament
pillow n. and v.t. (*pil'ō*) Soft cushion used as support for the head in bed
pilot n. and v.t. (*pī'lot*) (naut.) One who steers a ship
pin n. (*pin*) Short, rigid, pointed piece of wire with flattened head, used for fastening clothing, sheets of paper, etc
pinafore n. (*pin'a faw*(*r*)) Apron, piece of clothing worn over a dress etc. to keep it clean
pinch v.t. and i. (*pinch*) To squeeze, compress, between two objects, esp. thumb and first finger, *don't pinch*; to crush, (colloq.) to steal
pine 1) v.i. (*pīn*) To languish, waste away through sorrow, illness, etc.; to long for, long to do, something, *pine for a sight of home*
pine 2) n. (*pīn*) Genus *Pinus* of evergreen coniferous trees with needle-shaped leaves and cones; the timber of this tree
pineapple n. (*pin'ăpl*) Tropical plant of genus *Ananas*; its sweet, juicy fruit shaped like a pine-cone
pint n. (*pīnt*) Measure of liquid capacity equal to one-eighth of a gallon

pineapple

pioneer n. and v.i. and t. (*pī o nēr'*) one who prepares the way for others, esp. in exploring unknown lands or new fields of activity
pipe n. (*pīp*) Musical wind-instrument
hollow tube used for conveying liquids, gas (inc. steam or air), tube with a bowl used for smoking tobacco, *to smoke a pipe*
pirate n. and v.t. (*pī'rat*) Sea-robber
pistol n. and v.t. (*pis'tol*) Small fire-arm held in one hand
pit n. (*pit*) Cavity or hole in the ground; hole in the ground made for a purpose by artificial means, an excavation, *gravel-pit*
pitch 1) n. and v.t. (*pich*) Thick black substance obtained by distillation of coal-tar etc
pitch 2) v.t. and i. (*pich*) To fix, set up, in position, *pitch a tent*; to hurl, throw, toss, *pitch a ball to someone*; (mus.) to set the key of, *the tune is pitched too high to sing*
pitch 3) n. (*pich*) Habitual place or station of person or object, *at one's usual pitch* (cricket) prepared and levelled ground between the wickets
pitcher n. (*pich'er*) Large vessel with handle and spout, for holding liquids; large jug
pity n. and v.t. (*pi'ti*) Feeling of grief, sorrow, for the sufferings of another
place n. (*plās*) Any part or specific area in space, *I can't be in two places at once*

plaid n. (*plăd*) Long piece of woollen cloth, generally with tartan pattern, worn over the shoulders
plain 1) adj. (*plān*) Easy to perceive by the senses, clearly visible or audible; easy to understand, *plain language*; simple, without ornament or pattern, *a plain blue material*
plain 2) n. (*plān*) Area of flat, level, open country
plait n. and v.t. (*plăt*) Length of three or more interlaced strands of hair, etc
plan n. and v.t. (*plăn*) Proportionate drawing made on a flat surface, of designed or completed structure; a scheme, project, *his plans all came to nothing*; methodical arrangement of means of doing something, *to make plans for a journey*
plane 1) n. (*plān*) Any tree of genus *Platanus* of wide-spreading trees that periodically shed their old outer bark
plane 2) n. and v.t. (*plān*) Tool used in smoothing wood
planet n. (*plăn'et*) Any one of the celestial bodies which revolve in orbits about the sun
plank n. and v.t. (*plăngk*) Long, flat piece of timber
plant n. (*plahnt*) Any vegetable organism, as distinct from animal
plantation n. (*plăn tā'shun*) Group of growing trees; area on which certain crops are cultivated
plaster n. (*plah'ster*) General name for plastic substances used for coating wall surfaces, which harden when dry; layer of medicinal substance, with a backing of some fabric, *corn-plaster*; adhesive fabric, often with medicated gauze, used to protect a cut etc., *sticking-plaster*
plate n. (*plāt*) Shallow, flat utensil of porcelain etc., used for holding food at table
plateau n. (*plăt'ō*) Broad plain of elevated land
platform n. (*plat'fawm*) Level surface raised above the general level, esp. in assembly hall or at a railway station
platinum n. (*plăt'i num*) Rare metallic element, symbol Pt, very heavy
platoon n. (*pla tōōn'*) Subdivision of a company in an infantry battalion, commanded by a lieutenant
play 1) v.i. and t. (*plā*) to amuse oneself, engage in an activity for recreation and not as work; to take part in a specific game, *play tennis* the rules of the game; (fig.) behave fairly and honestly; **play tricks with** meddle with, misuse; **play second fiddle to** (fig.) occupy subordinate position to; **play something down** try to minimize it; **play ball with** be ready to co-operate with. (OE. *plegian*)
play 2) n. (*plā*) drama for the stage
pleasant adj. (*plez'ant*) Agreeable, having a pleasing quality
please v.i. and t. (*plēz*) To give pleasure to, satisfy, *that will please her*; to choose, prefer, like, think fit, *I shall do as I please*; as polite form of request, *please come in*
pleasure n. (*ple'zher*) Enjoyment, satisfaction, delight
pledge n. and v.t. (*plej*) Object given as security for fulfilment of obligation, contract, or engagement
plenty n. and adv. (*plen'ti*) Full supply, large quantity, abundance
pliable adj. (*pli'abl*) Capable of being bent, supple
plight n. (*plīt*) Condition, state; awkward predicament
plimsoll n. (*plim'sol*) Light canvas shoes with rubber sole
plod v.i. and t. (*plod*) To walk slowly, heavily, and laboriously; to work slowly, conscientiously, and laboriously
plot 1) n. and v.t. (*plot*) Small extent of ground

plum

plot 2) n. and v.t. and i. (*plot*) Secret scheme to effect specific end, *a plot to overthrow the government*
plough n. and v.t. and i. (*plow*) Agricultural implement having a blade or blades for cutting furrow in the ground, drawn by animals or a tractor
pluck v.t. and i. and n. (*pluk*) To gather, *pluck flowers*; pull out the feathers of (hen etc.)
snatch at, twitch with sudden force, take hold of and pull
plug n. and v.t. and i. (*plug*) Any object used to stop a hole
plum n. (*plum*) Tree of genus *Prunus*; its fruit, with sweet juicy flesh and smooth skin; (fig.) choicest of its kind, the pick
plumage n. (*plōōm'ij*) Bird's feathers collectively
plumber n. (*plum'er*) Person whose trade is to fit and repair pipes, cisterns, etc. in water supply and disposal and drainage systems of a building
plump adj. and v.t. and i. (*plump*) (Of the body) well-covered with flesh, on the fat side
plunder v.t. and i. and n. (*plun'der*) To seize property by violence
plunge v.t. and i. and n. (*plunj*) To immerse suddenly and rapidly in a liquid
plural n. and adj. (*plōō'ral*) Form of word denoting more than one
plus prep., adj., and n. (*plus*) With the addition of
pneumonia n. (*nū mō'ni a*) Illness characterized by inflammation of the lung
poach v.i. and t. (*pōch*) To trespass on private property and steal game or fish
pocket n. (*pok'et*) Small bag forming part of one's clothing, for carrying money or small objects in
poem n. (*pō'em*) Literary composition written in metrical form, usually expressing an intensely felt experience or experiences
point 1) n. (*point*) Sharp or tapering end, *point of a sword*; mark or dot made by a sharp end, esp. of pencil etc.; real or imagined mark or position in space or time, *point of departure*; particular division, heading, item entry, *go over a scheme point by point*; distinctive quality, characteristic, *painting is not my strong point*; a degree, mark on a scale, *boiling-point*; gist of an argument or remark, *you've missed my point*; purpose, use, *what is the point of that?*; small promontory or sea-cape

pointer

point 2) v.t. and i. (*point*) To direct attention to, indicate position or direction of, *the compass needle points to the magnetic north*; to direct (at or towards), *point a gun at someone*; give a point to, *point a pencil*; add force to, *point a moral*; fill in joints of brickwork with mortar, using the point of a trowel
point-blank adj. (*point blăngk'*) Aimed horizontally, direct, at close range
pointer n. (*poin'ter*) Person or thing that points, esp. indicator on dial etc.; breed of sporting dog trained to stand with body steady and nose directed towards game
poison n. and v.t. (*poi'zn*) Substance causing death or injury when absorbed into the system
poke v.t. and i. and n. (*pōk*) To thrust against, in, or into; push; grope, feel about, *poke into other people's business*
pole 1) n. (*pōl*) One of the two extremities of the earth's axis or of the celestial sphere; either of the two ends of a magnet or the terminal points of a battery or accumulator; (fig.) an opposite extreme, *they are poles apart*

pole 2) n. (*pōl*) Long, slender, rounded piece of wood etc

police n. and v.t. (*po lēs'*) Civil force for preservation of law and order

policy 1) n. (*pol'i si*) Art of government; plan, statement of principles and plans pursued by a governing body; specific plan pursued or put forward by a governing body or political party
policy 2) n. (*pol'i si*) Written statement of a contract, esp. of an insurance contract
polish v.t. and i. and n. (*po'lish*) To make smooth and glossy, esp. by rubbing
polite adj. (*po lit'*) Courteous
politics n. (*pol'it iks*) (pl.) Science or art of governing
poll n., and v.t. and i. (*pōl*) Register of voters; act or place of voting at election; number of votes cast; estimate of public opinion by scientific methods
pollute v.t. (*pol ōōt'*) To defile or to make unclean; contaminate
pony n. (*pōn'i*) Small horse
pool n. (*pōōl*) Small sheet of water or liquid, puddle; deep still place in river
poor adj. and n. (*pōōr*) Having no wealth, needy
pop v.t. and i. (*pop*) Tò make low explosive sound as of sudden release of air under pressure
pope n. (*pōp*) Bishop of Rome, head of R.C. Church
porcelain n. (*paw'sel in*) Fine semi-transparent earthenware
porch n. (*pawch*) Covered structure round entrance of building
pore n. (*paw(r)*) Minute opening (esp. in skin) by which fluids are exhaled or absorbed
pork n. (*pawk*) Pig flesh, fresh or salted for eating
porridge n. (*po'rij*) Oatmeal or other meal boiled in water or milk as food
port 1) n. (*pawt*) Harbour for protection and loading and unloading of ships; town having harbour; (fig.) place of refuge, shelter
port 2) n. (*pawt*) Gate; port-hole; opening in ship's side for gangway, loading etc
port 3) n. (*pawt*) Fortified sweet wine from Portugal
porter 1) n. (*pawt'er*) Doorkeeper or gatekeeper, esp. of hotel, public building etc
porter 2) n. (*pawt'er*) Man employed to carry burdens, esp. passengers' luggage at stations, airports etc
portion n. and v.t. (*paw'shun*) Part, share, or division
portrait n. (*pawt'rit*) Likeness of person in paint, drawing, photograph etc.; (fig.) description of person in words
portray v.t. (*pawt rā'*) To paint or draw likeness of (person); describe (person) in words
pose v.t. and i., and n. (*pōz*) To place in certain position or attitude, esp. as model for painting or photographing; propound (question, problem); pretend, to make oneself out as, *I don't pose as an expert*
position n. and v.t. (*poz ish'un*) Place or situation occupied by anything
positive adj. and n. (*poz'i tiv*) Definite, expressed without qualification, stated as a fact, *proof positive*; fully convinced, *to be positive about something*
possess v.t. (*po zes'*) To hold, own, occupy, *possess property*
possible adj. and n. (*pos'ibl*) Capable of happening, existing, or being done
post 1) n. (*pōst*) Upright stake set in the ground to act as a support, *door-post*
post 2) v.t. (*pōst*) To affix a notice etc. to a post or other conspicuous place, *post (up) an advertisement*; to announce by posting up a public notice
post 3) n. and v.t. (*pōst*) Place where a soldier etc. is on watch place of duty; place occupied by troops, esp. an outpost, *a chain of frontier posts*; outlying settlement, esp. for trading, *a trading-post*; any position, duty, to which someone is assigned, *to remain at one's post*; position, employment, job As v.t. to place soldier or other person at a post; allot a duty to.
the official transmission and delivery of messages, letters, and parcels
post 4) v.i. and t. (*pōst*) (hist.) dispatch a letter by post
postage n. (*pōst'ij*) Rate charged for postal conveyance; **postage stamp** printed adhesive label used to prepay postage on letters etc
poster n. (*pōs'ter*) One who posts notices; bill or placard displayed in a public place for advertising purposes etc
post-mortem adj. and n. (*pōst maw'tem*) Made, occurring, done, after death. As n., medical examination of a dead body to ascertain cause of death
postpone v.t. (*pōst pōn'*) To put off until a later time

postscript n. (*pōst'skript*) Addition to a letter, written below the signature and abbreviated P.S.
pot n. (*pot*) Rounded vessel for holding liquids or solids, for cooking food in, etc., *a stew-pot*
potato n. (*po tā'tō*) Edible tuber
potter n. (*pot'er*) Maker of earthenware pots and vessels; **potter's wheel** revolving horizontal disk on which clay is thrown and moulded. Hence: **pottery** n. earthenware; pots; the making of earthenware; workshop where pottery is made
pouch n. and v.t. (*powch*) Small bag or sac; anything resembling this in shape
poultry n. (*pōl'tri*) Domestic fowls kept for food
pounce n. and v.i. (*powns*) A sudden swoop down on something with intent to seize
pound n. (*pownd*) Standard unit of weight, 16 ounces
pour v.t. and i. (*paw (r)*) To cause to flow out in a stream, *please pour the tea out*
poverty n. (*pov'er ti*) State of being poor
powder n. and v.t. and i. (*pow'der*) Fine particles produced by pulverizing a substance
power n. (*pow'er*) Capacity for or exercise of, control, authority, *the power of the law*
practical adj. (*prak'tik al*) workable, *a practical scheme*; soundly functional, *a really practical ironing-board*
practice n. (*prăk'tis*) The performance of a thing (contrasted with theory), *to put an idea into practice*; habitual, customary action, regular performance, *a matter of common practice*; ceremonial observance or ritual, *Christian practices*; repeated exercise of some kind, done to acquire proficiency, *piano-practice*; the exercise of a profession; clients, patients etc. dealt with by members of a profession, *a doctor with a large practice*
practise v.t. and i. (*prak'tis*) To carry out (a theory) in action; put into practice; perform as a custom, *practise early rising*; follow a profession, art etc. *practise medicine*; train, exercise, in some activity to gain proficiency, *practise at the piano*
prairie n. (*prār'i*) Wide tract of mid-latitude grasslands, esp. in N. America
praise v.t. and n. (*prāz*) To express approval or admiration of
prance v.i. and n. (*prahns*) (Of a horse) to spring forward from the hind legs move about gaily and energetically
prank n. (*prăngk*) Mischievous trick, *to play a prank*.
pray v.i. and t. (*prā*) To beg (for) earnestly, *we pray your attention*; utter prayers (for a thing), address oneself to God *let us pray!*
prayer n. (*prār*) One who prays; act of praying to God; words addressed to God, *the Lord's Prayer*; formal request made to superior authority, *humble petition and prayer*
preach v.t. and i. (*prēch*) To proclaim, *preach the Gospel*; deliver (a sermon); make known a religious doctrine, *preach to the unconverted*; give moral advice to, esp. unasked and unwanted, *too fond of preaching to his staff*; to urge, *preach economy*
precede v.t. and i. (*prē sēd'*) To go, come, be, before, *lightning precedes thunder*
precious adj. (*pre'shus*) Of great value or price, *precious jewels*; highly valued, held dear, *precious memories*
precipice n. (*pre'si pis*) Sheer, perpendicular face of rock
precise adj. (*pre sis'*) Exact, clearly defined, *a precise statement*; strictly accurate, correct, exact
predict v.t. (*pre dikt'*) To foretell, prophesy
prefabricate v.t. (*prē făb'ri kāt*) To manufacture the parts of a building, ship, etc. in sections ready for assembly on site
prefer v.t. (*pre fur'*) To like better than
prefix n. and v.t. (*prē'fix*) Word placed before another word
pregnant adj. (*preg'nant*) With child in the womb
prehistoric adj. (*prē his to'rik*) Of the time before recorded history
premature adj. (*prem'a tūr*) Done, happening, before the normal time
premier adj. and n. (*prem'i er, prē'mi er*) First in rank or importance, principal
prepare v.t. and i. (*pre pār'*) To make ready for use, to get ready, make preparations
prescribe v.t. and i. (*pre skrib'*) To ordain, direct, *prescribed textbooks*; advise (medicine or treatment); lay down rules
prescription n. (*pre skrip'shun*) Act of prescribing; what is

prescribed, esp. written recipe for preparation of a medicine; the medicine itself
present 1) adj. (*pre'zent*) Being in the place in question, *how many were present?*; occurring, existing, now, *the present time*
present 2) n. (*pre'zent*) The present time; present tense; **for the present** for the moment; **at present** now
present 3) v.t. and i. (*pre zent'*) To introduce submit, lay before, put forward, *present a petition*
show, reveal, *present a bold front*; bestow as gift
present 4) n. (*pre'zent*) A gift
preserve v.t. (*pre zurv'*) To keep safe from harm, damage or decay
preside v.i. (*pre zid'*) To occupy the place of authority, esp. at a meeting, to take the chair; **preside over** be in charge of
president n. (*prez'i dent*) Title of various officers holding authority, esp. the head of government in the U.S.A. and other republics
press 1) v.t. and i. (*pres*) To exert force or weight upon so as to crush or compress, to squeeze, *to press grapes*
urge, request insistently, *press a debtor for money*
press 2) n. (*pres*) Act of pressing; what is to be pressed; what presses, *a wine-press*
printing; a printing
pressure n. (*presh'er*) Act of pressing; force exerted by pressing force exerted by one body against another
pretend v.t. and i. (*prit end'*) To feign, simulate; lay false claim to; play at being, imagine oneself as
pretty adj., adv., and n. (*prit'i*) Superficially but pleasantly attractive, pleasing; dainty, neat
prevent v.t. (*pri vent'*) To stop
preview n. (*prē'vū*) View or examination of play, film, exhibition etc. in advance of public presentation
previous adj. and adv. (*prē' vyus*) Preceding, earlier
price n. and v.t. (*pris*) Money value paid or asked for goods on sale, services offered, etc
prick v.t. and i. (*prik*) To pierce with sharp pointed object
prickle n., and v.t. and i. (*prik'l*) Tingling sensation of skin; spine of hedgehog etc.; small thorn
pride n. and v. reflex. (*prid*) Excessive pleasure and satisfaction felt in merits of one's achievements, wealth, position, etc
priest n. and v.t. (*prēst*) One whose office it is to perform sacred rites and act as intermediary between the people and God
primary adj. (*prim'er i*) Earliest, original; principal, most important; preparatory, rudimentary
prime 1) n. (*prim*) State of highest perfection, *he is in the prime of life*
prime 2) adj. (*prim*) First in time, rank or importance
primitive adj. and n. (*prim'iti v*) Of or at earliest stage of development or evolution; prehistoric; uncivilized
principal adj. and n. (*prin'sip al*) Most important; highest in rank
n. head of institution
print v.t. and i. (*print*) To reproduce words, illustrations, etc. by impressing on paper etc. with inked type, blocks, plates
prior 1) n. (*pri'er*) Superior of monastery
prior 2) adj. and adv. (*pri'er*) Earlier, previous
prison n. (*priz'on*) Place of confinement; building in which law-breakers are kept
private adj. and n. (*pri'vit*) Individual, personal, not public, *this is a private house*; secret, confidential, *the matter was kept private*; secluded, undisturbed
privilege n. and v.t. *(privi' lij)* Right, advantage, or immunity exclusive to one person, class, or group
prize n., adj., and v.t. (*priz*) Reward for merit or won in competition or game of chance
probable adj. and n. (*prob'a bl*) Likely to happen; likely to be true
probation n. (*prō bā'shun*) State or period of being tested; (law) system by which sentence is suspended on condition that offender is of good behaviour and reports regularly to appointed official
problem n. (*prob'lem*) Question involving uncertainty and difficulty
proceed v.i. (*pro sēd'*) To move (from or towards a place); begin, *let us proceed to business*; continue, *shall we proceed?*; act or behave, *how do we proceed?*
proceeds n. (*prō'sedz*) (pl.) Money raised by performance, sale, etc.; profit
process n. and v.t. (*prō'ses*) Method by which something is done; system of manufacture

procession n. and v.t. and i. (*prō sesh'un*) Number of persons or things proceeding in orderly succession, esp. in religious or festive ceremony
proclaim v.t. (*pro klām'*) To announce publicly and officially
procrastinate v.t. and i. (*prō kras'tin āt*) To defer action
procure v.t. (*pro kyo͞or'*) To obtain, acquire
prodigal adj. and n. (*prod'ig al*) Lavish, extravagant, wasteful of money
produce 1) v.t. and i. (*pro dūs'*) To bring forth, yield
produce 2) n. (*prod'ūs*) What is produced; harvest, crop, yield; product
profession n. (*pro fesh'un*) Occupation
proficient adj. and n. (*pro fish'ent*) Expert
profile n. and v.t. (*prō'fīl, prō'fēl*) Side view of face; outline drawing
profit n., and v.t. and i. (*prof'it*) Advantage, benefit
profound adj. (*pro fownd'*) Very deep; having great knowledge or insight, *he is a profound scholar*
programme n. and v.t. (*prō'gram*) Descriptive notice (e.g. order of events, those taking part) of concert, play, sports meeting, etc.; actual entertainment provided at concert, theatre, etc. or on radio or television; statement of policy or intentions, esp. of political party
progress 1) n. (*prō'gres*) Onward or forward movement; improvement, development
progress 2) v.t. (*prō gres'*) To move forward, advance
prohibit v.t. (*prō hib'it*) To forbid, esp. by law
project v.t. and i. (*pro jekt'*) and n. (*proj'ekt*) To throw, hurl with deliberate aim, esp. of beam of light; form mental picture of; cast (image) on screen by
projectile adj. and n. (*pro jekt'il*) Hurling, projecting; intended to be hurled. As n. missile
projector n. (*pro jekt'er*) One who forms projects; promoter of enterprise; apparatus for projecting films etc. on screen
prolong v.t. (*pro long'*) To make longer, extend; cause to last longer, spin out
promenade n., and v.t. and i. (*prom en ahd'*) Short leisurely walk taken for pleasure or exercise; place designed for walking about freely, esp. along sea front
prominence n. (*prom'in ens*) Condition of being prominent; projecting point of land. Hence: **prominent** adj. jutting out, projecting; distinguished, conspicuous; eminent, famous
promise n. (*prom'is*) Undertaking or guarantee about one's future conduct; thing promised; probability of success or fulfilment, *his work shows promise*
promontory n. (*prom'on tri*) A cape, high land jutting out to sea
promote v.t. (*prom ōt'*) To raise to higher rank
prompt 1) adj. and n. (*prompt*) Quick to act
prompt 2) v.t. and n. (*prompt*) To urge, incite; aid memory of, esp. of actor etc. who had forgotten his lines

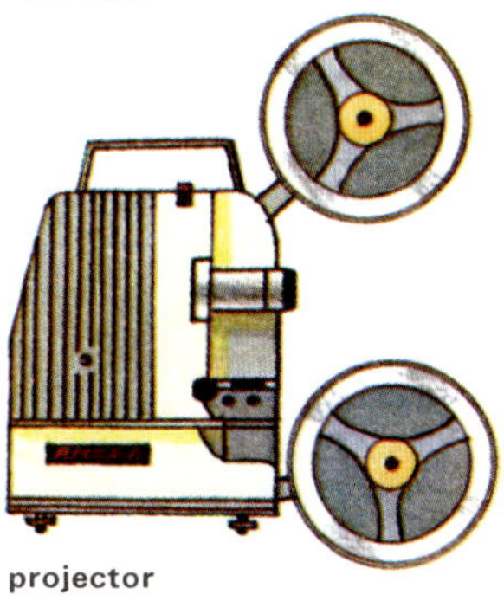

projector

promontory

pronoun n. (*prō'nown*) Word used in place of noun
pronounce v.t. and i. (*pro nowns'*) To utter, articulate (words)
pronunciation n. (*prō nun sē ā'shun*) Mannerof pronouncing,esp. generally accepted way of saying word, phrase, etc
proof n. (*prōōf*) Act or process of demonstrating that fact or statement is true
prop n., and v.t. (*prop*) Rigid support (stick, stake, etc.) holding up weight; (fig.) moral support, spiritual comfort; person who gives support
propaganda n. (*prop ag ăn'da*) Act or method of propagating doctrine, ideals, etc; books, broadcasts, films, literature, etc. used to this end; information, arguments, facts, etc. (often false or distorted) thus disseminated; organization for spreading doctrines
propagate v.t. and i. (*prop'ag āt*) To breed, multiply by natural reproduction; have offspring; disseminate, spread, transmit
propel v.t. (*pro pel'*) To cause to move forward; drive forward
propeller n. mechanism for propelling, esp. screw of ship or aircraft
proper adj. (*prop'er*) Apt, suitable, right, *this is the proper tool to use*; according to rule or custom, regular; one's own, *I saw it with my proper eyes*; accurate, correct; (colloq.) thorough, complete, *he's a proper scoundrel*; decent, modest

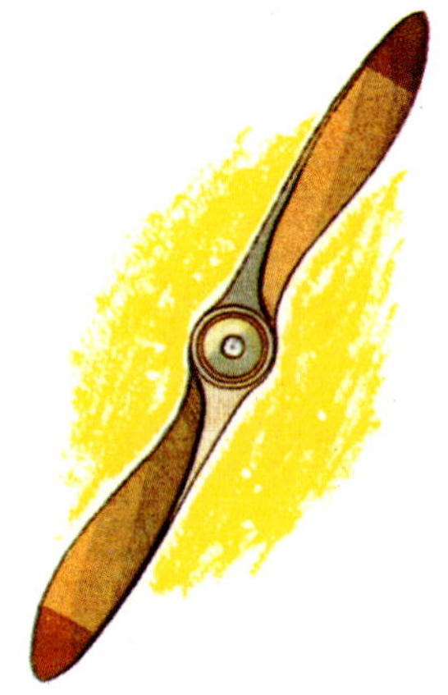

propeller

property n. (*prop'er ti*) What is owned, possessions, belongings
prophesy v.t. and i. (*prof'is i*) pret. and p.p. **prophesied** (*prof'is id*) To predict (event); foretell future
prophet n. (*prof'it*) one who foretells future
proportion n. and v.t. (*prop aw'shun*) Part or portion, *a small proportion of them were women*; ratio, comparative relation (in size, quantity, quality, arrangement, etc.)
proposal n. (*prop ōz'al*) Act of proposing; offer, esp. of marriage; thing proposed, suggestion
propose v.t. and i. (*prop ōz'*) To put forward (suggestion, scheme, plan, etc.) for consideration; nominate (person) as member of society; make offer of marriage
proprietor n. (*pro prī'et er*) Owner
prosecute v.t. and i. (*pros'ik ūt*) To take legal proceedings against
prospect n., and v.t. and i. (*pros'pekt*) Condition of facing in specified direction; view, landscape, vista, *the house has a wonderful prospect*; mental scene, plan, ambition, *do you have anything in prospect?*; (pl.) expectations esp. of success or advancement in a career; (mining) area giving promise of mineral deposit
prosper v.t. and i. (*pros'per*) To thrive, succeed
prosperity n. (*pros pe'ri ti*) State of prospering; good fortune, wealth
prosperous adj. (*pros'per us*) Successful, flourishing, thriving
protect v.t. (*pro tekt'*) To defend from harm, guard, keep safe
protest n. (*prō'test*) and v.t. and i. (*pro test'*) Expression of disapproval
prototype n. (*prō'tō tip*) Earliest form of a series; model, pattern
protractor n. (*pro trăk'ter*) Instrument for measuring angles
proud adj. and adv. (*prowd*) Having just awareness of one's merits or achievements; feeling oneself honoured, *I am proud to have served him*; indulging in feeling of unwarranted satisfaction in oneself; haughty, arrogant
prove v.t. and i. (*proov*) To demonstrate to be true or valid, establish as true
proverb n. (*prov'erb*) Short traditional saying expressing
provide v.t. and i. (*prō vid'*) To procure and supply, furnish
province n. (*prov'ins*) Large administrative division of a country

protractor

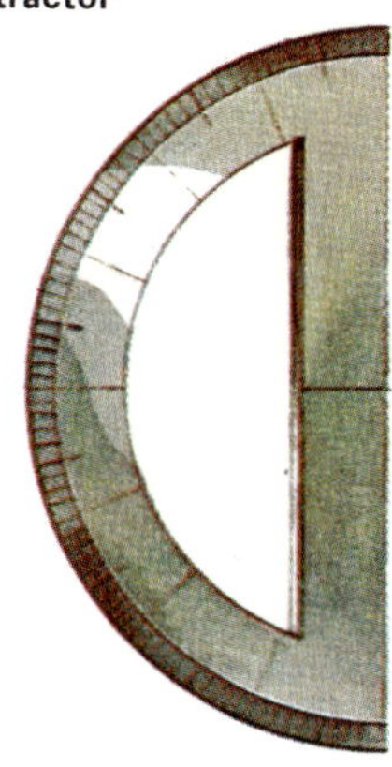

provision n. and v.t. (*prō vizh'un*) Act of providing (against, for): what is provided (pl.) stock or supply
provisional adj. (*prō vizh'un al*) Temporary, for the time being
prowl v.t. and i., and n. (*prowl*) To move about in search of plunder or prey; wander stealthily through
prudent adj. (*prōōd'ent*) Cautious
pry 1) v.i. (*prī*) To peer into, spy on
pry 2) v.t. (*prī*) To force (open) with lever
psychology n. (*sī kol'oj i*) Study of the mind, its nature, processes, habits, etc
public adj. and n. (*pub'lik*) As n. community; nation; that part of community interested or likely to be interested in specified idea, article, activity, etc
publication n. (*pub li kā'shun*) anything published, book, magazine, music, etc
publicity n. (*pub li'si ti*) act or practice of advertising; advertisements
publish v.t. (*pub'lish*) To make generally known; announce, music etc.) for sale
puddle n., and v.t. and i. (*pu'dl*) Shallow pool esp. of rain water
puff v.t. and i., and n. (*puf*) To emit (smoke, steam, etc.) in short repeated blasts; breathe heavily and jerkily, pant; be out of breath
pull v.t. and i. (*pōōl*) To exert such force upon something as to cause it to be drawn in direction of force, *the horse pulls the cart*
pulp n. and v.t. (*pulp*) Soft fleshy fibre, e.g. interior of fruit
pulpit n. (*pōōl'pit*) Raised box-like structure from which preacher delivers sermon
pulse n., and v.t. and i. (*puls*) Rhythmic throbbing of heart and blood stream, esp. throbbing of this felt at wrist; rate of this pulsation; rhythmic beating, vibration
pump n., and v.t. and i. (*pump*) Mechanical device for moving gases and liquids,
punch 1) n. and v.t. (*punch*) Instrument for making holes in paper, leather, metal, etc
punch 2) v.t. and n. (*punch*) To strike esp. with clenched fist
punch 3) n. (*punch*) Wine or spirit mixed with hot water or milk, flavoured with lemon and spice and sweetened
punctual adj. (*pungk'chōō al*) Observing appointed time, not late, prompt
punctuate v.t. (*pungk'chōō āt*) To insert commas, stops, etc. in passage of writing
puncture n., and v.t. and i. (*pungk'cher*) Prick, perforation, esp. one in pneumatic tire
punish v.t. (*pun'ish*) To penalize for wrong-doing
puny adj. (*pū'ni*) Weak, feeble, under-sized
pupil n. (*pū'pil*) One being taught by teacher opening in iris through which light reaches retina
puppet n. (*pup'it*) Doll, esp. small jointed figure worked by pulling wires or strings in toy theatre

pupil

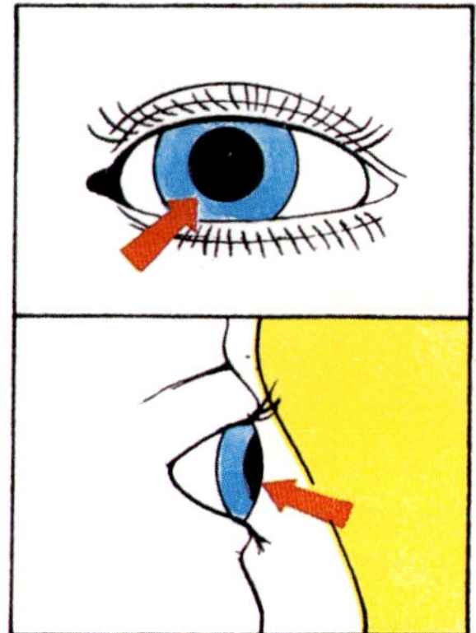

purchase v.t. and n. (*pur'chis*) To buy, acquire by payment
pure adj. (*pūr*) Clean, uncontaminated, *pure air*
purpose n. (*pur'pus*) Object, aim, *will this serve your purpose?*
purr v.i. and n. (*pur*) (of cats etc.) To make low vibrating sound expressing content or satisfaction
purse n. (*purs*) Small pouch usually of leather for carrying money
pursue v.t. (*pursū'*) To follow with intent to capture or kill; follow in pursuit; practise (occupation, activity, etc.)
pursuit n. (*pur sūt'*) Act of pursuing; chase, hunt; occupation, recreation, hobby or any other activity one follows
push v.t. and i. (*po͝osh*) To exert force against (object) tending to move it away
put v.t. and i. (*po͝ot*) pret. and p.p. **put** (*po͝ot*) To set, place, lay; bring into some relation or state
puzzle v.t. and i., and n. (*pu'zl*) To baffle, perplex, confuse; be perplexed by
pyjamas, (U.S.) **pajamas** n. (*pi jah'maz*) (pl.) Sleeping suit of jacket and trousers
pylon n. (*pi'lon*) Steel structure carrying overhead electric cables
pyramid n. (*pi'ra mid*) (geom.) ancient Egyptian monument

Q

quack 1) v.i. and n. (*kwăk*) To make a noise like a duck. As n., noise made by ducks. (Imit.)
quack 2) n. (*kwăk*) One who pretends to specialized knowledge, esp. in medicine or surgery

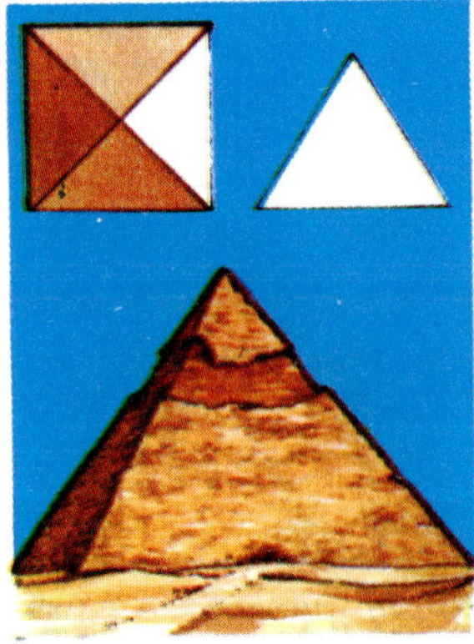

pyramid

quadrangle n. (*kwod'răngl*) Four-sided, four-angled plane figure; (arch.) rectangular court enclosed by buildings
quadruple adj., n., and v.t. (*kwod'ro͞opl*) Fourfold, *at a quadruple rate*. As n., a fourfold amount. As v.t., to multiply by four. Hence: **quadruplet** n. (*kwod'ro͞o plet*) one of four children born at one birth
quaint adj. (*kwānt*) Pleasing or attractive because unusual or old-fashioned
quake v.i. and n. (*kwāk*) (Of things) to shake, tremble, *the ground quaked beneath his feet*; (of persons) shake, tremble, esp. with fear. As n., a shake, an earthquake
qualify v.t. and i. (*kwol'i fi*) To give the necessary qualifications to, train and prepare for a particular employment etc
quality n. (*kwol'i ti*) What distinguishes one thing from another, its essential nature
quantity n. (*kwon'ti ti*) The property of anything that is measurable in terms of size, weight, number, amount, or extent; a specified amount or number, *a large quantity*
quarantine n. (*kwo'ran tēn*) Period of isolation of persons, animals, or things suspected of carrying infectious disease
quarrel 1) n. (*kwo'rel*) Dispute, contention, esp. when angry and heated
quarrel 2) v.i. (*kwo'rel*) To engage in a quarrel, argue heatedly
quarry 1) n. (*kwo'ri*) Any animal hunted by men or beasts or birds of prey
quarry 2) n. (*kwo'ri*) Pit from which stone is excavated
quarry 3) v.t. and i. (*kwo'ri*) To get from a quarry
quart n. (*kwawt*) Measure of liquid capacity, fourth part of a gallon
quarter 1) n. (*kwaw'ter*) One of four equal or corresponding parts, *a quarter of an hour* one of the four cardinal points of the compass, *the quarter from which the wind is blowing*; division of a town or district; part of a town occupied by a particular part of the population, mercy to a defeated enemy, *to give quarter*
quarter 2) v.t. and i. (*kwaw'ter*) To divide into four quarters

quarterly adj., adv., and n. (*kwaw'terli*) Happening each quarter of the year. As adv., once every quarter of the year. As n., a periodical published every three months
quartet(te) n. (*kwaw tet'*) A group of four, esp. four singers or players; piece of music arranged for four singers or players
quay n. (*kē*) Place on coast or riverside for the loading and unloading of cargo from vessels
queen n. and v.t. (*kwēn*) Woman ruling in her own right, *Elizabeth I, Queen of England*; wife of a king, *Queen Elizabeth, wife of George VI* (cards) court card next below the king; principal scoring piece in chess; large, fertile female of certain insects, *queen bee*
queer adj., n., and v.t. (*kwēr*) Odd, strange; doubtful, questionable; in poor health; slightly mad
quell v.t. (*kwel*) To suppress, crush
quench v.t. (*kwench*) To put out, extinguish, damp down, *quench a fire*; still, repress, *quench hope*; allay, slake (thirst)
query n. and v.t. (*kwē'ri*) A question, As v.t., to call in question, *I queried whether his word was reliable*; require confirmation or further explanation
quest n. and v.i. (*kwest*) Search, pursuit
question n. (*kwes'chun*) A request for information, an interrogation requiring a reply, *ask many questions*; subject of debate, point of discussion
queue n. and v.i. (*kū*) line of people one behind another waiting for their turn (to enter, buy something etc.); line of vehicles waiting to proceed. As v.i., to form a queue; wait in a queue
quick adj. (*kwik*) Lively in intellect, ready in understanding, *quick to learn*
quicken v.t. and i. (*kwi'ken*) To make alive, give life to; stir to action, hasten, *quicken one's steps*
quiet 1) adj. (*kwi'et*) Free from movement, noise, disturbance, or excitement, *a quiet street*; calm
quiet 2) n. (*kwi'et*) Absence of noise, silence
quieten v.t. and i. (*kwi'e ten*) To quiet
quill n. (*kwil*) Large feather; hollow stem of such a feather; object made from it, esp. a pen for writing; the spine of a porcupine
quilt n. and v.t. (*kwilt*) Thick bed-cover made by padding two layers of material with a soft substance and cross-stitching it into place
quintuplet n. (*kwin tū'plet*) Group of five things or persons; one of five children born at one birth, commonly abbreviated to *quin*
quit adj. and v.t. and i. (*kwit*) Released from an obligation, free, clear, *well quit of a bad bargain*. As v.t. and i., to leave, go away from, *quit a town*; depart, *notice to quit*
quite adv. (*kwit*) Entirely, *not quite finished*; almost, practically, as one might say, *he's quite a little man now*; fairly, largely, to a certain extent, *I didn't quite like his tone*
quits adj. or adv. (*kwits*) On even terms with
quiver 1) v.i. and t. and n. (*kwi'ver*) To tremble, shake, *his lips quivered*; to cause to quiver
quiver 2) n. (*kwi'ver*) Case for carrying arrows
quiz n. and v.t. and i. (*kwiz*) (modern use) game or test in which participants are asked questions on subjects of general knowledge
quoit n. (*koit*) Ring used in the game of quoits; (pl.) game in which players throw a quoit on to or near a peg
quota n. (*kwō'ta*) Proportional share, limited number or part previously assigned or allocated
quotation n. (*kwō tā'shun*) Act of quoting; what is quoted, esp. from a book, poem etc., *quotations from*

quoit

Wordsworth; statement of a price demanded for a commodity etc.; estimate of cost of specified work
quote v.t. and i. (*kwōt*) To repeat, cite in speech or writing (words written or spoken by another); state, estimate (a price)

R

rabbi n. (*răb'ī*) Jewish minister of religion
rabble n. (*ră'bl*) Ragged, disorderly, noisy mob of people
race 1) n. (*rās*) Division of mankind whose members share certain obvious physical characteristics; (bot.) variety that reproduces its own peculiarities; stock or breed of people; group of persons, animals, or plants connected by common descent
race 2) n. and v.t. and i. (*rās*) Contest of speed over given distance between persons or animals or vehicles competing against each other or against the clock As v.t. and i. to compete in speed
racial adj. (*rā'shal*) Pertaining to, due to, race; **racial discrimination** legal or social disadvantages imposed on some races; **racial prejudice** irrational hatred for or fear of men of another race. Hence: **racialism** n. race sentiments, prejudices and loyalties; view that race is of primary importance; **racialist** n. and adj.; **racially** adv
rack n. and v.t. (*răk*) Framework of bars for holding or storing plates, toast, clothes etc
racket 1) n. (*răk'it*) Oval gut- or nylon-strung bat used in tennis and related games
racket 2) n. and v.i. (*răk'it*) Confused, rowdy, clamorous noise; scheme for making illegal or immoral profits
radar n. (*rā'dah*) Apparatus using radio echoes for finding position of surrounding objects
radiant adj. and n. (*rā'dyant*) Emitting rays of light; shining brightly, *the radiant sunlight*; (fig.) bright with pleasure, joy, health
radiate adj., and v.t., and i. (*rā'di āt*) Having rays. As v.t. and i. to emit rays
Hence: **radiation** n.; **radiator** n. (*rā'di a tur*) that which radiates; device for heating by means of hot water, air or steam in pipes; device for cooling cylinders of petrol engine
radio n. and v.t. and i. (*rā'dyō*) Wireless telegraphy or telephony; wireless receiving set. As v.t. and i. to transmit (message) by radio
radioactive adj. (*rā'dyō ak'tiv*) (phys.) Spontaneously and continuously emitting charged atomic particles
radium n. (*rā'dyum*) Metallic element denoted by Ra, notable for its intense radioactivity
radius n. (*rā'dyus*) pl. **radii** (*rā dyi*) (geom.) Distance of a circle's circumference from its centre circular area centred
on a specified point, *she knows everyone within a ten-mile radius*
raffia n. (*ră'fya*) Long-leaved Madagascar palm, *Raphia ruffia*; cuticle of this plant used for tying up plants and making mats, hats etc
raffle n. and v.t. (*ră'fl*) Sale of article whereby tickets are sold and drawn by lottery, the prize being won by the winning ticket holder. As v.t. to dispose by a raffle
raft n. and v.t. (*rahft*) Flat structure of logs, planks etc. used as a conveyance on water
rafter n. and v.t. (*rahf'ter*) Sloping beam supporting frame of a roof
rag n. (*răg*) Torn, dirty, useless piece of cloth; tattered old garments
rage n. and v.i. (*rāj*) Furious anger (colloq.) fashionable craze, *all the rage*. As v.i. to be in a rage
raid n. and v.t. (*rad*) Sudden attack for purposes of plunder or destruction
As v.t. to make raid into or upon; to plunder
rail n. and v.t. (*rāl*) Wooden or metal bar; bar supported by brackets for hanging clothes on; balustrade on a staircase; one of the parallel steel lines forming the permanent way for trains and trams; railway, *to send by rail*; (pl.) fence; railway line
rain n. (*rān*) Condensed moisture of the atmosphere falling as small drops of water; (fig.) rapid succession or repetition (of blows, bullets etc.)
rainbow n. (*rān'bō*) Arched bow showing colours of the spectrum formed in the sky opposite the sun
raise v.t. and n. (*rāz*) To cause a rise; to lift; to build; to exalt; to promote; to increase the amount or value; to enhance; to inspire, *danger raised his spirits*; to suggest; to evoke; to rear, *lions raise their young*; to levy; to procure money, *I raised a loan, he raises money for charity*; to recruit, *a large army*

was raised; to speak, *no one raised his voice*
raisin n. (*rā'zen*) Dried grape.
rake n., and v.t. and i. (*rāk*) Long-handled agricultural and garden tool with horizontal bar of prongs for gathering hay, leaves, weeds etc. v.t. to scrape; to clear As v.i. to use a rake; (fig.) to search minutely, *to rake among old records*
rally v.t. and i., and n (*răl'i*) To reassemble, esp. disordered forces for further attack; to revive for further effort. As n. the act of rallying (sport) rapid interchange of strokes in tennis etc
ram n. and v.t. (*răm*) Adult male sheep As v.t. to crash into forcibly; to butt like a ram; to batter
ramble n. and v.i. (*răm'bl*) Irregular excursion; stroll. As v.i. to wander about; to roam; to saunter for pleasure; (fig.) to wander about in speech or writing
ramp n., and v.t. and i. (*rămp*) Slope; inclined plane connecting two different levels esp
ranch n. and v.i. (*rahnch*) Extensive farm for cattle or fruit etc. usually in U.S.
rancid adj. (*răn'sid*) Having a sour, stale smell or taste
random adj. and n. (*răn'dom*) Aimlessly; left to chance
range n., and v.t. and i. (*rānj*) Row; series; collection, *a range of mountains*; area; cooking stove; distance reached by hearing or sight; distance reached by projectile of gun; practice area for gun or rifle fire; maximum distance reached by vehicle, aircraft etc. without refuelling; (fig.) capacity, *his range of knowledge* As v.t. to set; to place in a row; to classify; to rove over; to traverse; to get the range of (with a gun etc.). As v.i. to move at large; to vary between two specified limits
rank 1) n., and v.t. and i. (*rănk*) Line of things or people; social class; eminence; degree of worth As v.t to place abreast or in line; to assign a rank. As v.i. to take rank; to belong to a certain rank
rank 2) adj. (*rănk*) Luxurious in growth; coarse; strong smelling; rancid; corrupt; loathsome
ransack v.i. (*răn'săk*) To search thoroughly; to plunder
ransom n. and v.t. (*răn'sum*) Price paid for release of prisoner
rap n., and v.t. and i. (*răp*) Quick, smart blow As v.t. and i. to knock lightly and sharply
rapid adj. and n. (*răp'id*) Very quick, swift; steep. As n. (usually pl.) rapid flow of water where river bed descends steeply
rare 1) adj. (*rār*) Thinly scattered; not dense, *the rare atmosphere of the mountains*; infrequent, *a rare occurrence*; unusual; precious; excellent
rare 2) adj. (*rār*) Nearly raw, underdone (of meat)
rascal n. (*rahs'kal*) Scoundrel, rogue; dishonest person
rash 1) n. (*răsh*) Eruption of the skin
rash 2) adj. (*răsh*) Hasty in action or judgement; reckless
raspberry n. (*rahz'be ri*) Plant *Rubus idaeus*; the fruit of this plant
rat n. and v.i. (*răt*) Small rodent
rate 1) n. (*rāt*) Proportion by which an unvarying relation between two things different in kind is measured, *30 miles an hour, 2d. per lb.*; price fixed or stated; (nav.) class of ship; (esp. pl.) local government tax calculated on value of property
rate 2) v.t. and i. (*rāt*) To estimate worth, *I do not rate his merits very highly*; to fix the rate; to assess for rating
rather adv. (*rah'ther*) More accurately, *the mail comes every day, or rather every weekday*; preferably, *I get up late rather than early*; in a modified way; more willingly or readily, *he would rather have died than refused*
ratify v.t. (*răt'i fi*) To confirm; to make valid; to approve
ration n. and v.t. (*răsh'un*) Fixed allowance of anything esp. food; (pl.) provisions As v.t. to limit distribution of anything esp. food to fixed quantities. (As ratio)
rational adj. (*răsh'un al*) Capable of reasoning; based on reason
rattle v.t. and i., and n. (*ră'tl*) To make or cause to make rapid succession of sharp clattering sounds As n. series of sharp clattering sounds plaything for babies that rattles
raucous adj. (*raw'kus*) Harsh; loud and coarse
ravage n., and v.t. and i. (*ră vij*) Devastation; waste As v.t. to devastate; to lay waste
rave v.i. and n. (*rāv*) To wander in mind; to speak incoherently; to rage; **to rave about** to speak

enthusiastically about
raven n. and adj. (*rā'ven*) Largest of the crow family
ravine n. (*ră vēn'*) Long deep gulley; narrow gorge
raw adj. and n. (*raw*) Natural; uncooked; untrained; inexperienced; sore; having the skin rubbed off; damp and chilly, *a raw wind*; crude, *raw manners*; undiluted, *raw spirit*; unprocessed, *wool is the raw material of the woollen textile industry*
ray n., and v.t. and i. (*rā*) Beam, shaft of light
rayon n. (*rā'on*) Artificial silk
razor n. (*rā'zer*) Sharp instrument for shaving off hair
re- pref. Back; again; against
reach v.t. and i., and n. (*rēch*) To stretch out, to extend; to grasp, take, or hand over with outstretched arm. As n. the act of reaching; distance to which hand can reach, *a boxer's reach, out of reach*; range of influence or power; distance, *within easy reach of home*
react v.i. (*rē akt'*) To respond to a stimulus
reaction n. (*rē ak'shun*) Response to a stimulus
read v.t. and i. (*rēd*) To look at and understand written or printed words, letters, or symbols (of instrument) to register, *the thermometer reads 98.4°F.*; to study for a degree, *he is reading law at Cambridge*
ready adj. and n. (*re'di*) Prepared; able to do something immediately; fit for immediate use; willing; quick; near at hand
real adj. and n. (*rē'al*) Actually existing; founded on fact, not imaginary or fictional; genuine, *the real thing*; true
realize v.t. (*rē'al iz*) To understand clearly; to become fully conscious or aware of; to achieve, *he realized his ambition*; to bring into existence as an accomplished fact; to convert into money by sale, esp. of property, securities
realm n. (*relm*) Kingdom
reap v.t. and i. (*rēp*) To cut (corn) with sickle, scythe, or reaping machine; to gather harvest; (fig.) to receive as reward for action or behaviour
rear 1) n. (*rēr*) What is behind; part of procession, marching troops etc. that comes last
rear 2) v.t. and i. (*rēr*) To raise; to lift; to breed; to nourish. As v.i. (of animals) to rise on hind legs
reason 1) n. (*rē'zon*) Capacity to think logically and draw conclusions; intellectual capacity; sanity, *he has lost his reason*; cause; justification, *give your reasons for being late*
reason 2) v.t. and i. (*rē'zon*) To base on reason; to persuade by argument; to think or discuss in logical manner
reassure v.t. (*rē a shoor'*) To dispel doubts, fears, anxieties of etc.; to give fresh confidence to
rebel 1) n. and adj (*re'bl*) One who defies authority esp. one who revolts against lawful government; one who resists discipline or rejects convention
rebel 2) v.i. (*re'bel'*) To act as a rebel (against); to revolt
recapitulate v.t. and i. (*rē kap it' yoo lāt*) To repeat main facts or arguments by way of summary or conclusion
recede v.i. (*ri sēd'*) To move backwards; to slope away or backwards; to fade into background; to slump slightly
receipt n. and v.t. (*ri sēt'*) Act of receiving; what is received; written acknowledgment of money or goods received
receive v.t. and i. (*ri sēv'*) To obtain or accept something offered, sent, gained, due, or dealt; to admit to one's presence; to entertain, welcome, *the host received his guests*
receiver n. (*ri sē'ver*) Who or what receives; apparatus that transforms broadcast waves into sound or light, radio or television set; earpiece of telephone; fence, *receiver of stolen goods*
recent adj. (*rē sent*) What has lately occurred
reception n. (*ri sep'shun*) Receiving or being received; admission; acceptance; formal and official welcome, *reception of official guests at 3 p.m.*; occasion for such a welcome, *wedding reception* receiving of radio signals or quality with which they are received
recess n. and v.t. (*ri ses'*) Temporary withdrawing from work or employment esp. of Parliament or court of law; retired secluded spot, *in the inmost recesses of the Alps*; creek in coastline; alcove, niche
recession n. (*ri ses'shun*) Act of withdrawing or retiring from a place; (econ.) slackening of trade
recipe n. (*re'si pi*) List of ingredients and instructions for

preparing food, drink, medical prescriptions etc
recital n. (*ri sī'tal*) Act of reciting; what is recited; detailed account; narrative; musical performance by soloist or small group
recitation n. (*re si tā'shun*) Act of declaiming in public a passage of prose or verse usually by heart
recite v.t. and i. (*ri sīt'*) To repeat aloud from memory esp. before an audience; give recitation
reckon v.t. and i. (*rek'on*) To count up, to calculate; to guess
recognize v.t. (*rek'og nīz*) To perceive by the senses as being particular person or thing previously known or known about; to admit as lawful, valid, or authentic; to acknowledge formally status of; to greet as acquaintance; to appreciate or acknowledge in some tangible way
recoil v.i. and n. (*rē koil'*) To spring back; to stagger back; (of gun) to kick
As n. act of recoiling esp. of gun when fired
recollect v.t. (*rek'o lekt*) To remember, recall, call to mind again
recommend v.t. (*rek om end'*) To speak or write favourably of, as suitable for a certain use or position, *his headmaster recommended him for the post*; to make acceptable; to entrust to the care of; to advise, *I recommended him to take his umbrella.*
recommendation n. (*rek om end ā'-shun*) act of recommending; that which recommends; qualities serving to recommend a person; letter of commendation
recompense v.t. and n.. (*rek'om pens'*) To requite, reward or punish; make amends to or for some wrong, loss, or injury undergone. As n. reward, compensation
reconcile v.t. (*rek'on sīl*) (often followed by *to* or *with*) To restore friendship; to make consistent or compatible with; to settle
reconnaissance n. (*ri kon'i sans*) Act of reconnoitring; (milit.) detailed investigation of enemy territory
reconnoitre v.t. and i., and n. (*rek on oi'ter*) To make reconnaissance of enemy territory; view; inspect
record 1) v.t. and i. (*ri kawd'*) To preserve in permanent fashion; set down in writing; make gramophone disc or magnetic tape of. As v.i. to make gramophone

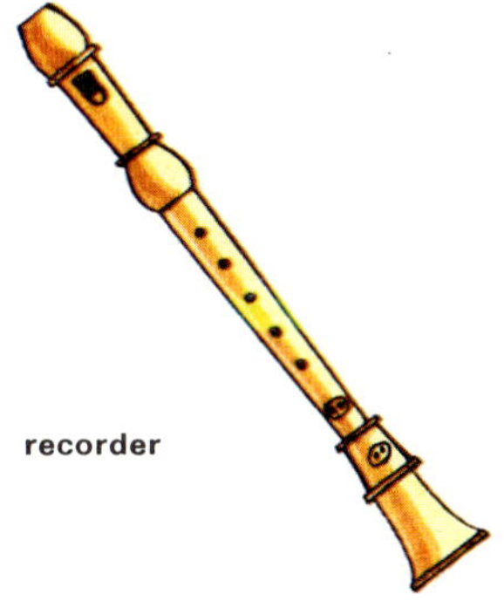
recorder

records. Hence: **recorder** n. one who or that which records apparatus for recording sounds or signals; (mus.) old form of flute with whistle head
record 2) n. (*rek'awd*) Register; written account of any proceeding or event; authentic representation of something past; flat disc with groove made by recording apparatus for reproduction on gramophone or record player; best performance yet accomplished (esp. in sport); (law) written copy of evidence and judgment of lawsuit preserved for future reference; list of person's previous crimes as known to the police; facts of person's character and behaviour as known to others
recover v.t. and i. (*ri ku'ver*) To get back or obtain again
As v.i. to regain health after sickness or injury
recreation n. (*rek rē ā'shun*) Act of relaxing body and mind after work; that which relaxes body and mind; amusement, diversion, entertainment, pastime, sport etc
recruit n., and v.t. and i. (*ri kroot'*) Newly and untrained enlisted person in organization esp. armed forces. As v.t. to seek or to enlist new members into organization esp. armed forces
rectangle n. (*rek'tăn gl*) Plane four-sided figure with four right angles
rectifiable adj. (*rek'ti fī a bl*) What may be corrected or rectified
rectify v.t. (*rek'ti fī*) To put right, correct, amend, remedy
rector n. (*rek'ter*) Priest of parish head of certain universities (esp. in Scotland etc.) and of educational or religious institutions
recuperate v.t. and i. (*ri koop'er*

āt) To restore to health. As v.i. to regain health; to recover from monetary losses
recur v.i. (*ri ker'*) To occur again or several times; to return to mind
redeem v.t. (*ri dēm'*) To buy back (property mortgaged or pawned); to recover by paying stipulated sum; to regain by diligence and effort; to atone for; to compensate for (often fault or defect), *his speech redeemed the meeting from boredom*; to set free
reduce v.t. and i. (*ri dūs'*) To diminish, make smaller or fewer
redundant adj. (*ri dun'dant*) Superfluous, unnecessary
reed n. and v.t. (*rēd*) Aquatic or marsh grass with long jointed stem; single straight stem of this; arrow made of this; musical pipe made of this; (mus.) vibrating part in mouthpiece of wind-instruments
reef 1) n. and v.t. (*rēf*) Horizontal portion of a sail that can be rolled or folded to reduce sail area
reef 2) n. (*rēf*) Ridge of rock, sand, shingle, or coral, at or just below water surface
reek v.i. and n. (*rēk*) To emit odour, stink, *the room reeks of stale tobacco smoke*
reel 1) n., and v.t. and i. (*rēl*) Rotary framework on which thread, cord, wire, cinema film etc. is wound; bobbin, spool
reel 2) n. (*rēl*) Lively Scottish dance; music for this
reel 3) v.i. (*rēl*) To stagger, to lurch from side to side, *he reeled to and fro like a drunkard*; to sway under the effects of a blow, to be giddy; (fig.) to be overwhelmed by some powerful emotional shock, *he reeled when he heard the tragic news*
refer v.t. and i. (*ri fer'*) To attribute, assign, *I referred his bad temper to indigestion*; to submit for decision or settlement, *the judge referred the case to a higher court*; to cite authority, *I refer you to the dictionary*
referee n., and v.t. and i. (*ref er ē'*) One to whom anything is referred; one appointed to settle dispute; (sport) umpire, person arbitrating between opponents. As v.t. and i. to act as referee in sporting contest
reference n. (*ref'rens*) Act of referring; person or thing referred to; indication of source of quotation or information, *references are listed at the end of each chapter*; allusion; connection, relation; person who will furnish information of ability, character and qualifications, often former employer; testimonial
refine v.t. and i. (*ri fīn'*) To purify
reflect v.t. and i. (*ri flekt'*) To throw back (light, heat, sound etc.) **to reflect on, upon** ponder over; consider carefully, *he reflected upon the problem before giving a decision*
reform v.t. and i., and n. (*ri fawm'*) To change for the better; to abandon or cause to abandon evil ways; to improve or cause to improve conduct, character, and habits; to remove social or political injustices. As n. act of reforming
refrain 1) n. (*ri frān'*) Line or verse repeated at intervals usually at end of each verse of poem or song
refrain 2) v.t. and i. (*ri frān'*) To abstain, *please refrain from singing*
refresh v.t. and i. (*ri fresh'*) To make fresh again; give new strength to
refrigerate v.t. and i. (*ri fri'je rāt*) To make or become cool; reduce to or keep at low temperature. Hence: **refrigeration** n. act of refrigerating; preservation of food by keeping in cold storage; **refrigerator** n. cabinet in which food is kept at low temperature for preservation; refrigerating machine
refuge n. (*ref'ūj*) Protection from danger or distress; any person, place, or course affording such protection raised piece in middle of busy street for the convenience of pedestrians. Hence: **refugee** n. one who flees for shelter esp. to foreign country to escape from political or religious persecution
refund v.t. and i. (*re fund'*), and n. (*rē'fund*) To reimburse; to make repayment
refuse 1) v.t. and i. (*ri fūz'*) To deny or decline (request, command etc.); to reject offer
refuse 2) n. and adj. (*ref'ūs*) What is rejected as useless; waste product, garbage, rubbish
regain v.t. (*ri gān'*) To recover possession of, *he regained consciousness*
regal adj. (*rē'gal*) Of, or belonging to a king
regard v.t. and i., and n. (*ri gahd'*) To gaze at, to stare at, *he was regarding me intently*; to pay attention to, *he does not regard*

my advice; to contemplate; to esteem, consider, *I regard him as a friend of mine* As n. steady gaze; esteem, consideration; attention
regatta n. (*ri gă'ta*) Race-meeting for boats
regent n. and adj. (*rē'jent*) One who governs or rules over kingdom during minority, absence, or disability of monarch.
regiment n. and v.t. (*rej'im ent*) Army unit consisting of varying number of battalions; (fig.) a vast number As v.t. to form into regiments; to organize into disciplined body or ordered system
register n., and v.t. and i. (*rej'is ter*) Written official record, e.g. of births, deaths, and marriages; book in which such record is kept; apparatus for regulating admission of air or heat; recording indicator; (mus.) compass of voice or instrumen As v.t. and i. to record in a register; to set down formally; to insure (mail, luggage etc.) against loss or damage in transit; (of instrument) to record automatically
Hence: **registration** n.; **registrar** n. official keeper of records or a register; **registry** n. act of entering in a register; place where registers are kept; **registry-office** where registers of births, deaths, and marriages are kept and where registrar performs civil marriages; office for supplying domestic servants
regret v.t. and n. (*ri gret'*) To feel sorry at, to grieve As n. grief esp. at loss of person or thing; remorse; disappointment.
regular adj. and n. (*reg'ū ler*) Conforming to some rule, plan, or arrangement; symmetrical, even, *he has regular features*; habitual, constant, recurring at set times, *it's past your regular bedtime*
regulate v.t. (*reg'ū lāt*) To govern by rule; to subject to rule; to adjust (machine, instrument) so that it works accurately; to cause to conform to standard or rate.
Hence: **regulation** n. act of regulating; prescribed rule, *you must keep within the regulation speed limit*
rehabilitate v.t. (*rē ha bil'i tāt*) To restore to former capacity (disabled person, criminal) by treatment and training; to restore to former position or rank
rehearsal n. (*rē hur'sal*) Act of rehearsing; practice performance (of play, music etc.) in preparation for public performance.
rehearse v.t. and i. (*rē hurs'*) To practise privately (play, music etc.) prior to public performance
reign n. and v.i. (*rān*) period during which monarch reigns
rein n. and v.t. (*rān*) Long strap attached to horse's bit by which to control or lead it
restrain; keep under control
reindeer n. (*rān'dēr*) Species of deer, *Rangifer tarandus*, found in N. Europe and Asia and used for drawing sledges
reinforce v.t. and n. (*rē in faws'*) To strengthen by additional men, material, or supplies
reinstate v.t. (*rē in stāt'*) To restore to former state or position
reject v.t. (*ri jekt'*) and n. (*rē'jekt*) To discard as worthless or unsatisfactory; to decline to accept
rejoice v.t. and i. (*ri jois'*) To feel joy; to be delighted
relate v.t. and i. (*ri lāt'*) To recount, narrate; bring into connection with or show connection between
relation n. (*ri lā'shun*) Act of relating; narration; way in which things correspond or differ connection by blood or marriage, kinsman
relative adj. and n. (*rel'a tiv*) Considered in relation to something else
relax v.t. and i. (*ri lăks'*) To loosen or cause to loosen; make less tense or rigid; make less severe
relay n., and v.t. and i. (*rē'lā*) Fresh group of workers, horses, hounds etc. to replace others tired through work

reindeer

As v.t. and i. to transmit broadcast originating from another station; to pass on information; to supply or arrange relays; **relay race** race between teams of which each member runs only part of the circuit consecutively

release v.t. and n. (*ri lēs'*) To set at liberty allow to be exhibited, published, or offered for sale on a certain date

relent v.i. (*re lent'*) To become less severe

relic n. (*rel'ik*) Part of body or personal possession of holy person kept as object of reverence; fragment, custom, belief etc. surviving from the past

relief 1) n. (*re lēf'*) Mode of carving in which design stands out from background

relief 2) n. (*re lēf'*) Alleviation of pain, distress, anxiety etc., *the treatment brought immediate relief* reinforcements

religion n. (*re li'jun*) Belief in and worship of God or gods one of the prevalent systems of faith and worship: the Christian, Hindu religion etc

religious adj. and n. (*re li'jus*) Of religion; believing in or practising a religion

relinquish v.t. (*re lin'kwish*) To resign, abandon, surrender, let go

relish n., and v.t. and i. (*rel'ish*) Distinctive taste, aroma, appetizing flavour; spice; (fig.) keenness

remain v.t. and i. (*ri mān'*), and n. To stay behind, be left over, As n. (usually pl.) persons or things left over; survivors; relics; ruins; corpse

remark v.t. and i., and n. (*ri mahk'*) To observe or notice, perceive; say or write by way of comment

remedy n. and v.t. (*rem'i di*) What cures disease, evil, trouble etc.

remember v.t. and i. (*ri mem'ber*) To call to mind (knowledge or past experience) greeting, *he wishes to be remembered to you*

remind v.t. (*ri mind'*) To cause to remember

remnant n. (*rem'nant*) The few things or people, or small quantity, that remain(s); scrap, fragment; goods esp. fabric left over and offered at reduced price after bulk has been sold

remorse n. (*ri maws'*) Strong sense of sorrow and regret caused by guilt

remote adj. (*ri mōt'*) Distant, far removed in space, time, spirit etc

remove v.t. and i., and n. (*ri-mōōv'*) To take, carry, move away; abolish; relieve (person) of his post; dismiss; change residence, *they've removed*

rendezvous n. and v.i. (*ron'dā-vōō*) Appointed meeting place

renew v.t. and i. (*ri nū'*) To make or become as good as new, restore to original state, renovate; give fresh energy to; begin again, repeat; grant again, prolong, *please renew my subscription to your journal*

renovate v.t. and i. (*ren'ō vāt*) To make as good as new by repairing; to restore to former state

renown n. (*ri nown'*) Celebrity, fame. Hence: **renowned** adj. famous, celebrated

rent 1) n., and v.t. and i. (*rent*) Periodical payment by tenant to landlord for use of premises, land etc.; payment for hire of anything

rent 2) n. (*rent*) Tear, hole, slit (in fabric)

repair v.t. and n. (*ri paer'*) To restore to good condition, to mend; to make good, to remedy

repeat v.t. and i., and n. (*ri pēt'*) To say or do again; recite by heart; spread (news, gossip etc.) abroad

repel v.t. (*ri pel'*) To drive back or away, repulse, inspire or fill with distaste

repent v.t. and i. (*ri pent'*) To feel sorrow or regret for and resolve to amend

replenish v.t. (*rē plen'ish*) To fill up again; to obtain fresh supplies of, restock

reply v.t. and i., and n. (*ri plī'*) To answer

report 1) v.t. and i. (*ri pawt'*) To give account of to inform against, *I shall report your carelessness to the manager*; to present oneself for duty or in answer to a summons, *you are to report to the police station*

report 2) n. (*ri pawt'*) statement of facts esp. after investigation; periodical account of progress at school, in commerce, industry etc.; written account of events for newspaper publication noise of explosion, *the gun went off with a loud report*

repose v.t. and i., and n. (*ri pōz'*) To rest, lay at rest

represent v.t. (*rep ri zent'*) To depict, portray, *the picture represents the death of Nelson*; to make out to be, *the hero is not what he is represented to be*; to show clearly, *war represents the*

es

folly of mankind; to convey; to symbolize, *the dove represents Peace*; to act on behalf of; to be Member of Parliament for
reprieve v.t. and n. (*ri prēv'*) To suspend or delay execution of sentence esp. death sentence upon
reprimand n. and v.t. (*rep'ri-mahnd*) Severe reproof, rebuke esp. when administered officially. As v.t. to reprove, rebuke
reproduce v.t. and i. (*rē prō dūs'*) To propagate; produce again; cause to grow afresh; make copy of
reptile n. and adj. (*rep'tīl*) (zoo.) Class Reptilia of cold-blooded, lung-breathing, crawling vertebrates covered with plates or scales
republic n. (*ri pub'lik*) Form of government without monarch; a country with this form of government
repulse v.t. and n. (*ri puls'*) To repel, drive back (attack, enemy); (fig.) rebuff, snub, reject (advances or offer)
reputation n. (*rep ū tā'shun*) Esteem or regard in which person or thing is commonly held, *he has not lived up to his reputation*
request n. and v.t. (*ri kwest'*) Act of asking for something, entreaty, petition; what is asked for, demand
require v.t. and i. (*ri kwīr'*) To need, *the problem requires careful consideration*; to order, demand
rescue v.t. and n. (*res'kū*) To set free from danger, confinement, harm etc
resemble v.t. (*ri zem'bl*) To be like
resent v.t. (*ri zent'*) To consider as personal affront or injury; to show or feel indignation at

or interest in property leased to another. (Lat. p.p. of *reservare* to keep back)
reserve 1) v.t. (*ri zerv'*) To keep for future use, *the boxer reserved his strength for the next round*; to keep as spare supply; set aside for use of particular person or persons; book (berth, seat etc.)
reserve 2) n. (*ri zerv'*) What is reserved state of being reserved, restraint, aloofness, reticence; deliberate withholding of truth; stretch of country protected for some particular use, *nature reserve*; (milit.) (pl.) armed forces held back from action until needed
reside v.i. (*ri zīd'*) To live (in or at) permanently or for a long time
resign v.t. and i. (*ri zīn'*) To give up, relinquish, abandon; give up office or post; (reflex.) yield, submit, accept with equanimity, *I resign myself to my fate*
resist v.t. and i. (*ri zist'*) To oppose, strive against, withstand, *he cannot resist temptation;* to be proof against, be unaffected by
resolute adj. (*rez'ō lūt*) Determined, unwavering, steadfast, fixed in purpose
resolve v.t. and i., and n. (*ri zolv'*) explain, solve, *the problem resolves itself*; to be determined
resource n. (*ri saws'*) Expedient, device, shift, *flight was his only resource*; source of distraction, *reading is a great resource* (pl.) stock, means of supplying requirements, natural source of wealth
respect n. and v.t. (*ri spekt'*) esteem, suitable deference, *I have the greatest respect for him*; particular aspect, *in some respects he is not reliable*
respiration n. (*res pi rā'shun*) Act of breathing
respirator n. (*respi rā' ter*) Apparatus worn over mouth and nose to protect lungs from smoke, fumes, gases, or cold air
respire v.t. and i. (*ris pīr'*) To breathe out; breathe; inhale and exhale air
respond v.i. and n. (*ris pond'*) To answer; to react to mental or physical stimulus, *a dog responds to kindness*
responsibility n. (*ris pon si bil'i ti*) State of being responsible; what one is responsible for; duty; obligation; trust
responsible adj. (*ris pon'si bl*) Answerable, liable to account; fit to undertake obligations; morally accountable for actions; trustworthy; involving responsibility
rest v.t. and i., and n. (*rest*) To place, lean, *he rested his elbows on the table*; to give repose or relief to, *the commander rested his troops*. As v.i. to cease from action or motion, to be quiet, *the seas never rest*; to sleep; to be dead; to rely, *I rest upon your promise*; to lean on, be supported by; to stand on. As n. cessation from motion or action; repose, sleep, *he has a rest after his lunch* that on or in which anything rests
restaurant n. (*res'ter a(ng)*) Establishment where meals may be bought and eaten
restore v.t. (*ri staw(r)'*) To bring back to former condition; to repair
restrain v.t. (*ris trān'*) To hold back or check; repress; restrict; confine
restrict v.t. (*ris trikt'*) To limit, confine; keep within bounds
result v.i. and n. (*ri zult'*) To follow as a consequence
As n. consequence; outcome; conclusion; (math.) answer following process of calculation
resurrect v.t. (*rez er ekt'*) To revive; to bring into use again; to restore to life; to raise from the dead. Hence: **resurrection n.** Christ's rising from the grave
retail 1) n., adj., and adv. (*rē'tāl*) Sale of goods in small quantities to ultimate consumer
retail 2) v.t. and i. (*rē tāl'*) To sell to consumer goods bought wholesale
retain v.t. (*ri tān'*) To hold or keep in possession; remember; keep back: engage services esp. by prepayment
retire v.t. and i. (*ri tīr'*) To withdraw; seek privacy; go to bed, *I shall retire early this evening*; retreat, *the enemy retired in good order*; give up office or employment, *he retired on a pension*
retreat v.i. and t., and n. (*ri trēt'*) To move backwards or away; abandon one's position or place; withdraw to safety; retire from an enemy
retrieve v.t. and i. (*ri trēv'*) To find and bring back; recover through some effort; rescue; regain possession of; restore. Hence: **retriever** n. person or thing that retrieves; dog trained to fetch game that has been shot
return v.t. and i. (*ri turn'*) To send, give, bring back, *I must return my book to the library*; yield; retaliate, give back in reply,

As v.i. to come or go back to same place, state, or condition
reunite v.t. and i. (*rē ū nit'*) To unite or be united again; join after separation
reveal v.t. (*ri vēl'*) To disclose to view
revenge n., and v.t. and i. (*ri venj'*) Act of taking vengeance on; malicious desire to do this
revenue n. (*rev'en ū*) Income
revere v.t. (*ri vēr'*) To regard with great respect
reverse 1) v.t. and i. (*ri vurs'*) To turn upside down or back to front; turn over or backwards; move or cause to move backwards, *he reversed his car into the garage*
reverse 2) adj. and n. (*ri vurs'*) Contrary, opposite,
As n., change or setback in course of events esp. misfortune, disaster, defeat etc.; contrary, opposite
review n., and v.t. and i. (*ri vū'*) Revision of situation; retrospective summary; critical evaluation of book, play, film, concert etc.; periodical containing articles, essays etc.; (milit.) formal inspection of troops. As v.t. to consider in retrospect; to revise; write press review of; inspect troops
revise v.t. and n. (*ri vīz'*) To examine again for purposes of correction or amendment; study afresh in preparation for examination; change (views), *I revised my opinion of him when I met him*
revival n. (*ri vī'val*) Act of reviving; state of being revived
revive v.t. and i. (*ri vīv'*) To return to life, consciousness, health, fashion etc.; recover from depression, exhaustion, neglect etc.; renew; flourish again
revolt v.t. and i., and n. (*ri vōlt'*) To seek to overthrow established authority; rebel
revolution n. (*rev ol ōō'shun*) Circular motion of a body on its axis or in orbit
complete change; reversal of attitude, belief, theory, conditions etc.; violent overthrow of existing political system
revolve v.t. and i. (*ri volv'*) To rotate or cause to rotate; to turn round; to move in circular course or orbit, *the Earth revolves both round the Sun and on its own axis*; (fig.) to revolve in the mind, to ponder over
revolver n. (*ri vol'ver*) Pistol fitted with revolving cylinder enabling it to be fired several times without reloading
reward n. and v.t. (*ri wawd'*) Return for service or merit, recompense, requital; money offered for restoration of lost property or information leading to arrest of criminal
rhetoric n. (*ret'er ik*) Art of speaking with elegance and persuasiveness
rheumatism n. (*rōōm'ăt izm*) Group of diseases causing pain and inflammation in muscles and joints
rhinoceros n. (*ri nos'er us*) Large mammal with thick hide creased into folds and with one or two

revolver

rhinoceros

horns on nose
rhubarb n. (*rōō'bahb*) Genus of large-leaved plants with fleshy stalks; variety of this of which stalks can be cooked and eaten
rhyme n., and v.t. and i. (*rim*) Correspondence of sound in words or final syllables esp. in terminating words of lines of verse; a verse of which line endings correspond in sound; poetry; poem As v.t. and i. to put into rhyme; to use as a rhyme; to form a rhyme; to compose verses in rhyme
rhythm n. (*ri'thm*) Regular variation of strong and weak stress in poetry; regular recurrence of events, phenomena, activities etc., *the rhythm of the seasons continues uninterrupted*; (mus.) accentuation and duration of notes in time
rib n. and v.t. (*rib*) One of curved bones extending from spine to enclose thorax; any long narrow strip slightly raised to form ridge-like protuberance
ribbon n. and v.t. (*rib'on*) Narrow band of silk, satin, or other fine material; length of this worn as decoration in clothes or hair; strip of this worn to suspend medal or to indicate membership of club, team etc. long narrow strip
rice n. (*rīs*) Cereal plant, *Oryza sativa*; white seed of this used as food
rich adj. and n. (*rich*) Abounding in money and possessions; wealthy; (of countries, periods, soil etc.) fertile, abundant in valuable materials or qualities; splendid; costly fatty, highly seasoned, (of food)
rid v.t. (*rid*) To free; drive away
riddle 1) n., and v.t. and i. (*rid'l*) Deliberately puzzling question,
riddle 2) n. and v.t. (*rid'l*) Coarse sieve for separating corn, gravel, cinders etc. As v.t. to sift with a riddle; pierce, perforate (with bullets)
ride v.t. and i., and n. (*rīd*), pret. **rode** (*rōd*), p.p. **ridden** (*rid'n*) To sit on or in and be borne along by (horse, bicycle, vehicle)
rider n. (*rī'der*) One who rides esp. on horseback
ridicule n. and v.t. (*ri'di kūl*) Contemptuous laughter; mockery, derision. As v.t. to treat with derision; expose to contempt; make fun of
rifle 1) v.t. (*rīf'l*) To ransack in search of loot
rifle 2) n. (*rīf'l*) Fire-arm with rifled barrel fired from shoulder
rig v.t. and i., and n. (*rig*) To equip with tackle and rigging Hence: **rigging** n. (naut.) system of ropes controlling masts and sails
right adj., adv., and n. (*rīt*) Correct, true, *he gave the right answer to my question*; most convenient, preferable, *the right man in the right place*; just, proper; sound, sane, *he is in his right mind*; comfortable, healthy, *the patient is as right as rain*; towards the east when facing north, opposite of left, *he writes with his right hand*; (pol.) Conservative
rigid adj. (*rij'id*) Stiff, not easily bent; immobile; (fig.) unyielding, severe, inflexible
rigour n. (*rig'er*) Severity, strictness
rim n. and v.t. (*rim*) Border, margin, brim: raised edge; (naut.) surface of the water; outer part of wheel where tyre fits
rind n. (*rīnd*) Peel of fruit and vegetables; bark; hard outer coating of cheese or bacon
ring 1) n., and v.t. and i. (*ring*) Anything in the form of a circular line or hoop; circular enclosure; circus arena; enclosed space for boxing or wrestling; hoop of gold or other metal worn as jewellery on finger, nose, or ear; group of persons or things forming a circle As v.t. and i. to encircle; to fit with a ring
ring 2) v.t. and i., and n. (*ring*) To sound, or to cause to sound with, clear resonant note

rice

As n. act of ringing; ringing sound
rink n. and v.i. (*rink*) Sheet of artificial ice for skating on; area for roller-skating
rinse v.t. and n. (*rins*) To cleanse with clean water; to put (clothes) in clean water to remove soap
riot n., and v.t. and i. (*ri'ot*) Violent disturbance of public peace by three or more persons; uproar; noisy festivity or enthusiasm; (fig.) profusion, *the flower border is a riot of colour* As v.t. and i. to take part in a riot; to raise a disturbance
rip v.t. and i., and n. (*rip*) To cut or tear open or apart
ripe adj. (*rip*) Mature, fully developed; ready (to be eaten, drunk, gathered, used etc.)
ripple n., and v.t. and i. (*rip'l*) Ruffling of water surface; gentle undulation or wave; soft sound that rises and falls, *we could hear a ripple of conversation*
rise 1) v.i. (*riz*) pret. **rose** (*rōz*), p.p. **risen** (*riz'n*) To get up from recumbent position; get out of bed; get to one's feet; ascend; to be raised; to end session, *the House rose at 1 a.m.*; to increase in force and volume, *the wind rose last night*; to become visible, *the sun rises in the east*; to originate, *the Thames rises in the Cotswolds*; to become successful, *he is a man likely to rise*; to swell; increase in rank, power, cost, or value; rebel, revolt; slope upwards; resurrect; (of fish) to come to surface of water
rise 2) n. (*riz*) Act of rising; upward motion; ascent; advance in rank, honour, fame; upward slope; increase in amount, intensity, value, volume etc.; increase in pay; amount of this; coming up of sun or moon; origin, source; movement of fish to surface
risk n. and v.t. (*risk*) Hazard of danger; chance of injury, harm, loss etc
rite n. (*rit*) Procedure in religious or other ceremony; formal observance; solemnly performed habit
rival n., adj., and v.t. (*ri'val*) One who competes with another As v.t. to compete against; to strive to equal or excel
river n. (*riv'er*) Stream of water flowing in natural course into sea, lake, or other river; (fig.) copious flow or stream
road n. (*rōd*) The highway; public metalled way for travelling; way, route
roam v.t. and i. (*rōm*) To wander over; to wander aimlessly
roar v.i. and n. (*raw(r)*) To cry with loud, deep, continuous sound As n. loud, deep, continuous sound (of animal, sea, laughter, pain, engine etc.)
roast v.t. and i., and n. (*rōst*) To cook by direct exposure to heat or in oven As n. operation of roasting; something roasted esp. joint of meat
rob v.t. (*rob*) To steal, often with violence
robe n., and v.t. and i. (*rōb*) Long, loose outer garment; ceremonial garment
robin n. (*rob'in*) Small red-breasted bird
robot n. (*rō'bot*) Automaton made to act like man; (fig.) machine-like person
robust adj. (*rō bust'*) Possessing great strength and vigour; sound, healthy
rock 1) n. (*rok*) Hard mineral matter of earth's crust; crag; boulder; projecting crag above or close to surface of sea; type of hard-boiled sweet
rock 2) v.t. and i., and n. (*rok*) To swing or cause to swing to and fro
rocket n., and v.t. and i. (*rok'it*) Projectile containing its own propellant; large jet-powered projectile driven through air or space used as lethal weapon or to place spacecraft etc. in orbit
rod n. (*rod*) Slender, straight stick; cane for corporal punishment cane used by anglers
rodent adj. and n. (*rō'dent*) Gnawing. As n. vertebrate that gnaws with chisel-edged incisor teeth; rodent animal.
rogue n. (*rōg*) Wandering beggar. dishonest person
roll 1) n. (*rōl*) Quantity of flexible material (cloth, paper etc.) coiled into a cylinder official document or register, esp. of schoolboys or soldiers; long reverberating sound, e.g. of drums or thunder; swaying movement
roll 2) v.t. and i. (*rōl*) To move or cause to move by turning over and over, *the coin rolled under the table*; spread out or level something with a roller, *he rolled the lawn*; form into a ball or cylinder, *he rolled himself a cigarette*; envelop, wrap; sway or rock; walk with swaying gait; make long reverberating sound; flow in waves
romance n., adj., and v.i.

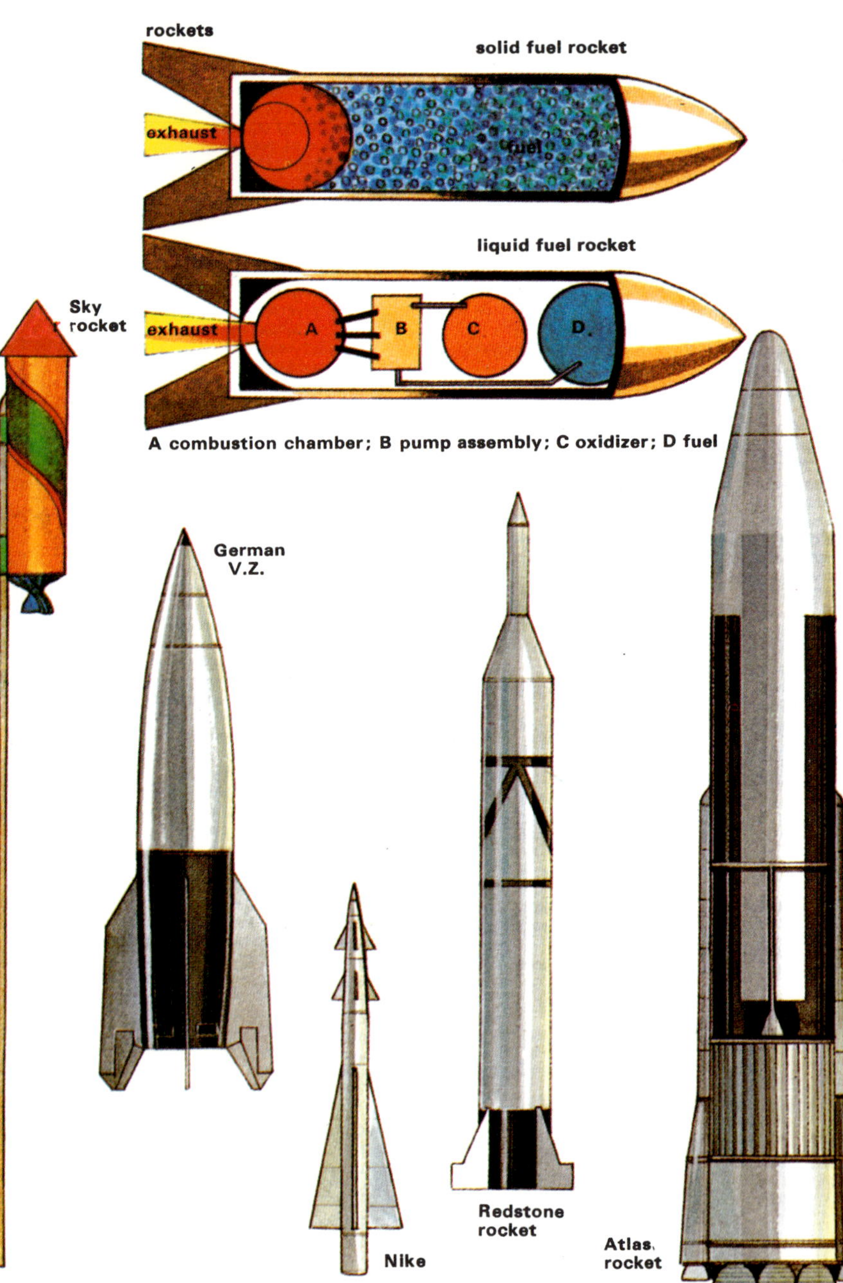
rockets
solid fuel rocket
exhaust
fuel
liquid fuel rocket
Sky rocket
exhaust
A
B
C
D.
A combustion chamber; B pump assembly; C oxidizer; D fuel
German V.Z.
Redstone rocket
Atlas rocket
Nike

(*rōmans', rō'mans*)
story, novel, film etc.
containing improbable plot, esp.
of idealized love
sentimental atmosphere
romantic adj. and n. (*rōman'tik*) Of or like romance
romp v.i. and n. (*romp*) To play boisterously and noisily
roof n. and v.t. (*rōōf*) Covering of top of building or vehicle As v.t. to cover with a roof
rook 1) n. and v.t. (*rōōk*) Large, black bird, *Corvus frugilegus,* nesting in colonies
rook 2) n. (*rōōk*) The castle in chess
room n. and v.i. (*rōōm*) Space, area, *there is plenty of room for all of us*; enclosed portion of house or building; (pl.) lodgings; opportunity, scope, *there is room for improvement.* As v.i. to share a room; lodge with
root 1) n., and v.t. and i. (*rōōt*) Part of plant that grows downwards and draws nourishment from soil; source, origin, *money is the root of all evil*; essential element, As v.t. and i. to plant deeply; fix firmly; form roots; to be or become firmly established
root 2) v.t. and i. (*rōōt*) To dig up, esp. with snout in search of food
rope n. and v.t. (*rōp*) Cord of some thickness formed of twisted strands As v.t. to join with rope
rose n. and adj. (*rōz*) Any of various wild or cultivated plants or their flowers of genus *Rosa*
rot n., and v.t. and i. (*rot*) Decay, As v.t. and i. to (cause to) decay, decompose; grow ill and wasted
rota n. (*rōt'a*) List showing duties to be done, or persons to do them
rotate v.t. and i., and adj. (*rō tāt'*) To revolve round an axis; to be done (planted etc.) in regular cycle of succession
rouge n. and v.t. (*rōōzh*) Red cosmetic for reddening cheeks
rough adj., n., adv., and v.t. (*ruf*) Not smooth or even; not polished; rocky; rugged; stormy, *the Channel crossing was rough*; harsh, *he spoke in a rough voice*; rugged in temper or manners; uncouth; cruel; clumsy; unfinished, approximate, *he drew a rough sketch*
round 1) adj. and n. (*rownd*) Having the form or approximate form of circle, sphere, ball, or cylinder, *the Earth is round*
As n. what is round; circle; sphere; circular slice; circular route or course; cycle; regular course of patrolling, visiting etc., beat, *the postman is on his rounds*; series of events or duties that return to beginning again
round 2) adv. and prep. (*rownd*) With circular motion, *the Earth goes round the Sun*; on all sides, to all points, *the hat was passed round*; by a different or indirect route. As prep. encircling; on all sides of; to all parts of, *he showed me round his house*
round 3) v.t. and i. (*rownd*) To make round; encircle; form into a circle; move round or about
roundabout n. and adj. (*rownd'abowt*)
circular enclosure at crossroads round which traffic travels in one direction
rouse v.t. and i. (*rowz*) To provoke; agitate; stimulate; to be stirred to action or interest; awaken
rout n. and v.t. (*rowt*)
disorderly retreat of defeated army. As v.t. to defeat utterly
route n. and v.t. (*rōōt*) Course travelled As v.t. to plan route
routine n. (*rōōtēn'*) Regular course of duties, habits, organization etc
rove v.t. and i. (*rōv*) To wander, roam (through); (of attention, eyes) move restlessly
row 1) n. (*rō*) Number of persons or things arranged in a line, *let us sit in the front row*
row 2) v.t. and i., and n. (*rō*) To propel (boat) by oars
row 3) n. and v.t. (*row*) Noisy disturbance; riot; quarrel. As v.t. to quarrel
royal adj. and n. (*roi'al*) Of, like, suited to, worthy of, a king or queen
royalty n. (*roil'ti*) State, office, or person of king or queen; sovereignty; member of royal family
payment to author, playwright, composer etc. according to number of books sold or of performances
rub v.t. and i., and n. (*rub*) To apply friction to surface of; wipe, clean, polish
rubber n. (*rub'er*) Person or thing that rubs; implement used for rubbing or cleaning
elastic material made from trees synthetically; small piece used for erasing pencil-marks etc

rudder

rubbish n. (*rub'ish*) Waste matter; litter; anything useless; (fig.) absurd idea, nonsense
rubble n. (*ru'bl*) Debris of demolished building etc
rucksack n. (*rŏŏk'săk*) Knapsack carried on back by straps round shoulders
rudder n. (*rud'er*) Vertical plate at stern of ship or aircraft by which it is steered
rude adj. (*rōōd*) Rough, primitive, *the Vikings used a rude method of navigation*; uneducated; discourteous, insolent; violent, abrupt, *he is in for a rude shock*
rue v.t. and i., and n. (*rōō*) To lament, repent, regret
ruffian n. (*ruf'yan*) Low and violent fellow; desperate character
ruffle v.t. and i., and n. (*ruf'l*) To disorder; disturb smoothness or calm As n. disturbance, agitation pleated
strip of fine cloth attached to border of garment, usually at wrist or neck
rug n. (*rug*) Large wrap or coverlet of thick woollen cloth; mat of wool, fur etc. laid on floor
ruin n., and v.t. and i. (*rōō'in*) Destruction; overthrow; what destroys or is destroyed; (pl.) remains of partly demolished city, building etc. As v.t. and i. to destroy; overthrow; bring to ruin
rule n., and v.t. and i. (*rōōl*) Established principle regulating conduct or procedure; regulation; custom
graduated steel or wooden bar for measuring As v.t. and i. to govern, reign, sway, regulate; settle as by rule, determine, *the chairman ruled that the motion was out of order*; to have power; to draw lines with a ruler
rummage v.t. and i., and n. (*rum'ij*) To ransack; make a search; disarrange while searching
rumour n. (*rōōm'er*) Current story not based on facts
run 1) v.i. and t. (*run*) pret. **ran** (*răn*), p.p. **run** (*run*) To progress swiftly over the ground by advancing feet alternately; to flee, *the thief ran for it*; proceed quickly; compete in a race; seek election; (of ship) travel fast; (of vehicle, machinery etc.) function, *my car runs well*; ply; continue in operation, *the play ran for a fortnight*; spread, *the news ran like wild-fire, the colour of my jacket has run*; flow, discharge matter, *his eyes were running*; extend, *the hedge runs along the road*; pursue in thought; (v.t.) chase; force; smuggle; cast, *he ran his eyes down the page*; discharge; draw; *run some water from the tap* manage, *he runs a garage*
run 2) n. (*run*) Act of running; distance or time of uninterrupted running; continuous succession of similar events; voyage, journey, trip; path; stretch of land for animals or fowls; slope for vehicle to run down; hole in garment caused by dropped stitch, ladder; (cricket) point scored by running successfully between wickets; (mus.) rapid series of notes; (theatre) unbroken series of performances
runaway n. and adj. (*run'a wā*) Person or thing that has run away
rung n. (*rung*) Step of ladder
rural adj. (*rōōr'al*) Pertaining to countryside; agricultural
rush 1) n. (*rush*) Aquatic plant of genus *Juncus* with pliant stem used when dry for basket-making etc
rush 2) v.t. and i., and n. (*rush*) To move or act, or cause to move or act, rapidly, impetuously, hastily, *he rushed out of the room, Parliament rushed the bill through*: to hurry; to bring or send in great haste; to take by storm; to flow or blow strongly, *the blood rushed to his head*. As n. forward movement in a burst of speed; sudden outburst, gush; bustle; sudden increase in work, demand, or activity
rustic adj. and n. (*rus'tik*) Of, in, or like the countryside

rush

rustle v.t. and i., and n. (*ru'sl*) To make or cause to make soft, crisp sound as of dry yet pliable things rubbing together, e.g. dry leaves, silk garments; (U.S.) to steal, esp. cattle or horses
rut n. (*rut*) Sunken groove made by wheels; well-worn groove; (fig.) settled habits; dreary routine

S

Sabbath n. (*săb'ath*) Day of rest and divine worship, Saturday for Jews, Sunday for Christians
sabotage n. and v.t. (*să'bo tahzh*) Wilful damage, esp. to machinery, plant, materials etc., by opponents in industry, war etc. As v.t., to perform an act of sabotage against
saccharin n. (*săk'a rin*) White crystalline powder, three hundred times sweeter than sugar, used as substitute for sugar in sweetening
sack 1) n. (*săk*) Large oblong bag of coarse material used for holding heavy goods such as coals
sack 2) v.t. (*săk*) To put, place in a sack; (colloq.) to dismiss from employment
sack 3) n. and v.t. (*săk*) Act of plundering a captured town etc. As v.t., to plunder; loot
sacrament n. (*săk'ra ment*) Ceremonial observance in the Christian Church
sacrifice v.t. and i. (*săk'ri fis*) To make a sacrifice of; give up as a sacrifice; offer a sacrifice
sad adj. (*săd*) Sorrowful, melancholy, *to feel sad*; causing sorrow
saddle n. and v.t. (*sădl*) Leather seat for rider on horse, bicycle, etc
safari n. (*sa fah'ri*) A hunting expedition; overland journey, esp. in Africa
safe 1) adj. (*sāf*) Secure, free from danger, hurt or injury, *safe from attack*; giving security, *a safe place to stay in*; unhurt and undamaged, *to return safe and sound*; not causing or likely to cause harm or danger, *this rope is quite safe*
safe 2) n. (*sāf*) Strong receptacle, usually of steel, for keeping valuables safely
safety n. (*sāf'ti*) State or quality of being safe
sag v.i. and n. (*săg*) To sink, bend downwards from the middle, bulge downwards, *the roof is sagging*; bend from the vertical, *the dead tree began to sag slowly*; (fig.) drop, *prices are sagging*; droop, *his spirits are sagging*
saga n. (*sah'ga*) Old heroic Icelandic or Norse prose epic; any romantic tale of heroism and adventure
sail 1) n. (*sāl*) Piece of canvas or other cloth spread to catch the wind and move a boat or ship forward; a ship, *not a sail in sight*; an excursion in a vessel, *go for a sail*; one of the arms of a windmill that is turned by the wind
sail 2) v.i. and t. (*sāl*) To move along on sea, lake, or river by means of sail(s); to travel in the water; to start on a sea voyage, to navigate, *sail a ship*
sailor n. (*sā'lor*) Seaman, one of the crew of a ship
sake n. (*sāk*) Cause, behalf, *do it for my sake*
salad n. (*săl'ad*) Cold dish consisting of lettuce or other vegetables
salary n. and v.t. (*săl'a ri*) Payment to employee for services other than manual labour, usually made monthly or quarterly
sale n. (*sāl*) Transfer of goods, property etc. from one person to another in return for money; act of selling; offering of goods for sale at reduced prices
sallow adj. (*săl'ō*) (Of complexions) yellowish in colour
salmon n. (*săm'on*) Species of large fish, *Salmo salar*, common in North Atlantic and adjacent waters, which comes into rivers and lakes to spawn; silvery pink or pale red colour
saloon n. (*sa lo͞on'*) Large

salmon

reception room; any large public room set aside for a specific purpose, *billiard saloon*; a closed-in motor car; large room on board a passenger ship
salt 1) n. (*sawlt*) Common salt, the naturally occurring form of sodium chloride, a white crystalline substance used as a seasoning in food and a preservative
salt 2) v.t. (*sawlt*) To season with salt
salute v.t. and i. and n. (*sa lūt'*) (milit. and naval) perform a prescribed action such as raising the hand to the forehead, firing guns etc
salvage n. and v.t. (*săl'vij*) The rescue of property from damage or loss by fire
salvation n. (*săl vā'shun*) Act of saving
same adj. (*sām*) (Preceded by *the*) identical, *meet me in the same place as yesterday*; similar, corresponding, unchanged, *the doctor gave me the same medicine as last time*; (as pron., used elliptically) the same thing, *they all say the same*
sample n. and v.t. (*sahmpl*) Part of anything, specimen, representing the quality or character of the whole, esp. single specimen of goods offered for sale
sanction n. and v.t. (*săngk'shun*) approval, encouragement for conduct etc. by general custom As v.t., to give sanction to
sand n. (*sănd*) Fine, loose, gritty substance found on sea-shore or river-bed
sandal n. (*săndl*) Type of shoe consisting of a sole with thongs or straps holding it on the foot
sandwich n. and v.t. (*sănd'wich*) Two pieces of bread and butter with jam, meat etc. between them
sane adj. (*sān*) Sound in mind, mentally normal
sanguine adj. (*săng'gwin*) cheerful, confident
sanitary adj. (*săn'i ta ri*) Of health or hygiene, esp. freedom from dirt or agents of infection
sanitation n. (*săn i tā'shun*) Measures to protect public health, esp. efficient drainage and sewage disposal
sap v.t. (*săp*) To drain away the vital energy or strength of, to weaken, *the climate sapped his health*
sarcasm n. (*sah'kăzm*) Mocking taunt intended to hurt the feelings
sari n. (*sah'ri*) Hindu woman's main garment, consisting of a cloth wound round the body
sash n. (*săsh*) Scarf worn round the waist or over one shoulder for ornament or as part of a military uniform.
one with counterweighted upper and lower frames, made to slide vertically one over the other
satellite n. (*săt'e līt*) follower; revolving round another, esp. a planet, *the moon is the Earth's satellite*; man-made object put into orbit round the Earth
satin n. (*săt'in*) Silk fabric with smooth lustrous surface
satire n. (*să'tīr*) Use of ridicule, mockery, irony etc. in writing or speech

sari

satisfaction n. (*să tis făk'shun*) Act of satisfying; state of being satisfied

satisfactory adj. (*sa tis făk'to ri*) Meeting one's desires or expectations, giving satisfaction

satisfy v.t. and i. (*săt'is fi*) To give contentment to, to gratify, *satisfy one's ambitions*

saturate v.t. (*săch'ū rāt*) To soak thoroughly

sauce n. and v.t. (*saws*) Kind of flavoured and thickened liquid used to enhance the flavour of food

sauna n. (*sow'na*) Steam bath, bathhouse, as in Finland

saunter v.i. and n. (*sawn'ter*) To stroll, walk slowly; loiter, linger. As n., a stroll, a leisurely walk

sausage n. (*so'sij*) Finely minced and seasoned meat, packed into a casing of skin

savage adj., n., and v.t. (*să'vij*) Wild, uncivilized, primitive, *a savage tribe* As n., human being in a very primitive stage of civilization, *the savages of the jungle*; a cruel person treat cruelly and brutally

save v.t. and i. (*sāv*) To rescue or preserve from danger, harm, injury etc

savour n. and v.t. and i. (*sā'ver*) Taste, flavour

savoury adj. and n. (*sā'ver i*) Having an appetizing taste or smell

saw n. (*saw*) Tool made in various forms, consisting of a strip of steel with a toothed edge, used for cutting purposes

saxophone n. (*săks'ō fōn*) Brass musical instrument with keys and a reed mouthpiece

saxophone

say 1) v.t. and i. (*sā*) To utter, express in words, *say that again*; repeat, recite by heart, *say a piece of poetry*; report, allege, *they say that . . .*; assert, utter an opinion, make a statement, *you have no right to say so*

say 2) n. (*sā*) In phrases **to have one's say** (be allowed) to express one's opinions

scab n. and v.i. (*skăb*) Dry crust formed over a healing wound or sore

scaffold n. (*skă'fold*) Temporary erection of timber or steel, used in the construction or demolition of a building to support workmen, tools, materials etc.; raised platform upon which criminals are executed

scald v.t. and n. (*skawld*) To injure the soft tissues of the body by contact with boiling water or steam

scale 1) n. and v.t. and i. (*skāl*) One of two shallow pans or dishes of a balance; (pl.) the weighing machine or balance itself

scale 2) n. and v.t. and i. (*skāl*) (zoo.) One of the thin, horny plates forming a protective covering of the skin of most fishes and reptiles

scale 3) n. and v.t. (*skāl*) System of grouping in a graduated order according to an accepted standard of relative rank, size, extent etc., *the social scale*; (math.) system of numeration, *the decimal scale*; relative dimensions of the representation of an object to those of the object itself, *the map has a scale of two inches to the mile*; series of graduated marks as on a ruler etc.; ruler or other instrument so marked; (mus.) series of sounds that subdivide the interval of the octave. As v.t., to climb up or over, reach the top by climbing; regulate according to a scale; ascertain the scale of

scalp n. and v.t. (*skălp*) Skin and hair of the top of the head; this part as stripped off for a trophy by Red Indians. As v.t., to strip off the scalp of

scalpel n. (*skăl'pel*) Straight, thin knife used by surgeons

scamp n. (*skămp*) Rascal, rogue

scamper v.i. and n. (*skăm'per*) To run off; run about gaily

scan v.t. and i. (*skăn*) To examine closely, scrutinize, *scan someone's face*
at perfunctorily, *he scanned the newspaper briefly while eating*

lunch; (elect.) to traverse repeatedly the surface of a television picture with a beam of light or electrons
scandal n. (*skăn'dal*) That which disgraces and damages the reputation of or shocks the feelings of, *his conduct is a scandal to the town*; feelings of disgrace, indignation so caused; malicious or damaging gossip about others
scant adj. and v.t. (*skănt*) Small, few in numbers, *a scant attendance*; inadequate in amount, *scant supplies of food*
scapegoat n. (*skāp'gōt*) blamed or punished for the wrongdoing of another or others
scar n. and v.t. (*skah(r)*) Mark left on body tissues after healing of a wound
scarce adj. (*skārs*) Not plentiful, rare, rarely come across, *a scarce book*
scarcely adv. (*skārs'li*) Barely, only just, hardly, *scarcely enough*; with difficulty, *I can scarcely put one foot before the other*
scare v.t. and n. (*skār*) To fill with sudden terror, strike fear into, *scared by a loud bang*
scarf n. (*skahf*) Length or square of silk, nylon, or other fabric worn about the neck or (by women) over the hair
scatter v.t. and i. (*skă'ter*) To fling about in various directions disperse, *scatter seed*; sprinkle with; break up, put to flight, *scatter the enemy*; be dispersed, run away, *the crowd scattered*
scene n. (*sēn*). Place where events of a play, novel etc. occur, *the scene is set in Roman London*; place where any event occurs, *the scene of the crime*; place represented on the stage of a theatre with backcloth etc., *scenes are changed in the intervals*; one of the subdivisions of an act of a play, *Act Three, Scene Two* view, something seen or spread out to view, with or without action, *scenes of merriment*
scenery n. (*sē'neri*) Painted representation of a scene for the stage; general appearance of a natural view, *mountain scenery*
scent 1) v.t. and i. (*sent*) To smell; to track by sense of smell; suspect, *scent a mystery*; impart fragrance to, *the flowers scent the whole room*; apply perfume to
scent 2) n. (*sent*) Odour, esp. a pleasant one
sceptre n. (*sep'ter*) Rod of gold carried by rulers on ceremonial occasions
schedule n. and v.t. (*shed'ūl*, (U.S.) *sked'ūl*) List, catalogue, giving details in tabular form. As v.t., to put into the form of a schedule; settle the time for an event to take place, *the meeting is scheduled for 10 a.m.*
scheme n. and v.i. and t. (*skēm*) Systematic arrangement or order, *a colour scheme*; programme of action, plan, *a scheme of political reform*; intrigue, *I distrust his little schemes*. As v.i. and t., to make schemes; design; arrange as a scheme
scholar n. (*skol'ar*) Learned man; expert in a subject a pupil; student, esp. undergraduate, elected after examination to a scholarship, and receiving an annual sum of money, specialized, detailed, and accurate knowledge; annual grant of money to a scholar for his maintenance while studying
school 1) n. (*skōōl*) Establishment for education, esp. of the young; the school buildings and grounds· pupils of a school collectively, *the school has a holiday today*; time when teaching is given, lessons, *school starts at 9 o'clock*; process of being educated in a school, *children of school age*; department of a university for the study of a particular subject
school 2) v.t. (*skōōl*) To educate, instruct; train, discipline. Hence: **schooling** n. education
science n. (*si'ens*) Systematized knowledge based on observation and tests and formulated as general principles and laws
scientific adj. (*si en tif'ik*) Of science and its methods
scissors n.pl. (*si'zerz*) Cutting tool consisting of two blades crossing each other and pivoted together at the middle, each with a loop at the end for finger and thumb, *a pair of scissors*
scoff n. and v.i. (*skof*) Expression of mockery, *scoffs and jeers*
scoop n. and v.t. (*skōōp*) Ladle with shallow bowl used for dipping or bailing liquids or shovelling up dry substances
scooter n. (*skōō'ter*) Child's toy consisting of a narrow short board used as foot-rest, and a steering-rod; small motor-bicycle with a low seat
scorch v.t. and i. and n. (*skawch*) To burn superficially, char the surface of
score 1) n. (*skaw(r)*) Cut, incision,

mark scratched or drawn, *his knife has made scores on the wood*; account, reckoning of money due, *to run up a score*; (in cricket and other games) runs, goals etc. made by player or team, *he made a good score today*
score 2) v.t. and i. (*skaw(r)*) To mark with scores; make or keep a score (in a game)
scorn n. and v.t. (*skawn*) Contempt, feeling or expression of disdain or derision
scoundrel n. (*skown'drel*) Rogue, villain, unprincipled person
scour v.t. and i. (*skow(r)*) To range over, search through thoroughly
(*skow(r)*) To clean by rubbing
scout n. and v.i. (*skowt*) Person, ship, or aircraft sent out to get information on the enemy's position and movements; member of the Boy Scout Movement
scowl v.i. and n. (*skowl*) To have a sullen, frowning look
scramble v.i. and t. and n. (*skrămbl*) To climb, clamber along using hands and feet; cook eggs by breaking into a saucepan with butter and heating
scrap n. and v.t. (*skrăp*) Small piece of anything; refuse, waste material; (pl.) odds and ends; pictures, newspaper cuttings, collected and pasted in a book
scrape v.t. and i. (*skrāp*) To clean, smooth a surface by rubbing with a sharp-edged tool; injure, graze, by contact with a sharp or rough surface, *scrape one's knee on a stone*; collect together by scraping or with difficulty, esp. to collect money, *scrape together*
scratch v.t. and i. (*skrăch*) To tear a surface lightly leaving a mark, tear with something sharp, *the cat scratched me*; be marked, scored, *he scratched his hand on the thorn*; to rub lightly as a relief for itching
scrawl v.i. and t. and n. (*skrawl*) To write or draw carelessly and hastily; make meaningless marks
scream v.i. and t. and n. (*skrēm*) To give a piercing cry, esp. of fear or pain
screech v.i. and t. and n. (*skrēch*) To shriek with a harsh, piercing sound
screen 1) n. (*skrēn*) Structure designed to give protection from wind, draughts, light etc. or to conceal something, esp. a portable folding framework used in a room any object giving shelter or concealment, *a smoke-screen*; white or silver surface on which films, colour transparencies etc. are projected
screen 2) v.t. (*skrēn*) To shelter, conceal, cut off, protect with or as with a screen; show something on a screen; make a film of; clean, grade (coal etc.) by passing through a sieve
scribble v.t. and i. and n. (*skribl*) To write hastily or illegibly; scrawl upon; to compose without regard to style
script n. (*skript*) Handwriting, as opposed to print a written document typescript, esp. of a play, talk to be broadcast etc
scroll n. (*skrōl*) Roll of parchment or paper
scrub 1) n. (*skrub*) Brushwood, small stunted trees or bushes; land covered with this
scrub 2) v.t. and i. and n. (*skrub*) To clean by hard rubbing, esp. with brush, soap, and water
scruff n. (*skruf*) Loose folds of skin at the back of the neck
scrutiny n. (*skrōō'ti ni*) Thorough and minute examination of anything
scuffle v.i. and t. and n. (*skufl*) To struggle; engage in a confused rough-and-tumble
scullery n. (*skul'e ri*) Room next to kitchen for washing dishes etc
sculpture n., and v.t. and i. (*skulp'cher*) Art of making representations or designs in stone, wood etc.; example of this art. As v.t. and i., to represent or design in sculpture; to decorate with sculptured figures; to practise the art of sculpture
scurry v.i. and n. (*sku'ri*) To scuttle, scamper
scuttle 1) n. (*skutl*) Container for coal at fireside
scuttle 2) v.i. and n. (*skutl*) To run away, hurry off
scythe n. and v.t. and i. (*sīth*) Tool with curved blade set at right-angles to long wooden pole with two handles projecting from it, used for cutting grass etc
sea n. (*sē*) The ocean, body of salt water covering the larger part of the earth's surface, *ships sail on the sea*; any of the various parts of this water, partly enclosed by land and considered as less than an ocean, *the Mediterranean Sea* expanse or mass of anything, *a sea of flame*
seal 1) n. and v.i. (*sēl*) Amphibious marine mammal with flippers

or webbed feet
seal 2) n. (*sēl*) Device stamped on wax, lead etc. by an engraved die and attached to a document to prove its authenticity
seal 3) v.t. (*sēl*) To affix a seal to; fasten or close by a seal, *seal a letter*; close tightly or completely.
seam n. and v.t. (*sēm*) Join where two pieces of cloth are sewn together
(geol. and min.) thin layer or stratum between two thicker strata, *a seam of coal*
search v.t. and i. (*surch*) To examine or scrutinize carefully in order to find or discover
season 1) n. (*sē'zon*) One of the divisions of the year distinguished by the weather, relative length of day and night etc
season 2) v.t. and i. (*sē'zon*) To render or become fit for use
seat 1) n. (*sēt*) What is sat upon or made to be sat upon, accommodation for sitting, *please use the cushion for a seat*; that part of a chair etc. that directly supports the body; the par⁺ of the body that sits, location,
site of a thing, place where something is carried on, *Westminster is the seat of British government*; principal residence on a private estate, usually in the country
seat 2) v.t. (*sēt*) To place in or on a seat, *seat oneself*; have seats for, *the hall will seat 500 people*
second 1) adj. (*se'kond*) Ordinal number of two; next to, following after, the first in space, time, position, a series, etc
second 2) adv. (*se'kond*) In the second place
second 3) n. (*se'kond*) one who supports another, esp. in a duel or boxing match
second 4) n. (*se'kond*) Sixtieth part of a minute; brief period of time, a moment; sixtieth part of a minute of angular measure
secret adj. (*sē'kret*) Hidden from the knowledge or view of others, designed for concealment
secretary n. (*sek're ta ri*) One employed to manage the correspondence, records etc. of an organization or person
section n. (*sek'shun*)
separate part made to be joined to other parts, *a section of a fishing-rod*; subdivision of a speech, piece of writing; subdivision of a class
secure adj. and v.t. (*se kūr'*) Free from anxiety, *to feel secure about the future*; free from danger, *secure from one's enemies*: firm, stable, *secure foundations*
security n. (*se kūr'i ti*) State of being secure or believing that one is secure; what gives security; something valuable, given as a pledge of repayment, *security for a loan*
sedative adj. and n. (*sed'a tiv*) Calming, soothing bodily or mental pain or agitation. As n., something producing a sedative effect, esp. a sedative drug
sediment n. (*sed'i ment*) Matter that settles to the bottom of a liquid
sedition n. (*se dish'un*) Unlawful actions or words directed against state authority; offence against the government not amounting to treason
see v.t. and i. (*sē*) pret. **saw** (*saw*), p.p. **seen** (*sēn*) To perceive visually; to understand, grasp intellectually; to experience, witness, come across, *he has seen years of hardship*; to have a vision or illusion of seeing, *see things in a dream*; to visualize, *I don't see myself doing that*: to look at, witness, examine, attend, *see a play*; to meet, come across, interview (someone)
seed n., and v.i. and t. (*sēd*) Fertilized germ of a plant
As v.i. and t. to produce seed
seek v.t. and i. (*sēk*) To look for, search out, *seek a new job*
seem v.i. (*sēm*) To appear to be, *he seems honest*
seep v.i. (*sēp*) (Of liquids) to ooze, percolate, leak
seesaw n. and v.i. (*sē'saw*) Board fastened at the middle to an upright support, so that each end can alternately rise and fall, used in a children's game
segment n., and v.t. and i. (*seg'ment*) A part into which a body may be divided, a section
segregate v.t. and i. (*seg're gāt*) To separate from others, isolate; become separated
seize v.t. and i. (*sēz*) (law) To put into possession of, take possession of; grasp, take possession of, forcibly or suddenly
seldom adv. (*sel'dom*) Rarely, not often
select adj. and v.t. (*se lekt'*) Chosen from a number, esp. on account of suitability, merit, etc
As v.t. to choose from a number, for particular purpose or on account of suitability etc

selfish adj. (*sel'fish*) Influenced primarily by one's own desires and pleasures; without care for others
sell v.t. and i. (*sel*) To transfer to another in return for a valuable consideration, usually money, *to sell a dog for £5*; to deal in, have for sale, *sell eggs*
semaphore n., and v.t. and i. (*sem'a faw(r)*) System of signalling by two movable arms on a post or by flags held in the hands, with various positions for letters of alphabet
semi- pref. (*sem'i*) Half, *semicircle*; partly, *semi-transparent*
send v.t. and i. (*send*) To cause to go, be carried, to dispatch, *to send a message*
senile adj. (*sē'nil*) Characteristic of old age
senior adj. and n. (*sē'nyor*) Older than another in years or standing; more advanced in education, rank etc., *senior pupils*
sensation n. (*sen sā'shun*) Feeling, sensual perception, *a sensation of cold*; state of excited emotion or deep interest, esp. in the public mind, *the news caused a sensation*
sense 1) n. (*sens*) Faculty of bodily sensation; any one of the bodily means of perception, *sense of smell* meaning, interpretation, *the sense of a word*
sense 2) v.t. (*sens*) To feel, perceive intuitively, realize, *sense that one is unwelcome*
sensitive adj. (*sens'i tiv*) Feeling readily and acutely; feeling too acutely, easily hurt physically or emotionally, *a sensitive child*
sentence n. and v.t. (*sen'tens*) (gram.) Words that express a coherent statement, question, wish or command; (law) statement of penalty imposed by a criminal court; the penalty itself, *a heavy sentence*
sentiment n. (*sen'ti ment*) The whole of one's feelings on a subject, attitude of mind
sentry n. (*sen'tri*) Military guard
separate 1) adj. (*sep'a rat*) Divided, disconnected, distinct, disunited, *cut into four separate parts*
separate 2) v.t. and i. (*sep'a rāt*) To make, become, keep, separate
sequel n. (*sē'kwel*) What follows or results from (an earlier event), *the sad sequel to his folly*; literary work continuing one that preceded it
serenade n., and v.t. and i. (*se're nād*) Music sung or played outdoors at night, esp. beneath a lover's window
serene adj. (*se rēn'*) Calm, peaceful, placid, undisturbed
sergeant n. (*sah'jent*) (milit.) Non-commissioned officer next above a corporal; police officer next above a constable
serial adj. and n. (*sēr'i al*) Of, in, forming a series, *in serial order*; appearing, issued in, parts or at intervals, *a serial story*
series n. (*sēr'ēz*) pl. **series** A number of similar or related things or events arranged or standing in graded order or successive relationship, *a series of coins*; a number of books of common format published successively
serious adj. (*sēr'i us*) Solemn, sober, grave, *a serious face*; in earnest, not in jest, *a serious offer*; important, requiring considered action, *a serious step to take*
sermon n. (*sur'mon*) Moral and religious address delivered during a church service
serpent n. (*sur'pent*) A snake
servant n. (*sur'vant*) One who serves; person employed by another to perform certain duties, esp. to attend to personal or domestic requirements
serve 1) v.t. and i. (*surv*) To be a servant to, be employed by, *to serve a master*; aid, help, assist, *can I serve you in any way?*; attend, wait upon, *to serve customers*; supply the wants of, *our delivery vans serve a large area*; present (food) at table, *to serve dinner*; fulfil, *serve a purpose*
serve 2) n. (*surv*) Act, style of serving; turn to serve (at tennis etc.)
service 1) n. (*sur'vis*) Act or occupation of serving or being a servant branch or department of public work, esp. of a government department, *the Diplomatic Service* something done to benefit a person, institution etc., *render services to one's country* (eccles.) the formal performance of religious worship or ritual; the serving of a customer, *service is poor in this hotel*
service 2) v.t. (*sur'vis*) To maintain or keep in good repair, *I have my car serviced regularly*
session n. (*sesh'un*) Formal meeting of a body for the transaction of business; period during which such a body meets regularly without a break

set 1) v.t. and i. (*set*) p. and p.p. set (*set*). To put (something) in a specified place or position, *set a plate on the table* appoint some duty for, direct to some action or task, *set a man to dig the garden* become stiff, hard, or firm, *set a jelly in the refrigerator*

set 2) n. (*set*) a group of similar or related objects or persons, esp. a collection forming a single whole, *a set of golf clubs*

settle v.t. and i. (*setl*) To set and place securely in, *settle oneself in a chair* to pay (a debt). As v.i., to go to a place as inhabitant, make one's home; assume a stable, lasting position, condition etc., *the weather seems to be settled at last*

several adj. and n. (*sev'er al*) Separate, distinct, various, *they went their several ways*; more than two but not very many, *several guests arrived today*

severe adj. (*si vēr'*) Strict, harsh, stern, serious; (of weather, illness etc.) intense, violent, *a severe frost*; exacting, rigorous, *a severe cross-examination*; (of style etc.) austere, simple

sew v.t. and i. (*sō*) p. **sewed**, p.p. **sewed** or **sewn** (*sōn*) To work with needle and thread; fasten together with stitches; make by stitching; stitch

sewage n. (*sū'ij*) Waste matter carried through sewers

sewer n. (*sū'er*) Underground conduit for removing sewage and surface waters from town etc. to a place of disposal

sex n. (*seks*) The total of characteristics that distinguish male from female organisms

sexton n. (*seks'ton*) Man who digs graves and tends the church and churchyard

shabby adj. (*shab'i*) Ragged, much worn; poorly dressed; mean, despicable, *a shabby trick*

shack n. (*shăk*) A hut, shed

shade 1) n. (*shād*) Comparative darkness caused by the cutting off of direct light, esp. sunlight, what shuts out light or softens its brilliance, *a lampshade*

shade 2) v.t and i. (*shād*) To cast shade on, shield from the light; cut off (light) from

shadow n. (*shăd'ō*) Patch of shade; dark shape thrown on to a surface by something intervening between it and the light, *the shadow of a dog* amount, *not a shadow of difference*; person who follows another closely or attends him

shaft n. (*shahft*) Stem, stock, of certain weapons, *shaft of an arrow* ray (of light); narrow, vertical opening, esp. one for a lift or leading down to a mine

shake 1) v.t. and i. (*shāk*) To move, be moved, violently or rapidly backwards and forwards or up and down, *to shake a bottle of medicine*; weaken the stability of, *the earthquake shook the house badly*

shake 2) n. (*shāk*) Shaking or being shaken; drink made by shaking two or more ingredients together, *a milk shake*

shallow adj., n., and v.i. (*shă'lō*) Of little depth; superficial

sham adj., n., and v.t. and i. (*shăm*) Not genuine

shame 1) n. (*shām*) Strong feeling of regret, self-disgust, guilt

shame 2) v.t. (*shām*) To cause shame to, cause someone to feel shame; to disgrace

shampoo v.t. and n. (*shăm pōō'*) To wash the hair with special powder, liquid etc. and water

shanty 1) n. (*shăn'ti*) Sailor's song

shanty 2) n. (*shăn'ti*) Small decrepit hut or shack, *shanty towns*

shape 1) n. (*shāp*) Outward form, outline, contour, *the shape of a man's head* clear, orderly conception or plan, *put one's ideas into shape*

share 2) v.t. and i. (*shār*) To give divide and distribute, *share (out) a cake among three people*; to participate with in the possession or use of a thing, *let us share the remainder between us*; have a share in, *share the cost with someone*

shark n. (*shahk*) One of a group of sea-fishes with rounded tapering body and mouth on the underside

sharp adj. (*shahp*) Keen, cutting, *a sharp edge*; piercing, *a sharp point*; acute, pointed, *a sharp nose*; abrupt, *a sharp turn*; steep, *a sharp hill*; shrill, *a sharp yelp*; distinctly seen or defined, *a sharp outline*; acrid, sour, *a sharp taste*

shatter v.t. and i. (*shăt'er*) To break to fragments, smash utterly

shave v.t. and i. and n. (*shāv*) To remove the hair from (the face etc.) with a razor, *have you shaved today?* pass close to without contact or with fleeting contact, *the car shaved the kerb*

shark

shawl n. (*shawl*) Piece of material worn over head or shoulders by women, or used to cover a baby
sheaf n. (*shēf*) pl. **sheaves** Bundle of reaped grain tied together; bundle of papers etc. laid or tied together, *a sheaf of papers*
shear v.t. and i. and n. (*shēr*) p.p. **sheared** or **shorn** (*shawn*) To cut with shears As n. (pl.) **shears, pair of shears** large scissor-like cutting tool used for shearing sheep, trimming hedges etc
sheath n. (*shēth*) Close-fitting cover for the blade of a weapon or tool
shed 1) v.t. (*shed*) To let fall, *the trees have shed their leaves*
shed 2) n. (*shed*) Small, roughly made structure
sheet n. (*shēt*) Large rectangular piece of cotton or linen cloth, used as bed-clothing thin, flat piece of any material, *a sheet of paper*
sheik(h) n. (*shāk*) Head of tribe or family in Arab and Moslem lands
shelf n. (*shelf*) Narrow flat projection in a cupboard, on a wall, etc., usually made of wood
shell n. (*shel*) Hard outer covering of many animal or vegetable objects, *the shell of an egg*; anything hollow and emptied of its contents, *only the shell of the house remained after the fire*; metal case filled with explosive and fired from a gun
shelter n. and v.t. and i. (*shel'ter*) State of safety from danger or annoyance; protection, cover that gives safety or shelter, *to find shelter from the rain*. As v.t. and i., to give shelter, safety, *shelter someone for the night*; take shelter, *shelter beneath a tree*
shepherd n. and v.t. (*shep'erd*) A man who tends sheep
sherry n. (*she'ri*) Dry brown wine of southern Spain
shield n. and v.t. (*shēld*) Piece of armour formerly carried on the left arm to protect the body in battle
shift v.t. and i. and n. (*shift*) To remove, get rid of, transfer, *shift the blame*; change the position of, *shift a chair across the room*; to move, change position, *shift from one foot to another*
shimmer v.i. and n. (*shim'er*) To shine fitfully, glisten
shin n. and v.i. (*shin*) Front part of the leg from knee to ankle
shine v.i. and t. (*shin*) To emit, reflect light; be bright, glow, be luminous, *the moon is shining tonight*; appear bright, cheerful, *a face shining with happiness*
shingle n. (*shing'gl*) Loose pebbles or stones as found on sea-beaches
ship n. (*ship*) Large ocean-going vessel
shirk v.t. and i. (*shurk*) To evade, try to escape (responsibility, duty, etc.)
shirt n. (*shurt*) Loose-fitting, sleeved garment worn by men under waistcoat, jacket etc.; woman's plain blouse
shiver v.i. and n. (*shiv'er*) To shake, tremble, esp. from cold, fear etc
shoal n. and v.i. (*shōl*) Large number of fish swimming together
shock 1) n. (*shok*) Violent blow or impact causing shaking, a jolt or jar, *the shock of the explosion*; (elect.) sensation caused by the discharge of electricity through the body
shock 2) v.t. and i. (*shok*) To cause shock to; fill with bewilderment, grief, disgust, disapproval etc
shoe n. (*shōō*) Covering for the foot, usually of leather, reaching to but not covering the ankle; flat crescent of metal fitted to a horse's hoof
shoot v.t. and i. (*shōōt*) pret. and p.p. **shot** (*shot*) To throw, propel, thrust forward swiftly and violently, *he was shot over his horse's head*; flash, dart suddenly, send out flashes, *shoot out beams*

of light; project (a missile) from a weapon of propulsion, *shoot a bullet from a rifle*; discharge (a weapon of propulsion), *don't shoot!*; wound or kill by firing a missile; pass over or through rapidly, *shoot the rapids in a canoe*; kill game by shooting in an area of land, *shoot a covert*; practise shooting as a sport; (cinema) to film (a sequence of events); throb with sudden pain, *shooting pains in the arm*; to bud, break, *the bushes will shoot again in the spring*

shop 1) n. (*shop*) Building where retail trade is carried on; workshop

shop 2) v.i. and t. (*shop*) To go to shops to buy things

shore n. (*shaw(r)*) Stretch of land immediately bordering on sea, estuary, or large lake

short adj. (*shawt*) Not having great length in space or time

shot n. (*shot*) One of the small lead pellets fired from a sporting or 'shot' gun; a number of these; what is fired from a gun; iron ball thrown in athletic competition

shoulder 1) n. (*shōl'der*) Either of the two projections on the body below and on either side of the neck

shoulder 2) v.t. (*shōl'der*) To take on the shoulders (also fig.), *shoulder a burden*

shout v.i. and t. and n. (*showt*) To utter a loud cry, to call; to speak loudly; to utter very loudly, *shout an order*

shove v.t. and i. and n. (*shuv*) To push

shovel n. and v.t. *(shuv'el)* Spade-like tool used for shifting loose hard material

show 1) v.t. and i. (*shō*) p.p. **shown** (*shōn*) To present to the sight, allow to be seen, *show one's tongue to a doctor* cause to understand, explain, *show the untruth of a story*; guide to, conduct, *show a visitor into the room*

show 2) n. (*shō*) Collection of things displayed or exhibited, *a dog show*

shower n. and v.t. and i. (*show'er*) Light or brief fall of rain, snow etc

shrapnel n. (*shrăp'nel*) Shell which bursts in the air and scatters bullets or pieces of metal

shred n. and v.t. and i. (*shred*) Small fragment, piece

shriek v.i. and t. and n. (*shrēk*) To utter a shrill, piercing cry

shrill adj. (*shril*) (Of sound, voice) high-pitched, piercing

shrink v.i. and t. (*shringk*) pret. **shrank** (*shrăngk*) p.p. **shrunk** (*shrungk*) To contract, become smaller or less

shrivel v.t. and i. (*shri'vel*) To curl up, shrink (through heat, frost etc.), *the grass shrivelled in the sun*

shrug v.t. and i. and n. (*shrug*) To lift (the shoulders) slightly as sign of doubt, nonchalance, helplessness etc

shudder v.i. and n. (*shud'er*) To tremble violently, shake with horror, disgust etc.

shuffle v.i. and t. and n. (*shufl*) To walk scraping the feet on the ground without lifting them; to mix objects together, esp. playing cards before a game

shun v.t. (*shun*) To avoid, have nothing to do with

shunt v.t. and i. and n. (*shunt*) To divert, esp. (rolling-stock) on a railway from one track to another

shut v.t. and i. (*shut*) To close, move into position to stop an opening, *shut the door!*; to fold, bring the folding parts of (something) together, *shut a book* catch or pinch by shutting something, *shut one's fingers in a door*

shutter n. and v.t. (*shut'er*) Hinged outer covering of wood etc. for a window

shy 1) adj. (*shī*) Self-conscious, bashful, timid, nervous

shy 2) v.i. (*shī*) (Of a horse) to swerve nervously aside

sick adj. and n. (*sik*) In bad health, ill

side 1) n. (*sīd*) One of the surfaces of an object

side 2) v.i. (*sīd*) Side with take the part of in a dispute

siding n. (*sī'ding*) Short track by the side of a main railway line

sieve n. and v.t. (*siv*) Utensil with a frame covered with network of wire, gauze etc., used for separating smaller from larger pieces or solids from liquids

sift v.t. and i. (*sift*) To separate by putting through a sieve

sigh v.i. and t. and n. (*sī*) Take a deep slow breath and exhale it audibly, to express boredom, sorrow etc

sight 1) n. (*sīt*) Faculty, power of seeing, *poor sight* something, someone odd or conspicuous, *what a sight you look!;* device to aid the vision when using rifle, telescope, etc

sight 2) v.t. (*sīt*) To see

sign 1) n. (*sīn*) That by which

anything is shown, indicated, or represented, *those clouds are a sign of rain;* word(s) or design on a board etc. to give warning or directions or to indicate trade or profession, *traffic signs*

sign 2) v.t. and i. (*sin*) To mark with a sign; put one's signature to (a document), *sign a letter*

signal n., and v.t. and i. (*sig'nal*) Message conveyed by signs, *a signal of distress;* device of distress; device for conveying a message, *the signals are against the train;* event or action indicating or inciting some other event or action, *his arrival was the signal for loud cheering*
As v.t. and i., to make a signal or signals to; send by signal; communicate by signalling

signature n. (*sig'na cher*) Person's name written by himself

signify v.t. and i. (*sig'ni fi*) To mean, make known or represent, by signs, symbols or words, *signify agreement by a nod;* be of importance, matter, *it doesn't signify much*

silence n. and v.t. (*si'lens*) Absence of sound

silhouette n. and v.t. (*siloo et'*) Picture in outline or profile made in black on white ground; profile or outline of someone or something seen against a light background

silly adj. and n. (*sil'i*) Foolish, stupid

silver 1) n. (*sil'ver*) Pure white metallic element, symbol Ag, and

silhouette

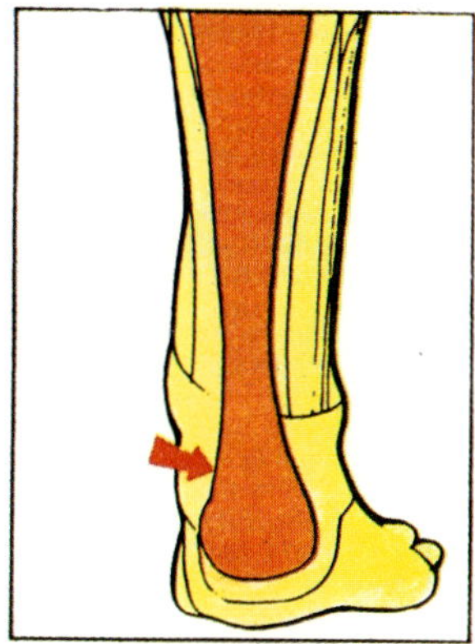

sinew

one of the precious metals; articles made of silver or plated with silver; coins of silver or formerly made of silver, *change this note into silver*

similar adj. (*sim'i lar*) Resembling

simple adj. and n. (*simpl*) not complex, easy to understand or do

simmer v.i. and t. and n. (*sim'er*) To boil gently; be in a state of suppressed anger or excitement

since adv., prep., and conj. (*sins*) From that time, after that time, *the house was bombed but has since been rebuilt;* from then till now, *he had a bad accident and has not been well since;* ago, *he died many years since.* As prep., after, from that time, *since I last wrote, I have been ill.* As conj., from the time when, *where have you been since we last met?;* because, *since you have failed, I will try*

sincere adj. (*sin sēr'*) (Of persons) honest, genuine; loyal; (of actions etc.) genuine, free from deceit, *a sincere devotion*

sinew n. (*sin'ū*) Tendon, fibrous tissue, uniting muscle and bone

sing v.t. and i. (*sing*) pret. **sang** (*săng*) p.p. **sung** (*sung*) To articulate with musical inflexions of the voice

singe v.t. and i. and n. (*sinj*) To burn superficially, scorch; become singed or scorched. As n., slight burn or scorch

single 1) adj. and n. (*sing'gl*) One only, not double or compound, *a single line railway;* designed for

done by, one person, *a single bed*
single 2) v.t. (*sing'gl*) To select, choose, separate, *single out for special attention;* cause to stand out, *abilities that single a man out for promotion*
singular adj. and n. (*sing'gūlar*) Of one person or thing, *first person singular;* uncommon, strange, *singular habits;* outstanding, *a man of singular courage.* As n., the singular number; word not in the plural
sinister adj. (*sin'is ter*) Evil; suggesting evil or coming disaster
sink 1) v.i. and t. (*singk*) pret. sank (*sănk*) p.p. **sunk** (*sunk*) To go or appear to go slowly downwards, esp. below the horizon or a surface
sink 2) n. (*singk*) Basin of porcelain, metal etc. with drainage outlet, placed below water taps and used for washing dishes etc
sip v.t. and i., and n. (*sip*) To drink in small quantities; to take a sip. As n., a small drink of liquid
sister n. (*sis'ter*) Female of the same parentage; one who acts like a sister; nurse in charge of a hospital ward; a nun
sit v.i. and t. (*sit*) pret. and p.p. sat (*săt*) To take or be in a position in which the weight of the upright body is supported by the buttocks resting on the ground or on a seat, *to sit on a chair;* to cover eggs for hatching, *the hens are sitting now*
site n. and v.t. (*sīt*) Place where something is, was, or is to be, *a site for a new school.* As v.t., to place, locate
situated adj. (*sit'ū ā ted*) Placed, having a certain position
situation n. (*sit ū ā'shun*) Position, condition, state of affairs; office, employment, job
size n. and v.t. (*sīz*) Relative dimensions, magnitude, or bulk, *a building of great size;* standard dimensions in which certain articles are made, *a shoe two sizes too small.* As v.t., to arrange according to size
skate 1) n. and v.i. (*skāt*) One of a pair of sharp-edged steel blades fitted to a boot and used for moving smoothly over ice; **roller-skate** skate with wheels instead of blades, used for sliding on any smooth surface. As v.i., to move on skates
skate 2) n. (*skāt*) Large flat fish
skeleton n. (*skel'e ton*) Bony

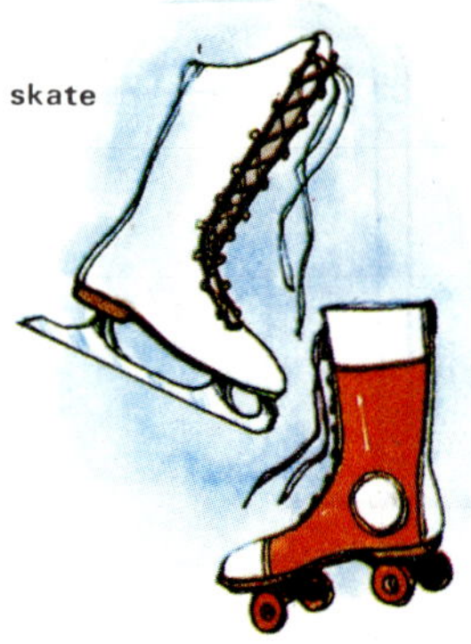
skate

framework of human or animal body, esp. without the soft tissues
sketch n., and v.t. and i. (*skech*) Rapid drawing in outline or wash; rough draft, outline, of anything; short descriptive article; short dramatic play
ski n. and v.i. (*skē, shē*) One of a pair of long narrow strips of wood, strapped to the feet for moving over frozen snow. As v.i., to use skis for moving over snow. Hence: **skier** n. one who skis
skid n. and v.i. (*skid*) side-slip or slide of wheels of motor-car or bicycle on a slippery road
skim v.t. and i. (*skim*) To remove matter floating on the surface (of a liquid), *skim the cream off milk;* glide lightly over (a surface), not touching or barely touching it, *the gull skimmed the sea;* read through rapidly and perfunctorily, *I shall skim this book*
skin v.t. and i. (*skin*) To remove the skin from
skip v.i. and t. and n. (*skip*) To leap about, gambol; to leap; to jump over a rope held in the hands and turned over the head and under the feet; to omit, *skip the dull parts of a book*
skipper n. (*skip'er*) Captain, esp. of a small merchant ship; (colloq.) captain of a side
skirmish n. and v.i. (*skur'mish*) Fight, often unpremeditated, between small bodies of troops
skirt n., and v.t. and i. (*skurt*) Outer garment worn by women, fitted at waist and covering part of the legs; lower part of a dress or other garment
As v.t. and i., to be on, pass along, the border of; to move, go close, to the border, *skirt along*

the edge of a cliff
skittles n.pl. (*skitlz*) Game in which a heavy wooden ball is bowled along an alley to knock down a number of bottle-shaped pieces of wood called nine-pins
skull n. (*skul*) Bony brain-casing of animals
sky n. (*skī*) Aerial region surrounding the earth; the upper atmosphere
slab n. (*slăb*) Thin, flat piece of any solid material, *a slab of cheese*
slack 1) adj., and v.t. and i. (*slăk*) Relaxed, not taut or tight, *a slack rope;* lazy, negligent, *slack in one's duties;* dull, not active, *business is slack;* slow-moving, sluggish, *a slack speed.* As v.t. and i., to be or become slack
slack 2) n. (*slăk*) Part of anything left slack or loose; slack water; small refuse coal; (pl.) loose-fitting trousers worn by women
slacken v.t. and i. (*slăk'en*) To become, cause to be, slack
slalom n. and v.i. (*slă'lom*) Ski-race between obstacles on a course. As v.i., to ski between obstacles on a course
slam v.t. and i. and n. (*slăm*) To shut violently and noisily, *slam a door;* put, throw, or knock down violently, *slam a book down on a table*
slander n. and v.t. (*slahn'der*) (law) Malicious report, uttered by words or gesture to damage a person's character As v.t., to utter slander concerning (someone)
slant v.i. and t., and n. (*slahnt*) To slope; cause to slant; put, place obliquely. As n., a slope; oblique position; **a slant on** (colloq.) point of view about (something), *a new slant on this problem*
slap v.t., n., and adv. (*slăp*) To strike with the open hand; **slap down** throw down with force As n., a blow with the open hand or something flat
slash v.t. and i., and n. (*slăsh*) To cut gashes in; to make long cuts in (a garment) in order to show the material beneath; to lash, strike at with a whip etc
slaughter n. and v.t. (*slaw'ter*) Slaying or killing, esp. of animals for food, or the indiscriminate mass killing of human beings
slave n. and v.i. (*slāv*) One whose person and labour are the legal property of another
slavery n. condition of being a slave; system of slave ownership
slay v.t. (*slā*) pret. **slew** (*slū*) p.p. **slain** (*slān*) To kill, murder
sled, sledge n. and v.i. and t. (*sled, slej*) Vehicle with runners and a low framework, for travelling over snow
sleek adj. and v.t. (*slēk*) (Of hair, animal's coat) smooth, glossy
sleep 1) n. (*slēp*) pret. and p.p. **slept** (*slept*) State of temporary unconsciousness recurring naturally in man every twenty-four hours; period during which one is asleep
sleep 2) v.i. and t. (*slēp*) To be or fall into a state of sleep; (colloq.) provide sleeping accommodation for, *we can sleep eight people if necessary*
sleepy adj. (*slē'pi*) Inclined to, ready for, sleep; (of places) quiet, inactive
sleet n. and v.i. (*slēt*) Fine snow mingled with rain; frozen rain
sleeve n. (*slēv*) Part of a garment covering the arm stiff envelope for disc of recorded music
slender adj. (*slen'der*) Small in width or circumference compared with length or height; slim; slight, scanty, *slender means*
sleuth n. and v.t. and i. (*slōōth*) (colloq.) Detective
slice n., and v.t. and i. (*slīs*) Thin, broad piece cut off something, *a slice of bread;* share, portion, *a slice of good luck;* broad flat blade for cutting, serving, etc., esp. fish
slick adj., adv., and n. (*slik*) Smooth, sleek; clever, smart, *a slick salesman*
slide 1) v.t. and i. (*slīd*) pret. and p.p. **slid** (*slid*) To move smoothly along with a gliding motion move or cause to move into a position quietly and unobserved, *she slid a coin into his hand*
slide 2) n. (*slīd*) Act of sliding; stretch of smooth ice, snow etc. on which to slide slip of glass used as a mount for objects under a microscope; colour transparency or picture on a glass plate, to be slid into a projector and shown on a screen
slight 1) adj. (*slīt*) Slender; frail, *a slight platform to carry such a heavy weight;* mild, inconsiderable, *slight differences;* trivial, *a slight book*
slight 2) v.t. and n. (*slīt*) To treat with contempt, to insult

slim adj., and v.t. and i. (*slim*) Slender; slight in degree or amount, *a slim chance.* As v.t. and i., to make slim; reduce one's weight
slime n. (*slīm*) Soft, moist, slippery substance, esp. mud
sling n., and v.t. and i. (*sling*) Strip of looped leather used to throw stones to a distance a loop used as a means of lifting or as a support, esp. for a broken arm
slink v.i. (*slingk*) pret. and p.p. slunk (*slungk*) To move in a furtive manner
slip 1) v.i. and t. (*slip*) To move or cause to move into a specified position quietly and easily, *the book slipped off his lap;* to place in position or remove quietly and furtively, *she slipped a coin into his hand;* to miss one's footing, stumble, esp. on a slippery surface to move from a normal or desired position, escape from a grasp or fastening, *the ball slipped from his fingers*
slip 2) n. (*slip*) Act of slipping; stumble; slight error or moral lapse; loose outer cover, *pillow-slip*; loose garment, esp. woman's petticoat; cutting from a plant; young, undeveloped person; thin strip or piece of anything, *a slip of paper*; sloping way on which vessels are built or repaired, a slipway; (cricket) one of the fielders behind the wicket on the off side; clay in a semi-liquid state for coating or decorating earthenware
slipper n. (*slip'er*) Loose, light shoe worn in the house
slit n. and v.t. (*slit*) A narrow opening or incision, *the slit of a letter-box.* As v.t., to make an incision in, cut open
slog v.i. and t., and n. (*slog*) To hit hard and wildly, *slog a ball*; slog at work hard at
slogan n. (*slō'gan*) Phrase symbolizing the aims or principles of a group or organization etc., *political slogans*
sloop n. (*slōōp*) Single-masted, fore-and-aft rigged vessel
slop n., and v.i. and t. (*slop*) A pool of spilt liquid; dirty waste water or other liquid from kitchen or bedrooms
slope n., and v.i. and t. (*slōp*) Inclined position or direction, *the slope of a roof*
slot n. and v.t. (*slot*) Narrow opening or groove through which an object may be inserted or along

sloop

which something may slide.
sloth n. (*slōth*) Mental and physical apathy, indolence
slouch n. and v.i. (*slowch*) Crouching attitude or way of walking
slough 1) n. (*slow*) Swamp, bog
slough 2) n., and v.t. and i. (*sluf*) Cast-off skin of a snake
sloven n. (*sluv'en*) Person careless in dress, habits etc., a dirty, lazy person
slow adj. (*slō*) Not quick, taking a long time, *a slow walker*; at less than the normal rate or speed, *a slow step*; not quick mentally, dull, *slow of wits*; not quickly moved, *slow to anger*; not lively, monotonous, *a slow book;* (of a surface) of such a nature as to cause objects moving over it to do so at a reduced rate, *a slow cricket pitch*; (of time) behind the correct time, *the clock is slow*
sludge n. (*sluj*) Thick, greasy mud; slushy snow; wet refuse, sewage
sluice n., and v.t. and i. (*slōōs*) Artificial channel for controlling the flow of water into or out of harbours, canal-locks, dams etc., esp. by means of a sluice-gate; the flow of water through such a channel or blocked above it
(colloq.) a wash down with water;
sluice-gate movable gate controlling flow of water in a sluice
slum n. and v.i. (*slum*) Street or area characterized by dirty, dilapidated, and overcrowded houses
slumber v.i. and t., and n. (*slum'ber*) To sleep

sluice-gate

slump n. and v.i. (*slump*) Steep or sudden fall in prices and demand; an economic depression; decline in value or reputation. As v.i., to sit down heavily, sit in a state of collapse, *slump in a chair;* (of prices etc.) to fall suddenly and steeply

slur v.t. and i., and n. (*slur*) To run syllables together so that they are indistinct

slush n. (*slush*) Liquid mud; melting snow

sly adj. (*slī*) Cunning, not frank, underhand

slyness n. (ON *slogr*)

smack 1) (*smăk*) Small fishing-boat

smack 2) n. and v.t. (*smăk*) Sharp sound of kissing, tasting, or of a blow with the open hand; a slap, blow, *to hit the ball a hard smack*

smack

small adj. (*smawl*) Not large in size, height, bulk, degree, extent etc., *a small house*; being few in number, amount, *a small audience*; insignificant, *small worries*

smart 1) v.i. and n. (*smaht*) To feel or cause a sharp but superficial pain, mental or physical, *eyes smart with tears*; feel hurt or resentful, *smart from an insult*

smart 2) adj. (*smaht*) Sharp, sudden and severe, *a smart blow;* quick, brisk, *a smart walk*; alert; witty; quick and clever, *smart at one's work*; capable, skilfully done. *a smart piece of work*; neat, clean, tidy, well-groomed, *you look very smart*; fashionable, modish, *the smart set*

smear n., and v.t. and i. (*smēr*) Mark made by a touch from something dirty, greasy, etc.

smelt v.t. (*smelt*) To heat (ore) so as to extract metal

smile n., and v.i. and t. (*smīl*) Pleased, happy, or amused expression, characterized by a parting of the lips and a lifting of their corners; the act of smiling

smirk v.i. and n. (*smurk*) To give a self-satisfied, fatuous smile

smite v.t. and i. (*smīt*) pret. **smote** (*smōt*) p.p. **smitten** (*smit'n*) (archaic) To strike, hit hard; to defeat utterly

smith n. (*smith*) Worker in iron or other metals, *blacksmith*. Hence: **smithy** n. blacksmith's workshop

smithereens n.pl. (*smith er ēnz'*) (colloq.) Small fragments

smock n. (*smok*) Loose garment, usually worn as an overall; child's loose dress

smocking n. (*smok'ing*) Decorative stitching in which material is stitched into small gathers in a kind of honeycomb.

smoke 1) n. (*smōk*) Fine particles given off by burning matter and held in suspension in the air

smoke 2) v.i. and t. (*smōk*) To give out smoke or visible vapour like smoke, *the horses were smoking after the race*; emit smoke in a wrong direction, esp. into a room, *the sitting-room chimney smokes badly*; draw in tobacco smoke from cigarette, pipe etc., and blow it out again, *to smoke a pipe* impregnate (meat etc.) with wood-smoke

smock

in order to preserve it, *to smoke herrings*
smooth 1) adj. (*smōōth*) (Of surfaces) free from roughness level, glossy, even, *smooth skin*; (of consistency) not lumpy, of even texture throughout, *a smooth paste*; (of motion) free from bumps or interruptions, *a smooth ride*
smooth 2) v.t. and i., and n. (*smōōth*) To make smooth or level; remove obstacles to make progress easy, *smooth away difficulties*
smoulder v.i. and n. (*smōl'der*) To burn slowly without flame
smudge v.t. and i., and n. (*smuj*) To smear, make a smear on; become blurred, smeared
smug adj. (*smug*) Self-satisfied
smuggle v.t. (*smugl*) To import or export goods secretly and illegally to avoid paying customs duties
snack n. (*snăk*) Light, usually hurried, meal
snag n. and v.t. (*snăg*) Rough, jagged projection; tear caused by such a projection, *a snag in a coat-sleeve*; unforeseen difficulty, *to discover a snag in someone's plans*
snake n. (*snāk*) Any member of the order *Ophidia*, scaly limbless reptiles
snap v.t. and i. (*snăp*) To break quickly and sharply, *snap a stick*; cause to make a sharp cracking sound, *snap a whip*; to bite, snatch with the teeth, *the dog snapped (at) my leg*; to bring together, shut or open, become fastened, with a short sharp noise or click, *snap down the lid of a box*; to take a snapshot of; have one's photograph taken in a snapshot; to speak curtly, irritably, *snap at a naughty child*
snare n. and v.t. (*snār*) Trap for catching birds and small animals
snarl v.i. and t., and n. (*snahl*) To show the teeth in a growl
snatch v.t. and i., and n. (*snăch*) Seize rapidly, grasp suddenly with the hand, grab; take, obtain quickly, seize the chance of having, *snatch a few hours of sleep*
sneak v.i. and t., and n. (*snēk*) To go silently and secretly, *sneak into a room*; (schoolboy slang) tell a teacher about the faults of others
sneer v.i. and n. (*sner*) To smile mockingly and contemptuously; to make mocking, contemptuous remarks, *sneer at someone's beliefs*
sneeze v.i. and n. (*snēz*) To expel air violently through nose and mouth
sniff v.i. and t., and n. (*snif*) To breath in through the nose, esp. so as to perceive a scent, *sniff a flower*; to breathe in sharply and audibly; to do this as an expression of disapproval
snigger v.i. and n. (*snig'er*) To utter a half-suppressed laugh, esp. at something improper. As n., a half-suppressed laugh, a giggle
snip v.t. and i., and n. (*snip*) To make a short clip or clips with scissors or shears
snipe v.i. and t. (*snip*) (milit.) To shoot (at) single enemy soldiers from a hiding place, usually at long range; to hit or kill in this way
snippet n. (*snip'et*) Small part or share, *snippets of information*
snivel v.i. and n. (*sni'vel*) To to whine, fret, complain tearfully
snob n. (*snob*) One who pays an exaggerated respect to rank, wealth, fashionable society etc., and despises persons of lower status
snoop v.i. (*snōōp*) To meddle, pry into matters that are not one's concern
snooze v.i. and n. (*snōōz*) To take a short sleep, to doze
snore v.i. and n. (*snaw(r)*) To breathe noisily and roughly while asleep
snorkel, schnorkel n. (*snaw'kel*) Device for breathing during underwater swimming; long air-tube by which a submarine takes in

fresh air while submerged
snort v.i. and t., and n. (*snawt*) To draw in air noisily and violently through the nose; to show contempt, disapproval etc. by this means
snout n. (*snowt*) Nose and muzzle of an animal; anything projecting from a mass, *the snout of a glacier*
snow 1) n. (*snō*) Small ice crystals formed from water vapour in the atmosphere and falling as soft white flakes
snow 2) v.i. and t. (*snō*) To cause to shower down like snow; to fall from the sky as snow; to scatter or come in large numbers or quantities, *congratulations snowed upon her*
snub v.t. and n. (*snub*) To rebuff, check, by contempt or coolness. As n., snubbing behaviour or words
snuff 1) v.t. and i. (*snuf*) To sniff, inhale through the nose
snuff 2) n. and v.i. (*snuf*) A sniff; (a pinch of) powdered tobacco to be sniffed up the nose. As v.i., to take snuff
snuff 3) v.t. and i. (*snuf*) To clip off (the wick of a candle)
snuffle v.i. and n. (*snufl*) To sniff continually, esp. through partially blocked nasal passages
snug adj. (*snug*) Sheltered from draughts and cold, cosy, *a snug parlour*
snuggle v.i. and t. (*snug'l*) To cuddle, lie close to, so as to be warm and comfortable
soak v.t. and i., and n. (*sōk*) To immerse or remain immersed in liquid until thoroughly saturated
soap n. and v.t. (*sōp*) Substance made from oils and fats and an alkali, used for washing and cleansing, *a bar of soap*
soar v.i. (*saw(r)*) (Of birds) to mount high in the air
sob v.i. and t., (*sob*) To draw rapid, convulsive breaths, usually from sorrow or pain and while crying, *she sobbed bitterly*; to express in sobs, *sob out one's grief*
sober adj., and v.t. and i. (*sō'ber*) Not drunk; not excited or exaggerated, *of a sober cast of mind*; moderate, temperate in disposition; subdued in colour
soccer n. (*sok'er*) Popular abbreviation of association football
sociable adj. (*sō'shabl*) (Of persons etc.) fond of company, friendly; marked by friendliness
social adj. and n. (*sō'shal*) Of the relations of people living in a community, *social laws*; living in groups characterized by mutual interdependence, *man is a social animal*; of organized human conduct and conditions, esp. of the grades of society, *one's social equals*; for companionship, *a social club*; sociable, *a social disposition*
socialism n. (*sō'shal izm*) Political theory advocating collective instead of individual ownership of capital and property
society n. (*sō sī'e ti*) System whereby men live together in organized communities; human life considered as existing in such communities, *the changing habits of society today*; any organized group of people forming a community, *many early societies were theocratic*; group or class of society, esp. group associated by common interests or occupation or distinguished by high rank, wealth, etc., *the world of society and fashion*; (attrib.) belonging to fashionable society, *a society hostess*; company, companionship, *the society of one's friends*; (with capital) association of persons organized with a purpose, *the Society of Friends*
sock n. (*sok*) Short stocking covering the ankle or reaching to just below the knee
soda n. (*sō'da*) Any of the various compounds of sodium, esp. common soda, *sodium carbonate*, used in glass-making, soap-boiling, etc., and baking soda, *sodium bicarbonate*, used in cooking; soda-water, *whisky and soda*
sodium n. (*sō'di um*) Metallic element, symbol Na, occurring naturally only in compounds, *sodium chloride*
sofa n. (*sō'fa*) Long, upholstered seat or couch, usually with back and arms
soft adj. (*soft*) Not resisting pressure, easily compressed or squeezed, not hard, easily cut or worked, *soft as butter*; not rough or harsh in texture, taste, or sound, *soft as silk*; gentle, *a soft breeze*, tender (in disposition), *a soft heart*
soften v.t. and i. (*sofn*) To make or become soft or softer
soil 1) n. (*soil*) Top layer of ground
soil 2) v.t. and i. (*soil*) To make or become dirty, *soil one's clothes*

sofa

solace n., and v.t. and i. (*sol'as*) What gives comfort, consolation; a consolation, pleasure. As v.t. and i., to provide solace (for)
solar adj. (*sō'lar*) Of the sun
solder n. and v.t. (*sōl'der*) Fusible alloy used for cementing metals together. As v.t., to unite with solder
soldier n. and v.i. (*sōl'jer*) Member of an army
sole 1) n. (*sōl*) Edible marine flatfish, *Solea vulgaris*
sole 2) n. and v.t. (*sōl*) Underside of the foot
sole 3) adj. (*sōl*) Only, single, alone, *the sole occupant*; exclusive, restricted to one person etc., *the sole rights*
solemn adj. (*sol'em*) serious, causing feeling of seriousness, *solemn occasions*; grave, not cheerful, *a solemn voice*
solicitor n. (*so lis'i tor*) A lawyer
solid adj. and n. (*sol'id*) Not liquid or gaseous, retaining its form under pressure, hard, firm, *solid bodies*; not hollow, having no empty spaces within it, *a solid tyre*
soliloquy n. (*so lil'ō kwi*) Utterance of one's thoughts aloud; speech uttered by a character in a play expressing his thoughts, often while alone on the stage
solitary adj. (*sol'i ta ri*) Being or living alone, *a solitary rider*; done, passed, alone, *solitary confinement*; little frequented, *a solitary hamlet*; sole, single, *not a solitary example*
solitude n. (*sol'i tūd*) State of being solitary, *to live in solitude*; a lonely place
solo n. and adv. (*sō'lō*) (mus.) Piece sung or played by a single performer (also attrib.); any performance by one person, *a solo flight*; card game for four players. As adv., alone, *to sail solo across the Atlantic*. Hence: **soloist** n. (mus.) one who gives a solo
solve v.t. (*solv*) Discover an answer to, find a way out of (a difficulty), *solve one's problems*
some adj. and pron. (*sum*) Person, number, quantity or thing not given a specific definition, *some child has broken the window*; more or less, approximately, *some fifty pounds*; one or other, *some day*; of a considerable degree, number, etc, *some way to go*; (colloq.) fine, great, *that was some game!* As pron., a certain unspecified number or quantity, *will you have some?*
son n. (*sun*) Male child of a parent
song n. (*song*) Singing; music for the voice, *to write a song*
soon adv. (*sōōn*) In a short time, *he will soon be here;* early, before the anticipated time, *we shall get there too soon;* without delay, readily, *he soon felt at home;* willingly, *I would as soon go home now*
soot n. and v.t. (*sōōt*) Black powdery substance deposited by fuel during imperfect combustion
soothe v.t. (*sōōth*) To calm, placate, *soothe a crying baby*
soprano n. (*sō prah'nō*) Female or boy's voice with highest singing range
sorcerer n. (*saw'ser er*) Wizard; magician aided by evil spirits. Hence: **sorceress** n. woman sorcerer; **sorcery** n. magic performed with the aid of evil spirits
sordid adj. (*saw'did*) Filthy, squalid
sore adj. and n. (*saw(r)*) (Of a part of the body) painful, tender to the touch As n., open wound, sore place on the body
sorrow n. and v.i. (*so'rō*) Unhappiness, grief, the opposite of joy, *to feel sorrow for*
sorry adj. (*so'ri*) Feeling regret or grief, *I am sorry to hear your sad news*
sort 1) n. (*sawt*) Group of persons or things having certain qualities in common, a class, category, *he's not my sort*
sort 2) v.t. and i. (*sawt*) To

separate things of one sort or kind from others; to arrange in groups
soufflé n. (*sōō'flā*) Sweet or savoury dish of eggs, milk etc. beaten to a froth and baked
soul n. (*sōl*) Non-material part in man
sound 1) n. (*sownd*) What is heard, a vibratory disturbance in the air perceived through the ear and sense of hearing
sound 2) v.t. and i. (*sownd*) To produce sound from, *sound a trumpet*; make a sound, *the bell sounds*; express by voice, *sound a note of triumph*
sound 3) adj. (*sownd*) In good condition, healthy; not diseased, decayed, or defective, *is this fruit sound?*; reliable, based on reason
sound 4) n. (*sownd*) Narrow channel of water joining two larger areas of water
sound 5) v.t. and i. (*sownd*) To measure the depth of (water); to try to ascertain someone's views, opinions etc
soup n. (*sōōp*) Liquid food made by cooking meat, vegetables etc. in water
sour adj., and v.t. and i. (*sowr*) (Of taste or smell) acid, sharp, tart; (of milk) rancid; (of the temper etc.) disagreeable, bitter
source n. (*saws*) Starting-point of a river; place of origin, cause of anything, *a source of infection*
south n. (*sowth*) Cardinal point of the compass opposite the north
souvenir n. (*sōō've nēr*) Small object kept as a reminder, a keepsake
soviet n. (*sov'iet*) Council forming a unit of local or national administration in the U.S.S.R.
sow 1) n. (*sow*) An adult female pig
sow 2) v.t. and i. (*sō*) To scatter, cast (seed) on the ground
spa n. (*spah*) Health-resort with a mineral spring. (*Spa*, in Belgium)
space n. and v.t. (*spās*) Limitless extension considered as an entity in which things may exist and move, *conditions of space and time*; distance between points and objects, *a space of 100 yards*; area, *enough space to work in*; period of time, *a space of two years*; the universe outside the earth's atmosphere
spade n. and v.t. (*spād*) A digging implement; any flat-bladed implement resembling this; the black suit of playing-cards marked with conventional representation of a spade
spaghetti n. (*spa get'i*) Kind of thin macaroni.
span n. (*spăn*) Distance between tip of thumb and tip of little finger when hand is fully extended, nine inches; short period or distance, *the brief span of human life*; whole extent of a measurement in time or space, *the span of a bridge*; space between supports
spangle n. and v.t. (*spăngl*) Small thin disc of shining metal, usually used to ornament a dress etc
spaniel n. (*spăn'yel*) Breed of dogs with long, silky hair and drooping ears
spank v.t. and i., and n. (*spănk*) To strike with open hand or a flat object
spanner n. (*spă'ner*) A hand tool for turning nuts and bolts; a wrench
spare adj. and n. (*spār*) Not plentiful, scanty, *a spare diet*; lean, *a spare figure*; left over, additional, available as desired, *spare cash*
sparkle v.i. (*spahkl*) To give out sparks or flashes of light
sparse adj. (*spahs*) Growing thinly, scarce, not abundant, *a sparse population*
spasm n. (*spăzm*) Involuntary contraction of muscle fibres
spastic adj. and n. (*spăs'tik*) Suffering from a type of physical disablement characterized by muscular spasms. As n., person suffering from this disablement
spate n. (*spāt*) Sudden flood, esp. of a river after rain; also fig., *a spate of complaints*
spatter v.t. and i., and n. (*spă'ter*) To sprinkle with drops of liquid, to splash, *spattered with mud*
speak v.i. and t. (*spēk*) To utter words without musical modulation
spear n. and v.t. (*spēr*) Throwing or thrusting weapon with a sharp-pointed head on a shaft
special adj. and n. (*spesh'al*) Of a particular sort, having a distinctive or exceptional character, *a special favour*; intended for a particular purpose, person, or thing, *a special correspondent*; detailed, intensive, *special study*; specific, *have you any special reason for saying so?*
species n. (*spē'shiz*) (biol.) Term of classification used to denote a group of allied individuals, larger than variety and smaller than

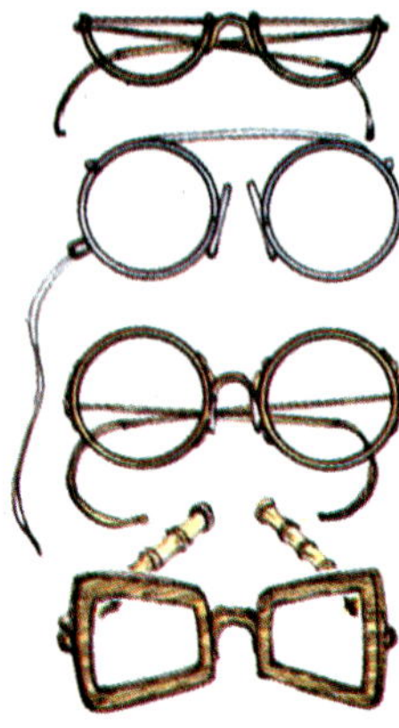

spectacles

genus; kind, sort, *he possessed a species of fierce pride*
specific adj. and n. (*spe sif'ik*) Of a distinct and definite sort, *a specific purpose*; definitely limited in force and meaning, precise, explicit, *a specific aim*; relating to a species
specify v.t. (*spe'si fī*) To make specific, particularize, *specify grounds of complaint*
specimen n. (*spe'si men*) One of a class, regarded as typical and representative of the whole class, esp. when preserved and exhibited, *a museum specimen*; part taken as typical of whole, *a specimen page from a book*
speck n. (*spek*) Small spot, mark, or stain; minute object, mark only just visible, *a speck of dust*
spectacle n. (*spek'takl*) Something looked at, esp. something displayed for inspection, *the air display was a fine spectacle*; something remarkable, esp. something arousing pity, contempt etc., *you look a sorry spectacle!*; (pl.) **(pair of) spectacles** pair of framed optical lenses, worn to correct faults in vision
spectator n. (*spek tā'tor*) An observer, one who watches.
spectre n. (*spek'ter*) Ghost
speech n. (*spēch*) Faculty of expressing meaning by speaking; a language, *the English speech*; particular manner of speaking, *indistinct speech*; a public address
speed n. (*spēd*) Swiftness, rapid movement, *at full speed*
speedometer instrument that shows speed at which a vehicle is travelling
spell 1) n. (*spel*) Magical formula, charm
spell 2) v.t. and i. (*spel*) pret. and p.p. **spelt** (*spelt*) To say or write in succession the letters constituting a word; (of the letters) to form a word; to result in, signify, *his injury spelt disaster for the team*; form words with right letters in right order, *learn to spell*
spend v.t. and i. (*spend*) pret. and p.p. **spent** (*spent*) To give in payment, exchange money for goods or services, *spend a lot on food*
sphere n. (*sfēr*) Solid figure, every point on whose surface is equidistant from the centre
sphinx n. (*sfingks*) Fabulous monster with human features and a lion's body, noted for asking insoluble riddles; sculptured stone figure of same
spice n. and v.t. (*spīs*) Aromatic, pungent preparation used in flavouring
spider n. (*spī'der*) Member of the order Araneida with eight legs and silk glands from which it spins webs to capture insects
spike n. and v.t. (*spīk*) Sharp pointed rod or projection
spill v.t. and i., and n. (*spil*) pret. and p.p. **spilt** (*spilt*) (Of liquid etc.) to upset, splash, or allow to upset or splash, out of a vessel, *spill milk from a jug*
spin v.t. and i. (*spin*) pret. **span** (*spăn*) or **spun** (*spun*), p.p. **spun** To draw and twist yarn etc. into thread; to perform the act or

sphinx

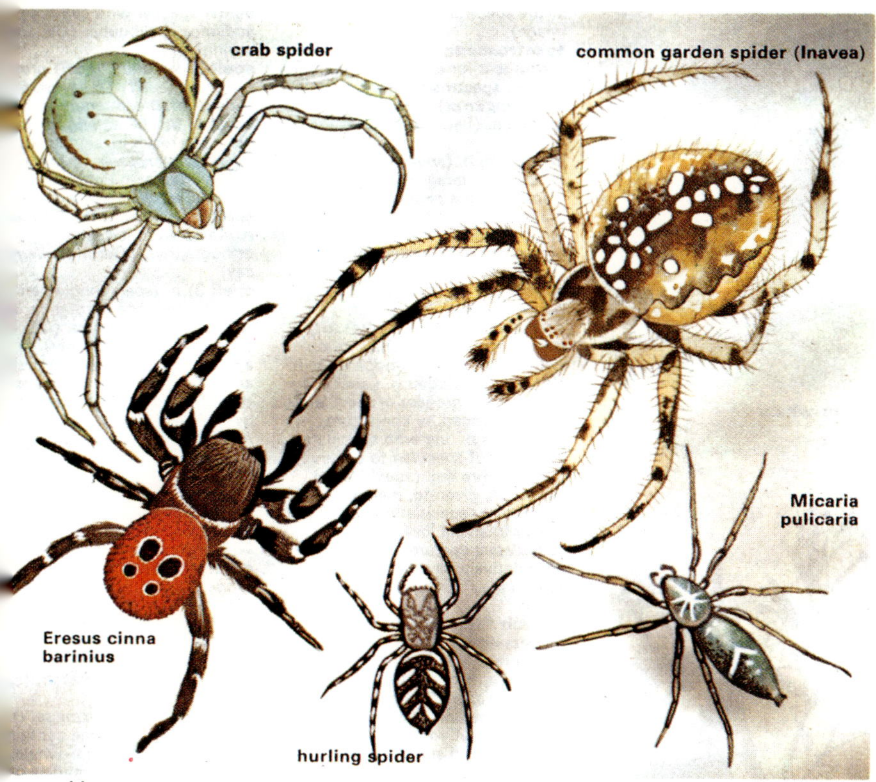

spiders

practice of spinning thread; to rotate or make rotate rapidly, *spin a top*

vertebral column; any stiff, pointed structure on a plant or animal, *the spines of a porcupine*; the back of a bound book

spinster n. (*spin'ster*) Unmarried woman

spire n. (*spīr*) Tapering, pointed structure above a tower; anything resembling this

spirit n. (*spi'rit*) Element in man considered to be immortal and non-material, in contrast to the body

(pl.) powerful alcoholic liquor produced by distillation

spiritual adj. and n. (*spi'ri chŏŏ al*) Of the spirit or soul, *spiritual existence*

spiritualism n. (*spi'ri chōō al izm*) Belief that the spirits of the dead communicate with the living

spit n. (*spit*) Long, thin rod or bar impaling meat for roasting; long, narrow point of land running out to sea

spite n. and v.t. (*spīt*) Malice, ill-will, *to do something from spite*; cause of dislike, grudge, *have a spite against someone*

splash v.t. and i. and n. (*splăsh*) (Of liquids) to scatter, cause to scatter or fly about, in drops, *splash wine on a dress*; to wet with drops of liquid, *splash the floor with water*

splendid adj. (*splen'did*) Magnificent

splint n. (*splint*) Strip of wood etc. tied to a limb to keep the two ends of a fractured bone in position

splinter n., and v.t. and i. (*splin'ter*) Small sharp fragment of hard material broken off from the main body. As v.t. and i. to break into splinters

split v.t. and i., including pret. and p.p. (*split*) To divide into two or more parts by fissure, esp. as result of pressure or a blow, *this wood splits easily*; to burst apart, burst open, *split someone's skull*; divide into parts, *split the profits*; to cause disunion, become disunited, *the party is split into factions*

spoil 1) n. (*spoil*) Goods taken by violence; profits, prizes, won by contest

spoil 2) v.t. and i. (*spoil*) To impair, do harm to, detract from the outward appearance of, detract from the pleasure or merit of, *holidays spoilt by bad weather*; to injure the character by excessive indulgence etc., *spoil a child*; to become impaired, deteriorate

spoke n. (*spōk*) Any one of the bars connecting the hub of a wheel with the outer rim

spokesman n. (*spōks'man*) One who speaks on behalf of others

sponge n., and v.t. and i. (*spunj*) Marine animal of the *Porifera* with fibrous skeleton; such skeleton used in cleaning because of its absorbent qualities; synthetic substance resembling such; sweet cake of light, soft consistency

sponsor n. and v.t. (*spon'sor*) One who accepts responsibility for another; one who first puts forward or takes responsibility (esp. financial) for a scheme, proposal, etc., *his firm are the sponsors of the new advertising campaign*. As v.t. to act as sponsor for. (Lat., 'a surety')

spontaneous adj. (*spon tā'ni us*) Arising from one's own free will or disposition, voluntary, *spontaneous admiration*

spook n. (*spōōk*) Ghost, apparition

spool n. and v.t. (*spōōl*) Reel, cylinder etc. on which something is wound, *a spool of thread*

spoon n. and v.t. (*spōōn*) Implement with long handle ending in a shallow bowl, used for raising or stirring liquids or food, *a teaspoon*

sporran n. (*spo'ran*) Pouch worn by Scottish Highlanders in front of the kilt

sport n., and v.t. and i. (*spawt*) Activity engaged in as a recreation

spot 1) n. (*spot*) Small marking, patch of different colour on, *a black cat with brown spots*; pimple on the skin

sporran

spot 2) v.t. and i. (*spot*) To mark with spots; see, recognize, detect, *spot an error*

spout v.i. and t., and n. (*spowt*) To burst, gush out, *blood spouting from a wound*; discharge (liquid) forcibly, *the whale spouts* As n. projection or lip at mouth of receptacle to direct flow of liquid when poured

sprain v.t. and n. (*sprān*) To strain tendons and muscles of a joint by sudden twist or wrench

sprawl v.i. and n. (*sprawl*) To sit or recline with limbs loosely spread out; (fig.) to be spread out irregularly over much space, to straggle, *sprawling suburbs of London*

spray n. and v.t. (*sprā*) Fine particles of liquid carried through the air by wind etc., *spray from a waterfall*; liquid disinfectant, perfume etc. driven in fine particles like spray by an atomizer etc.; atomizer etc. used to produce such a spray. As v.t. to scatter spray on

spread 1) v.t. and i. (*spred*) To make something cover a larger surface, esp. by pressing out and flattening, unfolding or unrolling, laying or scattering on, *to spread a cloth on the table*; to cover (a surface) by one of these means, *spread a table with a cloth*; to extend or be extended, *the grassy plains spread before us*; to disseminate, be disseminated, *to spread news*; to extend in time, *instalments may be spread over six months*

spread 2) n. (*spred*) Act or process of spreading, condition or extent of being spread, *the spread of a*

bird's wings; (colloq.) a feast, table spread with a large amount of food; kind of paste for spreading on bread and butter, *chocolate spread*
spring 1) v.i. and t. (*spring*) pret. **sprang** (*sprăng*), p.p. **sprung** (*sprung*) To leap, jump, *spring out of bed*; move suddenly, *the lid sprang open*; come rapidly into some position, condition etc., *spring into fame*; (of water etc.) gush up, flow forth; arise from, have origin in, *errors springing from carelessness*; sprout up, *weeds spring up everywhere*; come into existence, emerge, *difficulties sprang up on every side*; cause to move, recoil, happen, rapidly, *to spring a trap*; announce unexpectedly, *spring a surprise*
spring 2) n. (*spring*) Act, capacity of springing; device or appliance, often of coiled or twisted metal, that tends to return to its original shape or position after distortion by pressure, *it's held by a spring*; recoil, rebound; resilience, elastic quality, *his step has lost its old spring*; source, origin, motive, *springs of action*; source of water, flow of water rising or issuing naturally out of the earth; time of year between winter and summer, reckoned astronomically in northern hemisphere as March 22–June 21
sprinkle v.t. and i., and n. (*springkl*) To scatter in small drops or particles
sprint v.i. and n. (*sprint*) To run at full speed for a short distance
sprout v.i. and t., and n. (*sprowt*) To put forth shoots, begin to grow
spry adj. (*sprī*) Lively, nimble
spur n., and v.t. and i. (*spur*) Device on rider's heel with spike or spiked wheel for pricking horse's flanks; any sharp-pointed, spur-like object, *a mountain spur*; (fig.) incitement, stimulus, *the spur of ambition*
spy n., and v.t. and i. (*spī*) One engaged in discovering what is intended to be secret, esp. one employed by a government in espionage; one who observes another secretly
squabble n. and v.i. (*skwobl*) Undignified, petty quarrel. As v.i. to engage in squabbles
squad n. (*skwod*) Small group of persons acting together, esp. detachment of troops or police
squadron n. (*skwod'ron*) Body of cavalry (120–200 men); group of warships or military aircraft forming a unit
squalid adj. (*skwol'id*) Dirty
squall v.i. and t., and n. (*skwawl*) To cry out loudly, bawl, *a squalling baby*; to utter with a squall. As n. loud, harsh cry; sudden violent brief wind, often with rain or snow
squander v.t. (*skwon'der*) To spend extravagantly
square n. (*skwār*) Plane rectangular figure with four equal sides; object in the shape of a square; open space or place in a town, bounded by streets
squat v.i. and adj. (*skwot*) To sit on one's heels, to crouch with the legs drawn up to the body; to settle on land without permission
squawk v.i. and n. (*skwawk*) To utter a short harsh cry. As n. a short harsh cry
squeak n., and v.i. and t. (*skwēk*) Thin, shrill cry of fright or excitement, *the mouse squeaked in fear*; high piercing sound, *the chalk squeaked on the blackboard*
squeal n., and v.i. and tr (*skwēl*) A high, shrill cry louder than a squeak
squeeze v.t. and i., and n. (*skwēz*) To compress, press firmly, *squeeze someone's hand*; extract moisture by pressure, *squeeze a lemon dry*
squint n. and v.i. (*skwint*) Condition of eye movement in which both do not look in the same direction; (colloq.) look, glance; narrow observation hole through a wall
squirm v.t. and i., and n. (*skwurm*) To twist the body, wriggle; (fig.) to feel humiliated, embarrassed, *he squirmed at her words*. As n. squirming motion

squirrel

squirrel n. (*skwi'rel*) Arboreal, bushy-tailed rodent of genus *Sciurus*
squirt v.t. and i., and n. (*skwurt*) To eject (liquid) in thin jet or stream; spurt out in a jet
stab v.t. and i., and n. (*stăb*) To pierce, wound, with a pointed instrument
stable 1) adj. (*stābl*) Fixed, steady, *stable foundations*; resolute, steadfast, *a stable character*
stable 2) n. and v.t. (*stābl*) Building for keeping horses; a group of racehorses under one ownership
stack n. and v.t. (*stăk*) Large, regular pile of hay, straw etc.; any orderly heap; (colloq.) any large pile or amount, *stacks of work to do*; a cluster of chimneys
stadium n. (*stā'di um*) Sports arena consisting of open space surrounded by tiers of seats and enclosing walls
staff n. and v.t. (*stahf*) Rod or stick used as support, weapon, or badge of office, *a bishop's staff*; pole serving as a support, *a flag-staff*; organized group of persons working under a single direction, *the nursing staff of a hospital*; group of army officers engaged in planning and organization, *the General Staff*; (mus.) group of five horizontal and parallel lines and spaces on which notes are placed to indicate their pitch
stag n. (*stăg*) Male red deer
stage n. (*stāj*) A platform, raised scaffolding; raised platform in a theatre on which the play is performed; acting as a profession; the theatre, drama, *the medieval stage*; the scene of action; a stopping-place, *last stage in a bus journey*; distance between stopping-places; period of development, *at a late stage in his career*
stagger v.i. and t., and n. (*stă'ger*) To walk or move unsteadily or stumblingly; to disconcert, overwhelm, *I was staggered by the news*; to set, arrange (times of events etc.) so that they do not conflict, *to stagger*
stagnant adj. (*stăg'nant*) (Of water) not flowing, foul through lack of motion
stain v.t. and i., and n. (*stān*) To discolour, blemish, blot, *fingers stained with nicotine*; to mar, *a stained reputation*; to impart colour deliberately to the surface of, *to stain wood*

stair n. (*stār*) One of a series of steps
stake n. and v.t. (*stāk*) Strong wooden pole or stick, pointed for driving into the ground; post to which person was tied for execution by burning to death; what is risked in a wager, *to gamble for high stakes*
stale adj. and v.i. (*stāl*) Not fresh
stalk 1) n. (*stawk*) The stem of a plant
stalk 2) v.t. and i. (*stawk*) To walk with stately, dignified stride
stall n., and v.t. and i. (*stawl*) Compartment for one animal in a stable, cattle-shed etc.; small covered stand for selling goods in public open places, markets etc. As v.t. and i. to place, keep, in a stall; (of engines) to stop working; (of aircraft) cause to be, become, out of control through loss of speed
stallion n. (*stăl'yun*) Uncastrated male horse
stalwart adj. and n. (*stawl'wert*) Tall, muscular, robust; staunch and reliable in support of a cause
stamen n. (*stā'men*) (bot.) Pollen-bearing organ of a flower
stamina n. (*stă'mi na*). Staying-power, constitutional vigour
stammer v.i. and t., and n. (*stă'mer*) To speak with a nervous impediment, esp. to pause on certain sounds and repeat them; speak incoherently, hesitate in speaking; utter with a stammer
stamp v.t. and i. (*stămp*) To bring (one's foot) down heavily

stamen

and forcibly, *stamp the foot*; imprint (a design, mark etc.) by means of a die etc., *stamp one's signature on a circular*; affix a postal stamp to, *stamp an envelope*; imprint on the mind, *a scene stamped on the memory*
stand v.i. and t. (*stănd*); pret. and p.p. **stood** (*stŏŏd*) To have, take, keep an upright unsupported position, the weight of the body being balanced on the feet, *to be too weak to stand*; to remain undisturbed, *not a stone was left standing*; remain valid, *my words still stand*; be in a specific place, situation, *the house stands on a hill*; be in a specific state or condition, *to stand in awe of*; to cause to be, put, in an upright position, *stand a bottle on the table*; move into a particular position, *stand aside*; endure, tolerate, be proof against, *he can't stand the heat*; undergo, *stand trial*; treat (someone) to, *stand a friend a dinner*
staple 1) n. and v.t. (*stāpl*) U-shaped pointed metal bar driven into wood etc. to hold hooks, wire etc.; piece of wire to fasten sheets of paper together
staple 2) n. and adj. (*stāpl*) (hist.) Privileged market; chief product of a place, *the staple is rice*; leading factor, element etc., *a staple of conversation*; essential raw materials; thread, fibre, of wool or cotton. As adj., chief (of products, raw materials); basic, principal
star n. and v.i. and t. (*stah(r)*) Any natural heavenly body seen in the night sky, esp. if self-luminous
stare v.i. and t., and n. (*stār*) To look fixedly with wide-open eyes
start v.i. and t. (*staht*) To make a sudden, involuntary movement, *start with surprise*; to move, rise, spring suddenly, *to start back*; set out, begin, *we must start early*; displace or be displaced from, make or become loose, *the timbers have started*; begin (an action, journey etc.), *start work*; put in motion, cause to start, originate, give a start to, *start someone in a career*; arouse, *start a hare*
startle v.t. (*stahtl*) To alarm, cause shock of surprise to
starvation n. (*stah vā'shun*) Starving or being starved
starve v.i. and t. (*stahv*) To perish of hunger; suffer extreme hunger or want; deprive of nourishment
state 1) n. (*stāt*) Condition, quality, *a poor state of health*; rank, *persons in every state of life*; pomp, ceremony, dignity, *robes of state*; organized political community with definite frontiers, *a menace to the state*; government, political authority, of such a community, *the State has too much power*; division of a federal republic, *the United States of America*; civil (as opposed to ecclesiastical) government, *Church and State*
state 2) adj. (*stāt*) Of the state, *state papers*; of, for, ceremonial or formal occasions, *the state coach*
state 3) v.t. (*stāt*) To express in words, esp. carefully and clearly, *he stated his opinion at some length*
statesman n. (*stāts'man*) Person taking part in state government
static adj. (*stăt'ik*) At rest, stationary
station n. and v.t. (*stā'shun*) Place chosen by or assigned to someone for a purpose, *one's appointed station*; place, building etc. assigned to an organisation, *the fire-station*; stopping-place for railway trains, with associated buildings, platforms etc.; (Aust.) a sheep-farm; social position, rank, *a lowly station in life*; military or naval base
stationary adj. (*stā'shun a ri*) Motionless, not moving or changing, *to remain stationary*
stationer n. (*stā'shun er*) Dealer in all kinds of writing materials
statistics n.pl. (*sta tis'tiks*) Systematic collection and arrangement of numerical facts; the art and mathematics of such
statue n. (*stăch'ōō*) Representation of human or animal figure carved or modelled in the round
staunch 1) v.t. (*stawnch*) To stop or check a flow of blood
staunch 2) adj. (*stawnch*) Loyal, trustworthy, firm
stay v.t. and i. (*stā*) To delay, hold back, *stay the spread of a disease*; endure, last out, *stay the course*; remain, refrain from departure, *stay where one is*; reside temporarily, *stay in a hotel*
steady adj., and v.t. and i. (*sted'i*) Firmly supported, not liable to shake or fall, *hold a ladder steady*; uniform, constant, *a steady improvement*; regular in conduct, habits etc., *a steady young man*; unwavering, *a steady look*
steak n. (*stāk*) Thick slice of meat or fish for grilling or frying, *rump-steak*

steal v.t. and i. (*stēl*) To thieve, take or carry away unlawfully the property of another; to gain or win by stealth, *steal a kiss*; to move, come, go, silently and secretly, *steal out of the house*
steam 1) n. (*stēm*) Water in the state of vapour
steam 2) v.t. and i. (*stēm*) To give out steam or vapour; to move, work etc. by means of steam; to expose to steam, esp. for cooking, cleaning etc
steel n., adj., and v.t. (*stēl*) Alloy of iron and carbon with less than 2% carbon
steep 1) adj. (*stēp*) Ascending or descending sharply, at a considerable angle, *a steep hill*
steep 2) v.t. and i. (*stēp*) To soak, bathe in liquid
steeple n. (*stē'pl*) High tapering structure surmounting a building, esp. a church, and often ending in a spire
steer 1) n. (*stēr*) Young ox or bullock
steer 2) v.t. and i. (*stēr*) To direct the course of (a vessel motor-car etc.)
stem n., and v.t. and i. (*stem*) Main support, esp. the stalk of a plant or secondary stalk supporting flower, leaf etc.; stem-like part or structure, *the stem of a wine-glass*; (naut.) main upright timber or metal bar at bow of ship
stench n. (*stench*) Strong, offensive smell
step 1) n. (*step*) A footfall, act of stepping, *retrace one's steps*; space covered by a step, *it's only a few steps from here*; sound of a footfall; mode of walking, *a light step*; act performed with a view to effecting a purpose, *take steps to do something*; degree, stage in progression, *a big step forward*; place that supports the feet in moving from one level to another, *a flight of steps*
step 2) v.i. and t. (*step*) To take a step or steps, *step forward*; walk
stereophonic adj. (*ster i ō fon'ik*) (also shortened to **stereo**) (Of reproduced sound) giving the illusion of a three-dimensional effect to a listener; apparatus with two or more loudspeakers to give this effect
sterile adj. (*ste'ril*) Barren, incapable of reproduction in offspring; unproductive, *sterile soil*; containing no bacteria or moulds, *a sterile food-container*; barren of ideas or interest, *a sterile discussion*

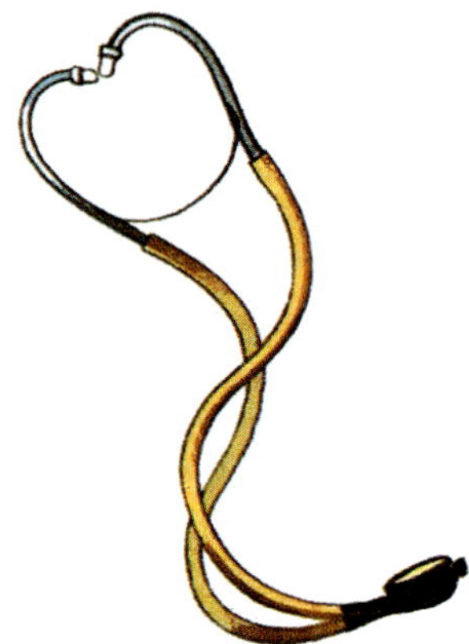

stethoscope

stern 1) adj. (*sturn*) Austere, severe, *a stern parent*; unrelenting, *a stern resolve*
stern 2) n. (*sturn*) Back part of ship or aircraft; hind quarters
stethoscope n. (*steth'ō skōp*) Instrument for listening to sounds of heart and breathing
stew v.t. and i., and n. (*stū*) To cook slowly in a small amount of liquid
stick 1) v.t. and i. (*stik*); pret. and p.p. **stuck** (*stuk*) To pierce, thrust (a pointed instrument) into, *stick a pin in one's finger*; (colloq.) to put, thrust, *stick one's tongue out*; to fasten, cause to adhere, *stick a stamp on a letter*; (colloq.) tolerate, endure, *I can't stick the noise any longer*; to remain with the point thrust in, *a knife sticking in the corpse*; to adhere, cling fast to, *stick like a limpet*; stop, *stick at home*; be unable to proceed, *the actor stuck half way through his speech*
stick 2) n. and v.t. (*stik*) Slender branch or twig of tree, *to gather sticks for a fire*; wood shaped and adapted for a special purpose, *walking stick*; slender, rod-shaped bar or piece (of chalk, charcoal, sealing-wax etc.)
stiff adj. and n. (*stif*) Not easily bent, rigid, *a stiff collar*; firm, not fluid, *a stiff paste*; not working freely, sticking, *a stiff lock*; great in volume, amount, etc., *a stiff breeze*; formal, constrained, *a stiff manner*; difficult, *a stiff climb*
stile n. (*stil*) Steps or similar device to facilitate passage over or through a fence, wall etc

still 1) adj., n., and v.t. (*stil*) Without motion or sound, *still waters*; (of a drink) not effervescent
still 2) adv. (*stil*) To this time, even now, *he is still asleep*; nevertheless, notwithstanding, *he's a bore; still, we must invite him*; even more, yet, *he is still smaller than his brother*
stilt n. (*stilt*) One of a pair of long poles with supports for the feet, used for raising a walker above the ground
stimulate v.t. (*stim'ū lāt*) To excite, cause, increase emotion or activity, *stimulate curiosity*
stimulus n. (*stim'ū lus*) Something that stimulates
sting 1) n. (*sting*) (zoo.) Sharp-pointed organ by which poison can be injected into a victim; (bot.) stiff hair which can inject irritant fluid; act of stinging; pain or wound caused by a sting; any sharp pain of body or mind, *the stings of hunger*; force, bite, *the wind has a sting in it*
sting 2) v.t. and i. (*sting*) pret. and p.p. **stung** (*stung*) To pierce, wound with a sting; to have the power to sting; cause a sharp smarting pain (to), *the rain stings my face*; to feel a sharp smarting pain; to provoke, *be stung to a sharp reply*
stink v.i. and t., and n. (*stingk*) pret. **stank** (*stănk*), p.p. **stunk** (*stunk*) To give out a strong unpleasant odour
stipend n. (*sti'pend*) Salary, esp. of a clergyman
stir v.t. and i. (*stur*) To set in motion, esp. to give a circular motion to, *stir one's tea*; rouse or be roused, *stir the imagination*; move, be in motion, *not a leaf stirred*
stirrup n. (*sti'rup*) Footrest for a horse-rider, consisting of hoop or ring hung by a strap from the saddle
stitch n., and v.t. and i. (*stich*) Single complete action of needle and thread when sewing stabbing pain in the side
stock 1) n. (*stok*) Main stem of tree or other plant; stem into which a graft is inserted; plant from which a cutting is taken; base, support, handle etc. of an object, *the stock of a rifle*; (pl.) frame on which a ship rests while building; (pl., hist.) framework in which the legs of criminals were publicly confined; descent, ancestry, *of noble stock*; goods on hand, material ready for use, *lay in a stock of sugar*; supply of anything, *the stock of human knowledge*; liquid in which bones, vegetables etc. have been boiled, used for making soup, gravy etc ; raw material for manufacture, *paper stock*; fragrant garden plant, gillyflower; money lent to a government at specified rate of interest; capital of a business company
stock 2) v.t. (*stok*) To have a stock of, keep in stock; supply or equip with
stomach n. and v.t. (*stum'ak*) Sac-like part of alimentary canal concerned in the digestion of food
stone n. (*stōn*) Single fragment of rock, *to throw stones*; solid mineral matter, esp. a block used for a specific purpose, *a grindstone*; precious stone, gem; concretion, esp. in kidneys or bladder; unit of weight, 14 lb
stool n. (*stōōl*) Seat without a back
stoop v.i. and t., and n. (*stōōp*) To bend body forwards and downwards
stop v.t. and i. (*stop*) To close by filling or obstructing, *stop a leak*; cause to cease motion, *stop the traffic*; cause cessation of, *rain stopped play*; withhold, *stop someone's wages*; impede, prevent, *nothing will stop me from going*; leave off, discontinue, *stop work*; halt, *the bus stops here*; (colloq.) remain for a time, *stop at a hotel*
storage n. (*staw'rij*) Storing or being stored; space used for

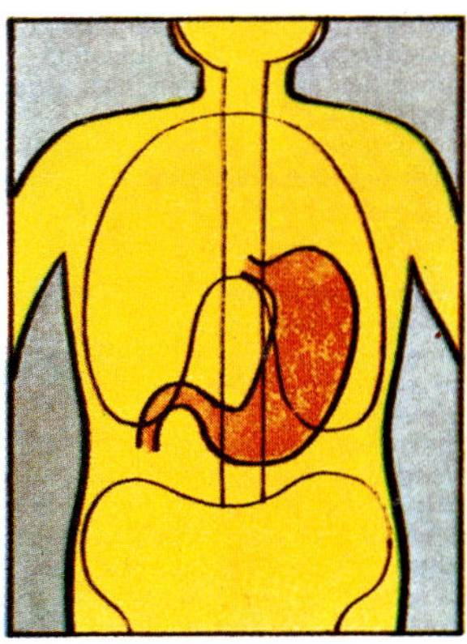

stomach

storing goods; charge made for storing goods
store n. and v.t. (*staw(r)*) Stock, accumulation of goods kept for use as needed, *a store of food*; goods of specific kind or for specific purpose, *naval stores*; accumulation of knowledge, *a store of learning*; storage-place, warehouse; shop, esp. one with many departments, *a department store*
storey, story n. (*staw'ri*) Floor level of a building; rooms etc. on one floor
stork n. (*stawk*) Large, long-legged and long-beaked wading bird of genus *Ciconia*
storm n., and v.i. and t. (*stawm*) Violent atmospheric disturbance, generally with strong wind, rain, and thunder and lightning; specific kind of storm, *a sand-storm*; loud expression of feeling by many people, *a storm of applause*; violent emotional upheaval, *a storm of indignation*; assault on a fortified place
story n. (*staw'ri*) Account of past events; account of imaginary or legendary events; anecdote, *he told some good stories of life abroad*
stout adj. and n. (*stowt*) Strong, durable, *a stout ship*; brave, intrepid, *a stout heart*; fat, *a stout figure*
stove n. (*stōv*) Apparatus burning fuel for heating or cooking
straggle v.i. (*străgl*) To stray or extend irregularly from the rest of a mass or in scattered groups, *the town straggles into the country*; to fall behind the main body, loiter in isolated groups, *don't straggle behind the rest of the class!*
straight 1) adj. (*strāt*) Without bend or curve, direct, *a straight line*; upright, *a straight back*; parallel to a given line or surface, level, *put a picture straight*; tidy, in order, *put a room straight*; frank, direct, *a straight answer*; honest, reliable, *straight dealing*
straight 2) n. (*strāt*) Condition of being straight; straight stretch of road, river etc
straight 3) adv. (*strāt*) Directly, in a straight line, *to walk straight*; by direct route, without detour or stops, *I shall go straight home*
straightforward adj. (*strātfaw'werd*) Honest, frank, *a straightforward answer*; simple, not complicated, *a straightforward problem*
straightway adv. (*strāt wā'*) At once, immediately
strain v.t. and i. (*strān*) To stretch tightly, *strain a rope to breaking-point*; exert (one's powers) to the utmost, *strain one's ears to hear*; fatigue or injure by over-exerting or stretching, *strain the eyes by too much reading* filter, percolate through a filtering substance, *strain soup*
strait n. (*strāt*) Narrow channel of water connecting two larger bodies of water, *Menai Strait*; (often pl.) trouble, difficult situation, *to be in great straits*
strand 1) n., and v.t. and i. (*strănd*) (poet.) Beach, shore. As v.t. and i. (of a ship) to run aground, cause to run aground. Hence: **stranded** adj. left helpless or destitute, *stranded in a foreign land*
strand 2) n. (*strănd*) Single thread, fibre etc. twisted together with others to form yarn, rope etc
strange adj. (*strānj*) Not before known, heard, seen, or experienced, *a strange face*; foreign, not one's own, *to follow strange gods*; odd, unaccustomed, *strange sights*; unfamiliar, *to be strange to a place*
stranger n. (*strān'jer*) Person one does not know; person from another town or country; one unacquainted, unfamiliar with, *a stranger to sorrow*
strap n. and v.t. (*străp*) Strip of leather or cloth, esp. with a buckle used for fastening or securing
strategy n. (*străt'eji*) Art of conducting a military campaign, esp. the art of moving armed forces into favourable positions for fighting; (fig.) skill in managing any affair
stratosphere n. (*străt'os fēr*) Upper part of the earth's atmosphere
stratum n. (*strāh'tum*) pl. **strata** Layer of sedimentary rock in the earth's crust
straw n. (*straw*) Stalk of grain, esp. wheat, oats etc.; stalks of grain collectively, as material for thatching, bedding etc
stray v.i., n., and adj. (*strā*) To wander, deviate, move away (from)
streak n., and v.t. and i. (*strēk*) Long, thin, often irregular line or band, *streaks of light*; (fig.) strain, trace, *a streak of humour in his make-up*
stream n. and v.i. (*strēm*)

Current, flow, of water or other liquid; river, brook, or rivulet; current, drift, *move with the stream*; (fig.) trend of events, opinions etc., *the main-stream of modern literature*; continuously moving crowd or series of objects, *a stream of cars*
street n. (*strēt*) Metalled road in a town, lined with buildings
strength n. (*strength*) Quality of being strong; bodily or intellectual power; toughness, durability, *the strength of a bridge*; power of resisting attacks, *the strength of a fortress*; power measured by numbers, *the enemy was there in strength*; source of power, support, *God is our strength*; intensity, potency, *the strength of a colour*; intellectual force, compelling power, *strength of an argument*
strenuous adj. (*stren'ū us*) Putting forth or needing great effort, *strenuous work*
stress n. and v.t. (*stres*) Strain, tension, *a time of stress*; force, intense pressure, *under stress of circumstances*; importance, weight, emphasis, *lay stress on correct diction*; emphasis used in uttering syllable(s) or word(s), *the stress is on the first syllable*; (mech.) force(s) exerted on a solid body
stretch v.t. and i., and n. (*strech*) To draw out to greater length or breadth, *stretch a glove to make it fit*; spread or pull to fullest extent, *stretch a rope tight*; be capable of extension, *this material stretches easily*; extend, reach, *the road stretched into the distance*; extend one's limbs, *he sat up and stretched*
strew v.t. (*strōō*) To scatter, sprinkle, spread irregularly
strict adj. (*strikt*) Precise, exact, definite, *the strict truth*; severe, inflexible, *strict discipline*
stride v.i. and t., and n. (*strīd*) pret. **strode** (*strōd*) To walk with long steps; to take one long step in crossing something, *stride across a brook*
strife n. (*strīf*) Conflict, struggle
strike 1) v.t. and i. (*strīk*) pret. and p.p. **struck** (*struk*) To hit, give a blow to, dash against, *strike a ball with a racket*; stab with a blow; collide with, *his foot struck on a stone*; produce by striking, *strike a light*; cause to light, be kindled by striking, *the match won't strike*; reach, arrive at, *strike a main road*; (cause to) sound, *a clock struck the hour*; make by stamping, *strike a medal*; fill with, *strike terror into someone*; impinge on the mind, *how does his work strike you?*; occur to the mind, *an idea has struck me*; to lower, take down, *strike a tent*
strike 2) n. and v.i. (*strīk*) Organized stoppage of work by employees till the employer considers their demands favourably
string n. (*string*) Slender rope, line or cord, used for tying; strip of ribbon or other material used for the same purpose, *apron-strings*; gut or wire cord of a musical instrument, *the strings of a harp*; series of objects, persons etc., *a string of horses*; series of objects threaded on a string, *a string of pearls*
strip v.t. and i., and n. (*strip*) To pull or tear off, *strip paper from a wall*; take away the covering or skin of, *strip a tree of its leaves*; deprive, despoil, *strip a man of his possessions*; take off one's clothes
stripe n. and v.t. (*strīp*) Long narrow strip or band on a surface
strive v.i. (*strīv*) pret. **strove** (*strōv*), **striven** (*striv'n*) To make great efforts; fight, struggle (with, against)
stroke 1) n. and v.t. (*strōk*) Act of striking, a blow, *a stroke of the axe*; single movement of the hand(s) or arm(s), esp. in games, *a stroke in golf*; single movement forming part of a regular series, *breast-stroke*; sound of a clock, *on the stroke of three*; mark made by single movement of the pen, pencil, brush etc., *fine strokes*; sudden attack of illness, esp. an

stroke

apoplectic seizure or sudden attack of paralysis; oarsman nearest stern of the boat, who sets the time of stroke. As v.t. act as stroke to, *stroke*
stroke 2) v.t. and n. (*strōk*) To pass the hand gently over the surface of, caress, *stroke a cat*
stroll n. and v.i. (*strōl*) A saunter, leisurely walk. As v.i. to saunter
strong adj. (*strong*) Physically, morally, or intellectually powerful, *strong arms*; tough, durable, *a strong rope*; fortified, easy to defend, *a strong position*; acting powerfully, *strong remedies* affecting a sense forcibly, *a strong smell*; well, *to feel quite strong again*; having a large proportion of the essential element, *strong coffee*; intense, firm, forcible, *strong opinions*
structure n. (*struk'cher*) Way in which something is built up, organized, or arranged, *the structure of a cell*; something that is constructed, esp. a building, *an imposing structure*
struggle v.i. and n. (*strugl*) To fight; strive; make great efforts to attain an end
stub n. and v.t. (*stub*) Short end of pencil, cigarette etc. left when the rest has been used or consumed As v.t. to strike (foot) against a hard object, *stub one's toe*
stubble n. (*stubl*) Short stalks of grain left standing in field after reaping
stubborn adj. (*stub'ern*) Resolute, determined, *stubborn courage*; (of persons) obstinate, self-willed
stud 1) n. and v.t. (*stud*) Kind of two-headed button used to fasten collar, shirt-front etc.; large-headed projecting nail or knob used to strengthen or ornament a surface
stud 2) n. (*stud*) Number of horses and mares kept for breeding, hunting, racing etc
studio n. (*stū'di ō*) Room designed as workroom of artist, photographer etc.; room used for production of cinema films, recordings, broadcasting etc.
study 1) n. (*stud'i*) Act of applying the mind to the acquisition of knowledge room in which studies are carried on
study 2) v.t. and i. (*stud'i*) To apply the mind to, engage in study
stuff 1) n. (*stuf*) Substance, matter, *his new medicine is nasty stuff*; worthless material or things; material or substance from which anything is made (also fig.)
stuff 2) v.t. and i. (*stuf*) To cram (objects) into a receptacle, fill tightly (with)
stumble v.i. and n. (*stumbl*) To trip up, miss one's footing, esp. by falling over some obstruction; fall into error or crime; speak haltingly, falter
stump n., and v.i. and t. (*stump*) Part of a tree-trunk remaining in earth when upper part has fallen or been felled; anything remaining after the main part has been removed, worn off etc., *the stump of a pencil*; (cricket) one of the three upright sticks forming the wicket
stun v.t. (*stun*) To make unconscious by a blow; shock, astound and confuse, *stunned by the tragic news*
stunt 1) v.t. (*stunt*) To check the growth or development of, *stunted trees*
stunt 2) n. (*stunt*) Feat of skill; showy performance
stupid adj. (*stū'pid*) Dull-witted, unintelligent, *a stupid action*
sturdy adj. (*stur'di*) Strong, hardy, vigorous.
stutter v.i. and t., and n. (*stu'ter*) To speak with involuntary hesitations, stammer
sty 1) n. (*stī*) Pigsty. (OE. *stig*)
sty 2), **stye** n. (*stī*) Inflamed swelling on the eyelid
style n. and v.t. (*stīl*) Mode of expression in writing or speech, manner, *a concise style*; fashion, design, esp. in dress; sort, kind, *style of behaviour*
subdue v.t. (*sub dū'*) To overcome, bring under control
subject 1) n. (*sub'jekt*) Person owing allegiance to particular State or ruler, *British subjects*; person or thing treated or dealt with in a particular way, *to be the subject of an experiment*; person liable to a specific condition etc., *a hysterical subject*; what is dealt with in writing, speech etc., *the subject of a play*; (mus.) theme, musical phrase upon which a composition is founded; circumstance, cause, *a subject for rejoicing*
subject 2) adj. (*sub'jekt*) Under authority, *a subject nation*; **subject to** liable to; dependent on, *the proposal is subject to approval*
sublet v.t. and i. (*sub let'*) To let to another a house, land etc. of which one is tenant

submarine (atomic)

submarine adj. and n. (*sub ma rēn'*) Living or designed for use below the surface of the sea, *submarine plants.* As n., submarine vessel
submerge v.t. and i. (*sub murj'*) To go or cause to go below the surface of the water; to cover with liquid
submit v.t. and i. (*sub mit'*) (reflex.) To yield, surrender, *submit oneself to another's authority*; proffer for consideration, judgement etc., *submit a scheme*; urge, forward, *he submitted that the plan was out of date*; give in to, *submit to control*
subscribe v.t. and i. (*sub skrib'*) To sign one's name to a document; pay, contribute, *subscribe money to charities*
subsequent adj. (*sub'se kwent*) Later, following; resulting, consequent
subside v.i. (*sub sīd'*) To sink down, *the floods have subsided*; (of ground) collapse, cave in; allow oneself to sink slowly, *subside into a chair*; decrease in volume, intensity etc., *the storm has subsided*
subsidy n. (*sub'si di*) Grant of public money to assist private enterprise or to an ally in war. Hence: **subsidize** v.t. (*sub'si dīz*) to give a subsidy to
elements, true meaning, of anything, *the substance of a speech*; material of which a thing consists stuff, *chemical substances*
substitute n., and v.t. and i. (*sub'sti tūt*) Person or thing used in place of, or acting instead of, another
subterranean adj. (*sub te rān'i an*) Underground
subtitle n. (*sub'tītl*) Secondary title of book etc.
subtract v.t. (*sub trăkt'*) Take away (a part, amount) from a quantity, *subtract two from four*
suburb n. (*sub'urb*) Part of town lying on its outskirts
subway n. (*sub'wā*) Underground pathway, esp. a passage beneath a busy street or railway line; (U.S.A.) tube railway
succeed v.t. and i. (*suk sēd'*) To follow, come after, be successor to, *night succeeds day*; be successful, accomplish one's purpose, *succeed in winning a race*
succumb v.i. (*suk um'*) To yield, be overcome by
such 1) adj. (*such*) Of that kind, similar, like, *I never saw such a thing before!*; emphatic, *such a fine day*; so great, so good etc., *such beauty!*
such 2) pron. (*such*) Such person(s) or thing(s), *if I offended you, such was not my intention*
suck v.t. and i., and n. (*suk*) To draw (liquid) into the mouth by the use of the lip muscles while inhaling, *suck lemonade through a straw*; draw liquid from, *suck oranges*; take into the mind, absorb, *suck knowledge into one's mind*; hold in the mouth and dissolve by licking etc., *suck a cough-sweet*; perform the action of sucking
suction n. (*suk'shun*) Act or process of sucking, esp. process of drawing fluid or gas into a vessel in which a partial vacuum has been created by withdrawing air; similar process by which surfaces are made to adhere together by withdrawing the air between them
sudden adj. and n. (*sud'en*) Happening, occurring, acting, done, unexpectedly and quickly, without warning, *a sudden shock*
sue v.t. and i. (*sōō*) To bring a legal action against
suet n. (*sōō'it*) Solid fat covering the kidneys etc. of oxen, sheep etc., used in cooking
suffer v.t. and i. (*suf'er*) To feel and endure mental or physical pain or distress, *suffer without complaint*; endure, undergo, *suffer pain*; allow, tolerate
suffice v.i. and t. (*su fīs'*) To be enough, *a few words will suffice*
sufficient adj. (*su fish'ent*) Enough, *to lack sufficient food*

suffocate v.t. and i. (*suf'ō kāt*) To cause difficulty in or stop respiration; have difficulty in breathing; kill by stopping respiration
suffrage n. (*suf'rij*) A vote, the right to vote. Hence: **suffragette** n. woman who agitated for female suffrage
sugar n. and v.t. (*sho͝o'gar*) Sweet crystalline substance obtained from various plants, esp. the sugar-cane or sugar-beet
suggest v.t. (*su jest'*) To propose, *suggest a plan*
suicide n. (*so͞o i sid*) Act of self-murder
suit 1) n. set of clothes made of the same material; one of four sets of playing-cards
suit 2) v.t. and i. (*sūt*) To be satisfactory to, *will lunch at midday suit you?*
suitable adj. (*sūt'abl*) Tending to suit, appropriate, proper
sullen adj. (*sul'en*) Persistently gloomy, morose
sulphur n. (*sul'fur*) Non-metallic element, symbol *S*, used to make sulphuric acid and in preparation of matches, fireworks etc. and in medicine
sultry adj. (*sul'tri*) Oppressively hot and damp
sum n., and v.t. and i. (*sum*) Total obtained by adding together numbers or amounts
summary adj. and n. (*sum'a ri*) Concise, brief and to the point, without many formalities, *summary justice*. As n. brief review, digest
summer n., v.i., and adj. (*sum'er*) Annual season of greatest heat, astron. June 21st to Sept. 22nd in northern hemisphere; the warmer half of the year, as contrasted with winter
summit n. (*sum'it*) Topmost point, also fig
summon v.t. (*sum'on*) To demand the presence of, require to carry out some action; gather together, *summon all one's energy*
sun 1) n. (*sun*) Central body of the solar system; its rays, sunlight, *to sit in the sun*; any similar star forming the centre of a planetary system
sun 2) v.t. (*sun*) To expose (oneself) to the rays of the sun
sundae n. (*sun'dā*) Ice-cream served with fruits in syrup
Sunday n. (*sun'dā*) First day of the week
sundry adj. and n. (*sun'dri*) Various, *sundry occasions*. As n. (pl.) miscellaneous items not separately listed
superb adj. (*so͞o purb'*) Magnificent
superficial adj. (*so͞o per fish'al*) Relating to the surface only, *a superficial wound*; not profound
superfluous adj. (*so͞o pur'flo͞o us*) More than is required
superintend v.t. (*so͞o per in tend'*) To oversee; control and direct
superior adj. and n. (*so͞o pēr'i or*) Higher, above, in excellence, skill, power etc., *superior strength*; higher in rank or grade; in greater number; of great excellence
supermarket n. (*so͞o'per mah ket*) Large self-service department store
supernatural adj. (*so͞o per năch'e ral*) Above or beyond control by natural laws; miraculous
superstition n. (*so͞o per sti'shun*) Belief in magic and the influence of inanimate objects on human life; irrational belief in the supernatural
supervise v.t. and i. (*so͞o'per viz*) To oversee, superintend
supper n. (*sup'er*) Last meal of the day
supple adj. (*supl*) Pliant, easily bent
supplement n. and v.t. (*sup'li ment*) What is additional to main purpose, in a book or magazine
supply v.t. and n. (*su pli'*) To provide (something needed or required), *cows supply us with milk*; make good, compensate for, *supply a need*
support v.t. and n. (*su pawt'*) To bear the weight of; sustain, maintain, *support a family*; strengthen, corroborate, *support a claim*; endure, put up with, *I will not support such insolence!*; help, further, aid by one's presence, *support a cause*
suppose v.t. (*su pōz'*) To assume tentatively, *let us suppose you are right*; imagine, guess, *I suppose him to be about thirty*; presuppose, *success normally supposes hard work*
suppress v.t. (*su pres'*) To restrain, prevent from occurring or developing; subdue, ban, eliminate, *suppress a book*; prevent from being known or seen, *suppress the facts*
sure adj. (*sho͞or*) Dependable, reliable, *a sure cure*; certain, *it's sure to rain*; confident, *be sure of one's facts*
surf n. (*surf*) Foamy water of breaking waves on shore or reef of rocks
surface n., adj., and v.t. and i. (*sur'fis*) Outer area of a thing, any

of the sides of an object, *the surface of the earth*; the outside, superficial appearance of anything, *surface virtues*

surfeit n. and v.t. (*sur'fit*) Excess

surgeon n. (*sur'jun*) Doctor practising surgery

surgery n. (*sur'jeri*) Medical treatment by operation and manipulative means; doctor's dispensary and consulting room

surname n. (*sur'nām*) Family name

surpass v.t. (*surpahs'*) To exceed or excel in quality, degree etc

surplice n. (*sur'plis*) White vestment worn by clergy and choir at divine service

surprise n. and v.t. (*surpriz'*) Unexpected action, event etc.; feeling aroused by this, *to my surprise he succeeded*

surrender v.t. and i., and n. (*suren'der*) To give up, relinquish, esp. under pressure, *surrender one's rights*; submit, yield oneself, to superior force, *surrender to the enemy*; give way to a specified mood, *surrender oneself to despair*

surround v.t. and n. (*surownd'*) To encircle, encompass

survey v.t. (*sur'vā*) To take a general view of an area or situation, *survey the scene*; measure and record the exact shape, features etc. of a piece of land, coast etc.; inspect the condition of a piece of property for purposes of valuation

survive v.t. and i. (*surviv'*) To outlive, exist longer than, remain alive after, *survive all one's children*; continue to exist, *not one of them survived*

surplice

suspect v.t., adj., and n. (*suspekt'*) To be inclined to believe in the existence of, think it probable, *he suspected an ambush*; doubt, mistrust, *suspect the truth of a story*; believe guilty, *suspect someone of lying*

suspend v.t. (*suspend'*) To hang from above, *lamps suspended from the ceiling*; postpone, delay, *suspend judgement*; exclude from duty for a period, *suspend a footballer for foul play*

suspense n. (*suspens'*) State of anxiety and uncertainty (about the result of some action or event)

sustain v.t. (*sustān'*) To hold up, support, *a roof sustained by columns*; uphold as right or just, *the court sustained his claim*; suffer, endure, *sustain injuries*; nourish, strengthen or support, *only hope sustained him*; maintain, *sustained efforts*

swab n. and v.t. (*swob*) Mop or pad for cleaning; (surg.) absorbent pad

swaddle v.t. (*swodl*) To wrap up in several layers of cloth, bandage, etc.; **swaddling-clothes** long strip of cloth formerly used for wrapping babies

swagger v.i. and n. (*swăg'er*) To walk or behave in self-satisfied, superior manner

swallow 1) v.t. and i., and n. (*swo'lō*) To pass food, drink etc. from the mouth through the gullet and into the stomach

swallow 2) n. (*swo'lō*) Passerine bird of any species of *Hirundo*, *Chelidon*, or *Cotile*, with forked tail

swamp n. and v.t. (*swomp*) Level tract of ground permanently under stagnant water

swan n. (*swon*) Large bird of genus *Cygneus*, with long neck and webbed feet

swarm n. and v.i. (*swawm*) Large number of insects, animals, persons etc., moving in an active cluster, esp. bees with a queen seeking a new home

swathe v.t. (*swāth*) To wrap, bind with a bandage

sway v.i. and t., and n. (*swā*) To move or cause to move slowly from side to side, *branches sway in the wind*; control or influence, *easily swayed by emotion*

swear v.t. and i. (*swār*); pret. **swore** *(swaw)*, p.p. **sworn** *(swawn)* To promise solemnly, bind oneself by oath, *swear to be faithful*

sweat n., and v.t. and i. (*swet*) Moisture exuded through pores of skin
sweater n. (*swe'ter*) Thick jersey
sweep 1) v.t. and i. (*swēp*) ; pret. and p.p. **swept** (*swept*) To remove (dust, dirt etc.) with brush or broom, clean by brushing, move quickly over, pass with a rush, pass over or along irresistibly or violently, *the storm swept the countryside* ; brush, move along lightly, and quickly, *sweep one's hand over harp-strings*
sweep 2) n. (*swēp*) Act of sweeping ; person who sweeps a chimney ; steady, powerful movement, flow, *the sweep of the tide*
sweet 1 adj. (*swēt*) Having the taste of sugar, *sweet apples*
sweet 2) n. (*swēt*) Anything with a sweet taste, esp. a small sweet-meat or a sweet dish eaten at a meal after the main dish
swell v.i. and t. (p.p. **swollen** (*swō'len*)), n., and adj. (*swel*) To increase in size, bulk, dimension, volume, intensity, or number, *the population has swelled recently* ; to be, cause to be, extended in a curve, to bulge out, *the sails swelled in the breeze*
swelter v.i. (*swel'ter*) To be, feel, extremely hot
swerve v.i. and t., and n. (*swurv*) To deviate, cause to deviate, from a straight line or course of progress
swift 1) adj. (*swift*) Rapid, fleet, *a swift runner* ; acting or happening promptly, *a swift reply*

swift

swift 2) n. (*swift*) Genus *Cypselus* of swallow-like birds with long pointed wings
swill v.t. and i., and n. (*swil*) To wash out, rinse, with water
swim v.i. and t., and n. (*swim*) pret. **swam** (*swăm*), p.p. **swum** (*swum*) To proceed through water by movements of limbs, fins, tail etc., *to swim under water*
swindle v.t. and i., and n. (*swindl*) To cheat, defraud, *I've been swindled*
swine n. (*swīn*) Pig ; pigs ; term of abuse for person regarded as disgusting or dishonourable
swing v.i. and t., and n. (*swing*) pret. and p.p. **swung** (*swung*) To move, cause, or allow to move backwards and forwards ; sway to and fro ; to hold suspended, *swing a lamp from a hook* ; turn, cause to turn, on or as on a pivot or hinge, *the door swung back* ; move with a free, easy movement, *he went swinging along the road*
As n. swinging movement ; rhythm, rhythmic movement, *the swing of music* seat suspended by ropes or chains, on which one sits and swings back-wards and forwards
swish v.t. and i., and n. (*swish*) To move, pass through the air with a hissing or whistling sound
swoon v.i. and n. (*swo͞on*) To faint. As n. fainting-fit
swoop v.i. and n. (*swo͞op*) To sweep down suddenly, descend in sudden attack, *the eagle swooped on its prey*
sword n. (*sawd*) Weapon consisting of sharp-edged blade tapering to a point, fixed in a hilt
syllable n. (*sil'a bl*) Speech sound or combination of sounds pronounced as a complete unit
syllabus n. (*sil'a bus*) Outline or summary of a course of studies ; such a course of instruction itself
symbol n. (*sim'bol*) Something that represents or stands for another thing, quality etc
sympathy n. (*sim'pa thi*) Community of feeling, under-standing, *there was perfect sympathy between husband and wife* ; sharing of another's griefs, compassion, *to feel sympathy for someone's misfortune*
symphony n. (*sim'fo ni*) (mus.) Orchestral composition of sub-stantial size, usually in three or four movements
symptom n. (*simp'tom*) Evidence of disease or disorder as

experienced by a patient, *he had all the symptoms of measles*; outward sign of the existence of something else, *the symptoms of fear*

synagogue n. (*sin'a gog*) Assembly of Jews for religious purposes; place set aside for such a meeting

syncopate v.t. and i. (*sin'kō pāt*) To compose or play (a piece of music) by altering the usual rhythm so that a note begins on a normally unaccented beat and is held on to the next accented beat

syndicate n. (*sin'di kat*) and v.t. (*sin'di kāt*) Group of businessmen combining to finance an enterprise

synopsis n. (*sin op'sis*) Comprehensive summary

syrup n. (*si'rup*) Saturated solution of sugar

system n. (*sis'tem*) Group of objects, units etc. forming a unity or functioning as a whole, *the solar system*

T

tab n. and v.t. (*tăb*) Tag, flap; end of shoelace; strip of material sewn to garment as distinguishing mark

table 1) n. (*tā'bl*) Piece of furniture consisting of flat surface of wood, marble etc. supported on legs at convenient height to allow seated person to eat, work etc. list of facts, figures, names etc., *he referred to the table of contents*

table 2) v.t. (*tā'bl*) To submit for discussion; make list of, tabulate

tableau n. (*tăb'lō*) Representation; picture; picture or composition represented by group of posed persons

tablet n. (*tăb'lit*) Flat slab of wood, stone etc. bearing inscription; flat piece of hard material on which to write; medicine or sweet in flat round form

tabloid n. (*tăb'loid*) Small round medicinal lozenge; newspaper that gives news in simple, concentrated form

tack n., and v.t. and i. (*tăk*) Short nail with broad head; long loose stitch for temporary fastening in needlework; (naut.) course of vessel esp. in relation to direction of wind

tackle n., and v.t. and i. (*tă'kl*) Mechanism for moving or lifting heavy weights, esp. system of ropes and pulleys; any equipment

tadpoles

or set of instruments, *fishing tackle, shaving tackle*; (football) attempt to rob opponent of ball. As v.t. and i. to manipulate by means of tackle; (fig.) to grapple with, to deal with, *let us tackle the problem immediately*; (football) to challenge opponent by a tackle

tact n. (*tăkt*) Ability to deal with embarrassing topic or situation without offending; instinctive ingenuity to say or do the right thing

tadpole n. (*tăd'pōl*) Frog, toad etc. in its first stage

tail n., and v.t. and i. (*tāl*) Part of backbone in vertebrates extending beyond trunk; any object resembling this; any trailing length; lowest or hindmost part of anything, *the tail*

take v.t. and i. (*tāk*) pret. **took** (*to͝ok*) p.p. **taken** (*tāk'n*) To carry away in hands; remove; gain possession of, seize, capture; gain, win, *he took first prize*; earn; understand, assume in the mind, *I take it we are all agreed*; consume, eat, drink, *have you taken your medicine?*; accept, endure, *you must take us as you find us*; perform, carry out, *the curate took the morning service*; catch, be infected with, *I have been taken ill*; avail oneself of; cause to come with one, *I took the dog for a walk*; write down, ascertain, *he took my name and address*; photograph; engage, hire, *we took a cottage for the summer*; experience, *I took pity on him*; choose, select, *I was* *forced to take sides*; be big enough to contain; succeed, *the vaccine did not take*

tale n. (*tāl*) Narrative, account, story, legend, anecdote

talent n. (*tăl'ent*) Natural aptitude for a specific activity

talk v.t. and i., and n. (*tawk*) To express in words, speak; converse; discuss, *it was much talked about*

tall adj. (*tawl*) (of person) High

talon n. (*tăl'on*) Claw esp. of bird of prey

tambourine n. (*tam bor ēn'*) Small shallow drum with tinkling metal disks attached to sides

tame adj. and v.t. (*tām*) Domesticated, freed of savagery; submissive, subdued; insipid, dull

tamper v.i. (*tamp'er*) To meddle with; interfere

tan n., adj., and v.t. and i. (*tan*) Bronze colour of sunburnt skin; golden brown colour; bark used in process of tanning hides. As adj. golden brown. As v.t. and i. to convert (hide into leather) by steeping in tannic acid; to make or become brown, esp. by exposure to sun

tandem adv., adj., and n. (*tan'dem*) (Placed) one behind or after another. As n. bicycle for two riders one behind the other

tang n. and v.t. (*tang*) Strong flavour or smell

tangent adj. and n. (*tan'jent*) Meeting at a point without intersecting it. As n. straight line touching curve without cutting it

tangerine n. (*tan jer ēn'*) Species of small, scented orange

tambourine

talons

tango n. and v.i. (*tang'gō*) South American dance; music for this

tank n. (*tangk*) Large cistern for storing water and other liquids; chamber in locomotive for water or in motor vehicle for petrol; (milit.) heavily armoured tracked vehicle mounted with guns

tanker n. (*tangk'er*) Ship or lorry built for carrying liquids, esp. petroleum in bulk

tantalize v.t. (*tant'al iz*) To tease (person etc.) by displaying or offering desirable object then withdrawing it; to torment by continually retracting proffered promise

tap 1) v.t. and i., and n. (*tăp*) To strike lightly, *he tapped the barometer*; to cause to strike lightly; to rap. As n. light blow or sound of this

tap 2) n. and v.t. (*tăp*) Device with control screw which stops or releases flow of liquid in pipe etc

tape n. and v.t. (*tāp*) Narrow strip of material used for fastening; such a strip stretched across race-track to indicate finishing line; roll or strip of paper on which telegraph messages are recorded; magnetic strip on which sounds are recorded

taper v.t. and i., and n. (*tāp'er*) To become or cause to become gradually narrower or thinner

tapestry n. (*tăp'est ri*) Hand-woven textile fabric into which are worked coloured designs

tar n. and v.t. (*tah*(*r*)) Thick, black, sticky liquid obtained by dry distillation of wood or coal, used for road surfaces, preservatives etc

tardy adj. (*tahd'i*) Slow to act, dilatory, sluggish; late; reluctant

target n. (*tah'git*) Board bearing

concentric circles set up to be shot at in archery, rifle shooting etc.; person or area at which shots, bombs, missiles etc. are aimed; (fig.) objective, *the target of the organ fund is £2,000*
tariff n. and v.t. (*tă'rif*) List of duties on imports and exports; rate of duty imposed on these; list of charges for items and services, esp. hotel price list
tarnish v.t. and i., and n. (*tahn'ish*) To lose or cause to lose lustre by exposure to damp, air etc.; (fig.) to stain, sully, *his reputation is tarnished*
tarot n. (*tă'rō*) Pack of 78 playing cards used for fortune-telling; game played with these
tarpaulin n. (*tah pawl'in*) Canvas treated with tar to render waterproof; sheet of this used as covering
tart 1) n. (*taht*) Pie containing fruit or jam, with or without top layer of pastry
tart 2) adj. (*taht*) Sharp to the taste, bitter, acid
tartan n. and adj. (*tah'tan*) Woollen fabric with coloured checks forming distinctive pattern denoting a Highland clan. As adj. made of or resembling a tartan
task n. and v.t. (*tahsk*) Specific piece of work, study, or labour
tassel n. and v.t. (*tăs'el*) Decorative pendant on dress, cap etc. made from bunch of threads, cord, or silk
taste 1) v.t. and i. (*tāst*) To test or perceive flavour of food or drink, *please taste the wine, I can taste garlic in the salad*; (fig.) to enjoy, to experience, *I have never tasted success*
taste 2) n. (*tāst*) Sense by which flavours are distinguished by tongue and palate; sensation experienced by this sense; sample, small portion, trace; natural or trained appreciation of what is aesthetically or intellectually pleasing, critical discernment of the artistic, *his house is decorated in excellent taste*; liking, preference, *I have no taste for air travel*
tattoo 1) n. and v.i. (*tăt'o͞o*) Military pageant presented usually at night
tattoo 2) v.t. and n. (*tăt'o͞o*) To decorate skin with indelible pictorial design by inserting coloured pigments into it
taunt v.t. and n. (*tawnt*) To reproach contemptuously, jeer at
taut adj. (*tawt*) Stretched tight
tavern n. (*tăv'en*) Inn, public house, hotel
tax v.t. and n. (*tăks*) To compel to pay contribution to national expenditure; subject to exacting demands, *the problem taxed his ingenuity*
taxi n. and v.i. (*tăks'i*) Motor-car plying for hire fitted with taximeter; **taxi-cab** taxi; **taxi-rank** place where taxis wait for fares. As v.i. to go by taxi; (of aircraft) to travel along ground prior to taking off or on landing
taximeter n. (*tăks'im ēt er, tăks im'it er*) Automatic device fitted to taxi indicating fare due
taxidermy n. (*tăks'i durm i*) Craft of preserving and stuffing animal skins in lifelike manner
tea n. (*tē*) Dried leaves of evergreen shrub, *Lycium chinense*; drink made by infusing these in boiling water; afternoon or early evening meal at which tea is served
teach v.t. and i. (*tēch*); pret. and p.p. **taught** (*tawt*) To impart knowledge or skill to, esp. by means of systematic instruction, *you cannot teach an old dog new tricks*; give lessons in school, educate
team n. and v.t. (*tēm*) Two or more domesticated animals harnessed together; number of players constituting a side in a game; group of persons working together
tease v.t. and n. (*tēz*) To make fun of
technical adj. (*tek'ni kal*) Of, by, or for industrial and mechanical arts and skills
tedious adj. (*tē'dyus*) Exhausting and boring, monotonously dull
teem v.t. and i. (*tēm*) To produce in abundance; contain in great numbers, *the forest teems with snakes*; be prolific
teenage adj. (*tēn'āj*) Of, for, or like an adolescent in his teens. Hence: **teenager** n
teens n. (*tēnz*) (pl.) Period of adolescence between 13 and 19 years of age
teetotal adj. (*tē tō'tal*) Advocating or observing total abstinence from intoxicating drinks
telegram n. (*tel'i gram*) Telegraphic message
telegraph n., and v.t. and i. (*tel'i grahf*)
Apparatus for transmitting signals, esp. by electrical impulses through wires. As v.t. and i. to transmit by

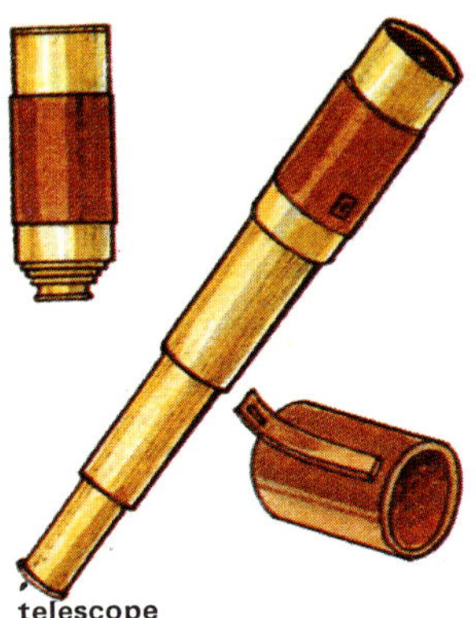

telescope

telegraph, send telegram, *telegraph me on your arrival*
telephone n., and v.t. and i. (*tel'ifōn*) Electric system of communication for transmitting speech over a distance through wires; transmitting and receiving instrument for this. As v.t. and i. to transmit by telephone; to use telephone
telescope n., and v.t. and i. (*tel'i skōp*) Optical instrument for making distant objects appear nearer and larger
television n. (*tel'i vi zhun*) System of transmitting by radio pictures of distant scenes for reproduction on receiving sets; receiving set for television
tell v.t. and i. (*tel*); pret. and p.p. **told** (*tōld*) To express in words, inform, *can you tell me the time?*; narrate, *tell me a story*; distinguish, *I cannot tell them apart*; divulge, reveal; command, *I told him to behave*
temper 1) v.t. and i. (*tem'per*) To moderate, modify, tone down
temper 2) n. (*tem'per*) Habitual or temporary state of mind, *he has a fiery temper, I am in a good temper today*; anger, irritation
temperament n. (*tem'per a ment*) Mental, moral, and emotional constitution
temperance n. (*tem'per ans*) Moderation, self-control; abstinence from alcoholic drinks
temperature n. (*tem'pra cher*) Condition or degree of heat or cold in body or atmosphere
tempest n. (*tem'pest*) Violent storm
temple n. (*tem'pl*) Building or place dedicated to a god; building used for worship, church
temporary adj. (*tem'per er i*) Lasting for limited time only, transient
tempt v.t. (*tempt*) To entice, incite; persuade (to do wrong)
tenant n. and v.t. (*ten'ant*) Person holding real estate for terminable period for payment of rent; occupant
tender 1) n. (*ten'der*) Railway truck carrying fuel and water immediately behind locomotive; vessel attending larger one to supply stores etc.; one who tends or looks after
tender 2) v.t. and i., and n. (*ten'der*) To offer (thanks, apologies etc.); to offer (payment) in satisfaction of claim; to offer to supply (goods, services etc.) under contract
tender 3) adj. (*ten'der*) Gentle; loving, affectionate; kind, considerate
tendon n. (*ten'don*) (anat.) Strong tissue which connects muscle and bone
tendril n. (*ten'dril*) Small, string-like shoot of climbing plants by which they cling for support
tennis n. (*ten'is*) Game for two or four players who strike ball with rackets over a net
tense 1) n. (*tens*) (gram.) Form taken by verb to indicate time (present, past, future etc.)
tense 2) adj. and v.t. (*tens*) Stretched tight, taut; (fig.) over-wrought, keyed up, alert, *there was a feeling of tense anticipation*
tent n. and v.i. (*tent*) Portable

tendril

shelter of canvas supported by poles and held taut by ropes
tentacle n. (*ten'ta kl*) Slender, flexible limb on some lower forms of animals used for gripping, exploring, and moving
tepid adj. (*tep'id*) Lukewarm, slightly warm
term 1) n. (*turm*) Limited period of time, *the president is elected for a term of five years*; fixed number of weeks of attendance at universities, schools etc. and when law courts are in session; (law) day fixed for payment esp. of rent; (med.) end of period of pregnancy; limit, boundary; word used to express definite conception in an art, science, profession etc.; (pl.) conditions esp. of payment, *our terms are ten guineas per week*; stated provisos of a contract; (pl.) mode of expression, *he introduced me in the most glowing terms*
term 2) v.t. (*turm*) To name, designate
terminate v.t. and i. (*turm'in āt*) To limit or bound; finish or cause to finish; bring to an end
terminus n. (*turm'i nus*) End, goal; end of railway line, bus-route etc.; station or depot at such a place
terrace n. and v.t. (*te'ras*) Raised level space, natural or artificial; flat level area bordering river, lake or sea, or cut out of side of hill; row of similar houses in street
terrible adj. (*te'ri bl*) Evoking horror or fear; terrifying; (colloq.) excessive, very bad, disappointing, *we are having terrible weather*
terrier n. (*te'ri er*) One of several breeds of small dogs kept as pets and used for hunting
terrify v.t. (*te'ri fi*) To frighten, to fill with horror
territory n. (*te'ri ter i*) Large region of land; single governmental division of country; dependent state, not entirely self-governing; (comm.) area assigned to one representative
terror n. (*te'ror*) Extreme fear
terrorism n. (*te'ror izm*) Policy of terror and intimidation. Hence:
terrorist n. one who favours terrorism; political fanatic who uses terror to gain his ends
test n. and v.t. (*test*) Critical examination or trial of person's or thing's qualities, As v.t. to submit to trial (person or thing) to ascertain merits of
testify v.t. and i. (*test'i fi*) To bear witness
testimonial n. (*test i mōn'ial*) Written statement by responsible person as to character, abilities, and qualifications of another
testimony n. (*test'i mon i*) (law) Written or oral statement under oath; what serves as proof or evidence
tether n. and v.t. (*teth'er*) Rope or chain used to tie grazing animal to peg while allowing it some freedom of movement; (fig.) extent of resources, strength, patience, authority etc., *I was at the end of my tether*. As v.t. to fasten (animal) with tether
text n. (*tekst*) Written or printed words forming literary work; original words and phrases used by author as distinct from later translation, paraphrase, commentary etc., *the translation follows the text too literally*; main body of book as distinct from preface, notes, index etc.; quotation from *Bible* esp. one used as basis of sermon; quotation from any source used as authority to support argument; theme, subject
textile n. and adj. (*teks'til*) Woven material, fabric. As adj. of or by weaving; woven; of textiles
than conj. and prep. (th*an*) Used to introduce second member in a comparison, *better safe than sorry, you are older than I am*
thank v.t. and n. (*thank*) To express gratitude to (someone) in speech or writing
thatch n. and v.t. (*thătch*) Roof covering made of straw or reeds
thaw v.t. and i., and n. (*thaw*) To cause (something frozen) to melt; (of snow, ice) to melt; (of weather) to become warm enough to melt ice; (fig.) to become friendly, less reserved
theatre n. (*thē'at er*) Large hall with stage for dramatic performances and seats for spectators; similar hall or room for lectures; place where some action takes place, *the theatre of war is in the Far East*
theft n. (*theft*) Act of stealing
their pron. and adj. (th*ār*) Possessive case of they; of them, *that is their book*
them personal pron. (th*em*) Obj. case of they, *do you know them?*
theme n. (*thēm*) Chief or recurring subject of writing, thought, conversation, argument etc
theology n. (*thē ol'oj i*) Systematic study of religion

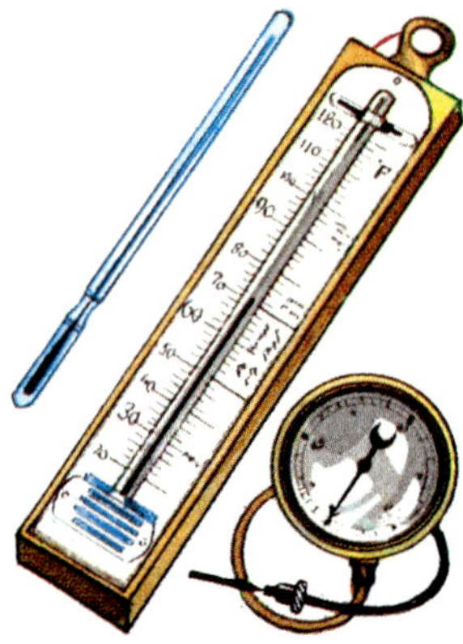
thermometer

thimble

theory n. (*thēr'i*) Speculative system based on and offering explanation of observed facts or phenomena, *Darwin's theory of evolution*; underlying laws and principles of a science, art etc., *I am studying the theory of music*; speculation; (colloq.) notion, fancy, *one of my pet theories is that*

therapy n. (*the'rapi*) Treatment intended to cure, e.g. *occupational therapy*

thermometer n. (*thurm'om it er*) Instrument for measuring temperature

Thermos n. (*thurm'os*) Vacuum flask used for keeping liquids at constant temperature. (Trade name)

thermostat n. (*thurm'ō stăt*) Device that regulates temperature automatically

they pron. (thā) Third person pl. nom.; those (people, things); those already referred to; people in general, *they say it is dangerous*

thick adj., n., and adv. (*thik*) Of considerable size between opposite surfaces, *the house has thick walls*; containing visible matter, *will you have thick or clear soup?*; muddy, cloudy; numerous, crowded, *the beach is thick with people*; closely packed, dense, *the forest is very thick*; dull-witted; (colloq.) intimate, *they are as thick as thieves*

thief n. (*thēf*) One who steals

thigh n. (*thī*) Part of human between knee and trunk

thimble n. (*thim'bl*) Rigid cap worn on finger for protection when sewing

thin adj., and v.t. and i. (*thin*) Having opposite surfaces close together, not thick, *a thin layer of paint*; lean, not plump, *she is very thin*; sparse, scanty, *the cream is thin*; (of liquids) having low density, *a thin oil*; (fig.) shallow, transparent, flimsy, *he offered* a *thin excuse*; fine, slender

thing n. (*thing*) Any animate or inanimate object made of material substance or in thought, *a garden is a lovesome thing*; fact; idea; subject; (pl.) personal possessions, baggage, clothes, etc., *I must pack my things*; act, circumstance, *that was a foolish thing to do*; (pl.) state of affairs, trade, business, *things are bad*; (colloq.) what is right, fitting, useful, *just the thing!*; (of person) expresses contempt, affection, pity etc., *you poor old thing*

think v.t. and i., and n. (*think*) pret. and p.p. **thought** (*thawt*) To reason within the mind; exercise reasoning faculties; meditate or reflect; believe without certainly knowing, be of opinion, *did you think it a good book?*; anticipate, surmise, *I think it will rain* consider to be

thirst n. and v.i. (*thurst*) Desire to drink; suffering caused by lack of water; (fig.) strong desire, longing, *I used to have a thirst for adventure*

this demonstrative adj. and adv. (th*is*) (Being) person or thing nearest to hand, last referred to, pointed out, etc.; used in contrast

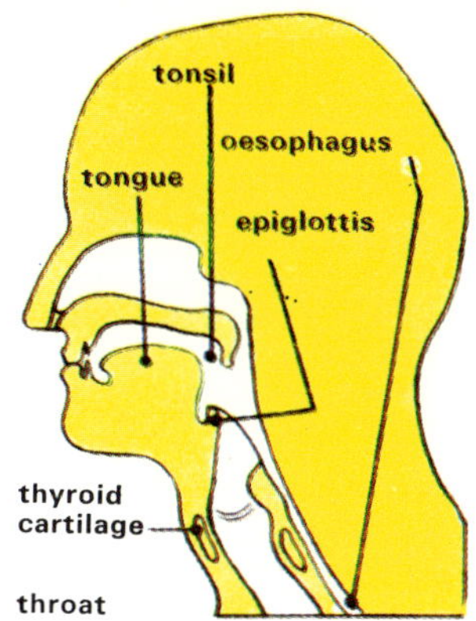

with *that, this window is closer than that one*; (of time) adj. referring to period of time now current, just passed, or immediately to come, *I shaved this morning, I shall be dining out this evening*
thistle n. (*thi's'l*) One of various prickly plants with purple or yellow flowers; national emblem of Scotland
thong n. (*thong*) Strip of leather used as strap or lash
thorn n. (*thawn*) Prickle on twigs and branches of certain trees and bushes
thorough adj. and prep. (*thu'rer*) Complete, entire, out-and-out, downright
though conj. (thō) Despite that, notwithstanding the fact that, *I shall try to come though I cannot promise*; nevertheless, *I wish you had told me though*
thought n. (*thawt*) Act or process of thinking; reasoned and logical ideas; reflection, consideration, *please give it a thought*; opinion, *have you any thoughts on the subject?*; body of ideas and opinions; small amount or degree, *may I have a thought more?*
thrash v.t. and i. (*thrăsh*) To beat severely, flog; thresh; beat grain from chaff; defeat decisively
thread n. and v.t. (*thred*) Fine cord (of silk, wool, cotton, etc.) used for sewing; filament; spiral groove of screw; logical connection, *I have lost the thread of my argument*
threat n. (*thret*) Act or statement declaring intention to hurt, punish, or damage; indication of probability of unpleasant occurrence, *there is a threat of rain*
thresh v.t. and i. (*thresh*) To beat (corn) so as to separate grain from chaff
threshold n. (*thresh'hōld*) Wooden plank or stone at entrance of dwelling, church, etc.; (fig.) beginning, *we are on the threshold of a new era*
thrift n. (*thrift*) Frugality, economical management
thrill v.t. and i., and n. (*thril*) To provoke deep emotional excitement; rouse the emotions of, *the actor thrilled his audience*; feel great enthusiasm, be deeply stirred
thrive v.i. (*thriv*) pret. **throve** *(thrōv)* **thrived** *(thrivd)* p.p. **thriven** (*thriv'n*) (Of person) to grow rich and/or successful; (of plants and animals) to multiply, grow vigorously; (of ideas etc.) to spread
throat n. and v.t. (*thrōt*) Passage in neck connecting mouth and nose with stomach and lungs, gullet, windpipe; front of neck
throb v.i. and n. (*throb*) To beat or pulsate rapidly; quiver or vibrate. As n. vibration, pulsation
throne n. and v.t. (*thrōn*) Chair of state, esp. for sovereign, bishop, etc.; (fig.) the sovereign, sovereign power, *Queen Victoria came to the throne in 1837*
throng n., and v.t. and i. (*throng*) Crowd of people, multitude

through prep., adv. and adj. (*thrōō*) From end to end or from side to side of, across; during; by means of, by agency of, *obtain it through your newsagent*; in the complete period, *July through September* (i.e. from beginning of July to end of September). As adv. from end to end or side to side, *please let me through*; **through and through** utterly, completely; **be through with** refuse to have further dealings with. As adj. passing right through, unobstructed; (of train, bus, etc.) doing whole journey without a break so that passengers need not change
throughout prep. and adv. (*thrōō owt'*) Through each and every part of; (of time) from beginning to end, *he slept throughout the lesson.* As adv. right through; in all respects, *he was badly treated throughout*
throw v.t. and i. (*thrō*) pret. **threw** (*thrū*), p.p. **thrown** (*thron*) To fling, cast, hurl through the air; cause to fly from hand in motion; *the fielder threw the ball*; (of horse or wrestler) bring (rider, opponent) to the ground; shape (pottery) on potter's wheel; twist (silk etc.) into threads; place hastily in position, *he threw on his clothes and hurried out*
thrust v.t. and i. (pret. and p.p. **thrust**), and n. (*thrust*) To push vigorously, jerk or push forward, *he thrust the bolt home*
thud v.i. and n. (*thud*) To fall on, collide with, or strike something with dull heavy sound. As n. dull heavy sound
thumb n. and v.t. (*thum*) Short thick finger set opposite other fingers in human hand; corresponding digit in animals
thump n., and v.t. and i. (*thump*) Dull sound produced by an impact; heavy blow
thunder n., and v.t. and i. (*thun'der*) Sound that follows flash of lightning
thus adv. (th*us*) In this manner; accordingly; to this extent
tick 1) n., and v.t. and i. (*tik*) Light tapping sound such as is made by watch or clock; symbol (√) used to indicate approval or correctness
tick 2) n. (*tik*) Any of various small blood-sucking parasites on men and animals
ticket n. and v.t. (*tik'it*) Written or printed piece of paper or card entitling holder to some privilege or service, e.g. to travel specified distance by public transport, to attend specified entertainment
tickle v.t. and i., and n. (*ti'kl*) Lightly to touch (skin) so as to produce slight irritation and usually laughter; to itch, *my nose tickles*
tide n., and v.t. and i. (*tīd*) The alternate rising and falling of the surface of the ocean and of connected bays, estuaries, rivers etc.; (fig.) tendency, trend
tidy adj., n., and v.t. (*tīd'i*) Arranged in good order, neat; (of person) habitually keeping things in order
tie 1) v.t. and i. (*tī*) To fasten or connect with rope, string, etc.; make a knot in, *he tied his shoe-laces*; restrict, bind, *he is tied to a wheel-chair*; do equally well with rival in a game, competition, examination, etc
tie 2) n. (*tī*) Strip of cloth worn round neck and knotted in front
tier n. (*tēr*) Horizontal row or rank esp. one of series placed one above another
tiff n. (*tif*) Trifling quarrel
tiger n. (*tiger*) Fierce carnivorous Asian feline, *Felis tigris*
tight adj. and adv. (*tīt*) Tied fast, firmly secured; closely packed; compact; close-fitting, *it's a tight fit*
till 1) n. (*til*) Cash-box with drawer used in shops
till 2) v.t. (*til*) To plough and sow. Hence: **tillage** n. (*til'ij*) agriculture, cultivated land; **tiller** n. one who tills
till 3) prep. and conj. (*til*) Until, up to the time of, *I stayed till the end.* As conj. up to the time when, *till death us do part*

tiger

timber n. and v.t. (*tim'ber*) Wood, esp. wood ready for use in building, carpentry, etc.; trees suitable for this
time 1) n. (*tīm*) Concept of past, present, and future; duration, continued existence, *it has stood the test of time*; particular point in this; portion of this, period, epoch, *in the time of the Romans*; system of measuring this, *what time is it?*; moment at which event occurs, *it is time I was going*; period in which it occurs, *it will take a long time*; normal or pre-arranged moment for something to happen, *what time is the bus?*; (mus.) style of movement depending on number and accentuation of beats in a bar; (pl.) period, era, age
time 2) v.t. (*tīm*) To measure duration of; record instant of; do or say opportunely
timid adj. (*tim'id*) Shy, lacking courage.
tin n. and v.t. (*tin*) Silvery-white malleable metal; container made of iron coated with tin (usually airtight and used for preserving food)
tinder n. (*tin'der*) Anything flammable to kindle fire from spark
tinge v.t. and n. (*tinj*) To tint, colour slightly; (fig.) modify slightly by mixture, *they are words tinged with malice*
tingle v.t. and i., and n. (*ting'gl*) To feel or cause to feel stinging sensation; smart; vibrate. As n. tingling sensation
tinker n., and v.t. and i. (*ting'ker*) One who repairs pots and pans etc
tinkle v.t. and i., and n. (*ting'kl*) To make or cause to make succession of metallic sounds; ring. As n. action or sound of tinkling
tinsel n., adj., and v.t. (*tin'sel*) Thin, shining, metallic material for decoration
tint n. and v.t. (*tint*) Hue, shade of colour
tiny adj. (*tīn'i*) Very small, minute
tip n. (*tip*) Extremity, esp. of tapering object, *only the tip of the iceberg can be seen*; slight push, pat; hint or advice; inside piece of information, esp. about horse-racing; gratuity given to waiters, porters etc. for services done; place where rubbish is dumped
tire v.t. and i. (*tīr*) To exhaust, weary; bore; (v.i.) grow weary; be bored by, have had enough of, *I am tired of reading*

toad

toad n. (*tōd*) Amphibian of genus *Bufo* resembling frog; **toad-in-the-hole** savoury dish of sausages baked in batter; **toadstool** inedible fungus resembling mushroom
toast n., and v.t. and i. (*tōst*) Slice of bread browned and crisped in front of fire; proposal to drink the health of someone (esp. woman) or thing (sentiment, institution, etc.)
tobacco n. (*to băk'ō*) Plant of genus *Nicotiana*; leaves of this dried and prepared for smoking, chewing, or as snuff
toboggan n. and v.i. (*to bog'an*) Light sledge for sliding down snowy slopes. As v.i. to ride on toboggan.
today adv. and n. (*too dā'*) On this day. As n. this day, *today is Monday*; the present time, *many of today's painters are abstract*
toe n., and v.t. and (v.i.) (*tō*) Digit of foot; fore-part of hoof; part of boot, shoe, or stocking that covers toes
toffee n. (*tof'i*) Sweet made of syrup, butter, sugar etc.
together adv. (*to geth'er*) In company; in union; one with another; in same place or time, *we were at school together*; uninterruptedly, on end; as well as
toil v.i. and n. (*toil*) To work hard
toilet n. (*toil'it*) Operation of dressing, making up, etc.; costume, style of dressing, esp. of women; lavatory
token n. (*tō'ken*) Sign, symbol (of affection etc.); what represents or is substitute for something else, esp. voucher representing money value exchangeable for goods

tomahawk

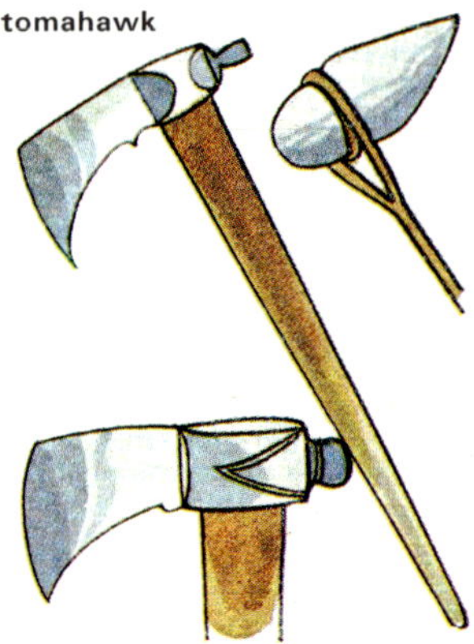

tolerance n. (*tol'erans*) Willingness to permit opinions, customs etc. differing from one's own
toll 1) n. (*tōl*) Payment for right to use road, bridge, etc
toll 2) v.t. and i., and n. (*tōl*) To cause (bell) to ring with slow measured sound; (of bell) to ring thus
tomahawk n. and v.t. (*tom'a hawk*) Light war and hunting hatchet used by Red Indians
tomato n. (*to mah'tō*, (U.S.) *to mā'tō*) Plant, *Lycopersicum esculentum*; red pulpy edible fruit of this
tomb n. (*tōōm*) Grave
tomorrow adv. and n. (*tōōmo'rō*) (On) the day after today
ton n. (*ton*) British measure of weight 2,240 lb

tomato

tone 1) n. (*tōn*) Sound, esp. with reference to its quality
tone 2) v.t. and i. (*tōn*) To give tone to; blend agreeably as to colour
tongs n.pl. (*tongz*) Implement consisting of two bars joined by pivot or spring used for grasping and lifting coal, sugar, etc
tongue n. and v.t. (*tung*) Organ of taste in animals and also of speech in man; power or method of speaking or expression, *she has a sharp tongue*; language, *her only tongue was Italian*; pin of buckle; leather flap under shoelace; clapper of bell; projecting point of land; projection to fit into groove
tonight adv. and n. (*tōō nīt'*) (On or during) this present night, the night of today
tonsil n. (*ton'sil*) One of two glandular bodies in throat
too adv. (*tōō*) Excessively; more than understood or specified purpose or standard, *you work too hard*; very; as well as, moreover
tool n., and v.t. and i. (*tōōl*) Implement, instrument, apparatus
toot v.t. and i., and n. (*tōōt*) To sound horn, esp. motor horn; to make noise like a horn. As n. sound of horn
top 1) n. (*top*) Highest part of anything, summit; upper part or surface; highest place, person, rank etc
top 2) adj. and v.t. (*top*) Of, on, or at the top; highest; utmost; first; best
top 3) n. (*top*) Wooden or metal toy usually pear-shaped which is made to spin on its point
topic n. (*top'ik*) Subject of conversation, discussion, or writing; general statement useful in developing argument
topple v.t. and i. (*top'l*) To fall or cause to fall (lit. and fig.)
topsy turvy adj. and adv. (*top si tur'vi*) Upside-down, in confusion
torch n. (*tawch*) Piece of wood soaked in flammable substance, used to give light when kindled
torment n. and v.t. (*taw'ment*) Severe suffering, pain of mind or body
tornado n. (*taw nā'dō*) West African or North American destructive local whirlwind
torpedo n. and v.t. (*taw pē'dō*) pl. **torpedoes** Self-propelled cigar-shaped apparatus, filled with explosives and used to destroy ships at sea

torpid adj. (*taw'pid*) Sluggish; dull, apathetic
torrent n. (*to'rent*) A violent rush, esp. a violent stream of water
torrid adj. (*to'rid*) Parched by the heat of the sun; very hot, *the torrid African sun*
tortoise n. (*taw'tus*) Slow-moving, four-legged reptile with hard shell
torture n. and v.t. (*taw'cher*) Extreme pain, agony of body or mind; act of inflicting extreme pain upon.
toss v.t. and i., and n. (*tos*) To throw with the hand, *toss a ball*; fling upwards, throw up with a quick, sharp movement, *the horse tossed its rider*; cause to rise up and down violently, *ships tossed by the waves*; (fig.) cause agitation of mind to; fling oneself about restlessly, *toss about in a bed*; to be agitated; be tossed about; spin a coin to decide a course of action. As n. act of tossing; fact of being tossed; tossing movement; **win (lose) the toss** guess correctly (incorrectly) whether heads or tails when a coin is tossed up
tot n. (*tot*) Small, young child
total adj., and v.t. and i., and n. (*tō'tal*) Entire, whole, complete
totter v.i. and n. (*tot'er*) To walk with shaky, faltering steps; to be shaky, in danger of falling; (fig.) be on the verge of ruin, *the empire tottered to its fall*
touch v.t. and i. (*tuch*) To come in contact with, be in contact, *the lowest branch touches the ground*; feel with hand or fingers, *please do not touch the exhibits*; come to, reach, *his head almost touches the ceiling*; concern oneself with, have to do with, esp. to play (an instrument), take (food), invest (money in), *I wouldn't touch those shares if I were you*; affect, concern, *he was touched with remorse when he heard the news*; handle, finger, lightly, *he only just touched you*; lay the hand on with a view to healing; practise doing this, *King James II often touched and was said to cure many*; impress, move, *touch the heart*; arouse (passions etc.), *his words touched her vanity*; deal with, affect, *what you say does not touch the issue*; be as good as, *there is nothing to touch a good sleep for relaxing you*; (slang) extract money from, *he touched me for £5*; **touch at** call at (a port); **touch down** (Rugby football) place the hand on the ball on the ground in area behind goal-posts
tough adj. and n. (*tuf*) (of material objects) Of close, firm consistency, pliable but not brittle, *tough leather*; (of persons or animals) strong, vigorous, robust; (of mind etc.) firm, tenacious; (of a task etc.) difficult, laborious, *a tough job*
tour n., and v.t. and i. (*tōōr*) A journey consisting of visits to different places; a round of visits, *tour of inspection*; (milit.) a turn of duty
tournament n. (*tōōr'na ment*) (hist.) Series of contests between mounted knights armed with lances, or series of tilting matches etc.; competition for a sports championship; competitive series of games of chess, etc
tourniquet n. (*tōōr'ni kā*) Device to stop bleeding by applying pressure with bandage or surgical apparatus that can be twisted tightly
tout n. and v.i. (*towt*) One who canvasses to obtain custom, esp. one who sells information about race-horses
tow v.t. and n. (*tō*) To pull along by rope or chain (esp. boat or broken-down vehicle)
toward(s) prep. (*tu wawd(z)'*) In the direction of, *towards the south*; in respect of, *to feel friendly towards someone*; round about, near, *towards dawn*; expressing direction of a tendency, *drifting towards war*
towel n. and v.t. (*tow'el*) Cloth used for drying something wet, esp. hands or body after washing
tower n. and v.i. (*tow'er*) A tall building, either standing alone or forming a lofty part of a building
town n. (*town*) Compact large settlement engaged primarily in non-agricultural employment
toxic adj. (*tok'sik*) Poisonous; caused by poison
toy n. and v.i. (*toi*) Child's plaything; any object meant for amusement only
trace 1) v.t. and i. (*trās*) To mark out, outline, *trace a plan on paper*; copy exactly by following lines of a map, design, etc. through transparent paper; to write, esp. laboriously; follow or discover something by means of tracks, clues, pieces of evidence, etc., *trace a criminal*; discover as

result of process of thought, *trace someone's fears to a childhood experience*; walk over, proceed along

trace 2) n. (*trās*) Mark left by anything passing, footprint, etc.; vestige, evidence left by earlier event, *every trace of the crime had been removed*; very small amount, *he showed not a trace of fear*

track n. and v.t. (*trăk*) Mark left by something that has passed along, *tracks of a vehicle in the mud*; footprint; path worn by use; course on which races are run; treaded metal belt used instead of tyres by vehicles such as tractors etc

tract 1) n. (*trăkt*) Wide expanse of land or water, *a tract of forest*; (anat.) a system in the body, *the digestive tract*

tract 2) n. (*trăkt*) Short treatise, usually on moral or religious subject

traction n. (*trăk'shun*) Act of drawing or pulling along; method by which drawing power is obtained, *motor traction*

tractor n. (*trăk'tor*) What is used for traction, esp. powerful vehicle used for pulling agricultural machinery or other equipment

trade 1) n. (*trād*) Act or business of buying and selling commodities; particular branch of this; group of persons engaged in a particular trade

trade 2) v.i. and t. (*trād*) To sell or exchange in commerce, buy and sell, barter

tradition n. (*tra dish'un*) Customs, beliefs, opinions etc. handed down verbally from generation to generation

traffic n. and v.i. (*tră'fik*) Act or process of buying and selling goods; movement of people and esp. vehicles to and fro, *there is a lot of traffic on the roads today*

tragedy n. (*traj e di*) Play for theatre or cinema, dealing with human sufferings and ending in disaster; a calamity in real life

trail n., and v.t. and i. (*trāl*) Mark, track, left by something that has passed; track followed by a hunter, path through wild country

train 1) v.t. and i. (*trān*) To give instruction and practice to (a person, animal), *train a horse for a race*; to practise; bring oneself to required physical condition for contest etc., *train for a boat-race*; to cause (plants) to grow in desired direction, *train roses up a wall*. Hence: **trainer** n. person who trains athletes, horses etc

train 2) n. (*trān*) Retinue; procession, cortège; trailing extension of a dress; series of railway coaches or trucks drawn as a unit

traitor n. (*trā'tor*) One who betrays a friend, cause, his country etc

tram n. (*trăm*) Large public vehicle carrying passengers and running on rails laid on a road; truck used underground for conveyance of coal

tramp v.i. and t., and n. (*trămp*) To walk heavily along; plod; go for a long walk; traverse by tramping. As n. vagabond who tramps the road

trample v.t. and i., and n. (*trămpl*) To tread under foot, crush

tranquil adj. (*trăng'kwil*) Calm; quiet

trans- pref. (*trănz*) Over, across; through; beyond

transact v.t. (*trahn zăkt'*) To carry through, conduct, (business etc.)

transcribe v.t. (*trahn skrib*) To copy in writing, esp. to reproduce in writing from shorthand notes

transfer v.t. and i. (*trahnz'fer*) To convey or move from one place to another, *transfer a cup from sideboard to table*; change from one bus, boat, etc., to another; convey (property etc.) into the possession of another; print a design, picture, from one surface to another

transform v.t. (*trahnz fawm'*) To change the shape and appearance of, to alter the nature of, *success transformed his character*

transfuse v.t. (*trahnz fūz'*) To transfer (liquid) from one vessel to another; transfer (blood) from veins of one human or animal to those of another; imbue. Hence: **transfusion** n

transgress v.t. and i. (*trahnz gres'*) To overstep, exceed, *transgress the bounds of friendship*; break (a law etc.); sin

transit n. (*trahn'zit*) Passage through; conveyance, *the transit of goods*

transition n. (*trahn zish'un*) Change, passage from one place, state etc. to another

translate v.t. (*trahnz lāt'*) To turn words written or spoken in one language into another

transmit v.t. (*trahnz mit'*) To send from one person or place to another

transparent adj. (*trahns pă'rent*) Allowing light to pass through so that objects behind can be clearly seen

transplant v.t. and i. (*trahns plahnt'*) (Of plants etc.) to take up and plant in another place; (of people) move from one place to another

transport 1) v.t. (*trahnz pawt'*) To carry (goods, persons) from one place to another; (hist.) send criminals to a distant penal settlement; (fig.) overwhelm, carry away, by powerful emotion, *transported with ecstasy*

transport 2) n. (*trahnz'pawt*) Conveying or being conveyed; ship or aircraft for carrying goods or passengers, esp. troops

trap n. and v.t. (*trăp*) Device for catching animals, birds etc., *mouse-trap*; (fig.) stratagem to deceive or mislead persons; anything having a deceptive appearance

trapeze n. (*tra pēz'*) Swinging horizontal bar suspended from two ropes, used by gymnasts and acrobats

trash n. (*trăsh*) Worthless stuff, rubbish; poor quality literature

travel v.i. and t. (*trăv'el*) To go, proceed, *travel into town*; make a journey, visit places, make a tour, *travel on the Continent*; travel as a salesman, *he travels* in *chemical products*; journey through, *travel the world*

traverse v.t. and n. (*tră'vers*) To pass across, over, *traverse the ocean*

tray n. (*trā*) Flat piece of wood etc. with a rim, for holding light articles, food etc., *a tea-tray*; container for papers, files etc., *the in-tray*

treacherous adj. (*trech'e rus*) Disloyal, false (to a friend, cause, etc.); unreliable, deceptive, *treacherous weather*

treacle n. (*trēkl*) Thick, syrupy substance produced in the process of refining sugar

tread v.i. and t. (*tred*) pret. **trod** (*trod*) p.p. **trodden, trod** To walk, step on, *tread on someone's toes*; press, trample, under the feet, *tread grapes*; beat down by treading, *tread a path through the grass*

treason n. (*trē'zon*) Treachery, esp. to one's country or ruler

treasure n. and v.t. (*trezh'er*) Valuables or money stored up, *buried treasure*; something of great value or importance, *art treasures*; highly valued person

treat v.t. and i. (*trēt*) To behave or act towards, *to treat animals kindly*; consider, *treat something as a joke*; deal with in a particular way, *treat a fruit tree with chemical sprays*; give medical or surgical care to, *treat a man for rheumatism*; deal with, discuss, *treat a subject thoroughly*; bear the cost of entertaining (another), *treat a friend to a drink*

treatment n. (*trēt'ment*) Act or way of treating, dealing with, someone or something; act of subjecting to particular process, *to try out a new treatment for cancer*

treaty n. (*trē'ti*) Negotiations, discussion of terms; agreement, esp. one agreed upon between different states

tree n. (*trē*) Plant with woody stem or trunk, larger than a shrub

trek v.i. and n. (*trek*) To make a long journey

trellis n. (*trel'is*) Light lattice-work of wood etc., esp. as used for training climbing-plants

tremble v.i. and n. (*trembl*) To be shaken with involuntary movements, as with fear, cold, etc.; shiver, *tremble with cold*; to be shaky, *his voice trembled*; to flutter; (fig.) feel intense anxiety

tremendous adj. (*tre men'dus*) Gigantic, enormous, formidable; (colloq.) implying importance, admiration etc., *he is a tremendous singer*

trench n., and v.t. and i. (*trench*) Ditch dug in the earth, esp. as ground cover for soldiers

trend n. and v.i. (*trend*) General tendency, direction, *the trend of modern fashion*

trespass v.i. and n. (*tres'pas*) To go unlawfully upon another's land

trial n. (*trī'al*) Testing, trying, proving, *to give something a trial*; something that afflicts, ill-fortune, *trials and tribulations*; judicial inquiry in court of law

triangle n. (*trī'ăngl*) Plane figure bounded by three lines forming three angles; object having approximately this form; musical instrument consisting of a three-cornered metal rod struck with a metal stick

tribe n. (*trīb*) Social unit

consisting of clans or families with common customs and institutions
tribute n. (*trī'būt*) Payment of sum (usually regularly) imposed by a conqueror; a tax; act or words showing admiration or approbation, *a tribute to the dead man*
trick n. and v.t. (*trik*) Something done in order to deceive, an artifice, dodge, swindle; an illusion, *trick of the imagination*; roguish prank, practical joke, *to play an amusing trick on someone*; personal mannerism, *odd tricks of pronunciation*; feat of conjuring, jugglery
trickle v.i. and t., and n. (*trikl*) To flow or cause to flow in a thin stream, *tears trickled down her face*
tricycle n. (*trī'sikl*) Three-wheeled bicycle
trifle n., and v.i. and t. (*trīfl*) Something of little value or importance, *to get upset over trifles*; sweet dish made of sponge cake, custard, fruit, cream etc
trigger n. and v.t. (*trig'er*) Lever for releasing a spring, esp. one releasing the hammer of a firearm
trigonometry n. (*tri go nom'e tri)* Branch of mathematics dealing with the relations of the sides and angles of triangles
trim adj., n., and v.t. and i. (*trim*) Neat; in good order. As n. neat or good condition, order, *in good trim*. As v.t. and i. to put in good order; adjust the burning of (a lamp), neaten (its wick), *trim the wick of a lamp*; adjust the sails of (a boat); ornament, attach edging to, *trim a hat*; modify one's principles or policy to suit circumstances etc., *a politician who is constantly trimming*
trinity n. (*trin'i ti*) Group of three, esp. the Father, Son, and Holy Ghost
trinket n. (*tring'ket*) Small ornament, jewel; worthless trifle
trio n. (*trē'ō*) Group of three persons or things; musical composition for three voices or instruments
trip v.i. and t., and n. (*trip*) To move nimbly with rapid steps; stumble through catching one's foot in an obstacle; cause to stumble or fall
triple adj., and v.t. and i. (*tripl*) Threefold
triplet n. (*trip'let*) Group of three; one of three children born at one birth
tripod n. (*trī'pod*) Stool, table etc. supported on three legs; a support with three legs, *camera tripod*
triumph n. and v.i. (*trī'umf*) Victory, achievement, success
trivial adj. (*tri'vi al*) Of little importance, *a trivial error*
trolley n. (*trol'i*) Light two- or four-wheeled hand-cart; small table on wheels or castors used for serving food; four-wheeled truck running on rails; overhead arm of electric tram-car or trolley-bus
trombone n. (*trom'bōn*) Brass wind instrument with bell-shaped end and sliding tube
troop n., and v.i. and t. (*troop*) A number, company, of people; (milit.) division of cavalry squadron corresponding to company in infantry regiment; (pl.) military forces. As v.i. and t. to move in large numbers, *people trooped out of the cinema*
trophy n. (*trō'fi*) Token, memorial, of victory; spoils of victory; prize awarded for a sporting contest, *tennis trophies*
tropic n. and adj. (*trop'ik*) Line of latitude 23° 28′ north of the equator (tropic of Cancer) or south of the equator (tropic of Capricorn) bounding the zone where sun shines vertically at noon for at least two days in the year
trot v.i. and t., and n. (*trot*) (Of a horse etc.) to move at a pace between walking and galloping; (of a person) to move with short, brisk steps
trouble v.t. and i., and n. (*trubl*) To stir, disturb, set into movement, *trouble the waters*; agitate, disturb, the mind, *troubled by someone's remarks*; pester

trombone

worry, *don't trouble me with such trivialities*; to be anxious, feel agitated; take pains, make an effort, *don't trouble to meet me*
trough n. (*trof*) Long, open vessel holding food or water for domestic animals
trousers n.pl. (*trow'zerz*) Outer garment covering the body from waist to ankle, having separate covering for each leg
trousseau n. (*trōō'sō*) Outfit of clothes and personal belongings for a bride
trout n. (*trowt*) pl. **trout**. Any of species of fish of genus *Salmo*; small spotted freshwater fish of this genus
trowel n. (*trow'el*) Implement with flat, diamond-shaped blade used for spreading mortar; hollow-bladed tool used in gardening
truant n. and adj. (*trōō'ant*) Person who absents himself from his duties for his own pleasure, esp. child who stays away from school
truce n. (*trōōs*) Cessation of hostilities by agreement between the hostile forces, usually for a considerable time
trudge v.i. and n. (*truj*) To walk laboriously and wearily
true adj., adv., and n. (*trōō*) Conforming to fact and reality, not false, *a true story*; faithful, loyal, *a true friend*; genuine, authentic, *the true heir to the throne*; accurate, exact, *a true copy*. As adv. truly. As n. exact position or adjustment, *to be out of true*
trumpet n., and v.t. and i. (*trum'pet*) Metal wind instrument giving high, powerful notes
trunk n. (*trungk*) Main stem of a tree; body of human or animal, without head or limbs; receptacle, esp. large box, with hinged lid, for conveying luggage while travelling; the proboscis or extended nose of an elephant
trust 1) n. (*trust*) Confidence, faith, in another's reliability, honour etc
trust 2) v.t. and i. (*trust*) To have confidence in, rely upon, *a man you can trust*
try 1) v.i. (*trī*) pret. and p.p. **tried** (*trīd*) To endeavour, attempt (to do something), *try to do your duty*; put to the test, test the properties of, test by experiment, *try how high you can jump*; judge (a person) in a court of law
try 2) n. (*trī*) An attempt,

trout

endeavour; (Rugby football) right to carry the ball in front of the goal and take a place-kick, the try alone counting three points
tub n., and v.t. and i. (*tub*) Wooden vessel, often in the form of a cask, used for holding water, washing clothes, etc
tube n. (*tūb*) Long hollow cylinder or pipe, *a test-tube*; organ of the body in the form of a tube, *bronchial tubes*; (colloq.) underground railway system in London
tuber n. (*tū'ber*) (bot.) Enlarged underground stem of a plant, such as the potato, containing buds
tuck v.t. and i., and n. (*tuk*) To draw together compactly, put or push away or under, *tuck a blouse into a skirt*
tug v.t. and i., and n. (*tug*) To pull suddenly and violently; pull hard (at). As n. act of tugging, a sudden hard pull; small powerful vessel used to tow larger ships or barges
tuition n. (*tū ish'un*) Teaching, instruction; what is taught
tumble v.t. and i., and n. (*tum'bl*) To stumble and fall; upset, overturn; disorder, rumple; turn somersaults; roll about; move hastily
tumbler n. (*tumb'ler*) Person or thing that tumbles; acrobatic clown; flat-bottomed drinking glass
tumour n. (*tū'mer*) Bodily swelling due to abnormal cell growth
tumult n. (*tū'mult*) Violent

confused uproar; public commotion

tune n., and v.t. and i. (*tūn*) Melody, air; correctness of pitch, *the piano is out of tune*; (fig.) agreement, harmonious relation, *the house is in tune with its surroundings*

tunic n. (*tūn'ik*) Loose, short-sleeved garment reaching to knees; close-fitting coat of soldier's, policeman's, etc. uniform

tunnel n., and v.t. and i. (*tun'el*) Underground passage esp. if artificially dug under hill, river, etc. for road or railway

turban n. (*tur'ban*) Eastern head-dress consisting of long strip of fabric wound round head

turbulent adj. (*tur'bū lent*) Unruly, tumultuous, violently agitated

tureen n. (*tū rēn'*) Deep covered dish for serving soup

turf n. and v.t. (*turf*) Soil-surface with grass roots growing in it

turkey n. (*turk'i*) Large bird of genus *Meleagris*, said to have origin in Turkey, and traditionally eaten on Christmas and Thanksgiving Days

turmoil n. (*tur'moil*) Tumultuous confusion, noisy agitation

turn v.t. and i. (*turn*) To cause to change direction, *turn your head the other way*; change direction, *turn right at the crossroads*; spin round, revolve, *he turned the key in the lock*; reverse, make to face in opposite direction; change, transform; become, be transformed, *his luck has turned*; shape on a lathe; translate; (of food) go bad, become sour; direct eyes or attention to; sicken, shock, *the sight of blood turns my stomach*; (milit.) get behind (enemy's line of battle); to have reached and passed specific time, *it has just turned seven o'clock, he has turned forty*

turnip n. (*turn'ip*) Plant of mustard family with fleshy roots used as vegetable and for feeding cattle

turpentine n. (*tur'pen tīn*) Oily secretion of pine trees; liquid used as solvent in mixing paints etc

turret n. (*tu'ret*) Small tower

tusk n. (*tusk*) Long tooth projecting from closed mouth as in elephant, walrus, etc

tussle n. and v.i. (*tu'sl*) Rough struggle, scuffle. As v.i. to struggle, wrestle

tutor n., and v.t. and i. (*tūt'er*) Private teacher; university teacher who directs studies of students

tweed n. (*twēd*) Rough woollen cloth woven from different coloured yarns

tweezers n. (*twe'zerz*) (pl.) Small pair of tongs for picking up delicate objects, plucking hair, etc

twig n. (*twig*) Small branch of tree

twilight n. (*twī'līt*) Half-light immediately before dawn or after sunset

twin adj. and n. (*twin*) Being one of two born at same birth

twine n., and v.t. and i. (*twīn*) Strong cord made of twisted strands of hemp etc. As v.t. and i. to twist together; to wind around; to interweave

twinge v.t. and i., and n. (*twinj*) To experience or affect with sudden, sharp spasm of pain. As n. such a pain

twinkle v.t. and i., and n. (*twin'kl*) To emit intermittent winking light; to glitter; to move rapidly to and fro; (of eyes) to sparkle, to show amusement

twirl v.t. and i., and n. (*twurl*) To revolve or cause to revolve quickly; to spin, to whirl. As n. circular motion

twist v.t. and i., and n. (*twist*) To plait together; to turn, bend, divert out of normal position, to distort (lit. and fig.), *I have twisted my ankle, he always twists my words*; to writhe; to render abnormal in outlook, emotions, etc.; (colloq.) to dance the twist; (slang) to swindle. As n. act of twisting; condition of being twisted, *full of twists and turns*; bend, kink; spinning motion; something twisted together; lump of coarse tobacco; modern dance

twitch v.t. and i., and n. (*twitch*) To jerk with sudden nervous movement; to move or contract muscle (esp. facial muscle) spasmodically. As n. sudden, uncontrollable muscular movement; sudden pull or jerk

twitter v.i. and n. (*twit'er*) (of birds) To chirp; (of humans) to chatter excitedly. As n. chirping or chattering sound; excited state

tycoon n. (*tī ko͞on'*) (colloq.) powerful businessman

type n., and v.t. and i. (*tīp*) Kind, variety, general class of a thing; representative member of class or group sharing certain characteristics; model, example, symbol

typhoon n. (*tī fo͞on'*) Violent cyclonic storm, hurricane

typical adj. (*tip'ik al*) True to type; wholly representative of its kind.
tyrant n. (*tī'rant*) Absolute ruler who maintains power by terrorism; harsh, oppressive. despotic ruler, master, etc.
tyre n. (*tīr*) Thick rubber band, either solid or filled with compressed air, encasing rim of wheel on motor vehicles etc., iron hoop encircling wooden wheel.

U

ugly adj. (*ug'li*) Repulsive, hideous; threatening, menacing, *an ugly situation*
ukelele n. (*ū ke lā'li*) Hawaiian musical stringed instrument like a guitar.
ulcer n. (*ul'ser*) An open sore discharging pus.
ultimate adj. (*ul'ti mat*) Last, furthest, *man's ultimate destiny*
ultimatum n. (*ul ti mā'tum*) Final statement of intentions or conditions, esp. when sent by one government to another and accompanied by a threat of force if the terms are rejected.
ultra- pref. (*ul'tra*) To an extreme
ultraviolet adj. (*ul tra vī'ō let*) (phys.) Of the electromagnetic waves at the limit of visibility at the violet end of the spectrum.
umbrella n. (*um brel'a*) Folding domed framework of ribs covered with nylon, silk etc., with a stick and handle, carried above the head for protection against rain
umpire n., and v.t. and i. (*um'pir*) Arbitrator, esp. one chosen to enforce the rules in a game and make necessary decisions
umpteen n. (*ump tēn'*) (slang) An indefinite large number
un- 1) pref. (*un*) Used to express negation before adjectives, adverbs, and nouns, *untidy, untidily, untidiness*
un- 2) pref. (*un*) Used before verbs to express reversal of the action, *undo*; separation, removal, *undress*
unanimous adj. (*ū năn'i mus*) (of persons) Agreeing in opinion; (of opinion etc.) held, agreed to, by all, *a unanimous vote of thanks.*
uncanny adj. (*un kăn'i*) Weird, mysterious.
uncle n. (*ungkl*) Brother of one's father or mother; husband of one's aunt
unconscious adj. and n. (*un kon'shus*) Not aware or knowing, *unconscious of danger*; not conscious, senseless, *to be unconscious after an accident*; involuntary, unintentional, *unconscious humour*; (of psychological processes) that cannot be made known to the conscious mind by direct effort of the will. As n., **the unconscious** (psych.). unconscious processes of the mind

ukelele

under prep., adj., and adv. (*un'der*) Below; in, at, to, a lower place or position than, *the stool is under the table*; in and covered by, *under the water*; beneath the surface of, *under the skin*; weighed down by, also fig., *to sink under a load of sorrow*; less in age, position, time, amount etc. than, *under three years of age*; indicating various conditions or states, esp. in course of, *under repair*; undergoing, *under torture*; controlled or governed by, *France under Napoleon*; implying obligation, *under contract*; indicating cover, disguise etc., *under a false name*; in the time of, *under British rule*
under-tenant. As adv. in a lower, inferior position, *to keep someone under*
under- pref. (*un'der*) Beneath, below, *underwear*; from beneath, *undermine*; inferior, subsidiary, *underling*; insufficient, not as much as necessary, *understaffed*.
undercover adj. (*un'der ku ver*) Secret, *undercover agent*
undercurrent n. (*un'der ku rent*) Current of water flowing beneath the surface; (fig.) tendency (of opinion, feeling etc.) not apparent on the surface, *an undercurrent of*

fear amid the rejoicings
undergo v.t. (*un der gō'*) ; pret. **underwent** (*un der went'*) ; p.p. **undergone** (*un der gon'*) To suffer, endure
undergraduate n. (*un der grăj' o͞o at*) University student who has not yet taken a degree
underground adv., adj. and n. (*un'der grownd*) Under the ground ; (fig.) secretly, surreptitiously, *an anti-government newspaper was produced underground*. As adj. beneath the surface of the ground, *an underground railway* ; (fig.) secret, esp. of forces opposing a government, *underground workers*. As n. underground railway
undergrowth n. (*un'der grōth*) Shrubs and small trees in a wood
underhand adv. and adj. (*un'der hănd*) (cricket etc.) With arm kept below the shoulder, *to bowl underhand* ; (fig.) secretly, deceitfully. As adj. (cricket etc.) delivered with the arm kept below the shoulder ; (fig.) secret, deceitful
undermine v.t. (*un der mīn'*) To dig away the ground underneath, weaken at the base, *a sea-wall undermined by the sea* ; to weaken, esp. secretly, *undermine someone's influence*
underneath adv. and prep. (*un der nēth'*) Beneath, below, in a lower place, *the river flows underneath*. As prep. under, below, *to crawl underneath a fence*
underpass n. (*un'der pahs*) Road or path that passes underneath another, to avoid crossing at the same level
underrate v.t. (*un der rāt'*) To estimate or value too low
undersell v.t. (*un der sel'*) To sell goods etc. at a lower price than (others)
understand v.t. and i. (*un der stănd'*) To perceive, comprehend, the meaning of, *can you understand what the lecturer means ?* ; to be able to interpret, *do you understand French ?* ; to grasp, take in, the idea of, *understand higher mathematics* ; to be informed of, *I understand from Mr Smith that all is well* ; to infer, assume, *do I understand that you refuse ?* ; to supply mentally something not expressed, *in 'he is fatter than I', the word 'am' is understood* ; to have understanding ; to be informed
understock v.t. (*un der stok'*) To have less stock than is desirable.
understudy n. and v.t. (*un'der stu di*) One who studies an actor's part so as to be able to play it in his absence ; a substitute
undertake v.t. (*un der tāk'*) ; pret. **undertook** (*un der to͝ok'*) ; p.p. **undertaken** (*un der ta'ken*) To take upon oneself, agree to do, *undertake a task* ; start, engage in, *undertake a journey* ; promise, affirm, *undertake that something is so*. Hence : **undertaking** n. what is undertaken, a task ; promise, obligation
undertaker n. (*un'der tā'ker*) One whose business is to undertake all duties connected with the burial of the dead
underwear n. (*un'der wār*) Underclothes
undo v.t. (*un do͞o'*) pret. **undid** (*un did'*) p.p. **undone** (*un dun'*) To untie, unfasten, *undo a button* ; annul, reverse what has been done, *undo the mischief one has done to others* ; (archaic) bring to ruin, ruin the fortunes, character of, *his carelessness will undo him one day*. Hence : **undoing** n. reversal of the past ; bringing to ruin ; cause of ruin, *drink was his undoing* ; **undone** adj. unfastened ; brought to ruin or misery
undulate v.i. (*un'dū lāt*) To be shaped in a series of alternate ridges and furrows, slight hills and valleys, *the land undulates to the horizon* ; to rise and fall in this way, *undulating waves*
undying adj. (*un dī'ing*) Everlasting, never-ending, *undying fame*
unearth v.t. (*un urth'*) To dig from the earth, *the dog unearthed a bone* ; (fig.) to discover, bring to light, by careful search, *unearth new facts about something*
unearthly adj. (*un urth'li*) Not of this world, supernatural, *an unearthly beauty* ; mysterious, frightening, *unearthly screams* ; (colloq.) unreasonable, *why are you still up at this unearthly hour ?*
uneasy adj. (*un ē'zi*) Uncomfortable in body or mind, *uneasy about the future* ; arising from, causing, uneasiness of mind, *uneasy dreams* ; showing lack of ease, *an uneasy manner*
unemployed adj. and n. (*un em ploid'*) Not being used, *unemployed capital* ; not occupied, not busy ; without a job. As n. **the unemployed** aggregate of persons out of work at any given time
unemployment n. (*un em ploi'-*

unicorn

ment) State of being out of work; number of workers out of work in a specific district or period, *statistics of unemployment*
unicorn n. (*ū'ni kawn*) Legendary animal, having the body and head of a horse, a lion's or horse's tail, and a single twisted horn in its brow
uniform adj. and n. (*ū'ni fawm*) Having the same shape, form etc., *coats of uniform size*; constant, unvarying, *maintain a uniform temperature*. As n. regulation form of dress worn as official and distinguishing costume, *school uniform*
unify v.t. (*ū'ni fi*) To form into one, reduce to unity; make uniform
unilateral adj. (*u ni lăt'e ral*) Of, on, affecting, done by, one side only, *unilateral disarmament*
union n. (*ū'ni on*) Uniting or being united; unit or unity resulting from this, esp. an association formed by the uniting of persons, groups etc.; a trade union act of joining in marriage; marriage, the married state; device for connecting together two pipes or rods
unique adj. (*ū nēk'*) Alone in kind or excellence; unequalled; unmatched, *a unique event*; (colloq.) remarkable, *to dress in a unique fashion*
unison n. (*ū'ni zon*) Harmony, agreement, in sound, esp. (mus.)
unit n. (*ū'nit*) A single object or person; group of objects or persons forming an entity or a convenient subdivision, *the borough is a unit of local government*; the numeral one; quantity or amount used as a standard of measurement, *the yard is a unit of length*
unite v.t. and i. (*ū nit'*) To form into a single whole, bring into union, join, *unite one country to another*; to join by or in marriage; to become a whole, become associated, act as one, *let us unite in resisting tyranny*
unity n. (*ū'ni ti*) State of being a unit or being united; agreement of aims, interests etc., *family unity*
universal adj. (*ū ni vur'sal*) Of the universe; affecting, done by, used by, held by, all, *a universal belief*
universe n. (*ū'ni vurs*) The whole system of suns, planets etc., existing in space; the whole of creation; (colloq.) the earth.
university n. (*ū ni vur'si ti*) Institution consisting of one or more colleges, where students are educated in the higher branches of learning, degrees are conferred, and research is carried out
unless conj. (*un les'*) If not, supposing that, except that, *I shall come unless it rains*
until prep. and conj. (*un til'*) Till, up to the time of, *wait until ten o'clock*. As conj. up to the time of, *wait until I arrive*
unusual adj. (*un ū'zhū al*) Rare, exceptional; unfamiliar, strange. Hence: **unusually** adv. in an unusual manner; (colloq.) extremely, *an unusually hot day*
up 1) adv. (*up*) Expressing transition to, or existence on, a higher level, *to go up to the top of a hill*; to or in a more important centre or the north of the country, *to travel up to Glasgow*; expressing change from inferior to superior or more highly developed physical, moral or social state, *to bring up a child*; expressing increase in intensity (also of feeling or mental activity), loudness, etc., *to speak up*; expressing increase in value, moral estimate, etc., *to go up in someone's opinion*; expressing coming into consideration, *it came up in conversation*; with verbs expressing finality, completeness, *to dry up*; expressing condition of being laid aside, out of use, inactive, *to put up one's sword*; after certain verbs of movement, *to pull up*; **up to** occupied with, *what are you up to?*; equal to, *he is not up to his brother's standard*; abreast of, *to catch up to (with) someone*

up 2) prep. (*up*) Expressing movement towards or existence at a higher level, *to go up a ladder*; expressing increase in importance, power etc., *to work one's way up a firm*; along the course of, esp. against the current, *to row up the stream*; along a road in a given direction from a particular spot, *walk up the road*; away from the sea, *to travel up (the) country*
uphold v.t. (*up hōld'*) To hold up, support; give moral support to, approve, *I cannot uphold his conduct*; to confirm, *uphold a ruling*
upholster v.t. (*up hōl'ster*) To furnish with carpets, curtains, furniture etc.; to stuff or cover (a chair etc.). Hence: **upholsterer** n. one whose trade is to upholster; **upholstery** n. materials used in upholstering; household furniture; trade of an upholsterer
upkeep n. (*up'kēp*) Maintenance; cost of maintenance
upon prep. (*u pon'*) On; upon is (preferred to *on* in certain usages), *once upon a time*
upper adj. and n. (*up'er*) Higher in physical or social position, dignity etc. As n. (usually pl.) part of shoe or boot above the sole Hence: **uppermost** adj. and adv. in the highest position, at the top
upright adj. and n. (*up'rit*) Erect; vertical; (fig.) honest, honourable; straightforward, *an upright businessman* As n. vertical support in any structure
uprising n. (*up'ri zing*) Rebellion, revolt
uproar n. (*up'raw(r)*) Great clamour, tumult, noisy disturbance
uproot v.t. (*up rōōt'*) To pull up by the roots; (fig.) eradicate, *uproot old customs*; remove from natural abode, *uproot someone from his homeland*
upset v.t. and i. and n. (*up set'*) To overturn, capsize, *upset a boat*; disturb, *upset someone's arrangements*; distress, make ill, *the sight of blood upsets me*; to be overturned. As n. (*up'set*) a fall, overturning; disturbance; state of disorder; a quarrel
upside-down adv. (*up sīd down'*) With the upper side below, *turn a chair upside-down*; in confusion, *the room was all upside-down*
upstairs adj., adv., and n. (*up stārz'*) To be on an upper storey, *an upstairs room*. As adv. towards, in, an upper storey, *to go upstairs*. As n. the upper rooms of a house
upstream adv. (*up strēm'*) Towards the source; moving against the stream or current
up-to-date adj. (*up tōō dāt'*) Of the present time; modern.
upward adj. (*up'ward*) Turned, moving, towards a higher position, *an upward glance*
urban adj. (*ur'ban*) Of or in a city or town, *urban population*
urbane adj. (*ur bān'*) Polished, refined, affable
urchin n. (*ur'chin*) mischievous, troublesome small boy
urge v.t. and n. (*urj*) To drive, push forward, *urge a horse on*; exhort, persuade, *urge someone to do something*; press, bring insistently to the attention, *urge upon someone the importance of a measure*. As n. powerful impulse, strong desire
urgent adj. (*ur'gent*) Important, needing prompt decision or action, *urgent necessity*; (of a person) demanding persistently, *an urgent suitor*; (of requests etc.) made insistently, *urgent enquiries*. Hence: **urgently** adv.; **urgency** n. stress, necessity; need for prompt action, *a matter of great urgency*; insistence
urine n. (*ū'rēn*) Liquid excrement secreted by the kidneys, passed into the bladder, and discharged
urn n. (*urn*) Vase of pottery or metal, usually with foot or pedestal and having a narrow neck, esp. as used for holding the ashes of the dead; large metal container with lid and tap, in which tea, coffee etc., may be kept hot
use 1) n. (*ūs*) Act of using; right or capacity to use, *lose the use of one's eyes*; opportunity, reason, for using or doing, *to find a use for left-overs*; usefulness, purpose served, *to be of use*
use 2) v.t. and i. (*ūz*) To employ for a purpose, *use a hammer*; put to use, put into operation, *use one's brain*; to consume, *use a ton of coal each winter*; to treat, handle, in a certain way, *use someone well*; have the use of, *may I use your telephone?*
used adj. (*ūzd*) Accustomed to; experienced in, *used to hard work*
usher n. and v.t. (*u'sher*) Official at a meeting etc. who admits people, shows them to their seats, keeps order etc. As v.t. to act as usher; show in, announce
usual adj. (*ū'zhōō al*) Customary, normal, frequently done or met

with, *all the usual people were there*; as **usual** in the ordinary way. Hence: **usually** adv. in the ordinary way.
usurp v.t. (*ū zurp'*) To take wrongful possession of.
utensil n. (*ū ten'sil*) Any tool or implement used for a specific purpose, esp. for domestic purposes, *kitchen utensils*.
utility n. (*ū til'i ti*) Quality of being useful.
utilize v.t. (*ū'til iz*) To put to use, find a use for.
utmost adj. and n. (*ut'mōst*) Outermost, farthest, *utmost limits*; to the greatest degree, *the utmost danger*. As n. the most or greatest possible, *do your utmost to succeed*.
utter 1) adj. (*u'ter*) Absolute, total, *utter ruin*; unconditional, *an utter denial*.
utter 2) v.t. (*u'ter*) To pronounce, produce audibly by the vocal organs, *not a sound was uttered*; put into circulation, *utter false coinage*.

V

vacancy n. (*vā'kan si*) State, condition, of being vacant.
vacant adj. (*vā'kant*) Empty, void, *vacant space*; uninhabited or untenanted, *a vacant house*; not booked, engaged, or occupied, *a vacant seat*; (of time) not filled with work or business, leisured; (of the mind) not active, idle.
vacate v.t. (*va kāt'*) To make vacant, leave unoccupied; go away from (a place or position).
vacation n. (*va kā'shun*) Act of vacating; fixed period in a year when work is suspended.
vaccinate v.t. (*văk'si nāt*) To inoculate with vaccine.
vaccine n. (*văk'sēn*) A preparation of any virus or micro-organism for introduction into the body for protection against infection by the same type of micro-organism(s).
vacuum n. (*văk'yōō um*) Space containing no matter or content, esp. one from which air has been removed; **vacuum-cleaner** apparatus used for removing dust etc. by suction; **vacuum-flask** double-walled vessel with a vacuum between the two walls, keeping the contents at a constant temperature.
vagabond adj. and n. (*văg'a bond*) Wandering, roaming, *a vagabond singer*. As n. a person of no fixed living-place; tramp; worthless fellow.

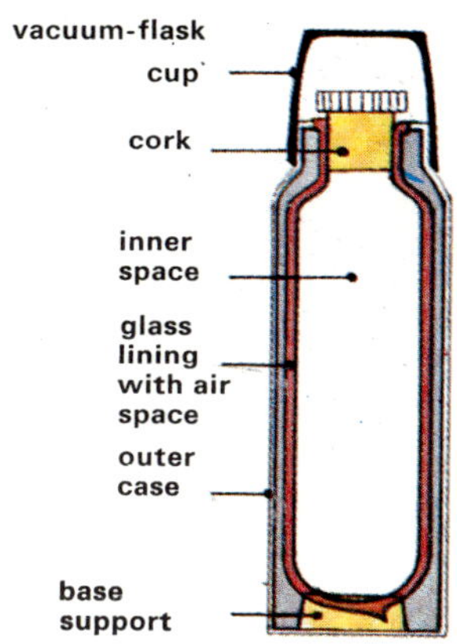

vague adj. (*vāg*) Undefined, not distinct, uncertain, *a vague outline*; not clearly expressed, *a vague statement*; (of persons, behaviour) uncertain, ambiguous, *he is vague as to what he wants*.
vain adj. (*vān*) Useless, without result or meaning, futile, baseless, *vain efforts*; conceited, *a vain man*.
vale n. (*vāl*) Valley.
valentine n. (*văl'en tin*) Card, letter, with messages of love, sent on St. Valentine's Day, Feb. 14th.
valet n. and v.t. (*văl'et, văl'ā*) Male personal servant.
valiant adj. (*văl'iant*) Brave.
valid adj. (*văl'id*) Sound in law, *a valid contract*; soundly based, *valid arguments*.
valley n. (*văl'i*) Tract of land between mountains or hills, often with river or lake; flat basin drained by river-system.
valuable adj. and n. (*văl'ū a bl*) Being of value, having material worth, *valuable pictures*; highly useful, *valuable information*. As n. (usually pl.) objects of value, *jewels and other valuables*.
valuation n. (*văl ū ā'shun*) Act of deciding or estimating the value of anything, *valuation of property*; value or price so estimated, *the two valuations differed*.
value n. and v.t. (*văl'ū*) Worth, quality of being useful or desirable, *the value of fresh air*; worth of anything when compared with other things, *this book will be of little value to you*; worth

estimated in terms of something for which it can be exchanged, esp. money, *property is increasing rapidly in value*; precise meaning, force, *the value of a word in a sentence*; (pl.) relative ethical standards, *moral values*. As v.t. to estimate the value of; attach a high degree of value to, *I value his friendship*

valve n. (*vălv*) Mechanical device to control the passage of air, liquid, gas etc. into or through a tube, pipe etc

vandal n. (*văn'dal*) One who spoils or destroys things, esp. things of beauty. Hence: **vandalism** n

vanish v.i. (*văn'ish*) To disappear suddenly and completely

vapour n. (*vā'per*) Substance in gaseous state

variation n. (*vār i ā'shun*) Varying from the normal, standard etc.; degree of change, *slight variation in temperature*; (mus.) development and elaboration of a theme

varied adj. (*var'id*) Having variety; changing from time to time, *a varied life*

variegated adj. (*vār'i e gā ted*) Diversified, esp. in colour

variety n. (*va rī'e ti*) Quality of being various, diversity; number of various things, *a variety of reasons*; different form or kind, a sort; form of entertainment in theatre or music-hall consisting of various short turns

varnish n. and v.t. (*vah'nish*) Solution of resin or resinous gum in spirits or oil used to give a protective gloss to a surface

vary v.i. and t. (*vār'i*) To change, alter, modify, diversify; become different in condition or quality

vase n. (*vahz*) Vessel of glass, pottery etc. for holding cut flowers or as ornament

vast adj. (*vahst*) Of great size, enormous

vat n. (*văt*) Large tub or storage vessel for liquids

vault 1) n. and v.t. (*vawlt*) Arched roof or ceiling; vaulted room, esp. underground, *wine vaults*; strongly guarded room in which safes are kept, *safety vault*; repository for the dead, *a family vault*

vault 2) v.i. and t., and n. (*vawlt*) To leap, spring by using one hand and arm as support, or with the help of a pole; **vaulting-horse** apparatus used in a gymnasium for practice in vaulting

veal n. (*vēl*) Flesh of a calf prepared for eating

veer v.i. (*vēr*) To shift in position or direction; (fig.) to change in feelings, opinion etc

vegetable adj. and n. (*vej'e tabl*) Of, from, affecting, composed of, plants or plant life. As n. any form of plant life, esp. edible leaves, stalks, roots etc. of plants cultivated for human food, *green vegetables*

vegetarian n. and adj. (*vej e tār'i an*) One who lives on a vegetable diet or diet excluding flesh. As adj

vegetate v.i. (*vej'e tāt*) To pass a passive existence like a plant

vegetation n. (*vej e tā'shun*) Vegetable growth; process of vegetating; the whole of the plants in a given area

vehicle n. (*vē'ikl*) Any conveyance on wheels for transport of persons or goods, *motor vehicle*; means or medium of communication or transmission, *he used his art as a propaganda vehicle*

veil n. and v.t. (*vāl*) Covering of net or fine material worn over face or head by women, esp. for protection, concealment, or fashion; (fig.) what obscures, *a veil of mystery*; **take the veil** become a nun. As v.t. to put a veil over; (fig.) conceal

vein n. (*vān*) One of the tubular vessels by which blood passes back to the heart and lungs; coloured streak or mark in stone, wood, etc

velocity n. (*ve los'i ti*) Rate of motion; speed, swiftness

velvet n. and adj. (*vel'vet*) A textile, wholly or partly of silk, with thick, soft nap on one side; any soft surface resembling velvet

veneer n. and v.t. (*ve nēr'*) Thin layer of wood, marble, ivory etc. glued as a surface over another material or material of inferior quality; (fig.) surface appearance (of politeness etc.) assumed to cover the true nature

venerable adj. (*ven'e rabl*) Worthy of respect, reverence or honour

vengeance n. (*ven'jans*) Exaction of retribution for having been wronged

vengeful adj. (*venj'fool*) Vindictive, revengeful

venison n. (*ven'i zon*) Flesh of deer, as food

ventilate v.t. (*ven'til āt*) To cause fresh air to circulate freely in (room or building etc.); (fig.) allow,

cause, to be freely discussed, *ventilate a grievance*
ventriloquism n. (*ven tril'ō kwism*) Art of modifying the voice so that the sound appears to come from a person or place at a distance from the speaker. Hence: **ventriloquist** n. person skilled in ventriloquism
venture n., and v.t. and i. (*ven'cher*) Undertaking of a hazardous nature. As v.t. and i. to risk, expose to risk, take the risk of, dare to go
veranda(h) n. (*ve răn'da*) Covered space built along the side(s) of a house to which it gives access
verb n. (*vurb*) Part of speech that expresses existence or action
verdict n. (*vur'dikt*) (law) Jury's decision in a tried cause; a judgment, decision, opinion
verge 1) n. (*vurj*) margin, edge, border, *the verge of a cliff*; **on the verge of** bordering on
verge 2) v.i. (*vurj*) To incline in a certain direction, *the car verged toward the centre*; (fig.) border on, *a remark verging on rudeness*
verger n. (*vur'jer*) a church official
verify v.t. (*ve'ri fi*) To show to be true, confirm, prove authentic
vermin n. (*vur'min*) Troublesome animals and obnoxious insects
versatile adj. (*vur'sa tīl*) Many-sided, talented in and adaptable to many subjects
verse n. (*vurs*) a set of lines of words so arranged and forming a poetic unity with definite structure
version n. (*vur'shun*) Translation or rendering, *the Authorized Version of the Bible*; account of something from a personal point of view, *his version of the incident differed from yours*
vertebra n. (*vur'te bra*) pl. **vertebrae** (anat.) Small bone or cartilage surrounding spinal cord. Hence: **vertebral column** the backbone; **vertebrate** adj. and n. (*vur'te brāt*) having a spinal column; belonging to the Vertebrata (Craniata), animals having a skull and skeleton of bone or cartilage; as n. a vertebrate animal
vertical adj. (*vur'ti kal*) upright, at right-angles to the plane of the ground, *a vertical wall*
vertigo n. (*vur'ti gō*) Giddiness, faintness, esp. when due to disturbance of balance etc.
very adj. and adv. (*ve'ri*) Truly and really, *in very truth*; used intensively or emphatically, *under my very eyes*. As adv. in a high degree, to a great extent, *very large*; absolutely, *the very same words*
vessel n. (*ves'el*) A hollow container, esp. for a liquid; a ship
vest n. (*vest*) Undergarment worn on the upper part of the body next to the skin
vestibule n. (*ves'ti būl*) Lobby, entrance-hall
vestige n. (*ves'tij*) Trace, sign left by something destroyed or vanished
veteran n. (*vet'e ran*) One old and experienced in a service, esp. in the armed forces; (attrib.) old and experienced, *a veteran campaigner*; (U.S.) any ex-serviceman
veterinary adj. (*vet e rin'a ri*) Of or concerned with the diseases of animals, esp. domestic animals, *a veterinary surgeon*
veto n. and v.t. (*vē'tō*) Prohibition, refusal to allow something to be said, done etc.; constitutional right so to prohibit. As v.t. to prohibit absolutely
vex v.t. (*veks*) To irritate, annoy, render mildly angry
via prep. (*vi'a*) By way of. (Lat., 'by the road')
viable adj. (*vi'abl*) capable of producing useful results, workable, *is that a viable alternative?*
viaduct n. (*vi'a dukt*) Bridge in the form of a series of arches

viaduct

carrying a road or railway or canal across a valley or ravine
vibrate v.i. and t. (*vī brāt'*) To quiver rapidly; swing backwards and forwards between two points; cause to vibrate
vice 1) n. (*vīs*) Moral weakness; immoral conduct, depravity; (in a horse) bad habit such as rearing
vice 2) n. (*vīs*) Device for gripping an object between two parts worked by a screw and holding it in a given position
vice- pref. (*vīs*) Acting as deputy for another or on behalf of another holding rank next below, *vice-admiral*
vicinity n. (*vi sin'i ti*) Nearness; neighbouring area
vicious adj. (*vish'us*) Practising, tending to, relating to, vice; malevolent, *a vicious look*; (of a horse) having bad habits
victim n. (*vik'tim*) Living creature offered as sacrifice to a god; person or animal who suffers from the ill-will of another, from his own defects, or from external circumstances, *a victim of poverty*
victor n. (*vik'tor*) One who wins or conquers
victory n. (*vik'to ri*) Success or conquest in battle or other contest or struggle; act of winning
view n. and v.t. (*vū*) Act of seeing; what is seen; range of vision; stretch of natural scenery; photograph, painting etc. representing this; mental estimate, *a clear view of a situation*; opinion, *to hold extreme views*; plan, purpose, intention, *to fall in with someone's views* As v.t. to look at, examine; consider, contemplate
vigil n. (*vij'il*) State of being awake, action of watching
vigilant adj. (*vij'i lant*) Watchful, alert, on guard against possible danger
vigour n. (*vig'or*) Mental or physical strength; energy, vitality
viking n. (*vī'king*) A Norse pirate
vile adj. (*vīl*) Base, depraved; (colloq.) of bad quality, atrocious, *vile weather*
villa n. (*vil'a*) Large house in its own grounds, (colloq.) detached suburban house with some ground
village n. (*vil'ij*) Small community in a rural district, larger than a hamlet and smaller than a town
villain n. (*vil'an*) A scoundrel, wicked person
vindictive adj. (*vin dik'tiv*) Revengeful
vine n. (*vīn*) The plant *Vitis*, esp. species *Vitis vinifera*, which bears grapes
vinegar n. (*vin'e gar*) Acid liquid
vintage n. and adj. (*vin'tij*) Grape-gathering; period in a season when this takes place
violate v.t. (*vī'ō lāt*) To treat with violence
violent adj. (*vī'ō lent*) Using, showing, great force or strength
violin n. (*vī ō lin'*) Stringed musical instrument of the viola family, played with a bow
violoncello n. (*vē ō lon chel'ō*) Bass viol, large instrument held between the player's knees (usually abbreviated to 'cello)
virile adj. (*vi'rīl*) Having, showing masculine characteristics
virtual adj. (*vur'chōō al*) For all intents and purposes, *he is the virtual head of the firm*
virtue n. (*vur'chōō*) Good quality, esp. moral
visa n. (*vē'za*) Endorsement on a passport permitting the holder to enter another state
visible adj. (*viz'ibl*) Able to be seen; in sight
vision n. (*vi'zhun*) Faculty of seeing; seeing, act of sight; imaginative perception, intuition, *the vision of a poet*; something seen; something visualized imaginatively or by supernatural means, *he saw a vision of the saint*
visit v.t. and i. (*viz'it*) To go to see a place or person, *visit a friend*; to inspect, *the doctor visits his patients*; to attack, *famine visited the land*
visual adj. (*vizh'ū al*) Relating to the sight
vital adj. (*vītal*) Having, relating to, life; full of vitality; essential, important, *vital to one's purpose*
vitamin n. (*vi'ta min*) Organic substance essential to metabolism that must come from outside in food
vivid adj. (*vi'vid*) Lively, vigorous, *a vivid imagination*; intense, bright, *vivid colouring*; clear and distinct, *a vivid description*
vocabulary n. (*vō kăb'ū la ri*) Range of words used by a speaker, author etc.; list of words used in a book etc., with translations or explanations of meaning
vocation n. (*vō kā'shun*) A calling, profession; talent for a particular calling, *to have a vocation for the law*
vodka n. (*vod'ka*) Spirituous drink

vocal chords

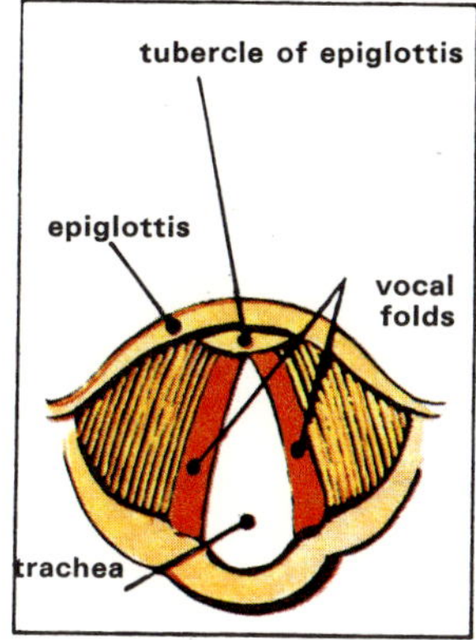

distilled from rye or potatoes, and drunk esp. in Russia.
vogue n. (*vōg*) Prevailing fashion
voice n. and v.t. (*vois*) Sound made by means of the mouth and human larynx; such sounds considered in relation to their quality etc., *a loud voice*; faculty of using the voice, *to lose one's voice*; (phon.) sound made by breath acting upon the organs of speech; anything resembling the human voice as a means of expressing ideas etc., *the voice of conscience*; opinion, wish, esp. in **have a voice in** have the right to express an opinion or influence a decision. As v.t. to express, *voice one's feelings*; (phon.) utter (sound, speech) with vibrations of the vocal chords.
void adj., n., and v.t. (*void*) Empty, vacant
empty space; a sense of loss, *his death left a void in our lives*.
volcano n. (*vol kā'nō*)
pl, **volcanoes** Hill or mountain composed wholly or largely of discharged matter, with a funnel or fissures to the depths of the earth through which ashes, lava, and gases are periodically or continuously ejected when the volcano is active
vole n. (*vōl*) Rodent of genus *Microtus*, resembling a rat
volley n., and v.t. and i. (*vol'i*) Discharge of a number of missiles more or less simultaneously; (tennis) hitting the ball before it touches the ground; (fig.) rapid succession of oaths, questions, etc. As v.t. and i. to discharge (as) a volley; (tennis) hit before ball touches ground.
volt n. (*vōlt*) Practical unit of electromotive force. Hence:
voltage n. electromotive force expressed in volts
volume n. (*vol'ūm*) A book, esp. one of a number completing a whole work; number of sheets, papers, periodicals bound together; a considerable amount, *a volume of smoke*; mass, solid content; space occupied by gas, liquid etc., measured in cubic units; (of sound) loudness
voluntary adj. and n. (*vol'un ta ri*) Acting willingly and freely, without being compelled
volunteer 1) (*vol un tēr'*) One who voluntarily offers to serve in any capacity, esp. military
volunteer 2) v.t. and i. (*vol un tēr'*) To offer freely and voluntarily; to offer oneself as a volunteer
vomit v.t. and i., and n. (*vom'it*) To bring back from the stomach through the mouth, to be sick; to discharge in large quantities, *that chimney vomits smoke*
vote n., and v.i. and t. (*vōt*) Expression of choice, opinion etc. concerning a resolution, motion, or choice of representative, by means of ballot, show of hands, etc.; choice thus expressed; the right to vote. As v.i. and t. to give a vote; establish, elect, defeat, by means of a vote, *vote someone into Parliament*
vouch v.i. (*vowch*) Chiefly in **to vouch for** to guarantee; confirm, *I can vouch for it that he will be ready*.
thing that vouches, esp. a document establishing that money has been paid; **meal voucher** ticket showing that payment for a meal has been made in advance
vow n. and v.t. (*vow*) Solemn promise or undertaking, usually made in the name of a god, *marriage vows*. As v.t. to make a vow, promise under oath to do, make, or give
vowel n. (*vow'el*) (phon.) Speech sound made without audible stoppage of the breath; letter, character, representing this: *a, e, i, o, u*.
voyage n. and v.i. (*voi'ij*) Journey by water, esp. a long sea journey.
vulnerable adj. (*vul'ne rabl*) Liable to be wounded, open to attack, criticism, *to be vulnerable to ridicule*.

vulture n. (*vul'cher*) Large bird of prey allied to hawks and eagles

W

wad n. and v.t. (*wod*) Lump of soft material for keeping things apart or in place, or used to stop up an opening thick pile of bank-notes
wade v.i. and t. and n. (*wād*) To walk through water, wet snow, or other substance that makes progress difficult
Hence: **wader** n. wading bird; (pl.) long waterproof garments covering feet and legs and coming up to the waist, used by anglers when wading, etc
wafer n. (*wā'fer*) Very thin flat biscuit, esp. one eaten with ices
waffle n. (*wofl*) Thin batter cake baked in an iron mould
waft v.t. and i., and n. (*woft*) To carry lightly and smoothly along, *a leaf wafted by the breeze*; drift, float, in the air. As n. act of wafting; breath of air, faint odour; smoothfloatingmovement
wag 1) v.t. and i. and n. (*wăg*) To move or cause to move up and down or to and fro with one end fixed, *his tail wagged furiously*
wag 2) n. (*wăg*) A humorist, a merry person full of laughable sayings
wage 1) n. (*wāj*) (Often pl.) payment for work
wage 2) v.t. (*wāj*) To undertake, carry on, *wage war*
wag(g)on n. (*wăg'on*) Strong, four-wheeled vehicle used for carrying heavy loads, usually pulled by horses; railway truck
waif n. (*wāf*) Homeless and destitute person, esp. a child
wail v.i. and t., and n. (*wāl*) To utter a shrill, loud, plaintive cry or sound, howl
waist n. (*wāst*) Narrower part of the body between ribs and hips, *a small waist*
wait v.i. and t. (*wāt*) To remain in expectancy, delay action, until a particular time or event, *don't wait if I'm late*; put off, postpone, *wait dinner for someone* Hence: **waiter** n. male servant who attends at table in restaurants, etc.; **waitress** n. woman waiter
wake 1) v.i. and t. (*wāk*) pret. **waked** (*wākd*) or **woke** (*wōk*) p.p. **waked** (*wākd*) or **woken** (*wōk'n*) To be, remain awake, *in our waking hours*; also **wake up**, become awake, stop sleeping
Hence: **waken** v.t. and i. to wake or cause to wake; **wakeful** adj. watchful; unable to sleep
wake 2) n. (*wāk*) Annual holiday and fair held in towns in northern England; vigil beside a corpse on the night before the funeral; festivities accompanying this
wake 3) n. (*wāk*) Track of smooth water behind moving vessel
walk 1) v.i. and t. (*wawk*) To move along by putting one foot alternately before the other, at a moderate pace, *walk steadily up and down*
go on foot, *to get out of a car and walk*; cause to walk, *walk a horse downhill*
walk 2) n. (*wawk*) Action of walking, manner of walking, excursion on foot, *go for a walk*; route traversed on foot
walkie-talkie n. (*wawk'i tawk'i*) (colloq.) Two-way radio telephone carried by police etc. for use in communicating with a headquarters or with users of similar sets
wall n. and v.t. (*wawl*) Construction, usually of brick or stone, erected as barrier, partition, or to enclose a space such as a room etc.; anything acting as a partition, *the walls of the heart* As v.t. to enclose with a wall; **wall up** block up (space etc.) with a wall
wallet n. (*wol'et*) Flat leather case or pocket-book for carrying papers, bank-notes etc
wallop v.t. and n. (*wol'op*) To beat, punch
wallow v.i. and n. (*wol'ō*) To roll about in water, liquid mud etc.; (fig.) revel in, indulge in to excess
walnut n. (*wawl'nut*) Edible nut in hard, rough shell; tree, *Juglans regia*, producing these nuts; hard timber of this tree, used in cabinet-making etc
walrus n. (*wawl'rus*) Large amphibious mammal allied to the seal, with long drooping tusks
waltz n., and v.i. and t. (*wawls*) Dance for couples, in three or two time, with smooth, even steps in a series of turns; music for accompanying such a dance. As v.i. and t. to dance a waltz; cause to waltz; move with a waltzing motion
wan adj. (*won*) Pallid, pale; sickly, tired-looking, *a wan smile*
wand n. (*wond*) Long, slender rod, esp. as used by conjurer or magician, or carried as symbol of authority by sheriff, steward etc
wander v.i. and t., and n.

(*won'der*) To move from place to place without specific purpose or route, to roam, *to wander through the woods*; leave the proper course, stray, *wander off the path*; fail to keep to the point or subject, become diffuse, *wander from the point*
wane v.i. and n. (*wān*) To diminish, lessen in intensity, power etc., *his popularity waned*
want v.t. and i. (*wont*) To lack, be deficient in, *he does not want intelligence*; need, require, *he wants someone to look after him*; wish for, have a desire for, *I want to go abroad this year*
war 1) n. (*waw(r)*) Open and large-scale hostilities between rival groups, esp. nations; science and tactics of warfare, *the art of war*; (fig.) any kind of struggle or conflict, *war against disease*
war 2) v.i. (*waw(r)*) To carry on a war
ward 1) n. (*wawd*) a minor under the control of a guardian administrative division of a town; section, room of a building, esp. of a hospital
ward 2) v.t. (*wawd*) **To ward off** avert, repel, *ward off a cold*
warden n. (*waw'den*) Person having authority over specific district, or appointed to carry out specific duties, *traffic-warden*
warder n. (*waw'der*) Prison guard, jailer
wardrobe n. (*wawd'rōb*) Large cupboard-like piece of furniture where clothes are kept; a person's stock of clothes
ware n. (*wār*) Manufactured articles, *hardware*; pottery, *stone ware*; (pl.) merchandise, articles for sale. Hence: **warehouse** n. and v.t. storehouse for goods before distribution to retailers etc
warm 1) adj. (*wawm*) Having a mild, pleasant degree of heat, *warm water*; used as equivalent of hot, *isn't this room warm!*; ardent, enthusiastic, *a warm welcome*; affectionate, *a warm heart*; vehement, heated, *the dispute grew warm*
warm 2) v.t. and i., and n. (*wawm*) To make or become warm or warmer
warn v.t. (*wawn*) To advise (someone) of possible danger
warp v.t. and i., and n. (*wawp*) To distort, put out of shape, esp. by twisting or bending; to become distorted, twisted
As n., distortion in an object caused by shrinkage etc. threads
running lengthwise in a fabric and crossed by the woof
warrant n. and v.t. (*wo'rant*) Justification, authority, *you have no warrant for that statement*; official means of authorization, esp. in documentary form
As v.t. to
justify, *nothing could warrant such rudeness*; vouch for, guarantee, *warranted pure silk*
warren n. (*wo'ren*)
tract of uncultivated land with many burrows where rabbits breed
wart n. (*wawt*) Small, hard growth on the skin
wary adj. (*wā'ri*) Cautious
wash 1) v.t. and i. (*wosh*) To make clean with or in water or other liquid, *wash one's hands*; wash oneself, *to wash in cold water*; (of materials etc.) stand washing without deterioration, *how does that dress wash?*; flow past, bathe, *the sea washes the cliffs*; scoop out, *rain has washed channels in the ground*; to carry away or along, *washed ashore by a wave*; flow, splash against or over, *a huge wave washed the boat*
wash 2) n. (*wosh*) Washing or being washed; clothes, linen etc. being washed or to be washed, *to have a large wash*; movement or flow of water, *the wash of the waves* thin application of water-colour, distemper etc., put on in liquid state
wasp n. (*wosp*) Family of insects with narrow waist and powerful sting

wasp

waste adj., v.t. and i., and n. (*wāst*) Not cultivated or occupied, unproductive, *waste land*; not wanted; superfluous, *waste products*
use extravagantly, *waste one's money*; lay waste; cause to shrink or lose vigour, substance etc., *wasted by disease*
As n. wasting or being wasted; amount lost by waste; refuse
watch 1) v.t. and i. (*woch*) To look at, observe attentively, *watch a procession pass*; observe with intent to protect, *the dog watched his clothes while he bathed*; look out (for), *watch (for) a favourable opportunity*
watch 2) n. (*woch*) Act of watching; vigil, look-out
timepiece usually enclosed in a flat round case and carried in the pocket or worn on the wrist
water 1) n. (*waw'ter*) Colourless odourless, tasteless liquid, composed of hydrogen and oxygen, *fish live in water*
water 2) v.t. and i. (*waw'ter*) To apply water to, sprinkle, irrigate, *water the plants*; provide with water, *water the horses*; dilute with water, *water the whisky*
watt n. (*wot*) The unit of electrical power
wave v.i. and t., and n. (*wāv*) To move or cause to move to and fro with curving, swelling motion, *waving corn*; (of line or surface) lie or cause to lie in a series of curves, undulate, *her hair waves naturally*; signal by waving the hand; express by a wave of the hand, *wave farewell*; signal to by waving, *wave someone away*
n. swelling, curving ridge on surface of sea etc.; any similar undulating movement
wave-like form or motion in which heat, light, sound, or electricity is carried or spread; waving movement, act of waving, *a wave of the hand*
wax 1) n. (*wăks*) Plastic yellow substance secreted by bees for the construction of cells; this material prepared, bleached, and purified for making candles etc
wax 2) v.t. (*wăks*) To cover, coat with, wax; treat with wax
wax 3) v.i. (*wăks*) To increase, grow larger, *the moon is waxing*
way n. (*wā*) Road, path, track, leading from one place to another, *a way across the fields*; route followed or to be followed (from one place to another), *the way home*; direction, *he went that way*; distance traversed or to be traversed between two points, *it's a long way from here*; progress; forward movement, momentum, *to gather (lose) way*; opportunity for progress or forward movement, *to clear the way*; method, plan, course of action, *the right way of doing something*; characteristic manner, custom or habit, *it's not his way to be mean*; range, sphere, *such a thing has never come my way*; state, condition, *things are in a bad way*; respect, point or detail, *can I help in any way?*
waylay v.t. (*wā lā'*) Ambush, lie in wait for in order to attack
weak adj. (*wēk*) Lacking in vigour, strength, firmness, durability etc., easily broken
weaken v.t. and i. (*wē'ken*) To make weaker, reduce strength or stability of, *the flood has weakened the bridge*; make less convincing, *weaken an argument*; grow weaker; become less assured, *he weakened after hearing my arguments*
wealth n. (*welth*) Plentiful supply, *a wealth of kindness*; abundance of material resources, riches, *a man of wealth*
weapon n. (*we'pon*) Instrument designed or used as means of offence or defence; organic means of defence, *the wasp's weapon is its sting*; means used to get the better in a conflict, *the strike is the workers' most powerful weapon*
wear v.t. and i. (*wār*) pret. **wore** (*wawr*) p.p. **worn** (*wawn*) To be clothed with, have on the body, as garment, *wear a new dress*
cause to diminish gradually, produce injury to, by friction or usage, *wear one's sock into holes*
last, remain unimpaired or in a certain condition, *these shoes will wear for years*; (of time) to pass, esp. slowly or tediously
weary adj., and v.t. and i. (*wēr'i*) Tired, fatigued
weasel n. (*wē'zel*) Small carnivore, *Mustela vulgaris*, allied to the stoat
weather 1) n. (*we'ther*) Atmospheric conditions as regards wind, clouds, temperature etc
weather 2) v.t. and i. (*we'ther*) To expose to action of weather, *to weather wood*; survive, come through successfully, *weather a crisis*

weave v.t. and i. and n. (*wēv*) pret. **wove** (*wōv*) p.p. **woven** (*wōv'n*) To make threads into a piece of material by intertwining on a loom
web n. (*web*) Network, esp. fig., *web of lies*; network of thread spun by spider etc., cobweb; membrane between toes of aquatic bird etc., *web-footed*
wed v.t. and i. (*wed*) To marry
wedding n. (*wed'ing*) Marriage ceremony
wedge n. and v.t. (*wej*) Piece of wood or metal tapered to thin edge at one end, used to split wood or rock or to drive between separate parts or objects so as to render them immovable
weed n., and v.t. and i. (*wēd*) Any plant growing where it is not wanted, esp. a wild plant among cultivated plants
v.t. and i. to clear (ground) of weeds
weeds n.pl. (*wēdz*) Mourning garments worn by widow
week n. (*wēk*) Period of seven successive days, esp. from a Sunday to the following Saturday inclusive
weep v.i. and t. and n. (*wēp*) pret. and p.p. **wept** (*wept*) To shed tears, cry; exude, show, moisture, *a weeping wound*
weft n. (*weft*) Threads interwoven with warp from selvedge to selvedge in weaving. (OE. *weft*)
weigh v.t. and i. (*wā*) To ascertain weight by means of scales or balances; consider critically, ponder over, *weigh the advantages and disadvantages of an action*; have a specified weight, *it weighs little*; possess significance, *such a consideration should not weigh with you*; **weigh down** press or pull down, *branches weighed down by fruit*; oppress, *weighed down by grief*
weight n. and v.t. (*wāt*) Gravitational force acting on a body in proportion to the mass of the body, *his weight is 140 lb*; heavy load, burden, *the bridge broke beneath the lorry's weight*; oppressive circumstances, event or conditions, *weight of sorrow*; significance, influence, importance, *an argument of great weight*; system of weighing
a heavy mass, esp. when used to keep something held down
weir n. (*wēr*) Small dam formed across river to control the flow of water; fence of stakes across a stream as trap for fish.
weird adj. (*wērd*) Strange
welcome 1) adj. and n. (*wel'kum*) Received with, giving, pleasure, *a welcome guest*
welcome 2) v.t. (*wel'kum*) To give a welcome to, accept with pleasure; show pleasure or satisfaction at an action, event, someone's arrival etc., *welcome someone to one's home*
weld v.t. and i., and n. (*weld*) To unite (pieces of metal) by hammering or pressure when the metal has been heated
welfare n. (*wel'fār*) State of comfort, health, etc., *enquire about someone's welfare*; **welfare state** one in which the welfare of all citizens is aided by government services of all kinds
well 1) n. and v.i. (*wel*) Shaft, usually lined with brick or stone, sunk in the ground to obtain water from a subterranean source; shaft by which oil is obtained from underground
deep enclosed space, esp. space in house in which the staircase is placed, *stairwell*
ink-well hollow in desk-top to contain an ink-pot. As v.i. to spring, flow up, from or as from a spring, *tears welled from her eyes*
well 2) adj., adv., and n. (*wel*) In good health, *you look well*; in a satisfactory condition, *all is not well with him*; advisable, desirable; lucky, fortunate, *it was well for you that you were alone*
wellingtons n.pl. (*wel'ing tonz*) Rubber or plastic boots reaching to the knees
west n., adv., and adj. (*west*) One of the cardinal points of the compass opposite to the east and marked by the setting of the Sun
western adj. and n. (*wes'tern*) Of, situated in, coming from, characteristic of, the west. As n. native of the west; (colloq.) cowboy film or novel
wet 1) adj. and n. (*wet*) Containing, covered, saturated with, liquid, *wet clothes*; marked by constant or abundant rain, *a wet day*
wet 2) v.t. (*wet*) To apply liquid to, make wet
whack v.t. and n. (*wăk*) To strike (someone or something) hard sharp, audible blow
whale n. and v.i. (*wāl*) Large fish-like marine mammal
wharf n. and v.t. (*wawf*) Timber

or stone structure where ships are loaded and unloaded
whatever adj. and pron. (*wot ev'er*) No matter what, *whatever excuse he makes, don't believe him.* As pron. anything, everything that, all that; no matter what, *whatever happens, I shall leave tomorrow*
wheat n. (*wēt*) Cereal plant of genus *Triticum*, bearing edible seeds; edible grain produced by this plant and ground into flour
wheel n., and v.t. and i. (*wēl*) Circular frame or disk capable of rotatory motion and used to facilitate the movement of a vehicle As v.t. and i. to cause (wheeled vehicle etc.) to move; propel (person, load etc.) in wheeled vehicle or barrow; (of line of troops etc.) swing round or cause to swing round on a pivot; move in a sweeping, circular course; ride a bicycle etc
whiff n. and v.i. (*wif*) A puff, breath, *a whiff of air*; a slight odour, *a whiff of the farmyard about him*
while n., v.t., and conj. (*wil*) Time, *stay for a while*
As v.t. **while** (**wile**)
away time cause time to pass in pleasant and leisurely manner. As conj. as long as, during the time that, *sit down while you wait*
whim n. (*wim*) Idea, passing fancy
whimper v.t. and i., and n. (*wim'per*) To cry fretfully and plaintively, utter weak frightened cries; utter in a whimpering voice. As n. whimpering cry, low, whining sob
whine v.t. and i., and n. (*win*) (of animal, child, siren etc.) To utter fretful, wailing cry; utter constant complaints, esp. about trifles; utter in whining tone. As n. wailing, plaintive cry; fretful and childish complaint
whip 1) v.t. and i. (*wip*) To strike with a lash, whip etc., beat, *whip a horse*; (colloq.) defeat, overcome; beat (eggs etc.) into a stiff consistency, *whipped cream*
whip 2) n. (*wip*) Flexible thong or lash attached to a handle for beating or thrashing
member of Parliament who ensures attendance of members at voting time etc
whippet n. (*wip'et*) Small crossbred greyhound trained for speed
whirl v.i. and t., and n. (*wurl*) To gyrate; spin or cause to spin rapidly as on a pivot, *a whirling top*; move or cause to move swiftly off, *he was whirled off in a taxi*; (of brain, senses) be giddy, reel; (of thoughts etc.) be confused. As n. whirling motion; (fig.) confusion of mind
whisk n., and v.t. and i. (*wisk*) Small bunch of feathers, straw, etc. for use as brush; light metal instrument for whipping eggs, cream etc. As v.t. and i. to remove by flicking or sweeping away; to wave, twitch, fling, *the cow whisked its tail*; beat with or as with a whisk, *whisk eggs*; move, depart, rapidly and abruptly, *whisk out of sight*
whisker n. (*wis'ker*) (Usually pl.) hair growing on the sides of a man's face; one of the long, stiff hairs growing at side of mouth of cat, tiger, etc
whisky, whiskey n. (*wis'ki*) Alcoholic liquor distilled from malted grain, esp. barley
whisper v.i. and t., and n. (*wis'per*) To speak, say (something) in a low voice, without vibration of the vocal chords; tell as a secret; circulate as a rumour, *strange things were whispered about him*; (of leaves etc.) make a faint sound like whispering
whist n. (*wist*) Card game for two pairs of players
whistle v.i. and t., and n. (*wisl*) To make a high shrill noise or note by forcing air or steam through a small opening, esp. breath through pursed-up lips; produce a tune in this way; pass swiftly with a whistling sound, *bullets whistled past him*; summon by whistling, *whistle a dog back*
tune. As n. sound produced by whistling; device for making such a sound, *a tin whistle*
white adj. (*wit*) Of the colour of fresh snow; not dark
whiz (z) n. and v.i. (*wiz*) Hissing, whirring sound made by a body flying through the air. As v.i. to rush through the air and make this sound. (Echoic)
who pron. (*hōō*) (obj.) **whom** (*hōōm*) (interrog.) What or which person?, *who is there?, to whom shall I send it?*; (rel.) that person, those persons, *I don't know the people who live there*
whole adj. and n. (*hōl*) Complete in all parts, unbroken,

intact, *there isn't a whole plate in the house*; all of anything, entire, *the whole town suffered from the earthquake*; sound in health
wholesale n., adj., and adv. (*hōl'sāl*) Sale of goods in bulk, esp. by manufacturer to retailer
wholesome adj. (*hōl'sum*) Favourable to health
whoop v.i. and n. (*hōōp*) To utter a loud cry or shout; **whooping-cough** infectious disease of children
why adv., n., and inter. (*wī*) (interrog. and rel.) For what cause or reason, *why are you going?, tell me why*
wick n. (*wik*) Twisted strands of thread set in middle of candle; piece of woven material immersed at one end in the oil of a lamp to conduct fuel to the flame at the other end. (OE. *wice*)
wicked adj. (*wik'ed*) Sinful, evil
wicker n. and adj. (*wik'er*) Fabric made of interwoven twigs, canes, etc
wicket n. (*wik'et*) Small door built into a larger door or gate; (cricket) set of stumps surmounted by a pair of bails, and defended by a batsman; the cricket pitch between wickets
wide adj. and adv. (*wīd*) Of great extent from side to side, broad, *a wide river*; of great extent, comprehensive, *a man of wide interests*; far from a specific point or objective, *the arrow is wide of the mark*
widow n. and v.t. (*wid'ō*) Woman whose husband is dead and who has not married again. As v.t. to make a widow. Hence: **widower** n. man who has not married again after his wife's death
wield v.t. (*wēld*) To have control or power over, have at one's command, *to wield influence*; handle, grasp by the hand and make use of, *wield an axe*
wife n. (*wīf*) pl. **wives** (*wīvs*) Married woman
wig n. (*wig*) Head-covering of false hair
wigwam n. (*wig'wom*) N. American Indian's conical tent of poles hung with hide, bark etc
wild adj. and n. (*wīld*) (of animals, birds etc.) Not tamed or domesticated; living in natural conditions; (of plants) uncultivated, not planted by man; (of man) savage, uncivilized; (of land) unsettled and

wigwam

uncultivated; disarranged, disorderly, *a state of wild confusion* violent, stormy, tumultuous, *a wild night*; excited, distracted, frenzied, *wild with delight*; rash, reckless, done or said at random, *a wild accusation*
wilderness n. (*wil'der nes*) Wild uncultivated region; desolate expanse, *a wilderness of waters*
wilful adj. (*wil'fōōl*) (of person or character) Self-willed, stubborn, headstrong
will n. (*wil*) Mental power by which a person consciously directs and determines his thoughts and actions, and influences those of others, *freedom of will* definite intention, desire or purpose, *against one's will* document in which a person declares how he wishes his property to be bestowed or used after his deatn
willing adj. (*wil'ing*) Ready and eager to help or do what is required
willow n. (*wil'ō*) Any tree or plant of genus *Salix*; a cricket-bat, as made of willow-wood
wilt v.i. and t. (*wilt*) To become or cause to become limp and drooping
wily adj. (*wī'li*) Full of wiles, cunning, *the wily old fox*
win 1) v.t. and i. (*win*) pret. and p.p. **won** (*won*) To gain, obtain, by effort, esp. as result of a contest etc., *win a prize*; achieve victory in, *win a race*; reach by effort, *win the summit*
win 2) n. (*win*) Act of winning

winch n. and v.t. (*winch*) Windlass, crank, or pulley. As v.t to move by using a winch

wind 1) n. (*wind*) Air set in motion by atmospheric conditions, *a gentle wind*; a similar movement of air caused mechanically, *wind from a bellows*; scent carried by the wind; (fig.) rumour, hint, esp. in **get wind of** hear as a rumour; breath, lung power, *sound in wind and limb*; flatulence; wordy, purposeless talk; (mus.) wind-instruments

wind 2) v.t. (*wind*) To wind of, give an opportunity of getting breath to, *we stopped to wind the horses.* (As above)

wind 3) v.i. and t. (*wind*) pret. and p.p. **wound** (*wownd*) To move or cause to move in a curving, twisting, or spiralling course, *the road winds up the hill;* to form (wool, string etc.) into a compact ball by twining (it) round or on to something; to enfold or wrap closely, embrace, *he wound his arms round me*; turn, cause to revolve, *wind a handle*; start a mechanism by winding, *wind a clock*

window n. (*win'dō*) Opening in wall or roof of a building, side of a closed vehicle etc., to admit light

wing n. and v.t. and i. (*wing*) One of the limbs of flight of a bird, insect, bat etc.; plane of an aeroplane or glider; lateral extension of a building; sides of stage; division of army working on the flank of the main body; (hockey, football) player on either extreme of the forward line; division of the Royal Air Force consisting of three squadrons; something like a wing in position or appearance, esp. membrane carrying certain seeds through the air
As v.t. and i. to give wings to; impel rapidly, *fear winged his steps*; travel on wings; wound in the wing or arm

wink v.i. and t., and n. (*wingk*) To close and open one or both eyes very quickly (of light, star, etc.) flash, shine fitfully, twinkle

winter n. and v.i. (*win'ter*) Cold season between autumn and spring, astronomically considered to be from Dec. 22nd to Mar. 20th in northern hemisphere, June 22nd to Sept. 21st in southern

wipe v.t. and i., and n. (*wip*) To clean or dry by rubbing gently with a cloth or other absorbent material, *wipe the floor*
Hence: **wiper** n. person or thing that wipes, esp. in compounds, *windscreen-wiper*. (OE. *wipian*)

wire n., and v.t. and i. (*wīr*) Fine thread of metal, single or made of threads twisted like cord
As v.t. and i. to fasten with or provide with wire; lay wire(s) in, for any purpose, *wire a house for electric light*; send a telegram

wireless adj. and n. (*wīr'les*) As n., wireless telegraphy or telephony; radio, communications or programmes of entertainment etc. transmitted by this means; instrument for receiving such communications or programmes, a radio set

wise adj. (*wīz*) Having, showing, springing from, sound judgement, prudence; possessing knowledge

wish 1) v.t. and i. (*wish*) To want, desire, long for, *do what you wish*; desire that, *I wish you wouldn't do that*; desire that oneself or another should have, *wish someone good luck;* express a desire in words, *wish someone farewell*

wish 2) n. (*wish*) Act of wishing; longing, desire; expression of this, *obey someone's wishes*; thing longed for, *you shall have your wish*

wistful adj. (*wist'fōōl*) Having, showing, unfulfilled longing

wit n. (*wit*) Mind, mental power; alertness of mind, *a man of quick wit*; quick appreciation of situation, *he had the wit to avoid trouble*; ability to perceive unexpected or humorous relations between ideas and express them in memorable, felicitous way, *the play is full of wit*; person noted for his humorous remarks, *he's a wit*

witch n. (*wich*) Woman supposed to possess occult powers and practise magic, esp. for evil purposes, a sorceress **witchcraft** power and practices of a witch; **witch-doctor** medicine man among primitive peoples

withdraw v.t. and i. (*with draw'*) pret. **withdrew** (*with drū'*) p.p. **withdrawn** (*with drawn'*) To pull or draw back, *withdraw one's head from a window*; recall, remove, *withdraw coins from circulation*; retire, move back, *the troops withdrew*; retract (one's word, promise etc.), *he has withdrawn his remark*

wither v.t. and i. (*wi'ther*) (Cause)

to shrivel up, wilt; (fig.) diminish, grow weaker
withhold v.t. (*with hōld'*) pret. and p.p. **withheld** (*with held'*) To keep back, refuse to give, *withhold permission*
within 1) adv. and n. (*with in'*) (archaic) On the inside. As n. the interior, *seen from within*
within 2) prep. (*with'in*) Inside, in the inner part of, within a place, *within the park are tennis courts*; not beyond the range, power, resources etc. of, *within call*; not exceeding the limits of specified time or distance, *within a few miles of home*
without 1) adv. and n. (*with owt'*) (archaic) On the outside. As n. the outside
without 2) prep. (*with owt'*) Not having or using, *without ceremony*; (archaic) on the outside of; **without fail** certainly; **that goes without saying** it is too obvious to be mentioned
withstand v.t. (*with stănd'*) pret. and p.p. **withstood** (*with stŏŏd'*) To oppose, resist, endure
witness n., and v.t. and i. (*wit'nes*) Evidence, testimony, *bear witness to*; person or thing providing evidence, esp. under oath in a court of law; person who adds his signature to that of the person who executes a document etc., in testimony of having seen the latter sign
As v.t. and i. to show, give evidence of, *her face witnessed her agitation*; be present at and see, *witness an accident*; give evidence, testify; add one's name to a document in declaration that one has seen it legally signed
wizard n. (*wiz'ard*) Person supposed to possess magic powers
wobble v.i. and t., and n. (*wobl*) To sway or cause to sway unsteadily from side to side, *the jelly wobbles*
woe n. (*wō*) (chiefly poet. or archaic) Grief, misery
wolf n. and v.t. (*wŏŏlf*) pl. **wolves** Carnivorous, savage quadrupeds of dog family
woman n. (*wŏŏ'man*) pl. **women** (*wi'men*) Adult person of the female sex
wonder 1) n. (*wun'der*) Person, object, etc. exciting surprised admiration, a marvel, miracle, *the seven wonders of the world*; feeling of mingled awe, surprise, and admiration, *to be filled with wonder*
wonder 2) v.i. and t. (*wun'der*) To experience wonder, to marvel, *I don't wonder at it*; feel curiosity about, desire to know, *I wonder who she is*
wood n. (*wŏŏd*) Large group of trees, esp. of natural growth; substance of which the hard part of a tree or shrub is composed, esp. as cut for use as timber
wool n. (*wŏŏl*) Soft hair of fleece of sheep or coat of goat, llama, etc.; thread or yarn made from this; fabric woven or knitted of wool; any substance resembling this, *cotton-wool*
word n. (*wurd*) Speech-sound or group of sounds used as a unit of spoken or written language, to represent an idea, object, action, relationship etc., *a word of two syllables*; written or printed symbol(s) representing this; (often pl.) thing said, speech, *his opening words*; order, spoken signal, *give the word to fire*; password; message, news, information, rumour, *I have had no word from him for a week*; promise, *to give one's word*
work 1) n. (*wurk*) Mental or physical activity carried out deliberately and with a purpose, *the work of building a house*; labour of specific kind regularly performed as means of livelihood, a trade, profession, etc., *what is his work?*; particular task or undertaking, *to have some work to do in the garden*
work 2) v.t. and i. (*wurk*) To make to do work, cause to act or operate, *work a machine*; to shape, prepare, by pressing, hammering etc., *work dough to the correct consistency*; to perform or achieve, do, effect, *to work a miracle*; expend effort upon, do work connected with, *work a farm* bring oneself, into specified condition, *work oneself into a temper*
world n. (*wurld*) The universe; the earth and heavens; the earth; the human race, mankind particular phase or section of society, *the ancient world*; particular sphere of activity or interest, persons connected with it, *the racing world*; one of the primary divisions of life on earth, *the animal world*
worm n. and v.t. (*wurm*) Legless invertebrate creeping animal, esp. the earthworm
worry v.t. and i., and n. (*wu'ri*)

To seize and shake in the teeth, *the cat worried a mouse*; pester, harass, esp. with repeated requests; to make or to be anxious or in discomfort, *don't let it worry you.* As n. worrying or being worried; something that causes one to be worried

worse adj., adv., and n. (*wurs*) Bad to a higher degree, *this path is worse than the other*; more ill, *he grew daily worse*; less satisfactory, *you will be no worse for the move.* As adv. in a worse manner, to a worse extent; to a greater degree, *it is snowing worse than before*

worst adj., adv., n., and v.t. (*wurst*) Bad to the highest possible degree, *the worst May for years*; most intense, *the worst frost for years.* As adv. in the worst manner. As n. what is worst, *tell me the worst*

worth adj. and n. (*wurth*) Having a certain value, *it is worth sixpence*; deserving of, meriting, *worth the trouble*; having property to the value of, *he must be worth a million by now*

As n. value or price, *a necklace of great worth*; excellence, admirable qualities; quantity of something of a specified value

wound 1) n. and v.t. (*wōōnd*) Injury to body in which the skin is pierced, cut etc., *an open wound* (fig.) injury to person's feelings. As v.t. to inflict a wound upon, to hurt

wrap v.t. and i., and n. (*răp*) To fold round, cover up in, *wrap a child in a shawl*; (fig.) surround with, *wrapped in an air of mystery*; hide, conceal, *wrap one's meaning in obscure language*

As n. material or garment used as wrapping or protection from the cold

wrath n. (*roth*) Great anger.

wreath n. (*rēth*) Circle made of twigs, leaves, flowers etc., placed on coffin, grave, memorial etc. or on the head as a garland

wreathe v.t. and i. (*reth*) To twist, wind, weave, esp. into a wreath; to encircle with a wreath; to clasp, entwine, *wreathe one's arms round someone*; (of smoke etc.) to move in a coiling, twining way

wreck n., and v.t. and i. (*rek*) Destruction, esp. of a ship by storm, rocks etc.; abandoned ship at sea or cast on shore; building, vehicle etc. destroyed or badly damaged; person whose health has been destroyed. As v.t. and i. to cause the wreck of. Hence: **wreckage** n. wrecking or being wrecked; wrecked material, fragments; **wrecker** n. one who deliberately causes destruction; one who causes shipwreck in order to plunder

wrench n. and v.t. (*rench*) Sudden, sharp twist or pull; tool for screwing nuts on or off; injury to muscle etc. inflicted by a wrench; painful emotion, esp. one felt at parting or separation

wrest v.t. (*rest*) To wrench away; extract by toil and effort

wrestle v.t. and i. (*res'l*) To struggle with an opponent by engaging him in a grip and trying to throw him

wretch n. (*rech*) Miserably unhappy or unfortunate person

wretched adj. (*rech'ed*) Miserable, unhappy

wriggle v.i. and t., and n. (*rig'l*) To move with rapid, jerky twistings

wring v.t. and n. (*ring*) pret. and p.p. **wrung** (*rung*) To squeeze and twist tightly; press out by doing this, *wring water from clothes*

wrinkle n., and v.t. and i. (*ring'kl*) Small crease or furrow on the skin or surface of something

wrist n. (*rist*) Joint between hand and fore-arm

write v.i. and t. (*rīt*) pret. **wrote** (*rōt*) p.p. **written** (*rit'n*) To make (symbols representing letters or words or numbers) on paper or other surface, *write legibly*; communicate in writing, tell by means of a letter, *write me all your news*; engage in literary composition, produce as a literary composition, *to write for a living*

writer n. (*ri'ter*) One who writes, esp. an author

writhe v.i. (*rīth*) To twist the body about, squirm

wrong 1) adj. (*rong*) Not morally right or just, *it is wrong to tell lies*; false, inaccurate, not true, *your calculations are wrong*; not as was intended, *he came on the wrong day*; mistaken, having misunderstood or been ignorant of, *he was wrong in what he said*; not well ordered, inopportune, unsuitable, *the wrong clothes for an occasion*

wrong 2) adv. (*rong*) In a wrong manner

wrong 3) n. (*rong*) What is unjust, evil, not morally right

wrong 4) v.t. (*rong*) To do

wrong to, treat unjustly or unkindly

X

xylophone n. (*zī'lo fōn*) Musical instrument of percussion consisting of a series of wooden bars, graduated in length and producing different notes when struck

Y

yacht n. and v.i. (*yot*) Light sailing-vessel; vessel, usually motor-driven, kept for pleasure-cruising

yap v.i. and n. (*yăp*) To utter sharp, shrill bark or series of barks

yard 1) n. (*yahd*) Enclosed space, esp. attached to a building or buildings, *farmyard*; enclosure for special purpose, *dockyard*

yard 2) n. (*yahd*) Standard unit of linear measure, equal to 3 feet or 36 inches

yarn n. and v.i. (*yahn*) Spun thread; (colloq.) a story; **spin a yarn** tell a story. As v.i. to tell yarns

yawn v.i. and n. (*yawn*) To take deep involuntary breath through wide-open mouth, esp. through tiredness or boredom; to be wide open. As n. act of yawning

year n. (*yēr*) Period of the earth's revolution round the sun, about 365¼ days; period beginning with 1st of January and ending with 31st of December; any period of 365 consecutive days

Hence: **yearly** adj. and adv. happening every year; happening once a year; as adv., every year, annually

yearling n. and adj. (*yēr'ling*) Animal one year old

yearn v.i. (*yurn*) To desire strongly, long for

yell v.i. and t., and n. (*yel*) To utter loud, strident cry, as in pain, terror etc.; utter with a yell. As n., sharp loud outcry

yeoman n. (*yō'man*) (hist.) Man owning and cultivating a small estate or farm; **Yeomen of the Guard** royal bodyguard now stationed at the Tower of London. Hence: **yeomanry** n. yeomen collectively; volunteer cavalry force formerly recruited from small farmers

yes adv. (*yes*) Expressing consent and agreement

yesterday adv. and n. (*yes'ter dā*) On the day last past. As n. the day last past

yet adv. and conj. (*yet*) Up to this time, until now, *he has not come yet*; up to that time in the past, *they had not yet arrived*; now, at this time, *I can't come yet*; still, even now, *he is yet alive* besides, in addition, *I have yet more to say*; at some future time, *he may yet win*

yield v.t. and i., and n. (*yēld*) To furnish, afford, produce, *trees yielding fruit;* surrender, relinquish, *yield a town to the enemy*; give oneself up, submit, *yield to force* n. amount produced, *a good yield per acre*

yoga n. (*yō'ga*) Hindu system of meditation

yoghourt, yoghurt, yogurt n. (*yōg'urt, yog'urt*) Sour fermented liquor made from milk

yolk n. (*yōk*) Yellow middle part of an egg

you pron. (*yōō*) Second pers. sing. and pl. personal pron.; indef. pron. one, anyone, *you never can tell*

young adj. and n. (*yung*) In the early stages of life, development etc., *a young man* recent, recently begun, *the night is still young*

youth n. (*yōōth*) State or period of being young, *friends of his youth*; a young man

yule n. (*yōōl*) Christmas season or festival; **yule-log** log burnt at Christmas

Z

zeal n. (*zēl*) Enthusiasm

zebra n. (*zeb'ra, zēb'ra*) Striped African quadruped related to the

zebra

horse and ass
zenith n. (*zen'ith*) Point in the sky vertically overhead; (fig.) highest point (of achievement, growth etc.), peak, *at the zenith of his powers*.
zephyr n. (*zef'er*) West wind; a light breeze.
zero n. (*zē'rō*) Nought, nothing
zest n. (*zest*) Gusto, keenness, *do something with zest*
zigzag n., adj., adv., and v.i. (*zig'zăg*) Line with a series of alternate right and left turns at sharp angles; anything resembling this in form, *a zigzag road*
zinc n. (*zingk*) Bluish-tinged white metallic element
zip n. (*zip*) a zip-fastener
zip-fastener a joining device consisting of two toothed metal edges interlocked by means of a sliding tab.
zodiac n. (*zō'di ak*) Imaginary belt of the heavens containing the path of the moon and the principal planets, divided into twelve sections called and represented by signs
zone n. and v.t. (*zōn*) Belt, area, distinguished in appearance, characteristics etc. from surrounding surface etc.; area with particular use, purpose etc., *war zone*; administrative division, *postal zone*
zoo n. (*zōō*) Zoological gardens, a collection of animals kept in confinement within a large park for exhibition or study.
zoology n. (*zō ol'o ji*) Branch of biology dealing with the form, structure, classification, of animals

KEY TO PRONUNCIATION

Symbol	As in:	Symbol	As in:	Symbol	As in:
a	above	*ī*	high	*ōōr*	gourd
ă	cat	*īr*	fire	*ow*	now
ā	date	*j*	jacket	*ow*(*r*)	flour
ār	bare	*k*	cat	*p*	put
ah	past	*kh*	loch	*r*	rat, beer
ah(*r*)	car	*ks*	exclaim	*s*	sit, city
aw	author	*kw*	queen	*sh*	shine
aw(*r*)	war	*l*	live, battle	*t*	time
b	bad	*m*	man	*th*	thin
ch	chase	*n*	nail	th	this
d	dad	*ng*	singer	*u*	mud
e	bet	(*ng*)	French 'bon'	*ur*	slur
ē	deed	*ng g*	finger	*ū*	tune
ēr	dear	*ngk*	think	*ūr*	pure
er	better	*o*	bomb	*v*	love
f	fog	*ō*	bone	*w*	wave
g	game	*oi*	boy	*y*	young
h	hear	*ŏŏ*	book, put	*z*	haze
i	him	*ōō*	loom	*zh*	vision

The accent (') follows the stressed syllable or syllables.

ABBREVIATIONS IN THE DICTIONARY

abs.	absolute	chem.	chemistry	esp.	especially
acc.	accusative	chron.	chronology	eth.	ethics
adj.	adjective	class.	classical	ethn.	ethnology
adv.	adverb	colloq.	colloquial	fem.	feminine
aeron.	aeronautics	comm.	commerce	fig.	figurative
agric.	agriculture	comp.	comparative	fut.	future
alg.	algebra	conj.	conjunction	gen.	genitive
anat.	anatomy	dat.	dative	geneal.	genealogy
anthrop.	anthropology	def.	definite	geog.	geography
antiq.	antiquities	dial.	dialect	geol.	geology
arch.	architecture	dim.	diminutive	geom.	geometry
archae.	archaeology	dram.	dramatic	ger.	gerund (ive)
arith.	arithmetic	eccles.	ecclesiastical	gram.	grammar
astron.	astronomy	econ.	economics	her.	heraldry
auxil.	auxiliary	elect.	electricity & electronics	hist.	history
bibl.	biblical			hort.	horticulture
biol.	biology	eng.	engineering	i.	intransitive
bot.	botany	entom.	entomology	imper.	imperative
cf.	compare	equiv.	equivalent	impers.	impersonal

ind.	indicative	opt.	optics	pron.	pronoun
indef.	indefinite	orig.	originally	prov.	provincial
inf.	infinitive	O.T.	Old Testament	proverb	proverb
inter.	interjection	p.	past	psych.	psychology
interrog.	interrogative	paint.	painting	pt.	participle
lang.	language	Parl.	Parliamentary	R.C.	Roman Catholic
lit.	literally	pass.	passive		
log.	logic	path.	pathology	reflex.	reflexive
masc.	masculine	philos.	philosophy	rel.	relative
math.	mathematics	phon.	phonetics	rhet.	rhetoric
mech.	mechanics	phot.	photography	Rom.	Roman
med.	medicine	phys.	physics	sc.	science
met.	metaphysics	physio.	physiology	sculp.	sculpture
metal.	metallurgy	pl.	plural	sing.	singular
meteor.	meteorology	poet.	poetry, poetical	spec.	specific
milit.	military	pol.	politics	subj.	subjunctive
min.	mineralogy	pop.	popular	super.	superlative
mus.	music	pos.	positive	surg.	surgical
myth.	mythology	p.p.	past participle	t.	transitive
n.	noun	pred.	predicate	tele.	telecom-munication
nat. hist.	natural history	pref.	prefix		
naut.	nautical	prep.	preposition	theol.	theology
nav.	naval	pres.	present	transl.	translation
neut.	neuter	pres. p.	present participle	typ.	typography
nom.	nominative			uncert.	uncertain
N.T.	New Testament	pret.	past (preterite tense)	v.	verb
numis.	numismatics			var.	variant
obj.	objective	print.	printing	vulg.	vulgar

SOME COMMON ABBREVIATIONS

A.A. Automobile Association.

A.A.A. Amateur Athletic Association.

A.B. able-bodied seaman.

A.B.A. Amateur Boxing Association.

abr. abridged; abridgement.

A.C. alternating current.

A.C.A. Associate of Institute of Chartered Accountants of England and Wales.

acc. account (also **acct., a/c**); accountant.

A.D. anno Domini, in the year of the Lord.

A.D.C. Aide-de-camp.

ad inf. *ad infinitum*, to infinity.

Adjt. Adjutant. **Adjt-Gen.** Adjutant-General.

ad lib. *ad libitum*, at pleasure.

Ala. Alabama.

Ald. Alderman.

a.m. *ante meridiem*, before midday.

amp. ampère.

anal. analysis; analogy.
anon. anonymous.
appro. approval, approbation.
approx. approximate.
A.R.A. Associate of Royal Academy.
A.R.A.M. Associate of Royal Academy of Music.
A.R.C.M. Associate of Royal College of Music.
A.R.I.B.A. Associate of the Royal Institute of British Architects.
A.S.A. Amateur Swimming Association.
at. wt. atomic weight.
A.W.O.L. absent without leave.

B.A. *Baccalaureus Artium*, Bachelor of Arts; British Association (for the Advancement of Science).
B.B.C. British Broadcasting Corporation.
Bart., Bt. Baronet.
B.C. Before Christ; British Columbia.
B.Ch. *Baccalaureus Chirurgiae*, Bachelor of Surgery.
B.C.L. Bachelor of Civil Law.
B.Com., B.Comm. Bachelor of Commerce.
B.D. Bachelor of Divinity.
B.D.S. Bachelor of Dental Surgery.
B.Econ. Bachelor of Economics.
B.Ed. Bachelor of Education.
B.E.M. British Empire Medal.
B.Eng. Bachelor of Engineering.
B. ès L. *Bachelier ès Lettres* (Fr.), Bachelor of Letters.
B. ès S. *Bachelier ès Sciences* (Fr.), Bachelor of Sciences.
biog. biographer; biography, biographical.
B.L. Bachelor of Law; Bachelor of Letters.
B.Litt. Bachelor of Literature.
B.M. Bachelor of Medicine; British Museum.
B.M.A. British Medical Association.
B.Mus. Bachelor of Music.
Bn. Baron.
bn. battalion.
B. of T. Board of Trade.
B.P. British Pharmacopoeia.
B.Phil. Bachelor of Philosophy.
B.Sc. Bachelor of Science.
B.S.I. British Standards Institution.
B.S.T. British Standard Time.
B.T.C. British Transport Commission.

C. Celsius; centigrade.
c., ct., cent. centum, a hundred.
Cantab. *Cantabrigiensis*, of Cambridge.
Centuar. *Cantuaria*, Canterbury.
C.B.E. Commander of the Order of the British Empire.
c.c. (or **cc.**). cubic centimetre(s).
C.D. Corps Diplomatique; Civil Defence.
Cdr. Commander.
C.D.S.O. Companion of the Distinguished Service Order.
cf. *confer*, compare.
C.F.G. *Confédération Générale du Travail*, General Confederation of Labour.
C.I.A. Central Intelligence Agency.
C.I.D. Criminal Investigation Department.
C.-in-C. Commander-in-Chief.
cir., circ. *circa, circiter, circum*, about.
C.M.G. Companion of the Order of St. Michael and St. George.

C.N.D. Campaign for Nuclear Disarmament.

Co. Company; County.

c/o. care of.

c.o.d. cash (or collect) on delivery.

C. of E. Church of England.

C.O.I. Central Office of Information.

Corp. Corporation

C.P. Communist Party.

Cpl. Corporal.

C.P.O. Chief Petty Officer.

cr. credit; creditor.

cres., cresc. crescendo; crescent.

C.S.M. Company Sergeant-major.

cu., cub. cubic.

C.U.P. Cambridge University Press.

C.W.S. Co-operative Wholesale Society.

D 500.

D.B.E. Dame Commander of the Order of the British Empire.

D.C. Da *capo* (It.), repeat from the beginning; (*elect*.) direct current; District of Columbia.

D.C.L. Doctor of Civil Law.

D.C.M. Distinguished Conduct Medal.

D.D. *Divinitatis Doctor*, Doctor of Divinity.

D.D.S. Doctor of Dental Surgery.

DDT Dichlorodiphenyltrichloroethane (diasone, an insecticide).

D.G. *Dei gratia*, by the grace of God.

diam. diameter.

dim. *diminuendo*, getting softer.

D.Lit. or **Litt.** *Doctor Litterarum* or *Litteraturae*, Doctor of Letters or Literature.

DNA deoxyribonucleic acid.

D.O.R.A. Defence of the Realm Act.

D.Ph. or **D.Phil.** *Doctor Philosophiae*, Doctor of Philosophy.

D.R. dead reckoning.

Dr. debtor; Doctor.

D.Sc. *Scientiae Doctor*, Doctor of Science.

D.Th. Doctor of Theology.

D.V. *Deo volente*, God willing.

E. & O.E. errors and omissions excepted.

Ebor. *Eboracum*. York.

eccles. ecclesiastical.

econ. economics.

E.E.C. European Economic Community (Common Market).

E.F.T.A. European Free Trade Association.

e.g., ex. gr. *exempli gratia*, for example.

elect. electricity; electronics.

emp. emperor.

entom. entomology.

e.o. *ex officio:* from office.

Ep. *Epistle.*

equiv. equivalent.

E.R. *Elizabeth Regina*, Elizabeth, Queen.

E.S.P. extra-sensory perception.

Esq., Esqr. Esquire.

est. established; estimated.

E.T.A. estimated time of arrival.

et al. *et alibi*, and elsewhere; *et alii, aliae,* or *alia*, and others.

etc., &c. *et ceteri* or *cetera*, and the others, and so forth.

et seq. or **sq.** (sing.), *et sequens*, **et sqq.** (pl.), *et sequentes* or *sequentia*, and the following.

exor. executor.

F. Fahrenheit.

f. *forte*; loud.

F.A. Football Association.
fac. facsimile.
F.A.O. Food and Agriculture Organization.
F.B.A. Fellow of the British Academy.
F.B.I. Federal Bureau of Investigation.
F.I.A.T. Fabbrica Italiana Automobili Torini (Italian Automobile Factory, Turin).
Fid. Def. *Fidei Defensor*, Defender of the Faith.
fig. figure, diagram.
F.M. Field-Mashal.
F.O. Foreign Office.
f.o.b. free on board.
fol. following.
F.P.A. Foreign Press Association.
F.R.A.M. Fellow of the Royal Academy of Music.
F.R.A.S. Fellow of the Royal Astronomical Society.
F.R.C.M. Fellow of the Royal College of Music.
F.R.C.O. Fellow of the Royal College of Organists.
F.R.C.P. Fellow of the Royal College of Physicians.
F.R.C.S. Fellow of the Royal College of Surgeons.
F.R.G.S. Fellow of the Royal Geographical Society.
F.R.I.B.A. Fellow of the Royal Institute of British Architects.
F.R.I.C. Fellow of the Royal Institute of Chemistry.
F.R.S. Fellow of the Royal Society.
F.R.S.A. Fellow of the Royal Society of Arts.

G.A.T.T. General Agreement on Tariffs and Trade.
G.B.E. (Knight or Dame) Grand Cross of the British Empire.
G.C. George Cross.
G.C.B. (Knight) Grand Cross of the Bath.
G.C.E. General Certificate of Education.
G.C.F. greatest common factor.
G.C.M.G. (Knight or Dame) Grand Cross of St. Michael and St. George.
G.C.V.O. (Knight or Dame) Grand Cross of (Royal) Victorian Order.
G.I. general issue: U.S. enlisted soldier.
G.H.Q. General Headquarters.
G.M. George Medal.
gm. gram(me).
G.M.T. Greenwich Mean Time.
G.P. general practitioner.

h. and c. hot and cold (water).
H.C.F. highest common factor.
H.E. His Excellency; His Eminence; high explosive.
H.F. high frequency.
H.H. His (or Her) Highness; His Holiness (the Pope).
Hi-Fi, hi-fi high fidelity.
H.M. His (or Her) Majesty.
H.M.I. His (or Her) Majesty's Inspector.
H.M.S. His (or Her) Majesty's Ship or Service.
H.M.S.O. His (or Her) Majesty's Stationery Office.
Hon. Honourable, Honorary.
h.p. horse-power.
H.Q. headquarters.
hr. hour
H.R.H. His (or Her) Royal Highness.

ib., ibid. *ibidem*, in the same place.
i/c in charge of.
I.C.I. Imperial Chemical Industries.
ICBM intercontinental ballistic missile.
ICFTU International Confederation of Free Trade Unions.
id. *idem*, the same.
i.e. *id est*, that is.
I.L.O. International Labour Organization.
I.M.F. International Monetary Fund.
inc., incorp. incorporated.
inc. including; inclusive
incog. *incognito* (It.), with concealed identity.
infra dig. *infra dignitatem*, beneath one's dignity.
I.N.R.I. *Iesus Nazarenus Rex Judaeorum*, Jesus of Nazareth King of the Jews.
in trans. *in transitu*, in transit.
I.O.M. Isle of Man.
I.Q. intelligence quotient.
i.q. *idem quod*, the same as.
I.R.A. Irish Republican Army.
IRBM intermediate range ballistic missile.
ital. italic

J.P. Justice of the Peace.
Jr., Jun., Junr. Junior.

K.B. Knight of the Bath; Knight Bachelor; King's Bench.
K.B.E. Knight Commander of the British Empire.
K.C. King's Counsel; King's College.
K.C.B. Knight Commander of the Bath.
K.C.M.G. Knight Commander of St. Michael and St. George.
K.C.V.O. Knight Commander of the (Royal) Victorian Order.
kg. kilogram(s).
K.G. Knight of the Garter.
K.G.C.B. Knight of the Grand Cross of the Bath.
K.K.K. Ku Klux Klan.
kl. kilolitre.
km. kilometre(s).
K.O., k.o. knock out.
Kt. Knight.
Kt. Bach. Knight Bachelor.
kw. kilowatt.

Lab. Labour (party).
lat. latitude.
L.C.M. lowest common multiple.
Lib. Liberal (party).
Lieut., Lt. Lieutenant.
Lit. Hum. *litterae humaniores*, humane letters, the humanities ('Greats').
Litt.D. *Litterarum Doctor*, Doctor of Letters.
LL.B. Bachelor of Laws.
log. logarithm.
long. longitude.
loq. *loquitur*, speaks.
L.R.A.M. Licentiate of the Royal Academy of Music.
LSD. lysergic acid diethylamide.
L.S.E. London School of Economics.
L.T.A. Lawn Tennis Association.

M. *Monsieur* (Fr.), Mr
m. metre; minute; million; masculine; maiden (over).
M.A. *Magister Artium*, Master of Arts.
max. maximum.

M.B. *Medicinae Baccalaureus*, Bachelor of Medicine.

M.B.E. Member of the Order of the British Empire.

M.C. Member of Congress; Master of Ceremonies; Military Cross.

M.D. *Medicinae Doctor*, Doctor of Medicine.

memo. memorandum.

Messrs. *Messieurs* (Fr.), Sirs, Gentlemen; used as pl. of Mr.

M.F.H. Master of Fox Hounds.

mg. milligram(me).

misc. miscellaneous; miscellany.

ml. millilitre

M.M. Military Medal.

mm. millimetre(s).

M.O. Medical Officer.

M.P. Member of Parliament; Military Police.

m.p.g. miles per gallon.

m.p.h. miles per hour.

M.R.C.P. Member of the Royal College of Physicians.

M.R.C.S. Member of the Royal College of Surgeons.

M.Sc. Master of Science.

M.T.B. motor torpedo-boat.

N.A.A.F.I. Navy, Army and Air Force Institute.

N.A.L.G.O. National Association of Local Government Officers.

NATO North Atlantic Treaty Organization.

N.B., n.b., *nota bene*, note well.

neg. negative.

nem. con. *nemine contradicente*, no one contradicting.

N.H.S. National Health Service.

non seq. *non sequitur*, it does not follow.

N.S.P.C.C. National Society for Prevention of Cruelty to Children.

N.S.W. New South Wales.

N.T. New Testament.

N.U.J. National Union of Journalists.

N.U.M. National Union of Mine-workers.

N.U.R. National Union of Railway-men.

N.U.S. National Union of Students.

O.A.P. Old Age Pension or Pensioner.

ob. *obiit*, died.

O.B.E. Officer of the Order of the British Empire.

O.C. Officer Commanding.

O.C.T.U. Officer Cadet Training Unit.

O.E.C.D. Organization for Economic Co-operation and Development.

O.H.M.S. On His (or Her) Majesty's Service.

op. cit. *opere citato*, in the work cited.

O.S. Ordnance Survey; outsize; ordinary seaman.

O.T. Old Testament.

p. *piano*, softly; page.

p.a. *per annum*, each year.

P. & O. Peninsular & Oriental (Steamship Co.).

pat. patent.

P.A.Y.E. Pay As You Earn (Income Tax).

P.E. physical education.

P.E.N. (International Association of) Poets, Playwrights, Editors, Essayists and Novelists.

per cent., *per centum*, by the hundred.

Ph.D. *Philosophiae Doctor*, Doctor of Philosophy.

P.M. *post meridiem*, after midday; Prime Minister; Provost Marshal.

P.M.G. Postmaster-General.

P.O. post-office; postal order; petty officer; pilot officer.

P.O.W. prisoner of war.

p.p. *per pro*, on behalf of; past participle.

P.P.S. *post postscriptum*, a later additional postscript; Parliamentary Private Secretary.

P.R. proportional representation; *Populus Romanus*, the Roman people.

P.R.O. Public Relations Officer.

PS. *postscriptum*, postscript, written after.

pseud. pseudonym.

P.T.O. please turn over.

Q.C. Queen's Counsel.

q.e.d. *quod erat demonstrandum*, which was to be proved.

q.e.f. *quod erat faciendum*, which was to be done.

q.e.i. *quod erat inveniendum*, which was required to be found out.

q.v. *quod vide*, which see.

R.A. Royal Academy or Academician; Royal Artillery.

R.A.C. Royal Automobile Club; Royal Armoured Corps.

R.A.D.A. Royal Academy of Dramatic Art.

R.A.F. Royal Air Force.

R.A.M. Royal Academy of Music.

R.A.M.C. Royal Army Medical Corps.

R.A.O.C. Royal Army Ordnance Corps.

R.C. Roman Catholic; Red Cross; right of centre (of stage).

R.C.M. Royal College of Music.

R.C.M.P. Royal Canadian Mounted Police.

R.C.P. Royal College of Physicians.

R.C.S. Royal College of Surgeons.

R.E. Royal Engineers.

recd. received.

R.E.M.E. Royal Electrical and Mechanical Engineers.

retd. returned; retired.

R.I.B.A. Royal Institute of British Architects.

R.I.P. *requiescat in pace*, may he (or she) rest in peace.

R.M. Royal Marines; Royal Mail.

R.M.S. Royal Mail Steamer.

R.N. Royal Navy; registered nurse.

R.N.L.I. Royal National Lifeboat Institute.

R.N.R. Royal Naval Reserve.

R.N.V.R. Royal Naval Volunteer Reserve.

R.S.M. Regimental Sergeant-Major.

R.S.P.C.A. Royal Society for the Prevention of Cruelty to Animals.

R.S.V.P. *répondez s'il vous plaît* (Fr.), reply, if you please.

Rt. Hon. Right Honourable.

Rt. Rev. Right Reverend.

S.E.A.T.O. South-East Asia Treaty Organization.

sic. 'so written'.

sig. signature.

S.R.N. State Registered Nurse.

s.s. steam ship.